NOTES OF
AND
BROTHE.

Henry James OM (15 April 1843 – 28 February 1916) was an American-British author regarded as a key transitional figure between literary realism and literary modernism, and is considered by many to be among the greatest novelists in the English language. He was the son of Henry James Sr. and the brother of renowned philosopher and psychologist William James and diarist Alice James.

He is best known for a number of novels dealing with the social and marital interplay between émigré Americans, English people, and continental Europeans. Examples of such novels include The Portrait of a Lady, The Ambassadors, and The Wings of the Dove. His later works were increasingly experimental. In describing the internal states of mind and social dynamics of his characters, James often made use of a style in which ambiguous or contradictory motives and impressions were overlaid or juxtaposed in the discussion of a character's psyche.(Source: Wikipedia)

Literary works:
Watch and Ward (1871)
Roderick Hudson (1875)
The American (1877)
The Europeans (1878)
Confidence (1879)
Washington Square (1880)
The Portrait of a Lady (1881)
The Bostonians (1886)
The Princess Casamassima (1886)
The Reverberator (1888)
The Tragic Muse (1890)
The Other House (1896)
The Spoils of Poynton (1897)
What Maisie Knew (1897)

NOTES OF A SON AND BROTHER

HENRY JAMES

PRINCE CLASSICS

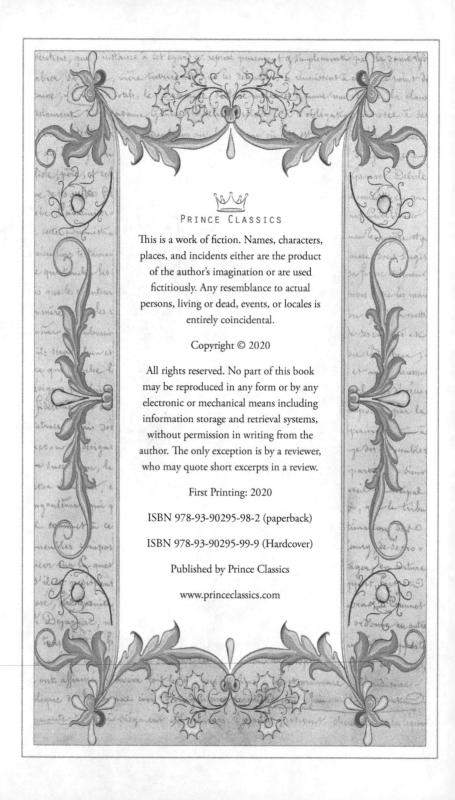

PRINCE CLASSICS

This is a work of fiction. Names, characters, places, and incidents either are the product of the author's imagination or are used fictitiously. Any resemblance to actual persons, living or dead, events, or locales is entirely coincidental.

Copyright © 2020

First Printing: 2020

ISBN 978-93-90295-98-2 (paperback)

ISBN 978-93-90295-99-9 (Hardcover)

Published by Prince Classics

www.princeclassics.com

Contents

I

It may again perhaps betray something of that incorrigible vagueness of current in our educational drift which I have elsewhere[1] so unreservedly suffered to reflect itself that, though we had come abroad in 1855 with an eye to the then supposedly supreme benefits of Swiss schooling, our most resolute attempt to tap that supply, after twenty distractions, waited over to the autumn of the fourth year later on, when we in renewed good faith retraced our steps to Geneva. Our parents began at that season a long sojourn at the old Hôtel de l'Écu, which now erects a somewhat diminished head on the edge of the rushing Rhone—its only rival then was the Hôtel des Bergues opposite, considerably larger and commanding more or less the view of that profiled crest of Mont-Blanc which used to be so oddly likened to the head and face of a singularly supine Napoleon. But on that side the shooting blue flood was less directly and familiarly under the windows; in our position we lived with it and hung over it, and its beauty, just where we mainly congregated, was, I fear, my own sole happy impression during several of those months. It was of a Sunday that we congregated most; my two younger brothers had, in general, on that day their *sortie* from the Pensionnat Maquelin, a couple of miles out of town, where they were then established, and W. J., following courses at the Academy, in its present enriched and amplified form the University, mingled, failing livelier recreation, in the family circle at the hotel. Livelier recreation, during the hours of completest ease, consisted mostly, as the period drew itself out, of those *courses*, along the lake and along the hills, which offer to student-life in whatever phase, throughout that blest country, the most romantic of all forms of "a little change"; enjoyed too in some degree, but much more restrictedly, by myself—this an effect, as I remember feeling it, of my considerably greater servitude. I had been placed, separately, at still another Institution, that of M. Rochette, who carried on an École Préparatoire aux Écoles Spéciales, by which was meant in particular the Polytechnic School at Zurich, with whatever other like curricula, always "scientific," might elsewhere be aimed at; and I had been so disposed of under a flattering misconception of my aptitudes that leaves me to-day even more wonderstruck than at that immediate season of my distress.

I so feared and abhorred mathematics that the simplest arithmetical operation had always found and kept me helpless and blank—the dire discipline of the years bringing no relief whatever to my state; and mathematics unmitigated were at the Institution Rochette the air we breathed, building us up as they most officiously did for those other grim ordeals and pursuits, those of the mining and the civil engineer, those of the architectural aspirant and the technician in still other fields, to which we were supposed to be addressed. Nothing of the sort was indeed supposed of me—which is in particular my present mystification; so that my assault of the preliminaries disclosed, feeble as it strikingly remained, was mere darkness, waste and anguish. I found myself able to bite, as the phrase was, into no subject there deemed savoury; it was hard and bitter fruit all and turned to ashes in my mouth. More extraordinary however than my good parents' belief—eccentric on their part too, in the light of their usual practice and disposition, their habit, for the most part, of liking for us after a gasp or two whatever we seemed to like—was my own failure to protest with a frankness proportioned to my horror. The stiffer intellectual discipline, the discipline of physics and of algebra, invoked for the benefit of an understanding undisputedly weak and shy, had been accepted on my side as a blessing perhaps in disguise. It had come to me by I know not what perversity that if I couldn't tackle the smallest problem in mechanics or face without dismay at the blackboard the simplest geometric challenge I ought somehow in decency to make myself over, oughtn't really to be so inferior to almost everyone else. That was the pang, as it was also the marvel—that the meanest minds and the vulgarest types approached these matters without a sign of trepidation even when they approached them, at the worst, without positive appetite. My attempt not therefore to remain abnormal wholly broke down, however, and when I at last withdrew from the scene it was not even as a conspicuous, it was only as an obscure, a deeply hushed failure. I joined William, after what had seemed to me an eternity of woe, at the Academy, where I followed, for too short a time but with a comparative recovery of confidence, such literary *cours* as I might.

I puzzle it out to-day that my parents had simply said to themselves, in serious concern, that I read too many novels, or at least read them too attentively—*that* was the vice; as also that they had by the contagion of their good faith got me in a manner to agree with them; since I could almost always enter, to the gain of "horizon" but too often to the perversion of experience, into any view of my real interests, so-called, that was presented to me with a dazzling assurance. I didn't consider certainly that I was so forming my mind, and was doubtless curious to see whether it mightn't, by a process flourishing in other applications, get to some extent formed. It wasn't, I think, till I felt the rapture of that method's arrest that I knew how grotesquely little it had done for me. And yet I bore it afterwards no malice—resorting again to that early fatalistic philosophy of which the general sense was that almost anything, however disagreeable, had been worth while; so unable was I to claim that it hadn't involved impressions. I positively felt the impressional harvest rather rich, little as any item of it might have passed at the time for the sort of thing one exhibits as a trophy of learning. My small exhibition was all for myself and consisted on the whole but of a dusty, spotty, ugly picture—I took it for ugly well-nigh to the pitch of the sinister. Its being a picture at all—and I clung to that—came from the personal and material facts of the place, where I was the only scholar of English speech, since my companions, with a Genevese predominance, were variously polyglot. They wondered, I couldn't doubt, what I was doing among them, and what lost lamb, almost audibly bleating, I had been charged to figure. Yet I remember no crude chaff, no very free relation of any one with any one, no high pitch, still less any low descent, of young pleasantry or irony; our manners must have been remarkably formed, and our general tone was that of a man-of-the-world discretion, or at the worst of a certain small bourgeois circumspection. The dread in the Genevese of having definitely to "know" strangers and thereby be at costs for any sort of hospitality to them comes back to me as written clear; not less than their being of two sorts or societies, sons of the townspeople pure and simple and sons of the local aristocracy perched in certain of the fine old houses of the Cité and enjoying a background of sturdily-seated lakeside villas and deeply umbrageous campagnes. I remember thinking the difference of type, complexion and general *allure* between these groups more marked, to all the senses, than any "social distinction" I had yet encountered. But the great thing was that I could so simplify our enclosing scene itself, round it in and make it compose—the dark, the dreary Institution, squeezed into a tall, dim, stony-faced and stony-hearted house at the very top of the Cité and directly in the rear of the Cathedral, portions of the apse of which seem to me to have straggled above or protruded toward it, with other odd extraneous masses than itself pressing still nearer. This simplification, quite luxuriously for my young mind, was to mere mean blackness of an old-world sordid order. I recognised *rich* blackness in other connections, but this was somehow of a harsh tradition and a tragic economy; sordid and strong was what I had from the first felt the place, though urging myself always to rub off history from its stones, and suffering thus, after a fashion, by the fact that with history it ought to be interesting and that I ought to know just how and why it was. For that, I think, was ever both the burden and the joy—the complication, I mean, of interest, and the sense, in the midst of the ugly and the melancholy, that queer crooked silent corners behind cathedrals wrought in their way for one, did something, while one haunted them, to the imagination and the taste; and that so, once more, since the generalisation had become a habit with me, I couldn't, seeing and feeling these things, really believe I had picked up nothing.

When I sat in a dusky upper chamber and read "French literature" with blighted M. Toeppfer, son of a happier sire, as I was sure the charming writer and caricaturist, in spite of cumbrous cares, must have been; or when, a couple of times a week and in the same eternal twilight (we groped almost lampless through the winter days, and our glimmering tapers, when they sparsely appeared, smelt of a past age), I worried out Virgil and Tite-Live with M. Verchère, or Schiller and Lessing with the ruddy noisy little professor of German, who sat always, the lesson long, in a light brown talma, the sides of which he caused violently to flap for emphasis like agitated wings, I was almost conscious of the breath of culture as I modestly aspired to culture, and was at any rate safe for the time from a summons to the blackboard at the hands of awful little M. Galopin, that dispenser of the paralysing chalk who most affected me. Extremely diminutive and wearing for the most part a thin inscrutable smile, the ghost of a tribute to awkwardness happily carried off, he found in our barren interviews, I believed, a charm to curiosity, bending afresh each time as over the handful of specimen dust, unprecedented product at its finest, extracted from the scratched soil of my intelligence. With M. Toeppfer I was almost happy; with each of these instructors my hour was unshared, my exploits unwitnessed, by others; but M. Toeppfer became a friend, shewed himself a *causeur*, brightened our lesson with memories of his time in Paris, where, if I am not mistaken, he had made, with great animation, his baccalauréat, and whence it was my possibly presumptuous impression he had brought back a state of health, apparently much impaired, which represented contrition for youthful spirits. He had haunted the parterre of the Théâtre Français, and when we read Racine his vision of Rachel, whom he had seen there as often as possible, revived; he was able to say at moments how she had spoken and moved, and I recall in particular his telling me that on her entrance as Phèdre, borne down, in her languorous passion, by the weight of her royal robes—"Que ces vains ornemens, que ces voiles me pèsent!"—the long lapse of time before she spoke and while she sank upon a seat filled itself extraordinarily with her visible woe. But where he most gave me comfort was in bringing home to me that the house commemorated, immortalised, as we call it, in the first of his father's Nouvelles Genevoises, La Bibliothèque de mon Oncle, was none other than the structure facing us where we sat and which so impinged and leaned on the cathedral walls that he had but to indicate to me certain points from the window of our room to reconstitute thrillingly the scenery, the drollery, the whimsical action of the tale. *There* was a demonstration I could feel important, votary and victim of the "scene," the scene and the "atmosphere" only, that I had been formed to be. That I called interesting lore—called it so at least to myself, though feeling it at the same time of course so little *directly* producible that I could perhaps even then have fronted this actually remote circumstance of my never having produced it till this moment. There abode in me, I may add, a sense that on any subject that did appeal and that so found me ready—such subjects being indeed as yet vague, but immensely suggestive of number—I should have grasped the confident chalk, welcomed the very biggest piece, not in the least have feared the blackboard. They were inscribed, alas for me, in no recognised course. I put my hand straight on another of them, none the less, if not on a whole group of others, in my ascent, each morning of the spring or the early summer sémestre, of the admirable old Rue de la Tour de Boël, pronounced Boisl, which, dusky, steep and tortuous, formed a short cut to that part of the Grand' Rue in which the Academy was then seated.

It was a foul and malodorous way—I sniff again, during the tepid weeks, its warm close air and that near presence of rank cheese which was in those days almost everywhere, for the nostril, the note of urban Switzerland; these things blessed me as I passed, for I passed straight to freedom and away from M. Galopin; they mixed with the benediction of the exquisite spring and the rapture, constantly renewed, though for too short a period, of my now substituting literary, or in other words romantic, studies for the pursuits of the Institution Rochette. I viewed them as literary, these new branches of research, though in truth they were loose enough and followed on loose terms. My dear parents, as if to make up to me, characteristically, for my recent absurd strain to no purpose, allowed me now the happiest freedom, left me to attend such lectures as I preferred, only desiring that I should attend several a week, and content—cherished memory that it makes of their forms with me— that these should involve neither examinations nor reports. The Academic authorities, good-natured in the extreme and accustomed to the alien amateur, appear to have been equally content, and I was but too delighted, on such lines, to attend anything or everything. My whole impression now, with my self-respect re-established, was of something exquisite: I was put to the proof about nothing; I deeply enjoyed the confidence shown in my taste, not to say in my honour, and I sat out lecture after lecture as I might have sat out drama, alternate tragedy and comedy, beautifully performed— the professor in each case figuring the hero, and the undergraduates, much more numerous, though not in general maturer than those of the Institution, where I had been, to my perception, every one's junior, partaking in an odd fashion of the nature at once of troupe and spectators. The scientific subjects, in a large suggestive way, figured tragedy, I seemed to feel, and I pushed this form to the point of my following, for conscience' sake, though not with the last regularity, lurid demonstrations, as they affected me, on anatomy and physiology; these in turn leading to my earnest view, at the Medical School, of the dissection of a *magnifique gendarme*—which ordeal brought me to a stand. It was by the literary and even by the philosophic *leçons* that the office of bright comedy was discharged, on the same liberal lines; at the same time that I blush to remember with how base a blankness I must have several times listened to H. F. Amiel, admirable writer, analyst, moralist. His name and the fact of his having been then a mild grave oracle of the shrine are all that remain with me (I was fit to be coupled with my cousin Anne King, named in another place, who, on the same Genevese scene, had had early lessons from the young Victor Cherbuliez, then with all his music in him, and was to live to mention to me that he had been for her "like any one else"); the shrine, not to say the temple itself, shining for me truly, all that season, with a mere confounding blur of light. Was it an effect of my intensity of reaction from what I had hated? was it to a great extent the beguiling beauty of a wonderful Swiss spring, into which all things else soothingly melted, becoming together a harmony without parts?—whatever the cause, I owed it to some accident only to be described, I think, as happy, that I moved, those three months, in an acutely enjoying and yet, as would at present appear, a but scantly comparing or distinguishing maze of the senses and the fancy. So at least, to cover this so thin report of my intelligence and my sum of acquisition and retention, I am reduced to supposing.

What essentially most operated, I make out, however, was that force of a renewed sense of William's major activity which always made the presumption of any degree of importance or success fall, with a sort of ecstasy of resignation, from my own so minor. Whatever he might happen to be doing made him so interesting about it, and indeed, with the quickest concomitance, about everything else, that what I probably most did, all the while, was but to pick up, and to the effect not a bit of starving but quite of filling myself, the crumbs of his feast and the echoes of his life. His life, all this Geneva period, had been more of a feast than mine, and I recall the sense of this that I had got on the occasion of my accompanying him, by his invitation, toward the end of our stay, to a students' celebration or carouse, which was held at such a distance from the town, at a village or small bourg, up in the Vaud back-country, that we had, after a considerable journey by boat and in heterogeneous and primitive conveyances, tightly packed, to spend two nights there. The Genevese section of the Société de Zoffingue, the great Swiss students' organisation for

brotherhood and beer, as it might summarily be defined, of which my brother
had become a member, was to meet there certain other sections, now vague
to me, but predominantly from the German-speaking Cantons, and, holding
a Commerce, to toast their reunion in brimming bowls. It had been thought
the impression might amuse, might even interest me—for it was not denied
that there were directions, after all, in which I *could* perhaps take notice; and
this was doubtless what after a fashion happened, though I felt out in the
cold (and all the more that the cold at the moment happened to be cruel),
as the only participant in view not crowned with the charming white cap of
the society, becoming to most young heads, and still less girt with the parti-
coloured ribbon or complementary scarf, which set off even the shabby—for
shabbiness considerably figured. I participated vaguely but not too excludedly;
I suffered from cold, from hunger and from scant sleeping-space; I found the
Bernese and the Bâlois strange representatives of the joy of life, some of them
the finest gothic grotesques—but the time none the less very long; all of
which, however, was in the day's work if I might live, by the imagination, in
William's so adaptive skin. To see that he was adaptive, was initiated, and to
what a happy and fruitful effect, that, I recollect, was my measure of content;
which was filled again to overflowing, as I have hinted, on my finding him
so launched at the Academy after our stretch of virtual separation, and just
fancying, with a freedom of fancy, even if with a great reserve of expression,
how much he might be living and learning, enjoying and feeling, amid work
that was the right work for him and comrades, consecrated comrades, that at
the worst weren't the wrong. What was not indeed, I always asked myself, the
right work for him, or the right thing of any kind, that he took up or looked
at or played with?—failing, as I did more than ever at the time I speak of, of
the least glimpse of his being below an occasion. Whatever he played with or
worked at entered at once into his intelligence, his talk, his humour, as with
the action of colouring-matter dropped into water or that of the turning-
on of a light within a window. Occasions waited on him, had always done
so, to my view; and there he was, that springtime, on a level with them all:
the effect of which recognition had much, had more than aught else, to say
to the charming silver haze just then wrapped about everything of which I
was conscious. He had formed two or three young friendships that were to

16

continue and to which even the correspondence of his later years testifies; with which it may have had something to do that the Swiss *jeunesse* of the day was, thanks to the political temperature then prevailing, in a highly inflamed and exalted state, and particularly sensitive to foreign sympathy, however platonic, with the national fever. It was the hour at which the French Emperor was to be paid by Victor Emmanuel the price of the liberation of Lombardy; the cession of Nice and Savoie were in the air—with the consequence, in the Genevese breast, of the new immediate neighbourhood thus constituted for its territory. Small Savoie was to be replaced, close against it, by enormous and triumphant France, whose power to absorb great mouthfuls was being so strikingly exhibited. Hence came much hurrying to and fro, much springing to arms, in the way of exercise, and much flocking to the standard— "demonstrations," in other words, of the liveliest; one of which I recall as a huge tented banquet, largely of the white caps, where I was present under my brother's wing, and, out of a sea of agitated and vociferous young heads, sprang passionate protests and toasts and vows and declaimed verses, a storm of local patriotism, though a flurry happily short-lived.

All this was thrilling, but the term of it, by our consecrated custom, already in view; we were transferred at a bound, for the rest of that summer of 1860, to the care, respectively, of a pair of kindly pedagogues at Bonn-am-Rhein; as to which rapid phase I find remembrance again lively, with a letter or two of William's to reinforce it. Yet I first pick up as I pass several young lines from Geneva, and would fain pick up too the drawing that accompanied them—this by reason of the interest of everything of the sort, without exception, that remains to us from his hand. He at a given moment, which came quite early, as completely ceased to ply his pencil as he had in his younger time earnestly and curiously exercised it; and this constitutes exactly the interest of his case. No stroke of it that I have recovered but illustrates his aptitude for drawing, his possible real mastery of the art that was yet, in the light of other interests, so utterly to drop from him; and the example is rare of being so finely capable only to become so indifferent. It was thanks to his later indifference that he made no point of preserving what he had done—a neglect that, still more lucklessly, communicated itself to his circle; so that we also let things go, let them again and again stray into the desert, and that what might be reproducible is but the handful of scraps that have happened not to perish. "Mother," he writes to his father in absence, "does nothing but sit and cry for you. She refuses to associate with us and has one side of the room to herself. She and the Aunt are now in the Aunt's room. Wilky and Bobby, at home for the day, are at church. It is a hard grey day. H. is telling a story to Louis Osborne, and I will try to make a sketch of them. There has been a terrible bise; the two Cornhill Magazines have come; Mrs. Thomas has been too sick to be at dinner, and we have seen something of some most extraordinary English people." Mrs. Thomas, of New York, was a handsome American widow with handsome children, all from the Avenue Gabriel in Paris, and with the boys enjoying life, among many little compatriots, at the admired establishment of M. Haccius, even as our small brothers were doing at that of M. Maquelin; yet with their destiny of ultimate Europeanisation, of finally complete absorption into the French system, already rather written for them—as a like history, for like foredoomed young subjects, was in those years beginning to be prefigured, through marriages of daughters and other such beguilements, almost wherever one looked. The extraordinary English people were perhaps an amiable family of whom I retain an image as conversing with our parents at the season when the latter were in their prompt flush of admiration for George Eliot's first novel, Adam Bede, then just given to the world and their copy of which they had rejoicingly lent to their fellow Anglo-Saxons. I catch again the echo of their consternation on receiving it back with the remark that all attempt at an interest in such people, village carpenters and Methodists, had proved vain—for that style of Anglo-Saxon; together with that of my own excited wonder about such other people, those of the style in question, those somehow prodigiously presented by so rare a delicacy, so proud a taste, and made thus to irradiate a strange historic light. It *referred* them, and to a social order, making life more interesting and more various; even while our clear democratic air, that of our little family circle, quivered as with the monstrosity. It might, this note that made us, in the parlance of to-day, sit up, fairly have opened to me that great and up to then unsuspected door of the world from which the general collection of monstrosities, its existence suddenly brought home to us, would doubtless stretch grandly away. The story I told Louis Osborne has quite passed from me, but not little Louis himself, an American child of the most charming and appealing intelligence, marked by some malady that was more or less permanently to cripple, or was even cruelly to destroy him, and whom it was a constant joy to aspire to amuse. His mother was schooling her elder son in the company of our own brothers, his father having established them all at Geneva that he might go for a tour in the East. Vivid to me still is the glimpse I happened to get one Sunday betimes of the good Maquelin couple, husband and wife, in deep mourning—a touch of the highest decency—who had come, with faces a yard long, to announce to Mrs. Osborne the death of her husband in the Holy Land, communicated to them, by slow letter, in the first instance. With little Louis on one's knee one didn't at all envy M. and Madame Maquelin; and than this small faint phantom of sociable helpless little listening Louis none more exquisite hovers before me.

With which mild memories thus stands out for me too the lively importance, that winter, of the arrival, from the first number, of the orange-covered earlier Cornhill—the thrill of each composing item of that first number especially recoverable in its intensity. Is anything like that thrill possible to-day—for a submerged and blinded and deafened generation, a generation so smothered in quantity and number that discrimination, under the gasp, has neither air to breathe nor room to turn round? Has any like circumstance now conceivably the value, to the charmed attention, so far as anything worth naming attention, or any charm for it, is anywhere left, of the fact that Trollope's Framley Parsonage there began?—let alone the still other fact that the Roundabout Papers did and that Thackeray thus appeared to us to guarantee personally, intimately, with a present audibility that was as the accent of good company, the new relation with him and with others of company not much worse, as they then seemed, that such a medium could establish. To speak of these things, in truth, however, is to feel the advantage of being able to live back into the time of the more sovereign periodical appearances much of a compensation for any reduced prospect of living forward. For these appearances, these strong time-marks in such stretches of production as that of Dickens, that of Thackeray, that of George Eliot, had in the first place simply a genial weight and force, a direct importance, and in the second a command of the permeable air and the collective sensibility, with which nothing since has begun to deserve comparison. They were enrichments of life, they were *large* arrivals, these particular renewals of supply—to which, frankly, I am moved to add, the early Cornhill giving me a pretext, even the frequent examples of Anthony Trollope's fine middle period, looked at in the light of old affection and that of his great heavy shovelfuls of testimony to constituted English matters; a testimony of course looser and thinner than Balzac's to *his* range of facts, but charged with something of the big Balzac authority. These various, let alone numerous, deeper-toned strokes of the great Victorian clock were so many steps in the march of our age, besides being so many notes, full and far-reverberating, of our having high company to keep—high, I mean, to cover all the ground, in the sense of the genial pitch of it. So it was, I remember too, that our parents spoke of their memory of the successive surpassing attestations of the contemporary presence of Scott; to which we might have replied, and doubtless after no great space began to reply, that our state, and even their later one, allowing for a certain gap, had nothing to envy any other. I witnessed, for that matter, with all my senses, young as I was, the never-to-be-equalled degree of difference made, for what may really be called the world-consciousness happily exposed to it, by the prolonged "coming-out" of The Newcomes, yellow number by number, and could take the general civilised participation in the process for a sort of basking in the light of distinction. The process repeated itself for some years under other forms and stimuli, but the merciless change was to come— so that through whatever bristling mazes we may now pick our way it is not to find them open into any such vales of Arcady. My claim for our old privilege is that we did then, with our pace of dignity, proceed from vale to vale.

II

My point at any rate, such as it is, would be that even at the age I had reached in 1860 something of the happier time still lingered—the time in which a given product of the press might have a situation and an aspect, a considerability, so to speak, a circumscription and an *aura*; room to breathe and to show in, margin for the casting of its nets. The occasion at large was doubtless shrinking, one could note—shrinking like the unlet "house" on a night of grandest opera, but "standing room only" was not yet everywhere the sign, and the fine deliberate thing could here and there find its seat. I really indeed might have held it the golden age of letters still, and of their fond sister leisure, with that quiet swim into our ken on its appointed day, during our Bonn summer, of the charming Once a Week of the prime, the prime of George Meredith and Charles Reade and J. E. Millais and George du Maurier; which our father, to bridge our separation from him, sent us, from Paris and elsewhere, in prompt and characteristic relief of our plotted, our determined strict servitude to German, and to the embrace of the sweet slim essence of which the strain of one's muscles round a circular ton of advertisement was not a condition attached. I should like to say that I rioted, all that season, on the supreme German classics *and* on Evan Harrington, with Charles Reade's A Good Fight, the assured little prelude to The Cloister and the Hearth, thrown in; and I should indeed be ready to say it, were not the expression gross for the really hushed piety of my attitude during those weeks. It was perhaps not quite till then that I fully emerged from the black shadow of the École Préparatoire aux Écoles Spéciales, not quite till we had got off beyond the blest Rhine at Basle that I ceased to hear and feel all but just behind me, portentous perhaps of another spring, the cold breath of the monster. The guttery Bonn-Gasse was during those weeks of the year close and stale, and the house of our good Herr Doctor Humpert, professor at the Bonn Gymnasium, in which I shared a room with my brother Wilky, contracted and dim, as well as fragrant through a range of assaults that differed only in kind and not at all in number from those of the street itself; and yet I held the period and the whole situation idyllic—the slightly odd sense of which was one's being to that extent attuned to the life of letters and of (oh the great thing!) impressions "gone in for." To feel a unity, a character and a tone in one's impressions, to feel them related and all harmoniously coloured, that *was* positively to face the æsthetic, the creative, even, quite wondrously, the critical life and almost on the spot to commence author. They had begun, the impressions—that was what was the matter with them—to scratch quite audibly at the door of liberation, of extension, of projection; what they were *of* one more or less knew, but what they were *for* was the question that began to stir, though one was still to be a long time at a loss directly to answer it.

There, for the present, was the rub, the dark difficulty at which one could but secretly stare—secretly because one was somehow ashamed of its being there and would have quickly removed one's eyes, or tried to clear them, if caught in the act of watching. Impressions were not merely all right but were the dearest things in the world; only one would have gone to the stake rather than in the first place confessed to some of them, or in the second announced that one really lived by them and built on them. This failure then to take one's stand in the connection could but come from the troubled view that they were naught without a backing, a stout stiff hard-grained underside that would hold them together and of which the terrible name was simply science, otherwise learning, and learning exclusively by books, which were at once the most beautiful and the most dreadful things in the world, some of them right, strikingly, showily right, some of them disgracefully and almost unmentionably wrong, that is grossly irrelevant, as for instance a bound volume of Once a Week would be, but remarkable above all for overwhelming number and in general for defiance of comprehension. It was true that one had from time to time the rare adventure of one's surprise at understanding parts of them none the less—understanding more than a very little, more than much too little; but there was no practical support to speak of in that, even the most one could ever hope to understand being a mere drop in the bucket. Never did I quite strike it off, I think, that impressions might themselves *be* science—and this probably because I didn't then know them, when it came to the point, as anything but life. I knew them but by that collective and unpractical—many persons would have said that frivolous—name; which saw me little further. I was under the impression—this in fact the very liveliest of what might have been called the lot—that life and knowledge were simply mutual opposites, one inconsistent with the other; though hovered about, together, at the same time, by the anomaly that when knowledge impinged upon life, pushed against her, as it were, and drove her to the wall, it was all right, and such was knowledge's way and title; whereas when life played the like tricks with knowledge nothing but shame for the ruder, even if lighter, party could accrue. There was to come to me of course in time the due perception that neither was of the least use—use to myself—without the other; but meanwhile, and even for much after, the extreme embarrassment continued: to whichever of the opposites one gave one's self it was with a sense of all but basely sacrificing the other. However, the conflict and the drama involved in the question at large was doubtless what was to make consciousness—under whichever of the two names one preferred to entertain it—supremely intense and interesting.

This then is by way of saying that the idyll, as I have called it, of the happy juncture I glanced at a moment back came from the fact that I didn't at all know how much I was living, and meanwhile quite supposed I was considerably learning. When, rising at some extraordinary hour of the morning, I went forth through the unawakened town (and the Germans, at that time, heaven knows, were early afoot too), and made for the open country and the hill, in particular, of the neighbouring Venusberg, long, low and bosky, where the dews were still fresh and ancient mummies of an old cloister, as I remember it, somewhere perched and exposed, I was doing, to my sense, an attuned thing; attuned, that is, to my coming home to bend double over Schiller's Thirty Years' War in the strenuous spirit that would keep me at it, or that would vary it with Goethe's Wahlverwandtschaften, till late in the warm afternoon. I found German prose much tougher than the verse, and thereby more opposed to "life," as to which I of course couldn't really shake off the sense that it might be worked as infinitely comprehensive, comprehensive even of the finest discriminations against it. The felicity, present but naturally unanalysed, was that the whole thing, our current episode, *was* exactly comprehensive of life, presenting it in particular as characteristically German, and therein freshly vivid—with the great vividness that, by our parents' vague wish, we were all three after or out for; in spite of our comparatively restricted use, in those days, of these verbal graces. Such therefore was the bright unity of our experience, or at least of my own share in it—this luck that, through the intensity of my wanting it to, all consciousness, all my own immediate, *tasted* German, to the great and delightful quickening of my imagination. The quickening was of course no such matter as I was to know nearly ten years later on plunging for the first time over the Alps into Italy; but, letting alone that I was then so much older, I had wondered about Italy, to put it embracingly, far more than I was constitutionally capable of wondering about Germany. It was enough for me at Bonn that I felt no lack of appetite—had for the time all the illusion of being on the way to something; to something, I mean, with which the taste of German might somehow *directly* mix itself. Every aspect and object round about was a part, at all events, of the actual mixture; and when on drowsy afternoons, not a little interspaced indeed, I attempted the articulate perusal of Hermann und Dorothea with our good Professor, it was like dreaming, to the hum of bees, if not to the aftertaste of "good old Rhenish," in some homely fruity eighteenth-century garden.

The good old Rhenish is no such false note in this reconstitution; I seem to see the Frau Doctorin and her ancient mildly-scowling sister Fräulein Stamm, who reminded me of Hepzibah Pyncheon in The House of the Seven Gables, perpetually wiping green hock-glasses and holding them up to our meagre light, as well as setting out long-necked bottles, with rather chalky cakes, in that forward section of our general eating-and-living-room which formed our precinct of reception and conversation. The unbroken space was lighted at either end, from street and court, and its various effects of tempered shade or, frankly speaking, of rather greasy gloom, amid which the light touch of elegance gleamed but from the polish of the glasses and the sloping shoulders of their bottle, comes back to me as the view of an intensely internal interior. I recall how oppressively in that apartment, how congestedly, as in some cage of which the wires had been papered over, I felt housed and disconnected; I scarce then, I think, knew what the matter was, but it could only have been that in all those summer weeks, to the best of my belief, no window was ever once opened. Still, there was the scene, the thick, the much-mixed chiaroscuro through which the two ladies of the family emerged from an exiguous retreat just off the back end of the place with ample platters of food; the almost impenetrable dusk of the middle zone, where the four or five of us, seated with our nutcracker-faced pastor, conveyed the food to our mouths with a confidence mainly borrowed from the play of his own deep-plunging knife; and then the forward, the festal extension, the privilege of occasionally lingering in which, or of returning to it for renewed refreshment, was a recognition both of our general minding of our business upstairs— left as we were to thumb our Flügel's Dictionary by the hour so long as we invoked no other oracle. Our drowsy Doctor invited no such approach; he smiled upon us as if unseen forefingers of great force had been inserted for the widening of his mouth at the corners, and I had the sense of his not quite knowing what to make of our being so very gently barbaric, or rather so informally civilised; he safely housed and quite rankly fed us, guided us to country walks and to the swimming-baths by the Rhine-side, introduced us to fruit-gardens where, on payment of the scantest tribute, we were suffered to consume off-hand bushels of cherries, plums and pears; suffered us to ascend the Drachenfels and to partake of coffee at Rolandseck and in other friendly open-air situations; but flung his gothic shadow as little as possible over my so passive page at least, and took our rate of acquisition savingly for granted.

This, in the optimism of the hour, I have no memory of resenting; the page, though slow, managed at the same time to be stirring, and I asked no more of any one or anything but that they should be with all due gothicism whatever they most easily might. The long vistas of the beeches and poplars on the other side of the Rhine, after we had crossed by the funicular ferry, gothically rustled and murmured: I fancied their saying perpetually "We are German woods, we are German woods—which makes us very wonderful, do you know? and unlike any others: don't you feel the spell of the very sound of us and of the beautiful words, 'Old German woods, old German woods,' even if you can't tell why?" I couldn't altogether tell why, but took everything on trust as mystically and valuably gothic—valuably because ministering with peculiar directness, as I gathered, to culture. I was in, or again I was "out," in my small way, for culture; which seemed quite to come, come from everywhere at once, with the most absurd conciliatory rush, pitifully small as would have been any list of the sources I tapped. The beauty was in truth that everything was a source, giving me, by the charmingest breach of logic, more than it at all appeared to hold; which was exactly what had not been the case at the Institution Rochette, where things had appeared, or at least had pretended, to hold so much more than they gave. The oddity was that about us now everything—everything but the murmur of the German woods and the great flow and magic name of the Rhine—was more ugly than beautiful, tended in fact to say at every turn: "You shall suffer, yes, indeed you *are* doing so (stick up for your right to!) in your sense of form; which however is quite compatible with culture, is really one of the finest parts of it, and may decidedly prove to you that you're getting it." I hadn't, in rubbing, with whatever weakness, against French and, so far as might be, against France, and in sinking, very sensibly, more and more into them, particularly felt that I was getting it *as* such; what I was getting as such was decidedly rather my famous "life," and without so much as thinking of the degree, with it all, of the valuable and the helpful.

Life meanwhile I had a good deal of at my side in the person of my brother Wilky, who, as I have had occasion elsewhere to say, contrived in those years to live, or to have every appearance of so doing, with an immediacy that left me far in the lurch. I was always still wondering how, while he had solved the question simply *ambulando*, which was for him but by the merest sociable stroll. This represented to me success—success of a kind, but such an assured kind—in a degree that was my despair; and I have never forgotten how, that summer, when the Herr Doctor did look in, did settle down a little to have the bristling page out with us, Wilky's share of the hour took on the spot the form of his turning at once upon our visitor the tables of earnest inquiry. He delighted, after this tribute of eagerness, to meet the Doctor's interrogative advance; but the communication so made was of anything and everything except the fruit of his reading (the act of reading was inhuman and repugnant to him), and I amazedly noted while I nursed my small hoard that anything he offered did in the event quite as well: he could talk with such charm, such drollery of candour, such unexpectedness of figure, about what he had done and what he hadn't—or talk at least before it, behind it and beside it.

26

We had three or four house-companions, youths from other places attending the Gymnasium and committed to our Professor's care, as to whom I could somehow but infer that they were, each in his personal way, inordinately gothic—which they had to be to supply to my mind a relation, or a substitute for a relation, with them; whereas my younger brother, without a scrap of a view of them, a grain of theory or formula, tumbled straight into their confidence all round. Our air for *him* was by just so much life as it couldn't have dreamed of being culture, and he was so far right that when the son of the house and its only child, the slim and ardent Theodor, who figured to me but as a case of such classic sensibility, of the Lieder or the Werther sort, as might have made, with the toss of a yellow lock or the gleam of a green blouse, the image for an Uhland or a Heine stanza, had imparted to him an intention of instant suicide under some resentment of parental misconception, he had been able to use dissuasion, or otherwise the instinct of then most freely fraternising, with a success to which my relish for so romantic a stroke as charmingly in Theodor's character and setting mightn't at all have attained. There is a small something of each of us in a passage of an ingenuous letter addressed by him from the midst of these conditions to his parents. I fondly catch, I confess, at any of these recoverable lights; finding them at the best too scant for my commemorative purpose.

Willy got his photograph this morning after three hours' hard work. From the post-office he was sent to the custom-house, and there was obliged to sign his name and to go to some neighbouring bookstore to buy a seal. On returning to the custom-house he was sent back to the post-office to get some document or other. After obtaining this article he turned his steps once more to the custom-house, where an insolent officer told him he must wait an hour. W. informed him that he would return at the end of the hour, and accordingly for the third time went to the C.H., and was conducted by the clerk to a cellar where the packages were kept, and there told to take off his hat. He obeyed, raging, and then was a fourth time sent to the P.O.— this time to pay money. Happily he is now in possession of his property. H. and he took a walk this afternoon to a fruit-garden, where plums, cherries, gooseberries and currants were abundant. After half an hour's good work H. left W. finishing merely the plums—the cherry and gooseberry course to come later. He was so enchanted that he thought H. a great fool to leave so soon. How does Paris now strike you? It can't be as nice as Bonn. You had better write to Bob.

Bob, our youngest brother, had been left at Geneva with excellent M. Maquelin and was at that time *en course*, over the Alps, with this gentleman and their young companions; a most desirable, delicious excursion, which I remember following in envious fancy, as it included a descent to the Italian Lakes and a push on as far as Genoa. In reference to which excursion I cull a line or two from a faded scrap of a letter addressed a little later by this youngest of us to his "Beloved Brother" William. "This is about our Grande Course. We started at 5 o'clock in the morning with our faces and hands all nicely washed and our nails clean. The morning was superb, and as we waited in the court the soft balmy air of the mountains came in bringing with it the melodious sound of the rappel for breakfast. This finished we bade adieu, and I could see the emotions of the kind and ever-watchful Madame Maquelin as a few silent drops trickled down her fair cheeks. We at last arrived at the boat, where we met Mr. Peters, a portly gentleman from the city of Philadelphia, with his two sweet sons, one twelve, the other seven years old, the eldest coming from Mr. E.'s school with no very good opinion of the principal— saying he had seen him in a state of tightness several times during his stay there." Mr. Peters appears to have been something of a pessimist, for, when at a later stage "it began to rain hard, and half the road was a foot deep in water, and the cocher had stopped somewhere to get lanterns and had at the same time indulged in certain potations which didn't make him drive any the straighter," this gentleman "insinuated that we had all better have been with our mothers." The letter records at some length the early phases of the affair, but under the weight of the vision of Italy it rather breaks down and artlessly simplifies. "Genoa is a most lively town, and there is a continual swarm of sailors in the street. We visited several palaces, among others that of Victor Emanuel, which is very fine, and the fruit is very cheap. We stayed there several days, but at last started for Turin, where we spent a Sunday—a place I didn't much like, I suppose because of that reason. We left Turin the next day on foot, but lost our road and had to come back." I recover even in presence of these light accents my shade of wonder at this odd chance that made the least developed of us the subject of what seemed to me even then a privilege of the highest intensity; and there again keeps it company my sense, through all the after years, that this early glimpse of the blest old Italy, almost too early though it appears to have but just missed being, might have done something towards preparing or enriching for Bob the one little plot of consciousness in which his deeply troubled life was to find rest. He was in the event also fondly to aim at painting, like two of his brothers; but whereas they were to fumble with the lock, in their very differing degree, only in those young years, he was to keep at it most as he grew older, though always with a perfect intelligence of the inevitable limits of the relation, the same intelligence that was so sharp and sad, so extraordinarily free and fine and detached in fact, as play of mind, play of independent talk and of pen, for the limits of his relation to many other matters. Singularly intelligent all round, yet with faculties that had early declined any consummation of acquaintance with such training as under a different sort of pressure he might have enjoyed, he had an admirable hand and eye, and I have known no other such capacity for absorbing or storing up the minutest truths and shades of landscape fact and giving them out afterward, in separation from the scene, with full assurance and felicity. He could do this still better even than he cared to do; I for my part cared much more that he should than he ever did himself, and then it was, I dare say, that I made the reflection: "He took in the picture of Italy, with his firm hard gift, having the chance while William and I were still, comparatively, small untouched and gaping barbarians; and it should always be in him to do at some odd fine moment a certain honour to that." I held to it that that sensibility had played in him more than by any outward measure at the time; which was perhaps indeed one of the signs within me of the wasteful habit or trick of a greater feeling for people's potential propriety or felicity or full expression than they seemed able to have themselves. At all events I was absolutely never to cease to remember for Bob, through everything—and there was much and of the most agitated and agitating—that he had been dipped as a boy into the sacred stream; to some effect which, thanks to two or three of his most saving and often so amusing sensibilities, the turbid sea of his life might never quite wash away.

William had meanwhile come to Bonn with us, but was domiciled with another tutor, younger and fairer and more of the world, above all more ventilated and ventilating, Herr Stromberg, whose defect might in fact have seemed that, with his constant exhibition of the stamp received by him from the writings of Lord Macaulay, passages of which he could recite by heart, and the circumstance that his other pupil, William's comrade for a time, was of unmitigatedly English, that is of quasi-Byronic association, he didn't quite rise to the full gothic standard. Otherwise indeed our brother moved on the higher plane of light and air and ease, and above all of enjoyed society, that we felt he naturally must. Present to me yet is the thrill of learning from him that his English fellow-pupil was the grandson, if I remember rightly the degree of descent, of Mary Chaworth, Byron's "first love," and my sense afterwards, in gaping at young Mr. Musters himself, that this independently romantic contact would have been more to my own private purpose at least than the most emphasised gothicism. None the less do I regain it as a part of my current vision that Frau Stromberg, who was young and fair, wrote tragedies as well as made pancakes—which were served to each consumer double, a thick confiture within being the reason of this luxuriance, and being also a note beyond our experience in the Bonn-Gasse; and that with the printed five acts of a certain "Cleopatra" before me, read aloud in the first instance to her young inmates and by my brother passed on to me, I lost myself in the view of I scarce knew what old-world Germanic grace, positively, or little court-city practice of the theatre: these things so lived in the small thick pamphlet, "grey paper with blunt type" and bristling, to my discomfiture, with descriptive stage directions, vast dense bracketed tracts, gothic enough in all conscience, as to which I could already begin to wonder whether such reinforcements of presentation proved more for or against the true expressional essence of the matter; for or against, that is, there being nothing at all so dramatic, so chargeable with meaning and picture, as speech, of whatever sort, made perfect. Such speculations, I may parenthesise, might well have been fostered, and doubtless were, by an impression that I find commemorated in a few lines of a letter of my father's to a friend in America—he having brought us on to Bonn, introduced us to our respective caretakers and remained long enough to have had an evening at the theatre, to which we accompanied him. "We had Ristori to play Mary Stuart for us last night—which was the vulture counterfeiting Jenny Wren. Every little while the hoarse exulting voice, the

30

sanguinary beak, the lurid leer of menace, and the relentless talons looked forth from the feathery mass and sickened you with disgust. She would do Elizabeth better." I recall the performance in every feature, as well as my absence of such reserves, though quite also the point to which I was impressed by the utterance of them; not that it didn't leave me at the same time free to feel that the heroine of history represented could scarce have been at all a dove-like, much less a wren-like person. She had indeed on Madame Ristori's showing prodigious resources of militant mobility—of what in fact would be called to-day mobilisation. Several years later on I was to see the actress play the same part in America; and then, if I am not mistaken, was to note scarce more than one point; the awful effect on *any* histrionic case, even on one so guardedly artful as hers, of having been dragged round the globe and forced home, so far as might be, to imperfect comprehensions. The big brush had come fairly to daub the canvas. Let the above, however, serve in particular to lead in as many examples of my father's singularly striking and personal habit of expression and weight of thought as these pages may find room for.

The one difficulty is that to open that general door into the limbo of old letters, charged with their exquisite ghostly appeal, is almost to sink into depths of concession. I yield here for instance to the claim of a page or two from William, just contemporary and addressed to our parents in Paris—and yield perhaps but for no better reason than that of the small historic value or recoverable charm that I am moved to find in its illustrative items. The reference of its later lines is to a contemporary cousin, young and blooming, by whom I have already ever so lightly brushed[2] and who figured quite with the grand air on our young horizon; the only daughter of the brightest of the Albany uncles (by that time lost and mourned) now on the tour of Europe with a pair of protective elders for her entrance upon life and at that hour surrounding our parents, her uncle and aunt, with a notably voluminous rustle of fresh Paris clothes, the far-spreading drapery of the more and more draped and flounced and "sloped" second Empire. This friendly frou-frou almost reached our ears, so sociable for us was every sound of her, in our far-off Rhineland. She was with her stature and shape the finest possible person to carry clothes, and I thought of her, with a revival of the old yearning envy, as now quite transcendently orphaned and bereft, dowered, directed and equipped.

Your hearts, I know, would have been melted if you had had a view of us this Sunday morning. I went directly after breakfast for the boys, and though H. had an "iron stomach-ache," as he called it, we went off together to that low wooded hill which the Aunt could see from her window when you were here, and walked about till dinner-time, H. being all the while in great pain. In one part we found a platform with a stone bench commanding a view of the whole valley, and, as we were rather tired, sat down on it, H. and Wilky each with a Once a Week, while I tried to draw the view in my pocket-book. We wondered what our beloved parents were doing at that moment, 11.30, and thought you must all have been in your salon, Alice at the window with her eyes fixed on her novel, but eating some rich fruit that Father has just brought in for her from the Palais Royal, and the lovely Mother and Aunt in armchairs, their hands crossed in front of them, listening to Father, who walks up and down talking of the superiority of America to these countries after all, and how much better it is we should have done with them. We wished, oh we wished we could have been with you to join in the conversation and partake of the fruit. We got up from the seat and went on with a heavy sigh, but in a way so fraternal, presenting such a sweet picture of brotherly unitedness and affection, that it would have done you good to see us.

And so it is every day that we meet for our shorter walks and talks. The German gets on slowly, but I notice a very marked improvement in talking. I have not kept at it so hard this last week as before, and I prevent H. from working his eyes out, which he seems on the whole rather less inclined to do. I am going to read as much as I can the rest of the time we are here. It seems a mere process of soaking, requiring no mental effort, but only time and steady patience. My room is very comfortable now I've got used to it, and I have a pair of slippers of green plush heavy and strong enough to last all my life and then be worn by my children. The photograph of our Zoffingen group has come, which gives me a moustache big enough for three lifeguardsmen. Tell us something more about Mary Helen. How long does she expect to stay in Europe, and who is this Dr. Adams—the man she is engaged to? She directs me to write to her in his care—so that I wish you would ask her, as she says she hopes to meet me, whether I shall still address her as Miss James? Of course it would be painful, but I think I could do it if Adams weren't there. Let the delicious little grey-eyed Alice be locked up alone on the day after the receipt of this with paper and envelopes to write a letter unassisted, uncorrected and unpunctuated to her loving brothers, who would send her novels and peaches if they could. What a blessing it is to have such parents, such a perfect Mother and magnificent Father and dear good Aunt and splendid little Sister!

I may mention that Mary Helen was not "engaged" to the gentleman above-mentioned, and was eventually to marry the late Alfred Grymes, originally of Louisiana. Also that a letter subsequent to this, apparently of the first days in September, sounds to his father the first note of my brother's definite personal preference, as he seemed lately and increasingly, though not in conditions markedly propitious, to have become aware of it, for an adoption of the "artistic career." It was an odd enough circumstance, in respect to the attested blood in our veins, that no less than three of our father's children, with two of his grandsons to add to these, and with a collateral addendum representing seven, in all, of our grandfather's, William James's, descendants in three generations, should have found the artistic career in general and the painter's trade in particular irresistibly solicit them.

I wish you would as you promised set down as clearly as you can on paper what your idea of the nature of Art *is*, because I do not, probably, understand it fully, and should like to have it presented in a form that I might think over at my leisure. I wish you would do so as fully as you conveniently can, so that I may ruminate it—and I won't say more about it till I have heard from you again. As for what your last letter did contain, what can I do but thank you for every word of it and assure you that they went to the right spot. Having such a Father with us, how can we be other than in some measure worthy of him?—if not perhaps as eminently so as the distance leads his fond heart to imagine. I never value him so much as when I am away from him. At home I see only his striking defects, but here he seems all perfection, and I wonder as I write why I didn't cherish him more when he was beside me. I beg darling old Mother's forgiveness too for the rude and dastardly way in which I snub her, and the Aunt for the impatience and violence I have always shown her. I shall be a perfect sherry-cobbler to both of them, and to the small Alice too, young as she may be for such treats.

I have just got home from dining with the boys and their Humperts; where I found the Doctor as genial as ever and the two old ladies perfect characters for Dickens. They have been so shut out from the world and melting together so long by the kitchen fire that the minds of both have become fused into one, and then seem to constitute a sort of two-bodied individual. I never saw anything more curious than the way they sit mumbling together at the end of the table, each using simultaneously the same comment if anything said at our end strikes their ear. H. pegs away pretty stoutly, but I don't think you need worry about him. He and Wilky appear to get on in great harmony and enliven themselves occasionally by brotherly trials of strength, quite good-natured, in their room, when excess of labour has made them sleepy or heavy. In these sometimes one, sometimes the other is victorious. They often pay me a visit here while I am dressing, which of course is highly convenient—and I have more than once been with *them* early enough to be present at Wilky's tumble out of bed and consequent awakening, with the call on the already-at-work H.: "Why the mischief didn't you stop me?" Wilky and I walked to Rolandseck yesterday afternoon, and after a furious race back to the station found ourselves too late for the train by a second. So we took a boat and rowed down here, which was delightful. We are going to put H. through a splashing good walk daily. A thousand thanks to the cherry-lipped, apricot-nosed, double-chinned little Sister for her strongly dashed-off letter, which inflamed the hearts of her lonely brothers with an intense longing to smack her celestial cheeks.

III

I have before me another communication of about the same moment, a letter addressed to his father in Paris within that month; from which, in spite of its lively interest as I hold, I cull nothing—and precisely because of that interest, which prescribes for it a later appearance in conditions in which it may be given entire. William is from this season on, to my sense, so livingly and admirably reflected in his letters, which were happily through much of his career both numerous and highly characteristic, that I feel them particularly plead, in those cases in which they most testify to his personal history, for the separate gathered presentation that happily awaits them. *There* best may figure the serious and reasoned reply drawn from him by some assuredly characteristic enough communication of our parent's own in respect to his declared preference for a painter's life over any other. Lost is this original and, in the light of later matters, sufficiently quaint declaration, and lost the paternal protest answered by my brother from Bonn and anything *but* infelicitous, on its side, so far as the truer apprehension went, under the showing of the time to come. The only thing was that our father had a wonderful way of being essentially right without being practically or, as it were, vulgarly, determinant, and that this relegation of his grounds of contention to the sphere of the non-immediate, the but indirectly urgent, from the point of view of the thing really to *do*, couldn't but often cause impatience in young breasts conscious of gifts or desires or ideals of which the very sign and warrant, the truth they were known by, was that they were susceptible of application. It was in no world of close application that our wondrous parent moved, and his indifference at the first blush to the manifestation of special and marketable talents and faculties, restlessly outward purposes of whatever would-be "successful" sort, was apt to be surpassable only by his delight subsequently taken in our attested and visible results, the very fruits of application; as to which the possibility, perhaps even the virtual guarantee, hadn't so much left him cold in advance as made him adversely and "spiritually" hot. The sense of that word was the most living thing in the world for him—to the point that the spiritual simply meant to him the practical and the successful, so far as he could get into touch with such denominations, or so far, that is, as he could face them or care for them *a priori*. Fortunately, as he had observational powers of the happiest, perceptions—perceptions of character and value, perceptions of relation and effect, perceptions in short of the whole—turned to the ground sensibly beneath our feet, as well as a splendid, an extraordinarily animated and, so far as he himself at least was concerned, guiding and governing soul, justice and generosity always eventually played up, the case worked itself happily out, and before we knew it he had found it quite the rightest of all cases, while we on our side had had the liveliest, and certainly the most amusing and civilising, moral or, as he would have insisted, spiritual recreation by the way.

My brother challenges him, with a beautiful deference, on the imputed damage to what might be best in a man by the professional pursuit of "art"— which he appears to have set forth with characteristic emphasis; and I take the example for probably one of the rarest in all the so copious annals of parental opposition to the æsthetic as distinguished from some other more respectable course. What was marked in our father's prime uneasiness in presence of any particular form of success we might, according to our lights as then glimmering, propose to invoke was that it bravely, or with such inward assurance, dispensed with any suggestion of an alternative. What we were to do instead was just to *be* something, something unconnected with specific doing, something free and uncommitted, something finer in short than being *that*, whatever it was, might consist of. The "career of art" has again and again been deprecated and denounced, on the lips of anxiety or authority, as a departure from the career of business, of industry and respectability, the so-called regular life, but it was perhaps never elsewhere to know dissuasion on the very ground of its failing to uplift the spirit in the ways it most pretends to. I must in fairness add, however, that if the uneasiness I here refer to continued, and quite by exception as compared with the development of other like episodes, during the whole of my brother's fortunately but little prolonged studio season, it was really because more alternatives swarmed before our parent's eyes, in the cause, than he could bring himself to simplify it by naming. He apprehended ever so deeply and tenderly his eldest son's other genius—as to which he was to be so justified; though this indeed was not to alter the fact that when afterwards that subject went in, by a wondrous reaction, for the pursuit of science, first of chemistry and then of anatomy and physiology and medicine, with psychology and philosophy at last piling up the record, the rich *malaise* at every turn characteristically betrayed itself, each of these surrenders being, by the measure of them in the parental imagination, so comparatively narrowing. That was the nearest approach to any plea for some other application of the spirit—that they *were* narrowing. When I myself, later on, began to "write" it was breathed upon me with the finest bewildering eloquence, with a power of suggestion in truth which I fairly now count it a gain to have felt play over me, that this too was narrowing. On the subsequent history of which high paradox no better comment could occur to me than my find of a passage in a letter long subsequently addressed to Mr. James T. Fields, then proprietor and editor of the Atlantic Monthly magazine—a letter under date of May 1868 and referring clearly to some published remarks on a certain young writer which did violence to the blessedly quick paternal prejudice.

I had no sooner left your sanctum yesterday than I was afflicted to remember how I had profaned it by my unmeasured talk about poor H. Please forget it utterly. I don't know how it is with better men, but the parental sentiment is so fiendish a thing with me that if anyone attempt to slay my young, especially in a clandestine way, or out of a pious regard (*e.g.*) to the welfare of the souls comprised in the diocese of the Atlantic, I can't help devoting him bag and baggage to the infernal gods. I am not aware of my animus until I catch, as yesterday, a courteous ear; then the unholy fire flames forth at such a rate as to leave me no doubt on reflection where it was originally lighted.

Almost all my dear father is there, making the faded page to-day inexpressibly touching to me; his passionate tenderness, his infinite capacity for reaction on reaction, a force in him fruitful in so many more directions than any high smoothness of *parti-pris* could be, and his beautiful fresh individual utterance, always so stamped with the very whole of him. The few lines make for me, after all the years, a sort of silver key, so exquisitely fitting, to the treasure of living intercourse, of a domestic air quickened and infinitely coloured, comprised in all our younger time. The renewed sense of which, however, has carried me for the moment too far from the straighter line of my narrative.

The author of the young letter of which I have deferred presentation met in Paris, shortly after that date, the other party to the discussion; and the impression of the endless day of our journey, my elder and my younger brothers' and mine, from Bonn to that city, has scarcely faded from me. The railway service was so little then what it has become that I even marvel at our having made our connections between our early rise in the Bonn-Gasse and our midnight tumble into bed at the Hôtel des Trois Empereurs in the Place du Palais Royal; a still-felt rapture, a revelation of the Parisian idea of bed after the rude German conception, our sore discipline for so many weeks. I remember Cologne and its cathedral almost in the bland dawn, and our fresh start thence for Strasbourg, now clearly recognised, alas, as a start back to America, to which it had been of a sudden settled that we were, still with a fine inconsequence, to return. We had seen Cologne cathedral by excursion from Bonn, but we saw Strasbourg, to my sorrow until a far later occasion soothed it, only as a mild monster behind bars, that is above chimneys, housetops and fortifications; a loss not made up to me by other impressions or particulars, vivid and significant as I found myself none the less supposing several of these. Those were the September days in which French society, so far as it was of the Empire at least, moved more or less in its mass upon Homburg and Baden-Baden; and we met it in expressive samples, and in advance and retreat, during our incessant stops, those long-time old stops, unknown to the modern age, when everyone appeared to alight and walk about with the animation of prisoners suddenly pardoned, and ask for conveniences, and clamour for food, and get mixed with the always apparently still dustier people of opposite trains drawn up for the same purposes. We appeared to be concerned with none but first-class carriages, as an effect of which our own was partly occupied, the livelong day, by the *gens* of a noble French house as to which we thus had frequent revelations—a pair of footmen and a lady's maid, types of servile impudence taking its ease, who chattered by the hour for our wonderstruck ears, treating them to their first echo of the strange underworld, the sustaining vulgarity, of existences classified as "great." They opened vistas, and I remember how when, much later, I came to consider the designed picture, first in Edmond About and then in Alphonse Daudet, of fifty features symptomatic of the social pace at which the glittering régime hurried to its end, there came back to me the breath of this sidewind of the frenzied dance that we had caught during those numerous and so far from edifying hours in our fine old deep-seated compartment. The impression, I now at any rate perfectly recover, was one that could feed full enough any optimism of the appointedly modest condition. It was true that Madame la Marquise, who was young and good-natured and pretty without beauty, and unmistakably "great," exhaling from afar, as I encouraged myself to imagine, the scented air of the Tuileries, came on occasion and looked in on us and smiled, and even pouted, through her elegant patience; so that she at least, I recollect, caused to swim before me somehow such a view of happy privilege at the highest pitch as made me sigh the more sharply, even if the less professedly, for our turning our backs on the complex order, the European, fresh to me still, in which contrasts flared and flourished and through which discrimination could unexhaustedly riot—pointing so many more morals, withal, if that was the benefit it was supposed to be, than we should find pretexts for "on the other side." We were to fall as soon as we were at home again to reading the Revue des Deux Mondes—though doubtless again I should speak here, with any emphasis, but for myself; my chin, in Europe, had scarce risen to the level of that publication; but at Newport in Rhode Island, our next following place of sojourn, I speedily shot up so as quite to bend down to it: it took its place therewith as the very headspring of culture, a mainstay in exile, and as opening wide in especial the doors of that fictive portrayal of a society which put a price, for the brooding young reader, on cases, on *cadres*, in the Revue parlance, already constituted and propitiously lighted. Then it was that the special tension of the dragged-out day from Cologne to Paris proved, on the absurdest scale, a preparation, justified itself as a vivid point of reference: I was to know what the high periodical meant when I encountered in its *études de mœurs* the blue-chinned corruptible, not to say corrupt, *larbin* and the smart soubrette; it was above all a blessing to feel myself, in the perusal of M. Octave Feuillet, an education, as I supposed, of the taste, not at a marked disadvantage; since who but the Petite Comtesse herself had swung her crinoline in and out of my prospect, or, to put it better, of my preserved past, on one of my occasions of acutest receptivity?

The truth was that acute, that quite desperate receptivity set in for me, under a law of its own—may really be described as having quite raged for me—from the moment our general face, by the restless parental decree (born not a little of parental homesickness and reinforced by a theory of that complaint on our own part, we having somehow in Europe "no companions," none but mere parents themselves), had been turned again to the quarter in which there would assuredly be welcomes and freedoms and unchecked appropriations, not to say also cousins, of both sexes and of a more and more engaging time of life, cousins kept and tended and adorned for us in our absence, together with the solicitation for our favour of possible, though oh so just barely possible, habitats before which the range of Europe paled; but which, nevertheless, to my aching fancy, meant premature abdication, sacrifice and, in one dreadful word, failure. I had had cousins, naturally, in the countries we were quitting, but to a limited degree; yet I think I already knew I had had companions in as full a measure as any I was still to know—inasmuch as my imagination made out one, in the complex order and the coloured air, almost wherever I turned; and, inasmuch as, further, to live by the imagination was to live almost only in that way, so to foresee the comparative, not to say the absolute, absence of tonic accent in the appearances complacently awaiting me, as well as to forecast in these appearances, at the best, a greater paucity, was really to enjoy a sharp prevision of dearth. Certain it is that those supreme moments of Paris, those after-days at the Trois Empereurs, were to flush for me, as they ebbed, with images and visions; judged by any achieved act of possession I hadn't assuredly much to give up, but intensity of sentiment, resting on a good disposition, makes for its own sake the most of opportunity, and I buried my associations, which had been in a manner till lately my hopes as well, with all decent dignity and tenderness. These more or less secret obsequies lent to our further brief delay a quality of suppressed excitement; the "old-world" hours were numbered too dreadfully—had shrunk but to a handful: I had waked up to that, as with a passionate even if private need for gathering in and saving, on the morrow of our reaching our final sticking-place: I had slipped from my so cushioned sleep, my canopied couch, to hang, from the balcony of our

quatrième, my brothers' and mine, over that Place du Palais Royal and up
against that sculptured and storied façade of the new Louvre which seemed
to me then to represent, in its strength, the capacity and chiselled rim of some
such potent vivifying cup as it might have been given us, under a happier
arrangement, to taste now in its fulness and with a braver sense for it. Over
against us on the great palace wall, as I make out—if not for that occasion then
for some other—were statues of heroes, Napoleon's young generals, Hoche,
Marceau, Desaix or whoever, such a galaxy as never was or should ever be
again for splendid monumental reference; and what it somehow came to was
that here massed itself the shining second Empire, over which they stood
straight aloft and on guard, like archangels of the sword, and that the whole
thing was a high-pitched wonder and splendour, which we had already, in our
small gaping way, got into a sort of relation with and which would have ever
so much more ever so thrillingly to give us. What it would give us loomed
but vaguely enough out of the great hum and the great toned perspective, and
withal the great noble expense, of which we had constant reminder; but that
we were present at something it would be always after accounted a privilege
to have been concerned with, and that we were perversely and inconsiderately
dropping out of it, and for a reason, so far as there might be a reason, that was
scarcely less than strange—all this loomed large to me as our interval shrank,
and I even ask myself before the memory of it whether I was ever again in
the later and more encompassing and accommodating years to have in those
places so rich a weight of consciousness to carry or so grand a presumption
of joy. The presumption so boldly entertained was, if you please, of what
the whole thing meant. It meant, immensely, the glittering régime, and that
meant in turn, prodigiously, something that would probably never be meant
quite to any such tune again: so much one positively and however absurdly
said to one's self as one stood up on the high balcony to the great insolence
of the Louvre and to all the history, all the glory again and all the imposed
applause, not to say worship, and not to speak of the implied inferiority, on
the part of everything else, that it represented. And the sense was of course
not less while one haunted at odd hours the arcades and glass galleries of the
Palais Royal close at hand—as if to store up, for all the world, treasures of
impression that might be gnawed, in seasons or places of want, like winter

pears or a squirrel's hoard of nuts, and so perhaps keep one alive, as to one's most vital faculty above-mentioned, till one should somehow or other be able to scramble back.

The particular ground for our defection, which I obscurely pronounced mistaken, was that since William was to embrace the artistic career—and freedom for this experiment had been after all, as I repeat that it was always in like cases to be, not in the least grudgingly granted him—our return to America would place him in prompt and happy relation to William Hunt, then the most distinguished of our painters as well as one of the most original and delightful of men, and who had cordially assured us that he would welcome such a pupil. This was judged among us at large, other considerations aiding, a sound basis for action; but never surely had so odd a motive operated for a break with the spell of Paris. We named the motive generally, I think, and to the credit of our earnest good faith, with confidence—and I am of course not sure how often our dear father may not explicatively have mentioned the shy fact that he himself in any case had gradually ceased to "like" Europe. This affects me at present as in the highest degree natural: it was to be his fortune for the rest of his life to find himself, as a worker in his own field and as to what he held most dear, scantly enough heeded, reported or assimilated even in his own air, no brisk conductor at any time of his remarkable voice; but in Europe his isolation had been utter—he had there had the sense of playing his mature and ardent thought over great dense constituted presences and opaque surfaces that could by their very nature scarce give back so much as a shudder. No more admirable case of apostolic energy combined with philosophic patience, of constancy of conviction and solitary singleness of production unperturbed, can I well conceive; and I certainly came later on to rejoice in his having had after a certain date to walk, if there was a preference, rather in the thin wilderness than in the thick. I dare say that when we returned to America toward the end of 1860, some five years and a half after our departure, it may have been with illusions not a few for him about the nature of the desert, or in other words about the degree of sensibility of the public, there awaiting him; but the pretext given him by his so prized and admired eldest son was at the worst, and however eccentric our action, inspiring: I alone of the family perhaps made bold not to say quite directly or literally that we went home to learn to paint. People stared or laughed when we said it, and I disliked their thinking us so simple—though dreaming too a little perhaps that they might have been struck with our patriotism. This however conveyed but a chill the more—since we didn't in the least go to our friend, who had been Couture's and Frère's pupil, who had spent years in France and of whom it was the common belief that you couldn't for the life of you tell him from a French painter, because he was patriotic; but because he was distinguished and accomplished, charming and kind, and above all known to us and thereby in a manner guaranteed. He looked, as people get to look under such enjoyed or even suffered exposures, extremely like a Frenchman, and, what was noteworthy, still more like a sculptor of the race than a painter; which doubtless had to do with my personally, though I hope, in present cultivated anxiety, not too officiously, sighing at all the explanation the whole thing took. I am bound to add none the less that later on, repatriated and, as to my few contacts, reassured, I found this amount, the apprehension of which had haunted me, no great charge; and seem even to make out that for the first six months of our Newport phase at least we might have passed for strikingly wise. For here was, beyond doubt, a genial, an admirable master; and here also—at such a rate did sparse individuals, scattered notches in the long plain stick, count—was John La Farge. Here moreover—here and everywhere about me, before we could quite turn round—was the War, with its infinite, its truly quite humiliating correction of my (as I now can but so far call it) fatuous little confidence that "appearances," on the native scene, would run short. They were in the event, taking one thing with another, never to hold out for me as they held during those four years. Wondrous this force in them as I at present look back—wondrous I mean in view of that indirectness of its play which my conditions confined me, with such private, though I must add, alas, such helplessly unapplied resentment, to knowing it by. If the force was great the attenuation of its reach was none the less preappointed and constant; so that the case must have come back again but to the degree—call it too, frankly, the force—of one's sensibility, or in other words the blest resource, the supremely breatheable and thereby nourishing and favouring air of one's imaginative life. There were of a truth during that time probably more appearances at one's command in the way of felt aspects, images, apprehended living relations and impressions of the stress of life, than during any other season one was to know; only doubtless with more of the work of their figuring to their utmost, their giving all they could, to do by one's self and, in the last resort, deep within one's breast. The point to be made just here, in any case, is that if we had not recrossed the sea, by way, rather, of such an anticlimax, to William Hunt, we should certainly with brief delay have found ourselves doing it, on the first alarm of War, for the experience I thus too summarily glance at and which I don't pretend to speak of as all my own.

IV

Newport, with repatriation accepted, would have been on many grounds inevitable, I think—as it was to remain inevitable for several years, and this quite apart from William's having to paint; since if I spoke just now of the sweep of our view, from over the water, of a continent, or well-nigh, waiting to receive us, the eligibility of its innumerable sites was a matter much more of our simplified, our almost distressfully uninvolved and unconnected state than of the inherent virtue of this, that or the other particular group of local conditions. Our parents had for us no definite project but to be liberally "good"—in other words so good that the presumption of our being so would literally operate anywhere and anyhow, would really amount in itself to a sort of situated state, a sufficient prime position, and leave other circumstances comparatively irrelevant. What would infallibly have occurred at the best, however, was what did punctually happen—its having to be definitely gathered that, though we might apparently be good, as I say, almost on any ground, there was but one place in which we should even at a restricted pitch be well: Newport imposed itself at that period to so remarkable a degree as the one right residence, in all our great country, for those tainted, under whatever attenuations, with the quality and the effect of detachment. The effect of detachment was the fact of the experience of Europe. Detachment might of course have come from many causes, but it truly came in most cases but from one, though that a fairly merciless: it came from the experience of Europe, and I think was on the whole regarded as—what it could only have been in the sphere of intimacy and secrecy felt to be—without an absolute remedy. As comparatively remedial Newport none the less figured, and this for sundry reasons into the detail of which I needn't go. Its rare distinction and precious attribute was that, being a watering-place, a refuge from summer heats, it had also, were the measure considerably stretched, possibilities of hibernation. We could, under stress, brave there the period from November to June; and it was to be under stress not to know what else to do. That was the pinch to which Europe reduced you; insidiously, fatally disconnected, you could but make the best, as a penalty, of the one marked point of reattachment. The philosophy of all of which was that to confess to disconnection was to confess by the same stroke to leisure—which involved also an admission, however rueful at once and deprecatory, of what might still at that time pass in our unregenerate country for something in the nature of "means." You had had the means, that is, to *become*, so awkwardly, detached—for you might then do that cheaply; but the whole basis of the winter life there, of that spare semblance of the Brighton life, the Folkestone life, the Bath or the Cheltenham or the Leamington life, was that your occupation or avocation should be vague enough; or that you shouldn't in other words be, like everyone you might know save a dozen or so at the most, in business. I remember well how when we were all young together we had, under pressure of the American ideal in that matter, then so rigid, felt it tasteless and even humiliating that the head of our little family was *not* in business, and that even among our relatives on each side we couldn't so much as name proudly anyone who was—with the sole exception of our maternal uncle Robertson Walsh, who looked, ever so benevolently, after our father's "affairs," happily for us. Such had never been the case with the father of any boy of our acquaintance; the business in which the boy's father gloriously *was* stood forth inveterately as the very first note of our comrade's impressiveness. *We* had no note of that sort to produce, and I perfectly recover the effect of my own repeated appeal to our parent for some presentable account of him that would prove us respectable. Business alone was respectable—if one meant by it, that is, the calling of a lawyer, a doctor or a minister (we never spoke of clergymen) as well; I think that if we had had the Pope among us we should have supposed the Pope in business, just as I remember my friend Simpson's telling me crushingly, at one of our New York schools, on my hanging back with the fatal truth about our credentials, that the author of *his* being (we spoke no more of "governors" than we did of "parsons") was in the business of a stevedore. That struck me as a great card to play—the word was fine and mysterious; so that "What shall we tell them you *are*, don't you see?" could but become on our lips at home a more constant appeal. It seemed wantonly to be prompted for our father, and indeed greatly to amuse him, that he should put us off with strange unheard-of attributions, such as would have made us ridiculous in our special circles; his "Say I'm a

46

philosopher, say I'm a seeker for truth, say I'm a lover of my kind, say I'm an author of books if you like; or, best of all, just say I'm a Student," saw us so very little further. Abject it certainly appeared to be reduced to the "student" plea; and I must have lacked even the confidence of my brother Bob, who, challenged, in my hearing and the usual way, was ready not only with the fact that our parent "wrote," but with the further fact that he had written *Lectures and Miscellanies James*. I think that when we settled awhile at Newport there was no one there who had written but Mr. Henry T. Tuckerman, a genial and graceful poet of the Artless Age, as it might still be called in spite of Poe and Hawthorne and Longfellow and Lowell, the most characteristic works of the first and the two last of whom had already appeared; especially as those most characteristic of Mr. Tuckerman referred themselves to a past sufficiently ample to have left that gentleman with a certain deafness and a glossy wig and a portly presence and the reputation, positively, of the most practised and desired of diners-out. He was to be recognised at once as a social value on a scene not under that rubric densely peopled; he constituted indeed such a note as would help to keep others of the vague definability in countenance. Clearly indeed it might happen that an association of vaguenesses would arrive in time, by fondly cleaving together, at the semblance of a common identity; the nature of the case then demanding, however, that they should be methodically vague, take their stand on it and work it for all it was worth. That in truth was made easy by the fact that what I have called our common disconnectedness positively projected and proclaimed a void; disconnected from business we could only be connected with the negation of it, which had as yet no affirmative, no figurative side. This probably would come; figures, in the void, would one by one spring up; but what would be thus required for them was that the void should be ample and, as it were, established. Not to be afraid of it they would have to feel it clear of everything and everyone they knew in the air actually peopled.

William Hunt, for that matter, was already a figure unmmistakable, superficially speaking unsurpassable, just as John La Farge, already mentioned, was so soon to prove to be. They were only two indeed, but they argued the possibility; and so the great thing, as I say, was that, to stand out, they should have margin and light. We couldn't all be figures—on a mere margin, the margin of business, and in the light of the general wonder of our being anything, anything *there*; but we could at least understand the situation and cultivate the possibilities, watch and protect the germs. This consciousness, this aim or ideal, had after all its own intensity—it burned with a pure flame: there is a special joy, clearly, in the hopeful conversion of the desert into the garden, of thinness into thickness, a joy to which the conversion of the thick into the mere dense, of the free into the rank or the close, perhaps gives no clue. The great need that Newport met was that of a basis of reconciliation to "America" when the habit, the taking for granted, of America had been broken or intermitted: it would be hard to say of what subtle secret or magic the place was possessed toward this end, and by a common instinct, I think, we didn't attempt to formulate it—we let it alone, only looking at each other hard, only moving gently, on the brave hypothesis, only in fine deprecating too rude and impatient, too precipitate a doubt of the spell that perhaps might work if we waited and prayed. We did wait and pray, accordingly, scantly-served though the board we might often have felt we had sat down to, and there was a fair company of us to do so, friendliest among whom to our particular effort was my father's excellent friend of many years Edmund Tweedy, already named in pages preparatory to these and who, with his admirable wife, presented himself as our main introducer and initiator. He had married, while we were all young in New York together, a manner of Albany cousin, Mary Temple the elder, aunt of the younger,[3] and had by this time "been through" more than anything, more than everything, of which there could be question for ourselves. The pair had on their marriage gone at once to Europe to live, had put in several years of Italy and yet had at last, particular reasons operating, returned to their native, that is to sterner, realities; those as to which it was our general theory, of so touching a candour as I look back to it, that they offered themselves at Newport in a muffling mitigating air. The air, material, moral, social, was in fact clear and clean to a degree that might well have left us but dazed at the circumjacent blankness; yet as to that I hasten to add too that the blowing out of our bubble, the planting of our garden, the correction of our thinness, the discovery, under stress, of such scraps of colour and conversation, such saving echoes and redeeming references as might lurk for us in each other, all formed in themselves an active, and might at last even grow to suggest an absolutely bustling, process.

48

I come back with a real tenderness of memory for instance to that felicity of the personal, the social, the "literary and artistic," almost really the romantic, identity responding, after a fashion quite to bring tears to the eyes, in proportion as it might have seemed to feel by some divine insufflation what it practically could stand for. What should one call this but the brave triumph of values conscious of having to be almost missionary? There were many such that in "Europe" hadn't had to be missionary at all; in Europe, as it were, one hadn't—comparatively—seen, if not the forest for the trees, then the trees for the forest; whereas on this other great vacuous level every single stem seemed to enjoy for its distinction quite the totality of the daylight and to rise into the air with a gladness that was itself a grace. Of some of the personal importances that acted in that way I should with easier occasion have more to say—I shall as it is have something; but there could perhaps be no better sample of the effect of sharpness with which the forces of culture might emerge than, say, the fairly golden glow of romance investing the mere act of perusal of the Revue des Deux Mondes. There was the charm—though I grant of course that I speak here all for myself, constitutionally and, face to face *with* myself, quite shamelessly an inquirer, a hunter, for charm—that whereas the spell cast had more or less inevitable limits in the world to which such a quality as the best things of the Revue, such a performance of the intellectual and expressional engagement as these suggested, was native and was thereby relative to other generally like phenomena, so it represented among *us*, where it had to take upon itself what I have already alluded to as all the work, far more than its face value. Few of the forces about us reached as yet the level of representation (even if here and there some might have been felt as trying for it); and this made all the difference. Anything suggestive or significant, anything promising or interesting, anything in the least finely charming above all, immensely counted, claimed tendance and protection, almost claimed, or at any rate enjoyed, worship; as for that matter anything finely charming does, quite rightly, anywhere. But our care, our privilege, on occasion our felt felicity, was to foster every symptom and breathe encouragement to every success; to hang over the tenderest shoots that betrayed the principle of growth—or in other words to read devoutly into everything, and as straight as possible, the very fullest meaning we might hope it would learn to have. So at least quite at first—and so again very considerably after the large interval and grim intermission represented by the War; during which interest and quality, to say nothing of quantity, at the highest pitch, ceased in any degree to fail us, and what might be "read into" almost any aspect without exception paled in the light of what was inevitably read out from it. It must be added at the same time that with its long duration the War fell into its place as part of life at large, and that when it was over various other things still than the love of peace were found to have grown.

Immediately, at any rate, the Albany cousins, or a particular group of them, began again to be intensely in question for us; coloured in due course with reflections of the War as their lives, not less than our own, were to become—and coloured as well too, for all sorts of notation and appreciation, from irrepressible private founts. Mrs. Edmund Tweedy, bereft of her own young children, had at the time I speak of opened her existence, with the amplest hospitality, to her four orphaned nieces, who were also our father's and among whom the second in age, Mary Temple the younger, about in her seventeenth year when she thus renewed her appearance to our view, shone with vividest lustre, an essence that preserves her still, more than half a century from the date of her death, in a memory or two where many a relic once sacred has comparatively yielded to time. Most of those who knew and loved, I was going to say adored, her have also yielded—which is a reason the more why thus much of her, faint echo from too far off though it prove, should be tenderly saved. If I have spoken of the elements and presences round about us that "counted," Mary Temple was to count, and in more lives than can now be named, to an extraordinary degree; count as a young and shining apparition, a creature who owed to the charm of her every aspect (her aspects were so many!) and the originality, vivacity, audacity, generosity, of her spirit, an indescribable grace and weight—if one might impute weight to a being so imponderable in common scales. Whatever other values on our scene might, as I have hinted, appear to fail, she was one of the first order, in the sense of the immediacy of the impression she produced, and produced altogether as by the play of her own light spontaneity and curiosity—not, that is, as through a sense of such a pressure and such a motive, or through a care for them, in others. "Natural" to an effect of perfect felicity that we were never to see surpassed is what I have already praised all the Albany *cousinage* of those years for being; but in none of the company was the note so clear as in this rarest, though at the same tune symptomatically or ominously palest, flower of the stem; who was natural at more points and about more things, with a greater range of freedom and ease and reach of horizon than any of the others dreamed of. They had that way, delightfully, with the small, after all, and the common matters—while she had it with those too, but with the great and rare ones over and above; so that she was to remain for us the very figure and image of a felt interest in life, an interest as magnanimously far-spread, or as familiarly and exquisitely fixed, as her splendid shifting sensibility, moral, personal, nervous, and having at once such noble flights and such touchingly discouraged drops, such graces of indifference and inconsequence, might at any moment determine. She was really to remain, for our appreciation, the supreme case of a taste for life as life, as personal living; of an endlessly active and yet somehow a careless, an illusionless, a sublimely forewarned curiosity about it: something that made her, slim and fair and quick, all straightness and charming tossed head, with long light and yet almost sliding steps and a large light postponing, renouncing laugh, the very muse or amateur priestess of rash speculation. To express her in the mere terms of her restless young mind, one felt from the first, was to place her, by a perversion of the truth, under the shadow of female "earnestness"— for which she was much too unliteral and too ironic; so that, superlatively personal and yet as independent, as "off" into higher spaces, at a touch, as all the breadth of her sympathy and her courage could send her, she made it impossible to say whether she was just the most moving of maidens or a disengaged and dancing flame of thought. No one to come after her could easily seem to show either a quick inward life or a brave, or even a bright, outward, either a consistent contempt for social squalors or a very marked genius for moral reactions. She had in her brief passage the enthusiasm of humanity—more, assuredly, than any charming girl who ever circled, and would fain have continued to circle, round a ballroom. This kept her indeed for a time more interested in the individual, the immediate human, than in the race or the social order at large; but that, on the other hand, made her ever so restlessly, or quite inappeasably, "psychologic." The psychology of others, in her shadow—I mean their general resort to it—could only for a long time seem weak and flat and dim, above all not at all amusing. She burned herself out; she died at twenty-four.

At the risk perhaps of appearing to make my own scant adventure the pivot of that early Newport phase I find my reference to William Hunt and his truly fertilising action on our common life much conditioned by the fact that, since W. J., for the first six months or so after our return, daily and devotedly haunted his studio, I myself did no less, for a shorter stretch, under the irresistible contagion. The clearness of the whole passage for me, the clearest impression, above all, of the vivid and whimsical master, an inspirer, during a period that began a little later on, of numberless devotions and loyalties, is what this fond memory of my permitted contact and endeavour still has to give me. Pupils at that time didn't flock to his gates—though they were to do so in Boston, during years, later on; an earnest lady or two, Boston precursors, hovered and flitted, but I remember for the rest (and I speak of a short period) no thorough-going élèves save John La Farge and my brother. I remember, for that matter, sitting quite in solitude in one of the grey cool rooms of the studio, which thus comes back to me as having several, and thinking that I really might get to copy casts rather well, and might in particular see myself congratulated on my sympathetic rendering of the sublime uplifted face of Michael Angelo's "Captive" in the Louvre. I sat over this effort and a few others for long quiet hours, and seem to feel myself again aware, just to that tune, of how happy I ought to be. No one disturbed me; the earnest workers were elsewhere; I had a chamber of the temple all to myself, with immortal forms and curves, with shadows beautiful and right, waiting there on blank-eyed faces for me to prove myself not helpless; and with two or three of Hunt's own fine things, examples of his work in France, transporting me at once and defying. I believed them great productions—thought in especial endless good of the large canvas of the girl with her back presented while she fills her bucket at the spout in the wall, against which she leans with a tension of young muscle, a general expression of back, beneath her dress, and with the pressure of her raised and extended bare arm and flattened hand: this, to my imagination, could only become the prize of some famous collection, the light of some museum, for all the odd circumstance that it was company just then for muddled me and for the queer figures projected by my crayon. Frankly, intensely—that was the great thing—these were hours of Art, art definitely named, looking me full in the face and accepting my stare in return—no longer a tacit implication or a shy subterfuge, but a flagrant unattenuated aim. I had somehow come into the temple by the back door, the *porte d'honneur* opened on another side, and I could never have believed much at best in the length of my stay; but I was there, day by day, as much as any one had ever been, and with a sense of what it "meant" to be there that the most accredited of pupils couldn't have surpassed; so that the situation to this extent really hummed with promise. I fail, I confess, to reconstitute the relation borne by my privilege to that of tuition "in the higher branches," to which it was quite time I should have mounted, enjoyed at the hands of the Reverend William C. Leverett, curate to the then "rector," Doctor Mercer, of that fine old high-spired Trinity Church in which had throbbed, from long before the Revolution as they used to say, the proud episcopal heart of Newport; and feel indeed that I must pretty well have shaken off, as a proved absurd predicament, all submission to my dilemma: all submission of the mind, that is, for if my share of Mr. Leverett's attention was less stinted than my share of William Hunt's (and neither had much duration) it failed to give me the impression that anything worth naming had opened out to me, whereas in the studio I was at the threshold of a world.

It became itself indeed on the spot a rounded satisfying world, the place did; enclosed within the grounds, as we then regarded them, of the master's house, circled about with numerous trees, as we then counted them, and representing a more direct exclusion of vulgar sounds, false notes and harsh reminders than I had ever known. I fail in the least to make out where the real work of the studio went forward; it took somewhere else its earnest course, and our separation—mine from the real workers, my indulged yet ignored state— kept me somehow the safer, as if I had taken some mild and quite harmless drug through which external rubs would reach me from a distance, but which left my own rubbing power, not to say my own smearing or smutching, quite free. Into the world so beautifully valid the master would occasionally walk, inquiring as to what I had done or would do, but bearing on the question with an easy lightness, a friendliness of tact, a neglect of conclusion, which it touches me still to remember. It was impossible to me at that time not so to admire him that his just being to such an extent, as from top to toe and in every accent and motion, the living and communicating Artist, made the issue, with his presence, quite cease to be of how one got on or fell short, and become instead a mere self-sacrificing vision of the picturesque itself, the constituted picturesque or treated "subject," in efficient figure, personal form, vivid human style. I then felt the man the great mystery could mark with its stamp, when wishing the mark unmistakable, teach me just in himself the most and best about any art that I should come to find benignantly concerned with me, for moments however smilingly scant. William Hunt, all muscular spareness and brownness and absence of waste, all flagrant physiognomy, brave bony arch of handsome nose, upwardness of strong eyebrow and glare, almost, of eyes that both recognised and wondered, strained eyes that played over questions as if they were objects and objects as if they were questions, might have stood, to the life, for Don Quixote, if we could associate with that hero a far-spreading beard already a little grizzled, a manner and range of gesture and broken form of discourse that was like a restless reference to a palette and that seemed to take for granted, all about, canvases and models and charming, amusing things, the "tremendously interesting" in the seen bit or caught moment, and the general unsayability, in comparison, of anything else. He never would have perched, it must be added, on Rosinante—he was fonder of horses even than of the method of Couture, and though with a shade of resemblance, as all simple and imaginative men have, to the knight of La Mancha, he least suggested that analogy as he passed in a spinning buggy, his beard flying, behind a favourite trotter. But what he perhaps most puts before me to-day is the grim truth of the merciless manner in which a living and hurrying public educates itself, making and devouring in a day reputations and values which represent something of the belief in it that it has had in *them*, but at the memory of which we wince, almost to horror, as at the legend of victims who have been buried alive. Oh the cold grey luminaries hung about in odd corners and back passages, and that we have known shining and warm! They serve at the most now as beacons warning any step not to come *that* way, whatever it does; the various attested ways it may not with felicity come growing thus all the while in number.

54

John La Farge became at once, in breaking on our view, quite the most interesting person we knew, and for a time remained so; he became a great many other things beside—a character, above all, if there ever was one; but he opened up to us, though perhaps to me in particular, who could absorb all that was given me on those suggestive lines, prospects and possibilities that made the future flush and swarm. His foreignness, which seemed great at that time, had gained a sharper accent from a long stay made in France, where both on his father's and his mother's side he had relations, and had found, to our hovering envy, all sorts of charming occasions. He had spent much time in Brittany, among kindred the most romantically interesting, people and places whose very names, the De Nanteuils of Saint-Pol-de-Léon, I seem to remember for instance, cast a spell across comparatively blank Newport sands; he had brought home with him innumerable water-colour sketches, Breton peasants, costumes, interiors, bits of villages and landscape; and I supposed him to have had on such ground the most delightful adventure in the world. How was one not to suppose it at a time when the best of one's education, such as that was, had begun to proceed almost altogether by the aid of the Revue des Deux Mondes, a periodical that supplied to us then and for several years after (or again I can but speak for myself) all that was finest in the furniture and the fittings of romance? Those beginnings of Newport were our first contact with New England—a New England already comparatively subdued and sophisticated, a Samson shorn of his strength by the shears of the Southern, and more particularly of the New York, Delilah; the result of which, still speaking for myself, was a prompt yearning and reaching out, on the part of the spirit, for some corrective or antidote to whatever it was that might be going, in the season to come, least charmingly or informingly or inspiringly to press upon us. I well recall my small anxious foresight as to a required, an indispensable provision against either assault or dearth, as if the question might be of standing an indefinite siege; and how a certain particular capacious closet in a house we were presently to occupy took on to my fond fancy the likeness at once of a store of edibles, both substantial and succulent, and of a hoard of ammunition for the defence of any breach—the Revue accumulating on its shelves at last in serried rows and really building up beneath us with its slender firm salmon-coloured blocks an alternative sphere of habitation. There will be more to say of this, bristling or rather flowering with precious particulars, if I stray so far; but the point for the moment was that one would have pushed into that world of the closet, one would have wandered or stumbled about in it quite alone if it hadn't been that La Farge was somehow always in it with us. That was in those years his admirable function and touch—that he affected me as knowing his way there as absolutely no one else did, and even as having risen of a sudden before us to bear us this quickening company. Nobody else, not another creature, was free of it to that tune; the whole mid-century New England—as a rough expression of what the general consciousness most signified—was utterly out of it; which made, you see, a most unequal division of our little working, or our totally cogitative, universe into the wondrous esoteric quarter peopled just by us and our friend and our common references, and the vast remainder of the public at large, the public of the innumerably uninitiated even when apparently of the most associated.

All of which is but a manner of expressing the intensity, as I felt it, of our Franco-American, our most completely accomplished friend's presence among us. Out of the safe rich home of the Revue, which opened away into the vastness of visions, he practically stepped, and into it, with all his ease, he mysteriously returned again: he came nearer to being what might have been meant concretely throughout it all—though meant most of course in its full-charged stream of fiction—than any other visiting figure. The stream of fiction was so constant an appeal to the charmed, by which I mean of course the predisposed, mind that it fairly seemed at moments to overflow its banks and take to its bosom any recognised, any congruous creature or thing that might happen to be within reach. La Farge was of the type—the "European," and this gave him an authority for me that it verily took the length of years to undermine; so that as the sense of those first of them in especial comes back to me I find it difficult, even under the appeal to me of the attempt, to tell how he was to count in my earliest culture. If culture, as I hold, is a matter of attitude quite as much as of opportunity, and of the form and substance of the vessel carried to the fountain no less than of the water-supply itself, there couldn't have been better conditions for its operating drop by drop. It operates ever much more, I think, by one's getting whatever there may happen to be out for one's use than by its conforming to any abstract standard of quantity or lustre. It may work, as between dispenser and subject, in so incalculably personal a manner that no chemical analysis shall recover it, no common estimate of forces or amounts find itself in the least apply. The case was that La Farge swam into our ingenuous ken as the figure of figures, and that such an agent, on a stage so unpeopled and before a scene so unpainted, became salient and vivid almost in spite of itself. The figure was at a premium, and fit for any glass case that its vivacity should allow to enclose it—wherein it might be surrounded by wondering, admiring and often quite inevitably misconceiving observers. It was not that these too weren't agents in their way, agents in some especial good cause without the furtherance of which we never should have done at all; but they were by that very fact specialised and stiffened, committed to their one attitude, the immediately profitable, and incapable of that play of gesture in which we recognise representation. A representative, a rounded figure, however, is as to none of its relations definable or announceable beforehand; we only know it, for good or for ill, but with something of the throb of elation always, when we see it, and then it in general sufficiently accounts for itself. We often for that matter insist on its being a figure, we positively make it one, in proportion as we seem to need it—or as in other words we too acutely miss the active virtue of representation. It takes some extraordinary set of circumstances or time of life, I think, either to beguile or to hustle us into indifference to some larger felt extension roundabout us of "the world"—a sphere the confines of which move on even as we ourselves move and which is always there, just beyond us, to twit us with the more it should have to show if we were a little more "of" it. Sufficiency shuts us in but till the man of the world—never prefigured, as I say, only welcomed on the spot—appears; when we see at once how much we have wanted him. When we fail of that acknowledgment, that sense as of a tension, an anxiety or an indigence relieved, it is of course but that the extraordinary set of circumstances, or above all the extraordinary time of life I speak of, has indeed intervened.

It was as a man of the world that, for all his youth, La Farge rose or, still better, bowed, before us, his inclinations of obeisance, his considerations of address being such as we had never seen and now almost publicly celebrated.

This was what most immediately and most iridescently showed, the truth being all the while that the character took on in him particular values without which it often enough, though then much more grossly, flourishes. It was by these enrichments of curiosity, of taste and genius, that he became the personality, as we nowadays say, that I have noted—the full freshness of all of which was to play but through his younger time, or at least through our younger apprehension. He was so "intellectual"—that was the flower; it crowned his being personally so finished and launched. The wealth of his cultivation, the variety of his initiations, the inveteracy of his forms, the degree of his *empressement* (this in itself, I repeat, a revelation) made him, with those elements of the dandy and the cavalier to which he struck us as so picturesquely sacrificing, a cluster of bright promises, a rare original and, though not at all a direct model for simpler folk, as we then could but feel ourselves, an embodiment of the gospel of esthetics. Those more resounding forms that our age was to see this gospel take on were then still to come, but I was to owe them in the later time not half the thrill that the La Farge of the prime could set in motion. He was really an artistic, an esthetic nature of wondrous homogeneity; one was to have known in the future many an unfolding that went with a larger ease and a shrewder economy, but never to have seen a subtler mind or a more generously wasteful passion, in other words a sincerer one, addressed to the problems of the designer and painter. Of his long later history, full of flights and drops, advances and retreats, experiment and performance, of the endless complications of curiosity and perversity, I say nothing here save that if it was to contradict none of our first impressions it was to qualify them all by others still more lively; these things belonging quite to some other record. Yet I may just note that they were to represent in some degree an eclipse of the so essentially harmonious person round whom a positive grace of legend had originally formed itself. I see him at this hour again as that bright apparition; see him, jacketed in black velvet or clad from top to toe in old-time elegances of cool white and leaning much forward with his protuberant and over-glazed, his doubting yet all-seizing vision, dandle along the shining Newport sands in far-away summer sunsets on a charming chestnut mare whose light legs and fine head and great sweep of tail showed the Arab strain—quite as if (what would have been characteristic of him) he had borrowed his mount from the adorable Fromentin, whom we already knew as a painter, but whose acquaintance as a writer we were of course so promptly to owe him that when "Dominique" broke upon us out of the Revue as one of the most exquisite literary events of our time it found us doubly responsive.

So, at any rate, he was there, and there to stay—intensely among us but somehow not withal of us; his being a Catholic, and apparently a "real" one in spite of so many other omnisciences, making perhaps by itself the greatest difference. He had been through a Catholic college in Maryland, the name of which, though I am not assured of it now, exhaled a sort of educational elegance; but where and when he had so miraculously laid up his stores of reading and achieved his universal saturation was what we longest kept asking ourselves. Many of these depths I couldn't pretend to sound, but it was immediate and appreciable that he revealed to us Browning for instance; and this, oddly enough, long after Men and Women had begun (from our Paris time on, if I remember) to lie upon our parents' book-table. *They* had not divined in us as yet an aptitude for that author; whose appeal indeed John reinforced to our eyes by the reproduction of a beautiful series of illustrative drawings, two or three of which he was never to surpass—any more than he was to complete his highly distinguished plan for the full set, not the least faded of his hundred dreams. Most of all he revealed to us Balzac; having so much to tell me of what was within that formidably-plated door, in which he all expertly and insidiously played the key, that to re-read even after long years the introductory pages of Eugénie Grandet, breathlessly seized and earnestly absorbed under his instruction, is to see my initiator's youthful face, so irregular but so refined, look out at me between the lines as through blurred prison bars. In Mérimée, after the same fashion, I meet his expository ghost—hovering to remind me of how he started me on La Vénus d'Ille; so that nothing would do but that I should translate it, try to render it as lovingly as if it were a classic and old (both of which things it now indeed is) and send it off to the New York weekly periodical of that age of crudest categories which was to do me the honour neither of acknowledging nor printing nor, clearly, since translations did savingly appear there, in the least understanding it. These again are mild memories—though not differing in that respect from most of their associates; yet I cherish them as ineffaceable dates, sudden milestones, the first distinctly noted, on the road of so much inward or apprehensive life. Our guest—I call him our guest because he was so lingeringly, so abidingly and supersedingly present—began meanwhile to paint, under our eyes, with devotion, with exquisite perception, and above all as with the implication, a hundred times beneficent and fertilising, that if one didn't in these connections consistently take one's stand on supersubtlety of taste one was a helpless outsider and at the best the basest of vulgarians or flattest of frauds—a doctrine more salutary at that time in our world at large than any other that might be sounded. Of all of which ingenuous intensity and activity I should have been a much scanter witness than his then close condisciple, my brother, had not his personal kindness, that of the good-natured and amused elder youth to the enslaved, the yearningly gullible younger, charmed me often into a degree of participation. Occasions and accidents come back to me under their wash of that distilled old Newport light as to which we more and more agreed that it made altogether exceptionally, on our side of the world, for possibility of the *nuance*, or in other words for picture and story; such for example as my felt sense of how unutterably it was the real thing, the gage of a great future, when I one morning found my companions of the larger, the serious studio inspired to splendid performance by the beautiful young manly form of our cousin Gus Barker, then on a vivid little dash of a visit to us and who, perched on a pedestal and divested of every garment, was the gayest as well as the neatest of models. This was my first personal vision of the "life," on a pedestal and in a pose, that had half gleamed and half gloomed through the chiaroscuro of our old friend Haydon; and I well recall the crash, at the sight, of all my inward emulation—so forced was I to recognise on the spot that I might niggle for months over plaster casts and not come within miles of any such point of attack. The bravery of my brother's own in especial dazzled me out of every presumption; since nothing less than that meant drawing (they were not using colour) and since our genial kinsman's perfect gymnastic figure meant living truth, I should certainly best testify to the whole mystery by pocketing my pencil.

I secured and preserved for long William's finished rendering of the happy figure—which was to speak for the original, after his gallant death, in sharper and finer accents perhaps than aught else that remained of him; and it wanted but another occasion somewhat later on, that of the sitting to the pair of pupils under Hunt's direction of a subject presented as a still larger challenge, to feel that I had irrecoverably renounced. Very handsome were the head and shoulders of Katherine Temple, the eldest of those Albany cousins then gathered at Newport under their, and derivatively our, Aunt Mary's wing, who afterwards was to become Mrs. Richard Emmet—the Temples and the Emmets being so much addicted to alliances that a still later generation was to bristle for us with a delightful Emmetry, each member of it a different blessing; she sat with endless patience, the serenest of models, and W. J.'s portrait of her in oils survives (as well as La Farge's, dealing with her in another view) as a really mature, an almost masterly, piece of painting, having, as has been happily suggested to me, much the air of a characteristic Manet. Such demonstrations would throw one back on regret, so far as my brother was concerned, if subsequent counter-demonstrations hadn't had it in them so much to check the train. For myself at the hour, in any case, the beautiful success with Kitty Temple did nothing but hurry on the future, just as the sight of the charming thing to-day, not less than that of La Farge's profil perdu, or presented ear and neck and gathered braids of hair, quite as charming and quite as painted, touchingly reanimates the past. I say touchingly because of the remembered pang of my acceptance of an admonition so sharply conveyed. Therefore if somewhat later on I could still so fondly hang about in that air of production—so far at least as it enveloped our friend, and particularly after his marriage and his setting up of his house at Newport, vivid proofs alike, as seemed to us all, of his consummate, his raffiné taste, even if we hadn't yet, I think, that epithet for this—it was altogether in the form of mere helpless admirer and inhaler, led captive in part by the dawning perception that the arts were after all essentially one and that even with canvas and brush whisked out of my grasp I still needn't feel disinherited. That was the luxury of the friend and senior with a literary side—that if there were futilities that he didn't bring home to me he nevertheless opened more windows than he closed; since he couldn't have meant nothing by causing my eyes to plunge so straight into the square and dense little formal garden of Mérimée. I might occasionally serve for an abundantly idle young out-of-doors model—as in fact I frequently did, the best perhaps of his early exhibitions of a rare colour-sense even now attesting it; but mightn't it become possible that Mérimée would meanwhile serve for me? Didn't I already see, as I fumbled with a pen, of what the small dense formal garden might be inspiringly symbolic? It was above all wonderful in the La Farge of those years that even as he painted and painted, very slowly and intently and belatedly—his habit of putting back the clock and ignoring every time-scheme but his own was matched only by his view of the constant timeliness of talk, talk as talk, for which no moment, no suspended step, was too odd or too fleeting—he remained as referentially and unexhaustedly bookish, he turned his back by the act as little on our theory of his omniscience as he ceased to disown his job, whatever it might be, while endlessly burying his salient and reinforced eyes and his visibly active organ of scent in some minutest rarity of print, some precious ancientry of binding, mechanically plucked, by the hazard of a touch, from one of the shelves of a stored collection that easily passed with us for unapproached.

He lost himself on these occasions both by a natural ease and by his early adoption and application of the principle of the imperturbable, which promised even from those days to govern his conduct well-nigh to the exclusion of every other. We were to know surely as time went on no comparable case of consistency of attitude—no other such prompt grasp by a nature essentially entire, a settled sovereign self, of the truth of what would work for it most favourably should it but succeed in never yielding the first inch of any ground. Immense every ground thus became by its covering itself from edge to edge with the defence of his serenity, which, whatever his fathomless private dealings with it, was never consentingly, I mean publicly, to suffer a grain of abatement. The artist's serenity, by this conception, was an intellectual and spiritual capital that must never brook defeat—which it so easily might incur by a single act of abdication. That was at any rate the case for the particular artist and the particular nature he felt himself, armour-proof as they became against the appeal of sacrifice. Sacrifice was fallibility, and one could only of course be consistent if one inveterately had hold of the truth. There was no safety or, otherwise, no inward serenity or even outward—though the outward came secondly—unless there was no deflection; none into the question, that is, of what might make for the serenity of others, which was their own affair and which above all seemed not urgent in comparison with the supreme artistic. It wasn't that the artist hadn't to pay, to pay for the general stupidity, perversity and perfidy, from the moment he might have to deal with these things; that was the inevitable suffering, and it was always there; but it could be more or less borne if one was systematically, or rather if one was naturally, or even, better still, preternaturally, in the right; since this meant the larger, the largest serenity. That account of so fine a case of inward confidence would indeed during those very first years have sinned somewhat by anticipation; yet something of the beauty—that is of the unmatched virtuosity—of the attitude finally achieved did even at the early time colour the air of intercourse with him for those who had either few enough or many enough of their own reserves. The second of these conditions sprang from a due anxiety for one's own interests, more or less defined in advance and therefore, as might be, more or less menaced; the other proviso easily went with vagueness—vagueness as to what things were one's interests, seeing that the exhibited working of an esthetic and a moral confidence conjoined on that scale and at play together unhampered would perhaps prove for the time an attraction beyond any other. This reflection must verily, in our relation, have brought about my own quietus—so far as that mild ecstasy could be divorced from agitation. I recall at all events less of the agitation than of the ecstasy; the primary months, certain aspects even of the few following years, look out at me as from fine accommodations, acceptances, submissions, emotions, all melted together, that one must have taken for joys of the mind and gains of the imagination so clear as to cost one practically nothing. They are what I see, and are all I want to see, as I look back; there hangs about them a charm of thrilled good faith, the flush and throb of crowding apprehensions, that has scarce faded and of which I can only wish to give the whole picture the benefit. I bottle this imponderable extract of the loitering summers of youth, when every occasion really seemed to stay to be gathered and tasted, just for the sake of its faint sweetness.

Some time since, in Boston, I spent an hour before a commemorative cluster of La Farge's earlier productions, gathered in on the occasion of his death, with the effect as of a plummet suddenly dropped into obscure depths long unstirred, that of a remembered participation, it didn't seem too much to say, in the far-away difficult business of their getting themselves born. These things, almost all finished studies of landscape, small and fond celebrations of the modest little Newport harmonies, the spare felicities and delicacies of a range of aspects that have ceased to appeal or to "count," called back into life a hundred memories, laid bare the very footsteps of time, light and uncertain though so often the imprint. I seemed so to have been there by the projection of curiosity and sympathy, if not by having literally looked in, when the greater number of such effects worked themselves out, that they spoke to me of my own history—through the felt intensity of my commission, as it were, to speak for my old friend. The terms on which he was ever ready to draw out for us the interesting hours, terms of patience as they essentially were for the edified party, lived again in this record, but with the old supposition of profit, or in other words the old sense of pleasure, of precious acquisition and intenser experience, more vivid than anything else. There recurs to me for instance one of the smallest of adventures, as tiny a thing as could incur the name and which was of the early stage of our acquaintance, when he proposed to me that we should drive out to the Glen, some six miles off, to breakfast, and should afterwards paint—we paint!—in the bosky open air. It looks at this distance a mythic time, that of felt inducements to travel so far at such an hour and in a backless buggy on the supposition of rustic fare. But different ages have different measures, and I quite remember how ours, that morning, at the neat hostel in the umbrageous valley, overflowed with coffee and griddle-cakes that were not as other earthly refreshment, and how a spell of romance rested for several hours on our invocation of the genius of the scene: of such material, with the help of the attuned spirit, may great events consent to be composed. My companion, his easel and canvas, his palette and stool and other accessories happily placed, settled to his subject, while I, at a respectful distance, settled to mine and to the preparation of this strange fruit of time, my having kept the impression as if it really mattered. It did indeed matter, it was to continue to have done so, and when I ask myself the reason I find this in something as rare and deep and beautiful as a passage of old poetry, a scrap of old legend, in the vagueness of rustling murmuring green and plashing water and woodland voices and images, flitting hovering possibilities; the most retained of these last of course being the chance that one's small daub (for I too had my easel and panel and palette) might incur appreciation by the eye of friendship. This indeed was the true source of the spell, that it was in the eye of friendship, friendship full of character and colour, and full of amusement of its own, that I lived on any such occasion, and that I had come forth in the morning cool and had found our breakfast at the inn a thing of ineffable savour, and that I now sat and flurriedly and fearfully aspired. Yes, the interesting ineffectual and exquisite array of the Boston "show" smote for me most the chord of the prime questions, the admirations and expectations at first so confident, even that of those refinements of loyalty out of which the last and highest tribute was to spring; the consideration, I mean, of whether our extraordinary associate, neither promptly understood nor inveterately accepted, might not eventually be judged such a colourist and such a poet that owners of his first felicities, those very ones over which he was actually bending, and with a touch so inscrutable, such "tonalities" of his own, would find themselves envied and rich. I remember positively liking to see most people stupid about him, and to make them out, I dare say, more numerously stupid than they really were: this perhaps in some degree as a bright communication of his own spirit—which discerned from so far off that of the bitterest-sweet cup it was abundantly to taste; and partly because the case would after that fashion only have its highest interest. The highest interest, the very highest, it certainly couldn't fail to have; and the beauty of a final poetic justice, with exquisite delays, the whole romance of conscious delicacy and heroic patience intervening, was just what we seemed to see meanwhile stow itself expectantly away.

This view of the inevitable fate of distinguished work was thus, on my part, as it comes before me again, of early development, and I admit that I should appear to antedate it hadn't I in renewed presence of each of the particular predestined objects of sacrifice I have glanced at caught myself in the very act of that invidious apprehension, that fondest contemporaneity. There were the charming individual things round the production of which I had so at once elatedly and resignedly circled; and nothing remained at the end of time but to test the historic question. *Was* the quiet chamber of the Boston museum a constitution of poetic justice long awaited and at last fully cognisant?—or did the event perhaps fail to give out, after all, the essence of

65

our far-away forecast? I think that what showed clearest, or what I, at any rate, most sharply felt, was the very difficulty of saying; which fact meant of course, I recognise, that the story fell a little short, alas, of rounding itself off. Poetic justice, when it comes, I gather, comes ever with a great shining; so that if there is any doubt about it the source of the doubt is in the very depths of the case and has been from the first at work there. It literally seems to me, besides, that there was more history and thereby more interest recoverable as the matter stood than if every answer to every question about it hadn't had a fine ambiguity. I like ambiguities and detest great glares; preferring thus for my critical no less than for my pedestrian progress the cool and the shade to the sun and dust of the way. There was an exquisite effort of which I had been peculiarly sure; the large canvas of the view of the Paradise Rocks over against Newport, but within the island and beyond the "second beach"—such were our thin designations! On the high style and the grand manner of this thing, even though a little uneasy before the absence from it of a certain crânerie of touch, I would have staked every grain of my grounded sensibility—in spite of which, on second thoughts, I shall let that faded fact, and no other contention at all, be my last word about it. For the prevailing force, within the Boston walls, the supreme magic anything was to distil, just melted into another connection which flung a soft mantle as over the whole show. It became, from the question of how even a man of perceptive genius had painted what we then locally regarded as our scenery, a question of how we ourselves had felt and cherished that scenery; which latter of these two memories swept for me everything before it. The scenery we cherished—by which I really mean, I fear, but four or five of us—has now been grossly and utterly sacrificed; in the sense that its range was all for the pedestrian measure, that to overwalk it was to love it and to love it to overwalk it, and that no such relation with it as either of these appears possible or thinkable to-day. We had, the four or five of us, the instinct—the very finest this must have been—of its scale and constitution, the adorable wise economy with which nature had handled it and in the light of which the whole seaward and insular extension of the comparatively futile town, untrodden, unsuspected, practically all inviolate, offered a course for the long afternoon ramble more in harmony with the invocations, or for that matter the evocations, of youth than we most of us, with appreciation so rooted, were perhaps ever to know. We knew already, we knew then, that no such range of airs would ever again be played for us on but two or three silver strings. They were but two or three—the sea so often as of the isles of Greece, the mildly but perpetually embayed promontories of mossy rock and wasted thankless pasture, bathed in a refinement of radiance and a sweetness of solitude which amounted in themselves to the highest "finish"; and little more than the feeling, with all this, or rather with no more than this, that possession, discrimination, far frequentation, were ours alone, and that a grassy rocky tide-washed, just a bare, though ever so fine-grained, toned and tinted breast of nature and field of fancy stretched for us to the low horizon's furthest rim. The vast region—it struck us then as vast—was practically roadless, but this, far from making it a desert, made it a kind of boundless empty carpeted saloon. It comes back to me that nobody in those days walked, nobody but the three or four of us—or indeed I should say, if pushed, the single pair in particular of whom I was one and the other Thomas Sargeant Perry, superexcellent and all-reading, all-engulfing friend of those days and still, sole survivor, of these, I thus found deeply consecrated that love of the long, again and again of the very longest possible, walk which was to see me, year after year, through so many of the twists and past so many of the threatened blocks of life's road, and which, during the early and American period, was to make me lone and perverse even in my own sight: so little was it ever given me then, wherever I scanned the view, to descry a fellow-pedestrian. The pedestrians came to succumb altogether, at Newport, to this virtual challenge of their strange agitation—by the circumstance, that is, of their being offered at last, to importunity, the vulgar road, under the invasion of which the old rich alternative miserably dwindled.

V

Nothing meanwhile could have been less logical, yet at the same time more natural, than that William's interest in the practice of painting should have suddenly and abruptly ceased; a turn of our affair attended, however, with no shade of commotion, no repining at proved waste; with as little of any confessed ruefulness of mistake on one side as of any elation of wisdom, any resonance of the ready "I told you so" on the other. The one side would have been, with a different tone about the matter and a different domestic habit than ours, that of my brother's awkwardness, accompanying whatever intelligence, of disavowal, and the other been our father's not unemphatic return to the point that his doubts, those originally and confidently intimated, had been justified by the fact. Tempting doubtless in a heavier household air the opportunity on the latter's part to recall that if he had perfectly recognised his son's probable progress to a pitch of excellence he had exactly not granted that an attainment of this pitch was likely in the least, however uncontested, to satisfy the nature concerned; the foregone conclusion having all the while been that such a spirit was competent to something larger and less superficially calculable, something more expressive of its true inwardness. This was not the way in which things happened among us, for I really think the committed mistake was ever discriminated against—certainly by the head of the family—only to the extent of its acquiring, even if but speedily again to fade, an interest greater than was obtainable by the too obvious success. I am not sure indeed that the kind of personal history most appealing to my father would not have been some kind that should fairly proceed by mistakes, mistakes more human, more associational, less angular, less hard for others, that is less exemplary for them (since righteousness, as mostly understood, was in our parent's view, I think, the cruellest thing in the world) than straight and smug and declared felicities. The qualification here, I allow, would be in his scant measure of the difference, after all, for the life of the soul, between the marked achievement and the marked shortcoming. He had a manner of his own of appreciating failure, or of not at least piously rejoicing in displayed moral, intellectual, or even material, economies, which, had it not been that his humanity, his generosity and, for the most part, his gaiety, were always, at the worst, consistent, might sometimes have left us with our small savings, our little exhibitions and complacencies, rather on our hands. As the case stood I find myself thinking of our life in those years as profiting greatly for animation and curiosity by the interest he shed for us on the whole side of the human scene usually held least interesting—the element, the appearance, of waste which plays there such a part and into which he could read under provocation so much character and colour and charm, so many implications of the fine and the worthy, that, since the art of missing or of failing, or of otherwise going astray, did after all in his hands escape becoming either a matter of real example or of absolute precept, enlarged not a little our field and our categories of appreciation and perception. I recover as I look back on all this the sense as of an extraordinary young confidence, our common support, in our coming round together, through the immense lubrication of his expressed thought, often perhaps extravagantly working and playing, to plenty of unbewildered rightness, a state of comfort that would always serve—whether after strange openings into a sphere where nothing practical mattered, or after even still quainter closings in upon us of unexpected importances and values. Which means, to my memory, that we breathed somehow an air in which waste, for us at least, couldn't and didn't live, so certain were aberrations and discussions, adventures, excursions and alarms of whatever sort, to wind up in a "transformation scene" or, if the term be not profane, happy harlequinade; a figuration of each involved issue and item before the footlights of a familiar idealism, the most socialised and ironised, the most amusedly generalised, that possibly could be.

Such an atmosphere was, taking one of its elements with another, doubtless delightful; yet if it was friendly to the suggested or imagined thing it promoted among us much less directly, as I have already hinted, the act of choice—choice as to the "career" for example, with a view of the usual proceedings thereupon consequent. I marvel at the manner in which the door appears to have been held or at least left open to us for experiment, though with a tendency to close, the oddest yet most inveterately perceptible movement in that sense, before any very earnest proposition in particular. I have no remembrance at all of marked prejudices on our father's part, but I recall repeated cases, in his attitude to our young affairs, of a disparagement suggested as by stirred memories of his own; the instance most present to me being his extreme tepidity in the matter of William's, or in fact of my, going, on our then American basis, to college. I make out in him, and at the time made out, a great revulsion of spirit from that incurred experience in his own history, a revulsion I think moreover quite independent of any particular or instrinsic attributes of the seat of learning involved in it. Union College, Schenectady, New York, the scene of his personal experiment and the natural resort, in his youth, of comparatively adjacent Albanians, might easily have offered at that time no very rare opportunities—few were the American country colleges that then had such to offer; but when, after years, the question arose for his sons he saw it in I scarce know what light of associational or "subjective" dislike. He had the disadvantage—unless indeed it was much more we who had it—of his having, after many changes and detachments, ceased to believe in the Schenectady resource, or to revert to it sentimentally, without his forming on the other hand, with his boys to place, any fonder presumption or preference. There comes out to me, much bedimmed but recognisable, the image of a day of extreme youth on which, during a stay with our grandmother at Albany, we achieved, William and I, with some confused and heated railway effort, a pious pilgrimage to the small scholastic city—pious by reason, I clearly remember, of a lively persuasion on my brother's part that to Union College, at some indefinite future time, we should both most naturally and delightedly repair. We invoked, I gather, among its scattered shades, fairly vague to me now, the loyalty that our parent appeared to have dropped by the way—even though our attitude about it can scarce have been prematurely contentious; the whole vision is at any rate to-day bathed and blurred for me in the air of some charmed and beguiled dream, that of the flushed good faith of an hour of crude castle-building. We were helped to build, on the spot, by an older friend, much older, as I remember him, even than my brother, already a member of the college and, as it seemed, greatly enjoying his life and those "society" badges and trinkets with which he reappears to me as bristling and twinkling quite to the extinction of his particular identity. This is lost, like everything else, in the mere golden haze of the little old-time autumn adventure. Wondrous to our sensibility may well have been the October glamour—if October it was, and if it was not it ought to have been!—of that big brave region of the great State over which the shade of Fenimore Cooper's Mohawks and Mohicans (if this be not a pleonasm) might still have been felt to hang. The castle we had built, however, crumbled—there were plenty of others awaiting erection; these too successively had their hour, but I needn't at this time stoop to pick up their pieces. I see moreover vividly enough how it might have been that, at this stage, our parents were left cold by the various appeal, in our interest, of Columbia, Harvard and Yale. Hard by, at Providence, in the Newport time, was also "Brown"; but I recover no connection in which that mystic syllable swept our sky as a name to conjure with. Our largest licence somehow didn't stray toward Brown. It was to the same tune not conceivable that we should have been restored for educational purposes to the swollen city, the New York of our childhood, where we had then so tumbled in and out of school as to exhaust the measure, or as at least greatly to deflower the image, of our teachability on that ground. Yale, off our beat from every point of view, was as little to be thought of, and there was moreover in our father's imagination no grain of susceptibility to what might have been, on the general ground, "socially expected." Even Harvard, clearly—and it was perhaps a trifle odd—moved him in our interest as little as Schenectady could do; so that, for authority, the voice of social expectation would have had to sound with an art or an accent of which it had by no means up to that time learned roundabout us the trick. This indeed (it comes to saying) is something that, so far as our parents were concerned, it would never have learned. They were, from other preoccupations, unaware of any such pressure; and to become aware would, I think, primarily have been for them to find it out of all proportion to the general pitch of prescription. We were not at that time, when it came to such claims, in presence of persuasive, much less of impressive, social forms and precedents—at least those of us of the liberated mind and the really more curious culture were not; the more curious culture, only to be known by the positive taste of it, was nowhere in the air, nowhere seated or embodied.

Which reflections, as I perhaps too loosely gather them in, refresh at any rate my sense of how we in particular of our father's house actually profited more than we lost, if the more curious culture was in question, by the degree to which we were afloat and disconnected; since there were at least luxuries of the spirit in this quite as much as drawbacks—given a social order (so far as it *was* an order) that found its main ideal in a "strict attention to business," that is to buying and selling over a counter or a desk, and in such an intensity of the traffic as made, on the part of all involved, for close localisation. To attend strictly to business was to be invariably *there*, on a certain spot in a certain place; just as to be nowhere in particular, to *have* to be nowhere, told the queer tale of a lack or of a forfeiture, or possibly even of a state of intrinsic unworthiness. I have already expressed how few of these elements of the background we ourselves had ever had either to add to or to subtract from, and how this of itself did after a fashion "place" us in the small Newport colony of the despoiled and disillusioned, the mildly, the reminiscentially desperate. As easy as might be, for the time, I have also noted, was our footing there; but I have not, for myself, forgotten, or even now outlived, the particular shade of satisfaction to be taken in one's thus being in New England without being of it. To have originally been of it, or still to have had to be, affected me, I recall, as a case I should have regretted—unless it be more exact to say that I thought of the condition as a danger after all escaped. Long would it take to tell why it figured as a danger, and why that impression was during the several following years much more to gain than to lose intensity. The question was to fall into the rear indeed, with ever so many such secondary others, during the War, and for reasons effective enough; but it was afterwards to know a luxury of emergence—this, I mean, while one still "cared," in general, as one was sooner or later to stop caring. Infinitely interesting to recover, in the history of a mind, for those concerned, these movements of the spirit, these tides and currents of growth—though under the inconvenience for the historian of such ramifications of research that here at any rate I feel myself warned off. There appeared to us at Newport the most interesting, much, of the Albany male cousins, William James Temple—coming, oddly enough, first from Yale and then from Harvard; so that by contact and example the practicability of a like experience might have been, and doubtless was, put well before us. "Will" Temple, as we were in his short life too scantly to know him, had made so luckless, even if so lively a start under one alma mater that the appeal to a fresh parentship altogether appears to have been judged the best remedy for his case: he entered Harvard jumping, if I mistake not, a couple of years of the undergraduate curriculum, and my personal memory of these reappearances is a mere recapture of admiration, of prostration, before him. The dazzled state, under his striking good looks and his manly charm, was the common state; so that I disengage from it no presumption of a particular plea playing in our own domestic air for his temporary Cambridge setting; he was so much too radiant and gallant and personal, too much a character and a figure, a splendid importance in himself, to owe the least glamour to settings; an advantage that might have seemed rather to be shed on whatever scene by himself in consenting to light it up. He made all life for the hour a foreground, and one that we none of us would have quitted for a moment while he was there.

In that form at least I see him, and no revival of those years so puts to me the interesting question, so often aimlessly returned upon in later life, of the amount of truth in this or that case of young confidence in a glory to come— for another than one's self; of the likelihood of the wonders so flatteringly forecast. Many of our estimates were monstrous magnifications—though doing us even at that more good than harm; so that one isn't even sure that the happiest histories were to have been those of the least liberal mistakes. I like at any rate to think of our easy overstrainings—the possible flaw in many of which was not indeed to be put to the proof. That was the case for the general, and for every particular, impression of Will Temple, thanks to his early death in battle—at Chancellorsville, 1863; he having, among the quickened forces of the time, and his father's record helping him, leaped to a captaincy in the regular Army; but I cling to the idea that the siftings and sortings of life, had he remained subject to them, would still have left him the lustre that blinds and subdues. I even do more, at this hour; I ask myself, while his appearance and my personal feeling about it live for me again, what possible aftertime could have kept up the pitch of my sentiment—aftertime either of his or of mine. Blest beyond others, I think as we look back, the admirations, even the fondest (and which indeed were not of their nature fond?) that were not to know to their cost the inevitable test or strain; they are almost the only ones, of the true high pitch, that, without broken edges or other tatters to show, fold themselves away entire and secure, even as rare lengths of precious old stuff, in the scented chest of our savings. So great misadventure have too often known at all events certain of those that were to come to trial. The others are the *residual*, those we must keep when we can, so to be sure at least of a few, sacrificing as many possible mistakes and misproportions as need be to pay but for two or three of them. There could be no mistake about Gus Barker, who threw himself into the fray, that is into the cavalry saddle, as he might into a match at baseball (football being then undreamt of), and my last reminiscence of whom is the sight of him, on a brief leave for a farewell to his Harvard classmates after he had got his commission, crossing with two or three companions the expanse of Harvard Square that faced the old Law School, of which I found myself for that year (1862-63) a singularly alien member. I was afterwards sharply to regret the accident by which I on that occasion missed speech of him; but my present vision of his charming latent agility, which any motion showed, of his bright-coloured wagging head and of the large gaiety of the young smile that made his handsome teeth shine out, is after all the years but the more happily uneffaced. The point of all which connections, however, is that they somehow managed to make in the parental view no straight links for us with the matter-of-course of college. There were accidents too by the aid of which they failed of this the more easily. It comes to me that, for my own part, I thought of William at the time as having, or rather as so much more than having, already graduated; the effect of contact with his mind and talk, with the free play of his spirit and the irrepressible brush of his humour, couldn't have been greater had he carried off fifty honours. I felt in him such authority, so perpetually quickened a state of intellect and character, that the detail or the literal side of the question never so much as came up for me: I must have made out that to plenty of graduates, or of the graduating, nothing in the nature of such appearances attached. I think of our father moreover as no less affected by a like impression; so extremely, so immensely disposed do I see him to generalise his eldest son's gifts as by the largest, fondest synthesis, and not so much proceed upon them in any one direction as proceed *from* them, as it were, in all.

Little as such a view might have lent itself to application, my brother's searching discovery during the summer of 1861 that his vocation was not "after all" in the least satisfyingly for Art, took on as a prompt sequel the recognition that it was quite positively and before everything for Science, physical Science, strenuous Science in all its exactitude; with the opportunity again forthcoming to put his freshness of faith to the test. I had presumed to rejoice before at his adoption of the studio life, that offering as well possible contacts for myself; and yet I recall no pang for his tergiversation, there being nothing he mightn't have done at this or at any other moment that I shouldn't have felt as inevitable and found in my sense of his previous age some happy and striking symptom or pledge of. As certain as that he had been all the while "artistic" did it thus appear that he had been at the same time quite otherwise inquiring too—addicted to "experiments" and the consumption of chemicals, the transfusion of mysterious liquids from glass to glass under exposure to lambent flame, the cultivation of stained fingers, the establishment and the transport, in our wanderings, of galvanic batteries, the administration to all he could persuade of electric shocks, the maintenance of marine animals in splashy aquaria, the practice of photography in the room I for a while shared with him at Boulogne, with every stern reality of big cumbrous camera, prolonged exposure, exposure mostly of myself, darkened development, also interminable, and ubiquitous brown blot. Then there had been also the constant, as I fearfully felt it, the finely speculative and boldly disinterested absorption of curious drugs. No livelier remembrance have I of our early years together than this inveteracy, often appalling to a nature so incurious as mine in *that* direction, of his interest in the "queer" or the incalculable effects of things. There was apparently for him no possible effect whatever that mightn't be more or less rejoiced in as such—all exclusive of its relation to other things than merely knowing. There recurs to me withal the shamelessness of my own indifference—at which I also, none the less, I think, wondered a little; as if by so much as it hadn't been given me to care for visibly provoked or engineered phenomena, by that same amount was I open to those of the mysteriously or insidiously aggressive, the ambushed or suffered sort. Vivid to me in any case is still the sense of how quite shiningly light, as an activity and an appeal, he had seemed to make everything he gave himself to; so that at first, until the freshness of it failed, he flung this iridescent mantle of interest over the then so grey and scant little scene of the Harvard (the Lawrence) Scientific School, where in the course of the months I had had a glimpse or two of him at work. Early in the autumn of 1861 he went up from Newport to Cambridge to enter that institution; in which thin current rather than in the ostensibly more ample began to flow his long connection with Harvard, gathering in time so many affluents. His letters from Cambridge during the next couple of years, many of them before me now, breathe, I think, all the experience the conditions could have begotten at the best; they mark the beginning of those vivacities and varieties of intellectual and moral reaction which were for the rest of his life to be the more immeasurably candid and vivid, the more numerous above all, and the more interesting and amusing, the closer view one had of him. That of a certainty; yet these familiar pages of youth testify most of all for me perhaps to the forces of amenity and spontaneity, the happy working of all relations, in our family life. In such parts of them as I may cite this will shine sufficiently through—and I shall take for granted thus the interest of small matters that have perhaps but that reflected light to show. It is in a letter to myself, of that September, dated "Drear and Chill Abode," that he appears to have celebrated the first steps of his initiation.

Sweet was your letter and grateful to my eyes. I had gone in a mechanical way to the P.O. not hoping for anything (though "on espère alors qu'on désespère toujours,") and, finding nothing, was turning heavily away when a youth modestly tapped me and, holding out an envelope inscribed in your well-known character, said, "Mr. J., this was in our box!" 'Twas the young Pascoe, the joy of his mother—but the graphic account I read in the letter he gave me of the sorrow of my mother almost made me shed tears on the floor of the P.O. Not that on reflection I should dream——! for reflection shows me a future in which she shall regard my vacation visits as "on the whole" rather troublesome than otherwise; or at least when she shall feel herself as blest in the trouble I spare her when absent as in the glow of pride and happiness she feels at the sight of me when present. But she needn't fear I can ever think of *her* when absent with such equanimity. I oughtn't to "joke on such a serious subject," as Bobby would say though; for I have had several pangs since being here at the thought of all I have left behind at Newport—especially gushes of feeling about the *place*. I haven't for one minute had the feeling of being at home here. Something in my quarters precludes the possibility of it, though what this is I don't suppose I can describe to you.

As I write now even, writing itself being a cosy cheerful-looking amusement, and an argand gas-burner with a neat green shade merrily singing beside me, I still feel unsettled. I write on a round table in the middle of the room, with a fearful red and black cloth. Before me I see another such-covered table of oblong shape against the wall, capped by a cheap looking-glass and flanked by two windows, curtainless and bleak, whose shades of linen flout the air as the sportive wind impels them. To the left are two other such windows, with a horse-hair sofa between them, and at my back a fifth window and a vast wooden mantel-piece with nothing to relieve its nakedness but a large cast, much plumbago'd, of a bust of Franklin. On my right the Bookcase, imposing and respectable with its empty drawers and with my little array of printed wisdom covering nearly *one* of the shelves. I hear the people breathe as they go past in the street, and the roll and jar of the horse-cars is terrific. I have accordingly engaged the other room from Mrs. Pascoe, with the little sleeping-room upstairs. It looks infinitely more cheerful than this, and if I don't find the grate sufficient I can easily have a Franklin stove put up. But she says the grate will make an oven of it.... John Ropes I met the other day at Harry Quincy's room, and was very much pleased with him. Don't fail to send on Will Temple's letters to him and to Herbert Mason, which I left in one of the library's mantelpiece jars, to use the Portuguese idiom. Storrow Higginson has been very kind to me, making enquiries about tables etc. We went together this morning to the house of the Curator of the Gray collection of Engravings, which is solemnly to unfold its glories to me to-morrow. He is a most serious stately German gentleman, Mr. Thies by name, fully sensible of the deep vital importance of his treasures and evidently thinking a visit to them a great affair—to *me*. Had I known how great, how tremendous and formal, I hardly think I should have ventured to call. Tom Ward pays me a visit almost every evening. Poor Tom seems a-cold too. His deafness keeps him from making acquaintances. Professor Eliot, at the School, is a fine fellow, I suspect; a man who if he resolves to do a thing won't be prevented. I find analysis very interesting *so far*! The Library has a reading-room, where they take all the magazines; so I shan't want for the Rev. des 2 M. I remain

with unalterable sentiments of devotion ever, my dear H., your Big Brother
Bill.

This record of further impressions closely and copiously followed.

Your letter this morning was such a godsend that I hasten to respond
a line or two, though I have no business to—for I have a fearful lesson to-
morrow and am going to Boston to-night to hear Agassiz lecture (12 lectures
on "Methods in Nat. Hist."), so that I will only tell you that I am very well
and my spirits just getting good. Miss Upham's table is much pleasanter than
the other. Professor F. J. Child is a great joker—he's a little flaxen-headed
boy of about 40. There is a nice old lady boarder, another man of about 50,
of aristocratic bearing, who interests me much, and 3 intelligent students.
At the other table was no conversation at all; the fellows had that American
solemnity, called each other Sir, etc. I cannot tell you, dearest Mother, how
your account of your Sunday dinner and of your feelings thereat brought
tears to my eyes. Give Father my ardent love and cover with kisses the round
fair face of the most kiss-worthy Alice. Then kiss the Aunt till you get tired,
and get all the rest of them to kiss *you* till you cry hold enough!

This morning as I was busy over the 10th page of a letter to Wilky in
he popped and made my labour of no account. I had intended to go and see
him yesterday, but found Edward Emerson and Tom Ward were going, and
so thought he would have too much of a good thing. But he walked over this
morning with, or rather without them, for he went astray and arrived very
hot and dusty. I gave him a bath and took him to dinner, and he is now
gone to see Andrew Robeson and E. E. His plump corpusculus looks as
always. I write in my new parlour whither I moved yesterday. You have no
idea what an improvement it is on the old affair—worth double the cost,
and the little bedroom under the roof is perfectly delicious, with a charming
outlook on little back yards with trees and pretty old brick walls. The sun is
upon *this* room from earliest dawn till late in the afternoon—a capital thing
in winter. I like Miss Upham's very much. Dark "aristocratic" dining-room,
with royal cheer. "Fish, roast beef, veal cutlets, pigeons!" says the splendid,
tall, noble-looking, white-armed, black-eyed Juno of a handmaid as you sit
down. And for dessert a choice of three, *three*, darling Mother, of the most

succulent, unctuous (no, not unctuous, unless you imagine a celestial unction without the oil) pie-like confections, always 2 platesful—my eye! She has an admirable chemical, not mechanical, combination of cake and jam and cream which I recommend to Mother if she is ever at a loss; though there is no well-stored pantry like that of good old Kay Street, or if there is it exists not for miserable me.

This chemical analysis is so bewildering at first that I am "muddled and bet" and have to employ almost all my time reading up. Agassiz is evidently a great favourite with his Boston audience and feels it himself. But he's an admirable earnest lecturer, clear as day, and his accent is most fascinating. Jeffries Wyman's lectures on Comp. Anatomy of Verts. promise to be very good; prosy perhaps a little and monotonous, but plain and well-arranged and nourris. Eliot I have not seen much more of; I don't believe he is a *very* accomplished chemist, but can't tell yet. We are only about 12 in the Laboratory, so that we have a very cosy time. I expect to have a winter of "crowded life." I can be as independent as I please, and want to live regardless of the good or bad opinion of every one. I shall have a splendid chance to try, I know, and I know too that the native hue of resolution has never been of very great shade in me hitherto. I am sure that that feeling is a right one, and I mean to live according to it if I can. If I do so I think I shall turn out all right.

I stopped this letter before tea, when Wilky the rosy-gilled and Frank Higginson came in. I now resume it by the light of a taper and that of the moon. Wilky read H.'s letter and amused me "metch" by his naive interpretation of Mother's most rational request that I should "keep a memorandum of all moneys I receive from Father." He thought it was that she might know exactly what sums her prodigal philosopher really gives out, and that mistrust of his generosity caused it. The phrase has a little sound that way, as H. subtly framed it, I confess!

The first few days, the first week here, I really didn't know what to do with myself or how to fill my time. I felt as if turned out of doors. I then received H.'s and Mother's letters. Never before did I know what mystic depths of rapture lay concealed within that familiar word. Never did the same being look so like two different ones as I going in and out of the P.O. if I bring a letter with me. Gloomily, with despair written on my leaden brow I stalk the street along towards the P.O., women, children and students involuntarily shrinking against the wall as I pass—thus,[4] as if the curse of Cain were stamped upon my front. But when I come out with a letter an immense concourse of people generally attends me to my lodging, attracted by my excited wild gestures and look.

Christmas being sparely kept in the New England of those days, William passed that of 1861, as a Cambridge letter of the afternoon indicates, without opportunity for a seasonable dash to Newport, but with such compensations, nearer at hand as are here exhibited. Our brother Wilky, I should premise, had been placed with the youngest of us, Bob, for companion, at the "co-educational" school then but a short time previously established by Mr. F. B. Sanborn at Concord, Massachusetts—and of which there will be more to say. "Tom" Ward, already mentioned and who, having left the Concord school shortly before, had just entered Harvard, was quickly to become William's intimate, approved and trusted friend; the diversion of whose patient originality, whose intellectual independence, ability and curiosity from science and free inquiry to hereditary banking—consequent on the position of the paternal Samuel Gray Ward as the representative for many years in the United States of the house of Baring Brothers—he from the first much regretted: the more pertinently doubtless that this companion was of a family "connected" with ours through an intermarriage, Gus Barker, as Mrs. S. G. Ward's nephew, being Tom's first cousin as well as ours, and such links still counting, in that age of comparatively less developed ramifications, when sympathy and intercourse kept pace as it was kept between our pairs of parents.

I have been in Boston the whole blest morning, toted round by the Wards, who had as usual asked me to dine with them. I had happily provided myself with an engagement here for all such emergencies, but, as is my sportive wont, I befooled Tom with divers answers, and finally let him believe I would come (having refused several dazzling chances for the purpose) supposing of course I should see him here yesterday at Miss Upham's board and disabuse him. But the young viper went home right after breakfast—so I had to go into Boston this morning and explain. Wilky had come up from Concord to dine in said Commonwealth Avenue, and I, as it turned out, found myself in for following the innocent lamb Lily up and down the town for two hours, to hold bundles and ring bells for her; Wilky and Tom having vanished from the scene. Clear sharp cold morning, thermometer 5 degrees at sunrise, and the streets covered with one glare of ice. I had thick smooth shoes and went sliding off like an avalanche every three steps, while she, having india-rubbers and being a Bostonian, went ahead like a swan. I had among other things to keep her bundles from harm, to wipe away every three minutes the trembling jewel with which the cold *would* with persistent kindness ornament my coral nose; to keep a hypocritic watchful eye on her movements lest she fall; to raise my hat gracefully to more and more of her acquaintances every block; to skate round and round embracing lamp-posts and door-scrapers by the score to keep from falling, as well as to avoid serving old lady-promenaders in the same way; to cut capers 4 feet high at the rate of 20 a second, every now and then, for the same purpose; to keep from scooting off down hills and round corners as fast as my able-bodied companion; often to do all these at once and then fall lickety-bang like a chandelier, but *when* so to preserve an expression of placid beatitude or easy nonchalance despite the raging fiend within: oh it beggars description! When finally it was over and I stood alone I shook my companion's dust from my feet and, biting my beard with rage, sware a mighty oath unto high heaven that I would never, while reason held her throne in this distracted orb, *never* NEVER, by word, look or gesture and this without mental reservation, acknowledge a "young lady" as a human being. The false and rotten spawn might die before I would wink to save it. No more Parties now!—at last I am a Man, etc., etc.!

My enthusiasm ran very high for a few minutes, but I suddenly saw that I was a great ass and became sobered instantly, so that on the whole I am better for the circumstance, being a sadder and a wiser man. I also went to the Tappans' and gave the children slight presents; then, coming home to my venal board, behaved very considerately and paternally to a young lady who sat next to me, but with a shade of subdued melancholy in my manner which could not have been noticed at the breakfast-table. Many times and bitterly to-day have I thought of home and lamented that I should have to

81

be away at this merry Christmastide from my rare family; wondering, with Wilky, if they were missing us as we miss them. And now as I sit in the light of my kerosene, with the fire quietly consuming in the grate and the twilight on the snow outside and the melancholy old-fashioned strains of the piano dimly rising from below, I see in vision those at home just going in to dinner; my aged, silvered Mother leaning on the arm of her stalwart yet flexible H., merry and garrulous as ever, my blushing Aunt with her old wild beauty still hanging about her, my modest Father with his rippling raven locks, the genial auld Rob and the mysterious Alice, all rise before me, a glorified throng; but two other forms, one tall, intellectual, swarthy, with curved nose and eagle eye, the other having breadth rather than depth, but a goodly morsel too, are wanting to complete the harmonious whole. Eftsoons they vanish and I am again alone, *alone*—what pathos in the word! I have two companions though, most all the time—remorse and despair! T. S. Perry took their place for a little, and to-day they have not come back. T. S. seemed to enjoy his visit very much. It was very pleasant for me to have him; his rustic wonder at the commonest sights was most ludicrous, and his conversation most amusing and instructive.

The place here improves to me as I go on living in it, and if I study with Agassiz 4 or 5 years there is nothing I should like better than to have you all with me, regular and comfortable. I enclose another advertisement of a house—but which would be too small for us, I believe, though it might be looked at. I had a long talk with one of A.'s students the other night, and saw for the first time how a naturalist may feel about his trade exactly as an artist does about his. For instance Agassiz would rather take wholly uninstructed people—"for he has to unteach them all they have learnt." He doesn't let them so much as look into a book for a long while; what they learn they must learn for themselves and be *masters* of it all. The consequence is he makes Naturalists of them—doesn't merely cram them; and this student (he had been there 2 years) said he felt ready to go anywhere in the world now with nothing but his notebook and study out anything quite alone. A. must be a great teacher. Chemistry comes on tolerably, but not so fast as I expected. I am pretty slow with my substances, having done but 12 since Thanksgiving and having 38 more to do before the end of the term.

Comment on the abundance, the gaiety and drollery, the generous play of vision and fancy in all this, would seem so needless as to be almost officious, were not the commentator constantly, were he not infinitely, arrested and reminded and solicited; which is at once his advantage and his embarrassment. Such a letter, at all events, read over with the general key, touches its contemporary scene and hour into an intensity of life for him; making indeed the great sign of that life my brother's signal vivacity and cordiality, his endless spontaneity of mind. Every thing in it is characteristic of the genius and expressive of the mood, and not least, of course, the pleasantry of paradox, the evocation of each familiar image by its vivid opposite. Our mother, *e.g.*, was not at that time, nor for a good while yet, so venerably "silvered"; our handsome-headed father had lost, occipitally, long before, all pretence to raven locks, certainly to the effect of their "rippling"; the beauty of our admirable aunt was as happily alien either to wildness or to the "hanging" air as it could very well be; the "mystery" of our young sister consisted all in the candour of her natural bloom, even if at the same time of her lively intelligence; and H.'s mirth and garrulity appear to have represented for the writer the veriest ironic translation of something in that youth, I judge, not a little mildly—though oh *so* mildly!—morose or anxiously mute. To the same tune the aquiline in his own nose heroically derides the slightly relaxed line of that feature; and our brother Wilky's want of physical "depth" is a glance at a different proportion. Of a like tinge of pleasantry, I may add, is the imputation of the provincial gape to our friend T. S. Perry, of Newport birth and unintermitted breeding, with whom we were to live so much in the years to come, and who was then on the eve of entering Harvard—his face already uninterruptedly turned to that love of letters, that practice of them by dauntless and inordinate, though never at all vulgarly resonant, absorption which was to constitute in itself the most disinterested of careers. I had myself felt him from the first an exemplary, at once, and a discouraging friend; he had let himself loose in the world of books, pressed and roamed through the most various literatures and the most voluminous authors, with a stride that, as it carried him beyond all view, left me dismayed and helpless at the edge of the forest, where I listened wistfully but unemulously to the far-off crash from within of his felled timber, the clearing of whole spaces or periods shelf by shelf or great tree by tree. The brother-in-law of John La Farge, he had for us further, with that reviving consciousness of American annals which the War was at once so rudely and so insidiously to quicken in us, the glamour of his straight descent from the Commodores Perry of the Lake Erie in the war of 1812, respectively, and of the portentous penetration of Japan just after the mid-century, and his longer-drawn but equally direct and so clean and comfortable affiliation to the great Benjamin Franklin: as these things at least seemed to me under my habit (too musing and brooding certainly to have made for light loquacity) of pressing every wind-borne particle of personal history—once the persons were only other enough from myself—into the service of what I would fain have called picture or, less explicitly, less formulatedly, romance.

These, however, are but too fond insistences, and what mainly bears pointing out is my brother's already restless reach forth to some new subject of study. He had but lately addressed himself, not without confidence, to such an investigation of Chemistry as he might become conscious of a warrant for, yet the appeal of Agassiz's great authority, so much in the air of the Cambridge of that time, found him at once responsive; it opened up a world, the world of sentient life, in the light of which Chemistry faded. He had not, however, for the moment done with it; and what I at any rate find most to the point in the pages before me is the charm of their so witnessing to the geniality and harmony of our family life, exquisite as I look back on it and reflected almost as much in any one passage taken at hazard as in any other. He had apparently, at the date of the following, changed his lodging.

President Felton's death has been the great event of the week—two funerals and I don't know how many prayers and sermons. To-day I thought I would go to University chapel for the sake of variety and hear Dr. Peabody's final word on him—and a very long and lugubrious one it was. The prayer was a prolonged moan in which the death (not in its consequences, but in itself) was treated as a great calamity, and the whole eulogy was almost ridiculously overcharged. What was most disagreeable throughout was the wailing tones, not a bit that of simple pagan grief at the *loss*—which would have been honest; but a whine consciously put on as from a sense of duty, and

84

a whine at nothing definite either, only a purposeless clothing of all his words in tears. The whole style of the performance was such that I have concluded to have nothing more to do with funerals till they improve.

The walking here has been terrible with ice or slush these many weeks, but over head celestial. No new developments in this house. The maniac sometimes chills my very marrow by hoarsely whispering outside the door, "Gulielmo, Gulielmo!" Old Sweetser sits in his dressing-gown smoking his pipe all day in a little uncomfortable old *bathroom* next door to me. He may with truth be called a queer cuss. The young ladies have that very nasty immodest habit of hustling themselves out of sight precipitately whenever I appear. I dined with Mrs. —— yesterday all alone. She was quite sick, very hoarse, and *he* was in the country, so that on the whole it was a great bore. She is very clumsy in her way of doing things, and her invitation to me was for the wife of an artist—not artistic!

I am now studying organic Chemistry. It will probably shock Mother to hear that I yesterday destroyed a pockethandkerchief—but it was an old one and I converted it into some sugar which though rather brown is very good. I believe I forgot to tell you that I am shorn of my brightest ornament. That solitary hirsute jewel which lent such a manly and martial aspect to my visage is gone, and the place thereof is naked. I don't think anyone will know the difference, and moreover it is not dead, it only sleeps and will some day rise phoenix-like from its ashes with tenfold its former beauty. When Father comes will he please bring Ganot's Physique *if H. doesn't want it?*

In none of these earlier communications from Cambridge is the element of affectionate pleasantry more at play than in those addressed to his sister.

Charmante jeune fille, I find the Tappans *really* expected me to bring you to them and were much disappointed at my failure. Ellen has grown very fat and big. Mary calls everybody "horrid." Lyly Barker is with the Wards. I haven't seen her yet, but shall do so on Saturday, when I am also to dine with the Hunts. I hope your neuralgia, or whatever you may believe the thing was, has gone and that you are back at school instead of languishing and lolling about the house. I send you herewith a portrait of Prof. Eliot, a very fair likeness, to grace your book withal. Write me whenever you have the slightest or most fleeting inclination to do so. If you have only one sentence to say, don't grudge paper and stamps for it. You don't know how much good you may do me at an appropriate time by a little easy scratching of your graceful nimble pen.

In another apostrophe to the same correspondent, at the same season, his high spirits throw off the bonds of the vernacular.

Est-ce que tu songes jamais à moi comme moi je songe à toi?—oh je crois bien que non! Maintes fois dans la journée l'image d'une espèce d'ange vêtue de blanc avec de longs boucles noirs qui encadrent une figure telle que la plupart des mortels ne font que l'entrevoir dans leur rêves, s'impose à mes sens ravis; créature longue et fluette qui se dispose à se coucher dans une petite chambrette verte où le gaz fait un grand jour. Eh, oua, oua, oua! c'est à faire mourir de douleur. Mais je parie que tout de même pas une étincelle ne vibre pour moi dans les fibres de ton cœur endurci. Hélas, oublié de mes parents et de mes semblables, je ne vois, où que je regarde, qu'un abîme de désespoir, un gouffre noir et peuplé de démons, qui tôt ou tard va m'engloutir. Tu ne m'écris jamais sauf pour me soutirer des objets de luxe. La vaste mère me déteste, il n'y a que le frère qui me reste attaché, et lui par esprit d'opposition plus que par autre chose. Eh mon Dieu, que vais-je devenir? En tout cas je vais clore cette lettre, qui s'est allongée malgré moi. Ton frère, James William.

Of the same bright complexion is this report, addressed to his parents, of the change of lodging already noted.

The presence of the Tweedys has been most agreeable and has contributed in no small degree to break the shock of removal to these new rooms, which are not near so cosy as the old; especially with the smoking of my stove, which went on all the first two days. That has been stopped, however, and the only trouble is now to get the fire alight at all. I have generally to start it 3 or 4 times, and the removal of the material of each failure from the grate is a fearful business. I have also to descend to the cellar myself to get my coal, and my "hod," as Ma Sweetser, my land-lady, calls it, not being very much bigger than a milk-pitcher, doesn't add to the charm. The coal is apt to drop on the stairs, and I have to pick it all up. At present the stove fills the room with a nephitic and pestilential gas, so that I have to keep the window open. I went last night with the Tweedys to the concert for which they came up, and with them this morning to hear Wendell Phillips. This Sweetser family is worthy of Dickens. It consists of a Mr. and Miss S., Mr. S.'s three gushing girls, a parrot and a maniac. The maniac is very obstreperous. Her husband left her boarding here 3 months ago and went to Cuba. When she got mad he was written to, but has sent no reply, and they are keeping her. For the Aunt's sake I keep my drawer locked against her at night. Old Sweetser is a riddle I hope to do justice to at some future time, but can't begin on now. His sister shakes like an aspen whenever she is spoken to. Oh I forgot the most important character of all, the black wench who "does" the room. She is about 20 years old and wears short frocks, but talks like Alice Robeson and has an antediluvian face about as large as the top of a flour-barrel.

I can really keep my hand from nothing, of whatever connection, that causes his intensity of animation and spontaneity of expression to revive. On a Sunday evening early in 1862 he had

just returned from Milton, and, after removing from my person a beetle, sit down to write you immediately. Ever since 10.30 this A.M. the beetle s'est promené à l'envi sur ma peau. The first feeling I had of his becoming attached to it made me jump so as to scare an old lady opposite me in the car into fits. Finding him too hard to crush I let him run, and at last got used to him though at times he tickled me to excruciation. I ache in every limb and every cranny of my mind from my visit.... They had the usual number of stories, wonderful and not wonderful, to tell of their friends and relatives (of Stephen somebody, *e.g.*, who had a waggon weighing several tons run over his chest without even bruising him, and so on). They are very nice girls indeed all the same. I then went, near by, to the Forbes's in a state of profuse perspiration, and saw handsome Mrs. F. and her daughters, and a substitute for Governor Andrew in the person of his wife; after which I returned here, being driven back in the car, as I perceived on the front platform, by our old familiar— familiar indeed!—friend William (I mean our Irish ex-coachman) whom age doesn't seem to render more veracious, as he told me several very big stories about himself: how he smashed a car to pieces the other night, how he first gave the alarm of the great fire, etc.

I went to the theatre the other night, and, asking a gentleman to make room for me, found him to be Bob Temple, who had arrived in Boston that day. He looks very well and talks in the most extraordinary way you ever heard about Slavery and the wickedness of human society, and is apparently very sincere. He sailed for Europe on Wednesday. I exhorted him to stop over at Newport, but he wouldn't. There was something quite peculiar about him—he seemed greatly changed. I can tell you more at home, but wish I might have seen more of him. I have been the last three nights running to hear John Wilkes Booth, the "young American Roscius." Rant, rant, rant of the most fearful kind. The worst parts most applauded, but with any amount of fire and energy in the passionate parts, in some of which he really becomes natural.... You don't know what a regular Sévigné you have in Alice. I blush for my delinquencies toward her, but bow my head with meek humility, contented to be her debtor all my life and despairing of ever repaying her the value of her letters. Mother and Aunt I pine to see, and the honest Jack Tar of the family, the rough Bob, with his rude untutored ways!

Traps for remembrance I find set at every turn here, so that I have either to dodge them or patiently to suffer catching. I try in vain for instance merely to brush past the image of our kinsman Robert Temple the younger, who made with his brother Will the eldest pair in that house of cousins: he waylays, he persuades me too much, and to fail of the few right words for him would be to leave a deep debt unrepaid—his fitful hovering presence, repeatedly vivid and repeatedly obscured, so considerably "counted" for us, pointing the sharpest moral, pointing fifty morals, and adorning a perpetual tale. He was for years, first on the nearer and then little by little on the further, the furthest, horizon, quite the most emphasised of all our wastrels, the figure bristling most with every irregular accent that we were to find ourselves in any closeness of relation with. I held him for myself at least, from far back, a pure gift of free-handed chance to the grateful imagination, the utmost limit of whose complaint of it could be but for the difficulty of rendering him the really proper tribute. I regarded him truly, for a long time, as a possession of the mind, the human image swung before us with most of the effect of strong and thick and inimitable colour. If to be orphaned and free of range had affected my young fancy as the happy, that is the romantic, lot, no member of the whole cousinship, favoured in that sense as so many of them were, enjoyed so, by my making out, the highest privilege of the case. Nothing, I could afterwards easily see, had been less inevitable and of a greater awkwardness of accident than his being, soon after the death of his parents, shipped off from Albany, in pursuit of an education, to an unheard-of school in a remote corner of Scotland; which fact it was, however, that played for me exactly the bright part of preparing to show with particular intensity what Europe again, with the opportunity so given, was going to proceed to. It thus shone out when after the lapse of several years he recurred to our more competent view that, quite richly erratic creature as he might appear, and to whatever degree of wonder and suspense, of amusement and amazement, he might wind us up, the rich alien influence, full of special queernesses and mysteries in this special connection, had complacently turned him out for us and had ever so irretrievably and ineffaceably stamped him. He rose before us, tall and goodlooking and easy, as a figure of an oddly *civilised* perversity; his irreverent challenging humour, playing at once, without mercy, over American aspects, seemed somehow not less cultivated than profane—just which note in itself caused the plot beautifully to thicken; for this was to distinguish and almost embellish him throughout a long career in which he was to neglect no occasion, however frankly forbidding, for graceless adventure, that he had the pure derisive, the loose and mocking mind, yet initiated, educated, almost elegantly impudent, in other words successfully impertinent, and which expressed itself, in particular by the pen, with a literary lightness that we used to find inimitable. He had dangled there, further off and nearer, as a character, to my attention, in the sense in which "people in books" were characters, and other people, roundabout us, were somehow not; so that I fairly thought of him (though this more, doubtless, with the lapse of time) very much as if we had owed him to Thackeray or Dickens, the creators of superior life to whom we were at that time always owing most, rather than to any set of circumstances by which we had in our own persons felt served; that he was inimitable, inimitably droll, inimitably wasted, wanton, impossible, or whatever else it might be, making him thus one with the rounded and represented creature, shining in the light of art, as distinguished from the vague handful of more or less susceptible material that had in the common air to pass for a true concretion. The promise of this had been, to my original vision, in every wind-borne echo of him, however light; I doubtless put people "into books" by very much the same turn of the hand with which I took them out, but it had tinged itself with the finely free that, proceeding in due course from his school at Fochabers to the University of Aberdeen (each sound and syllable of this general far cry from Albany had in itself an incoherence!) he had encountered while there the oddest of all occasions to embrace the Romish faith. In the same way it ministered to the vivid, even if baffled, view of him that he appeared then to have retreated upon the impenetrable stronghold of Nairn, described by him as a bleak little Scotch watering-place which yet sufficed to his cluster of predicaments: whence he began to address to his bewildered pair of Albany guardians and trustees the earlier of that series of incomparably amusing letters, as we judged them, the arrival of almost any one of which among us, out of the midst of indocilities at once more and more horrific and more and more reported with a desperate drollery, was to constitute an event so supremely beguiling that distressful meanings and expensive remedies found themselves alike salved to consciousness by the fact that such compositions could only be, for people of taste, enjoyable. I think of this hapless kinsman throughout as blest with a "form" that appealed to the finer fibres of appreciation; so that, variously misadventurous as he was ever to continue, his genius for expression again and again just saved him—saved him for bare life, left in his hand a broken piece of the effective magic wand, never perhaps waved with anything like that easy grace in an equally compromised interest.

It was at any rate as if I had from the first collected and saved up the echoes—or so at least it seems to me now: echoes of him as all sarcastically and incorrigibly mutinous, somewhat later on, while in nominal charge of a despairing *pasteur* at Neuchâtel—followed by the intensified sense of him, after I scarce remember quite what interval, on his appearing at Newport, where his sisters, as I have mentioned, had been protectively gathered in, during the year, more or less, that followed our own installation there. Then it was that we had the value of his being interesting with less trouble taken to that end—in proportion to the effect achieved—than perhaps ever served such a cause; it would perhaps scarce even be too much to say that, as the only trouble he seemed capable of was the trouble of quite positively declining to interest on any terms, his essential Dickensism, as I have called it, or his Thackerayan tint if preferred, his comedy-virtue in fine, which he could neither disown nor, practically speaking, misapply, was stronger even than his particular sardonic cynicism, strongly as that was at last to flower. I won't in the least say he dazzled—that was reserved for his so quite otherwise brilliant, his temporarily triumphant, younger brother, at whom I have already glanced, who was on no possible terms with him, and never could have been, so that the difficulty of their relation glimmers upon me as probably half the good reason for the original queer despatch of the elder to about the remotest, the most separating, point in space at which "educational advantages" could be conceived as awaiting him. I must have had no need by that time to be dazzled, or even to be charmed, in order more or less fondly, often indeed doubtless fearfully, to apprehend; what I apprehended being that here was a creature quite amusedly and perceptively, quite attentively and, after a fashion, profitably, living without a single one of the elements of life (of the inward, I mean, those one would most have missed if deprived of them) that I knew as most conducive to animation. What could have roused more curiosity than this, for the time at least, even if there hadn't been associated with it such a fine redolence, as I then supposed it, of the rich and strange places and things, as I supposed *them*, that had contributed to making him over? He had come back made—unless one was already, and too conveniently or complacently, to call it unmade: *that* was the point (and it certainly wasn't Albany that ever would have made him); he had come back charged, to my vision, with prodigious "English" impressions and awarenesses, each so thoroughly and easily assimilated that they might have played their part as convictions and standards had he pretended to anything that would in that degree have satisfied us. He never spoke of his "faith," as that might have been the thing we could have held him to; and he knew what not too gracelessly to speak of when the sense of the American grotesque in general and the largely-viewed "family" reducibility to the absurd in particular offered him such free light pasture. He had the sign of grace that he ever perfectly considered my father—so far as attitude, distinct from behaviour, went; but most members of our kinship on that side still clung to this habit of consideration even when, as was in certain cases but too visible, they had parted with all sense of any other. I have preserved no happier truth about my father than that the graceless whom, according to their own fond term, he, and he alone of all of us, "understood," returned to him as often and appealed to him as freely as those happier, though indeed scarce less importunate, in their connection, who found attraction and reason enough in their understanding *him*. My brother's impression of this vessel of intimations that evening at the Boston theatre, and of his "sincerity" and his seeming "greatly changed," doesn't at all events, I feel, fail in the least to fit into one of those amplifications upon which my incurable trick of unwillingness wholly to sacrifice any good value compromised by time tends to precipitate me with a force that my reader can scarce fear for me more than I fear it for myself. There was no "extraordinary way" in which our incalculable kinsman *mightn't* talk, and that William should have had for the hour the benefit of his general truth is but a happy note in my record. It was not always the case that one wished one "might have seen more of him," but this was only because one had had on any contact the sense of seeing so much. That produced consequences among which the desire for more might even be uncannily numbered. John Wilkes Booth, of the same evening, was of course President Lincoln's assassin-to-be, of whose crudely extravagant performance of the hero of Schiller's Robbers I recall my brother's imitative description—I never myself saw him; and it simplifies his case, I think, for distracted history, that he must have been quite an abominable actor. I appear meanwhile to have paid William at Cambridge a visit of which I have quite oddly lost remembrance—by reason doubtless of its but losing itself in like, though more prolonged, occasions that were to follow at no great distance and that await my further reference. The manner of his own allusion to it more than suffices.

The radiance of H.'s visit has not faded yet, and I come upon gleams of it three or four times a day in my farings to and fro, but it has never a bit diminished the lustre of far-off shining Newport, all silver and blue, and of this heavenly group below[5]—all being more or less failures, especially the two outside ones. The more so as the above-mentioned H. could in no wise satisfy my craving for knowledge of family and friends—he didn't seem to have been on speaking terms with anyone for some time past, and could tell me nothing of what they did, said or thought, about any given subject. Never did I see a so-much uninterested creature in the affairs of those about him. He is a good soul, though, in his way, too; and less fatal than the light fantastic and ever-sociable Wilky, who has wrought little but disaster during his stay with me; breaking down my good resolutions about food, keeping me from all intellectual exercise, working havoc on my best hat by wearing it while dressing, while in his nightgown, while washing his face, and all but going to bed with it. He occupied my comfortable arm-chair all the morning in the position represented in the fine plate that accompanies this letter—but one more night though, and he will have gone, and no thorn shall pierce the side of the serene and hallowed felicity of expectation in which I shall revel till the time comes for returning home, home to the hearth of my infancy and budding youth. As Wilky has submitted to you a résumé of his future history for the next few years, so will I of mine, hoping it will meet your approval. Thus: one year Chemistry, then one term at home. Then one year with Wyman, followed by a medical education. Then five or six years with Agassiz; after which probably death, death, death from inflation and plethora of knowledge. This you had better seriously consider. So farewell till 8.45 some Sunday evening soon. Your bold, your beautiful, your blossom!

"I lead, as ever," he meanwhile elsewhere records, "the monotonous life of the scholar, with few variations."

We have very general talk at our table, Miss Upham declaiming against the vulgarity of President Lincoln and complacently telling of her own ignorance as to the way the wind blows or as to the political events going on, and saying she thinks it a great waste of time and of "no practical account" to study natural history. F. J. Child impresses one as very witty and funny, but leaves it impossible to remember what he says. I took a walk with the Divinity student this splendid afternoon. He told me he had been walking yesterday with one of the Jerseymen and they had discussed the doctrine of a future state. The Jerseyman thought that if the easy Unitarian doctrines were to become popular the morals of the community would be most terribly relaxed. "Why," said the other, "here you are in the very thick of Unitarianism; look about you—people are about as good as anywhere." "Yes," replied the Jerseyman, "I confess to you that that is what has *staggered* me, and I don't understand it yet!"

I stretch over to the next year, 1863, for the sake of the following to his sister.

Chérie charmante, I am established in a cosy little room, with a large recess with a window in it containing bed and washstand, and separated from the main apartment by a rich green silk curtain and a large gilt cornice. This gives the whole establishment a splendid look. I found when I got back here that Miss Upham had raised her price; so great efforts were made by two of us to form a club. But too little enthusiasm was shown by any one else, and it fell through. I then with that fine economical instinct which distinguishes me resolved to take breakfast and tea, of my own finding and making, in my room, and only pay Miss Upham for dinners. Miss U. is now holding forth at Swampscott, so I asked to see her sister Mrs. Wood and learn the cost of the 7 dinners a week. She with true motherly instinct said that I should only make a slop with my self-made meals in my room, and that she would rather let me keep on for 4.50, seeing it was me. I said she must first consult Miss Upham. She returned from Swampscott saying that Miss U. had sworn she would rather pay *me* a dollar a week than have me go away. Ablaze with economic passion I cried "Done!"—trying to make it appear that she had made me a formal offer to that effect. But she then wouldn't admit it, and after much recrimination we separated, it being agreed that I should come for 4.50, *but tell no one.* So mind *you* don't either. I now lay my hand on my heart and confidently look to my Mother for that glance of approbation which she must bestow. Have I not redeemed any weaknesses of the past? Though part of my conception fails, yet it was boldly planned and would have been a noble stroke.

I have been pretty busy this week. I have a filial feeling toward Wyman already. I work in a vast museum at a table all alone, surrounded by skeletons of mastodons, crocodiles and the like, with the walls hung about with monsters and horrors enough to freeze the blood. But I have no fear, as most of them are tightly bottled up. Occasionally solemn men and women come in to see the museum, and sometimes timid little girls (reminding me of thee, my love, only they are less fashionably dressed), who whisper "Is folks allowed here?" It pains me to remark, however, that not all the little girls are of this pleasing type, many being bold-faced jades. Salter is back here, but morose. One or two new students and Prof. Goodwin, who is very agreeable. Also William Everett, son of the great Edward, very intelligent and a capital scholar, studying law. He took honours at the English Cambridge. I send a photograph of General Sickles for your and Wilky's amusement. It is a part of a great anthropomorphological collection which I am going to make. So take care of it, as well as of all the photographs you will find in the table-drawer in my room. But isn't he a bully boy? Desecrate the room as little as possible. If Wilky wants me as an extra nurse send for me without hesitation.

VI

These returns to that first year or two at Newport contribute meanwhile to filling out as nothing in the present pages has yet done for me that vision of our father's unsurpassable patience and independence, in the interest of the convictions he cherished and the expression of them, as richly emphatic as it was scantly heeded, to which he daily gave himself. We took his "writing" infinitely for granted—we had always so taken it, and the sense of him, each long morning, at his study table either with bent considering brow or with a half-spent and checked intensity, a lapse backward in his chair and a musing lift of perhaps troubled and baffled eyes, seems to me the most constant fact, the most closely interwoven and underlying, among all our breaks and variations. He applied himself there with a regularity and a piety as little subject to sighing abatements or betrayed fears as if he had been working under pressure for his bread and ours and the question were too urgent for his daring to doubt. This play of his remarkable genius brought him in fact throughout the long years no ghost of a reward in the form of pence, and could proceed to publicity, as it repeatedly did, not only by the copious and resigned sacrifice of such calculations, but by his meeting in every single case all the expenses of the process. The untired impulse to this devotion figured for us, comprehensively and familiarly, as "Father's Ideas," of the force and truth of which in his own view we were always so respectfully, even though at times so bewilderedly and confoundedly persuaded, that we felt there was nothing in his exhibition of life that they didn't or couldn't account for. They pervaded and supported his existence, and very considerably our own; but what comes back to me, to the production of a tenderness and an admiration scarce to be expressed, is the fact that though we thus easily and naturally lived with them and indeed, as to their more general effects, the colour and savour they gave to his talk, breathed them in and enjoyed both their quickening and their embarrassing presence, to say nothing of their almost never less than amusing, we were left as free and unattacked by them as if they had been so many droppings of gold and silver coin on tables and chimney-pieces, to be "taken" or not according to our sense and delicacy, that is our felt need and felt honour. The combination in him of his different vivacities, his living interest in his philosophy, his living interest in us and his living superiority to all greed of authority, all overreaching or overemphasising "success", at least in the heated short run, gave his character a magnanimity by which it was impossible to us not to profit in all sorts of responsive and in fact quite luxurious ways. It was a luxury, I to-day see, to have all the benefit of his intellectual and spiritual, his religious, his philosophic and his social passion, without ever feeling the pressure of it to our direct irritation or discomfort. It would perhaps more truly figure the relation in which he left us to these things to have likened our opportunities rather to so many scattered glasses of the liquor of faith, poured-out cups stood about for our either sipping or draining down or leaving alone, in the measure of our thirst, our curiosity or our strength of head and heart. If there was much leaving alone in us—and I freely confess that, so far as the taking any of it all "straight" went, my lips rarely adventured—this was doubtless because we drank so largely at the source itself, the personally overflowing and irrigating. What it then comes to, for my present vision, was that he treated us most of all on the whole, as he in fact treated everything, by his saving imagination—which set us, and the more as we were naturally so inclined, the example of living as much as we might in some such light of our own. If we had been asked in our younger time for instance what *were* our father's ideas, or to give an example of one of them, I think we should promptly have answered (I should myself have hastened to do so) that the principal was a devoted attachment to the writings of Swedenborg; as to whom we were to remember betimes, with intimate appreciation, that in reply to somebody's plea of not finding him credible our parent had pronounced him, on the contrary, fairly "insipid with veracity." We liked that partly, I think, because it disposed in a manner, that is in favour of our detachment, of the great Emanuel, but when I remember the part played, so close beside us, by this latter's copious revelation, I feel almost ashamed for my own incurious conduct. The part played consisted to a large extent in the vast, even though incomplete, array of Swedenborg's works, the old faded covers of which, anciently red, actually apt to be loose, and backed with labels of impressive, though to my sense somewhat sinister London imprint, Arcana

Coelestia, Heaven and Hell and other such matters—they all had, as from other days, a sort of black emphasis of dignity—ranged themselves before us wherever, and however briefly, we disposed ourselves, forming even for short journeys the base of our father's travelling library and perhaps at some seasons therewith the accepted strain on our mother's patience. I recall them as inveterately part of our very luggage, requiring proportionate receptacles; I recall them as, in a number considerable even when reduced, part of their proprietor's own most particular dependence on his leaving home, during our more agitated years, for those speculative visits to possible better places (than whatever place of the moment) from which, as I have elsewhere mentioned, he was apt to return under premature, under passionate nostalgic, reaction. The Swedenborgs were promptly out again on their customary shelves or sometimes more improvised perches, and it was somehow not till we had assured ourselves of this that we felt *that* incident closed.

Nothing could have exceeded at the same time our general sense—unless I all discreetly again confine myself to the spare record of my own—for our good fortune in never having been, even when most helpless, dragged by any approach to a faint jerk over the threshold of the inhabited temple. It stood there in the centre of our family life, into which its doors of fine austere bronze opened straight; we passed and repassed them when we didn't more consciously go round and behind; we took for granted vague grand things within, but we never paused to peer or penetrate, and none the less never had the so natural and wistful, perhaps even the so properly resentful, "Oh I say, do look in a moment for manners if for nothing else!" called after us as we went. Our admirable mother sat on the steps at least and caught reverberations of the inward mystic choir; but there were positive contemporary moments when I well-nigh became aware, I think, of something graceless, something not to the credit of my aspiring "intellectual life," or of whatever small pretensions to seriousness I might have begun to nourish, in the anything but heroic impunity of my inattention. William, later on, made up for this not a little, redeeming so, to a large extent, as he grew older, our filial honour in the matter of a decent sympathy, if not of a noble curiosity: distinct to me even are certain echoes of passages between our father and his eldest son that I assisted at, more or less indirectly and wonderingly, as at intellectual "scenes," gathering from them portents of my brother's independent range of speculation, agitations of thought and announcements of difference, which could but have represented, far beyond anything I should ever have to show, a gained and to a considerable degree an enjoyed, confessedly an interested, acquaintance with the paternal philosophic *penetralia*. That particular impression refers indeed to hours which at the point I have reached had not yet struck; but I am touched even now, after all the years, with something exquisite in my half-grasped premonitory vision of their belonging, these belated discussions that were but the flowering of the first germs of such *other*, doubtless already such opposed, perceptions and conclusions, to that order of thin consolations and broken rewards which long figured as the most and the best of what was to have been waited for on our companion's part without the escape of a plaint. Yet I feel I may claim that our awareness of all that was so serenely dispensed with—to call it missed would have been quite to falsify the story and reflect meanly on the spirit—never in the least brutally lapsed from admiration, however unuttered the sentiment itself, after the fashion of raw youth; it is in fact quite distinct to me that, had there been danger of this, there came to us from our mother's lips at intervals long enough to emphasise the final sincerity and beauty a fairly sacred reminder of that strain of almost solely self-nourished equanimity, or in other words insuperable gaiety, in her life's comrade, which she had never seen give way. This was the very gaiety that kept through the years coming out for us—to the point of inviting free jokes and other light familiarities from us at its expense. The happiest household pleasantry invested our legend of our mother's fond habit of address, "Your father's *ideas*, you know—!" which was always the signal for our embracing her with the last responsive finality (and, for the full pleasure of it, in his presence). Nothing indeed so much as his presence encouraged the licence, as I may truly call it, of the legend—that is of our treatment *en famille* of any reference to the attested public weight of his labours; which, I hasten to add, was much too esoteric a ground of geniality, a dear old family joke, not to be kept, for its value, to ourselves. But there comes back to me the impression of his appearing on occasion quite moved to the exuberance of cheer—as a form of refreshment he could draw on for a stronger and brighter spurt, I mean—by such an apology for resonance of reputation as our harmless, our of course utterly edgeless, profanity represented. It might have been for him, by a happy stretch, a sign that the world *did* know—taking us for the moment, in our selfish young babble, as a part of the noise of the world. Nothing, at the same time, could alter the truth of his case, or can at least alter it to me now: he had, intellectually, convictionally, passionally speaking, a selfless detachment, a lack of what is called the eye for effect—always I mean of the elated and interested order—which I can but marvel at in the light of the rare aptitude of his means to his end, and in that of the beauty of both, though the stamp was doubtless most vivid, for so differing, so gropingly "esthetic" a mind as my own, in his unfailingly personal and admirable style. We knew he had thoroughly his own "unconventional" form, which, by the unspeakable law of youth, we managed to feel the distinction of as not platitudinous even while we a bit sneakingly felt it as quotable, on possible occasions, against our presence of mind; the great thing was at all events that we couldn't live with him without the sense that if his books resembled his talk and his character—as we moreover felt they couldn't help almost violently doing—they might want for this, that or the other which kept the conventional true to its type, but could as little fail to flush with the strong colour, colour so remarkably given and not taken, projected and not reflected, colour of thought and faith and moral and expressional atmosphere, as they could leave us without that felt side-wind of their strong composition which made after all so much of the air we breathed and was in the last resort the gage of something perpetually fine going on.

It is not too much to say, I think, that our religious education, so far as we had any, consisted wholly in that loose yet enlightening impression: I say so far as we had any in spite of my very definitely holding that it would absolutely not have been possible to us, in the measure of our sensibility, to breathe more the air of that reference to an order of goodness and power greater than any this world by itself can show which we understand as the religious spirit. Wondrous to me, as I consider again, that my father's possession of this spirit, in a degree that made it more deeply one with his life than I can conceive another or a different case of its being, should have been unaccompanied with a single one of the outward or formal, the theological, devotional, ritual, or even implicitly pietistic signs by which we usually know it. The fact of course was that his religion was nothing if not a philosophy, extraordinarily complex and worked out and original, intensely personal as an exposition, yet not only susceptible of application, but clamorous for it, to the whole field of consciousness, nature and society, history, knowledge, all human relations and questions, every pulse of the process of our destiny. Of this vast and interesting conception, as striking an expression of the religious spirit surely as ever was put forth, his eldest son has given an account[6]—so far as this was possible at once with brevity and with full comprehension—that I should have been unable even to dream of aspiring to, and in the masterly clearness and justice of which the opportunity of the son blends with that of the critic, each character acting in perfect felicity, after a fashion of which I know elsewhere no such fine example. It conveys the whole sense of our father's philosophic passion, which was theologic, by my direct impression of it, to a degree fairly outdistancing all theologies; representing its weight, reproducing its utterance, placing it in the eye of the world, and making for it the strong and single claim it suggests, in a manner that leaves nothing to be added to the subject. I am not concerned with the intrinsic meaning of these things here, and should not be even had they touched me more directly, or more converted me from what I can best call, to my doubtless scant honour, a total otherness of contemplation, during the years when my privilege was greatest and my situation for inquiry and response amplest; but the active, not to say the obvious, moral of them, in all our younger time, was that a life of the most richly consequent flowed straight out of them, that in this life, the most abundantly, and above all naturally, communicated *as* life that it was possible to imagine, we had an absolutely equal share, and that in fine I was to live to go back with wonder and admiration to the quantity of secreted thought in our daily medium, the quality of intellectual passion, the force of cogitation and aspiration, as to the explanation both of a thousand surface incoherences and a thousand felt felicities. A religion that was so systematically a philosophy, a philosophy that was so sweepingly a religion, being together, by their necessity, as I have said, an intensity of relation to the actual, the consciousness so determined was furnished forth in a way that met by itself the whole question of the attitude of "worship" for instance; as I have attempted a little to show that it met, with a beautiful good faith and the easiest sufficiency, every other when such came up: those of education, acquisition, material vindication, what is called success generally. In the beauty of the whole thing, again, I lose myself—by which I mean in the fact that we were all the while partaking, to our most intimate benefit, of an influence of direction and enlargement attended with scarce a single consecrated form and which would have made many of these, had we been exposed to intrusion from them, absurdly irrelevant. My father liked in our quite younger period to read us chapters from the New Testament and the Old, and I hope we liked to listen to them—though I recall their seeming dreary from their association with school practice; but that was the sole approach to a challenge of our complete freedom of inward, not less than our natural ingenuity of outward, experience. No other explicit address to us in the name of the Divine could, I see, have been made with any congruity—in face of the fact that invitations issued in all the vividest social terms, terms of living appreciation, of spiritual perception, of "human fellowship," to use the expression that was perhaps oftenest on his lips and his pen alike, were the very substance of the food supplied in the parental nest.

The freedom from pressure that we enjoyed in every direction, all those immunities and exemptions that had been, in protracted childhood, positively embarrassing to us, as I have already noted, before the framework, ecclesiastical and mercantile, squared at us as with reprobation from other households, where it seemed so to conduce to their range of resource—these things consorted with our yet being yearned over or prescribed for, by every implication, after a fashion that was to make the social organisation of such invidious homes, under my subsequent observation of life, affect me as so much bleak penury or domestic desert where these things of the spirit, these genialities of faith were concerned. Well do I remember, none the less, how I was troubled all along just by this particular crookedness of our being so extremely religious without having, as it were, anything in the least classified or striking to show for it; so that the measure of other-worldliness pervading our premises was rather a waste, though at the same time oddly enough a congestion—projecting outwardly as it did no single one of those usual symptoms of propriety any of which, gathered at a venture from the general prospect, might by my sense have served: I shouldn't have been particular, I thought, as to the selection. Religion was a matter, by this imagination, to be worked off much more than to be worked in, and I fear my real vague sentiment to have been but that life would under the common equipment be somehow more amusing; and this even though, as I don't forget, there was not an item of the detail of devotional practice that we had been so much as allowed to divine. I scarce know why I should have wanted anything more amusing, as most of our coevals would have regarded it, than that we had from as far back as I could remember indulged in no shade of an approach to "keeping Sunday"; which is one of the reasons why to speak as if piety could have borne for us any sense but the tender human, or to speak at all of devotion, unction, initiation, even of the vaguest, into the exercises or professions, as among our attributes, would falsify altogether our mere fortune of a general liberty of living, of making ourselves as brightly at home as might be, in that "spiritual world" which we were in the habit of hearing as freely alluded to as we heard the prospect of dinner or the call of the postman. The oddity of my own case, as I make it out so far as it involved a confused criticism, was that my small uneasy mind, bulging and tightening in the wrong, or at least in unnatural and unexpected, places, like a little jacket ill cut or ill sewn, attached its gaping view, as I have already more than enough noted, to things and persons, objects and aspects, frivolities all, I dare say I was willing to grant, compared with whatever manifestations of the serious, these being by need, apparently, the abstract; and that in fine I should have been thankful for a state of faith, a conviction of the Divine, an interpretation of the universe—anything one might have made bold to call it—which would have supplied more features or appearances. Feeling myself "after" persons so much more than after anything else—to recur to that side of my earliest and most constant consciousness which might have been judged most deplorable—I take it that I found the sphere of our more nobly supposititious habitation too imperceptibly peopled; whereas the religious life of every other family that could boast of any such (and what family didn't boast?) affected my fancy as with a social and material crowdedness. That faculty alone was affected—this I hasten to add; no directness of experience ever stirred for me; it being the case in the first place that I scarce remember, as to all our young time, the crossing of our threshold by any faint shade of an ecclesiastical presence, or the lightest encounter with any such elsewhere, and equally of the essence, over and above, that the clerical race, the pre-eminently restrictive tribe, as I apprehended them, couldn't very well have agreed less with the general colour of my fondest vision: if it be not indeed more correct to say that I was reduced to *supposing* they couldn't. We knew in truth nothing whatever about them, a fact that, as I recover it, also flushes for me with its fine awkwardness—the social scene in general handsomely bristling with them to the rueful view I sketch, and they yet remaining for us, or at any rate for myself, such creatures of pure hearsay that when late in my teens, and in particular after my twentieth year, I began to see them portrayed by George Eliot and Anthony Trollope the effect was a disclosure of a new and romantic species. Strange beyond my present power to account for it this anomaly that amid a civilisation replete with "ministers"—for we at least knew the word—actively, competitively, indeed as would often appear quite violently, ministering, so little sense of a brush against approved examples was ever to attend me that I had finally to draw my nearest sufficiency of a true image from pictures of a social order largely alien to our own. All of which, at the same time, I allow myself to add, didn't mitigate the simple fact of my felt—my indeed so luxuriously permitted—detachment of sensibility from everything, everything, that is, in the way of great relations, as to which our father's emphasis was richest. *There* was the dim dissociation, there my comparative poverty, or call it even frivolity, of instinct: I gaped imaginatively, as it were, to such a different set of relations. I couldn't have framed stories that would have succeeded in involving the least of the relations that seemed most present to *him*; while those most present to myself, that is more complementary to whatever it was I thought of as humanly most interesting, attaching, inviting, were the ones his schemes of importances seemed virtually to do without. Didn't I discern in this from the first a kind of implied snub to the significance of mine?—so that, in the blest absence of "pressure" which I just sought here passingly to celebrate, I could brood to my heart's content on the so conceivable alternative of a field of exposure crammed with those objective appearances that my faculty seemed alone fitted to grasp. In which there was ever the small torment of the fact—though I don't quite see to-day why it should not have been of a purely pleasant irritation—that what our parent most overflowed with was just the brave contradiction or opposition between all his parts, a thing which made for perfect variety, which he carried ever so easily and brightly, and which would have put one no less in the wrong had one accused him of knowing only the abstract (as I was so complacently and invidiously disposed to name it) than if one had foolishly remarked on his living and concluding without it. But I have already made clear his great mixed range—which of course couldn't *not* have been the sign of a mind conceiving our very own breathing humanity in its every fibre the absolute expression of a resident Divinity. No element of character, no spontaneity of life, but instantly seized his attention and incurred his greeting and his comment; which things could never possibly have been so genially alert and expert—as I have, again, before this, superabundantly recorded—if it had not fairly fed on active observation and contact. He could answer one with the radiant when one challenged him with the obscure, just as he could respond with the general when one pulled at the particular; and I needn't repeat that this made for us, during all our time, anything but a starved actuality.

None the less, however, I remember it as savouring of loss to me—which is my present point—that our so thoroughly informal scene of susceptibility seemed to result from a positive excess of familiarity, in his earlier past, with such types of the shepherd and the flock, to say nothing of such forms of the pasture, as might have met in some degree my appetite for the illustrational. This was one of the things that made me often wish, as I remember, that I might have caught him sooner or younger, less developed, as who should say; the matters that appeared, however confusedly, to have started his development being by this measure stranger and livelier than most of those that finally crowned it, marked with their own colour as many of these doubtless were. Three or four strongest pages in the fragment of autobiography gathered by his eldest son into the sheaf of his Literary Remains describe the state of soul undergone by him in England, in '44, just previous to the hour at which Mrs. Chichester, a gentle lady of his acquaintance there, brought to his knowledge, by a wondrous chance, the possibility that the great Swedenborg, from whom she had drawn much light, might have something to say to his case; so that under the impression of his talk with her he posted at once up to London from the neighbourhood of Windsor, where he was staying, possessed himself of certain volumes of the writings of the eminent mystic (so-called I mean, for to my father this description of him was grotesque), and passed rapidly into that grateful infinitude of recognition and application which he was to inhabit for the rest of his days. I saw him move about there after the fashion of the oldest and easiest native, and this had on some sides its own considerable effect, tinged even on occasion with romance; yet I felt how the *real* right thing for me would have been the hurrying drama of the original rush, the interview with the admirable Mrs. Chichester, the sweet legend of his and my mother's charmed impression of whom had lingered with us—I admired her very name, there seeming none other among us at all like it; and then the return with the tokens of light, the splendid agitation as the light deepened, and the laying in of that majestic array of volumes which were to form afterward the purplest rim of his library's horizon and which I was thus capable, for my poor part, of finding valuable, in default of other values, as coloured properties in a fine fifth act. It was all a play I hadn't "been to," consciously at least—that was the trouble; the curtain had fallen while I was still tucked in my crib, and I assisted but on a comparatively flat home scene at the echo of a great success. I could still have done, for the worst, with a consciousness of Swedenborg that should have been graced at least with Swedenborgians—aware as I was of the existence of such enrolled disciples, ornaments of a church of their own, yet known to us only as persons rather acidly mystified by the inconvenience, as we even fancied them to feel it, of our father's frankly independent and disturbingly irregular (all the more for its being so expressive) connection with their inspirer. In the light or the dusk of all this it was surely impossible to make out that he professed any faint shade of that clerical character as to his having incurred which we were, "in the world," to our bewilderment, not infrequently questioned. Those of the enrolled order, in the matter of his and their subject of study, might in their way too have raised to my regard a fretted vault or opened a long-drawn aisle, but they were never at all, in the language of a later day, to materialise to me; we neither on a single occasion sat in their circle, nor did one of them, to the best of my belief, ever stray, remonstrantly or invitingly, into ours; where Swedenborg was read not in the least as the Bible scarce more than just escaped being, but even as Shakespeare or Dickens or Macaulay was content to be—which was without our arranging or subscribing for it. I seem to distinguish that if a fugitive or a shy straggler from the pitched camp did turn up it was under cover of night or of curiosity and with much panting and putting off of the mantle, much nervous laughter above all—this safe, however, to become on the shortest order amusement easy and intimate. That *figured* something in a slight way—as at least I suppose I may infer from the faint adumbration I retain; but nothing none the less much attenuated what I suppose I should have denounced as the falsity of our position (meaning thereby of mine) had I been constitutionally at all voluble for such flights. Constructionally we had all the fun of licence, while the truth seemed really to be that fun in the religious connection closely depended on bondage. The fun was of course that I wanted in this line of diversion something of the coarser strain; which came home to me in especial, to cut the matter short, when I was present, as I yielded first and last to many an occasion for being, at my father's reading out to my mother with an appreciation of that modest grasp of somebody's attention, the brief illusion of publicity, which has now for me the exquisite grace of the touching, some series of pages from among his "papers" that were to show her how he had this time at last done it. No touch of the beautiful or the sacred in the disinterested life can have been absent from such scenes—I find every such ideally there; and my memory rejoices above all in their presentation of our mother at her very perfectest of soundless and yet absolutely all-saving service and trust. To have attempted any projection of our father's aspect without an immediate reference to her sovereign care for him and for all of us as the so widely open, yet so softly enclosing, lap of all his liberties and all our securities, all our variety and withal our harmony, the harmony that was for nine-tenths of it our sense of her gathered life in us, and of her having no other—to have so proceeded has been but to defer by instinct and by scruple to the kind of truth and of beauty before which the direct report breaks down. I may well have stopped short with what there would be to say, and yet what account of us all can pretend to have gone the least bit deep without coming to our mother at every penetration? We simply lived by her, in proportion as we lived spontaneously, with an equanimity of confidence, an independence of something that I should now find myself think of as decent compunction if I didn't try to call it instead morbid delicacy, which left us free for detachments of thought and flights of mind, experiments, so to speak, on the assumption of our genius and our intrinsic interest, that I look back upon as to a luxury of the unworried that is scarce of this world. This was a support on which my father rested with the absolute whole of his weight, and it was when I felt her listen with the whole of her usefulness, which needed no other force, being as it was the whole of her tenderness and amply sufficing by itself, that I understood most what it was so to rest and so to act. When in the fulness of the years she was to die, and he then to give us time, a few months, as with a beatific depth of design, to marvel at the manner of his acceptance of the stroke, a shown triumph of his philosophy, he simply one day consciously ceased, quietly declined to continue, as an offered measure of his loss of interest. Nothing— he had enabled himself to make perfectly sure—was in the least worth while without her; this attested, he passed away or went out, with entire simplicity, promptness and ease, for the definite reason that his support had failed. His philosophy had been not his support but his suspension, and he had never, I am sure, felt so lifted as at that hour, which splendidly crowned his faith. It showed us more intimately still what, in this world of cleft components, one human being can yet be for another, and how a form of vital aid may have operated for years with such perfection as fairly to have made recognition seem at the time a sort of excess of reaction, an interference or a pedantry. All which is imaged for me while I see our mother listen, at her work, to the full music of the "papers." She could do that by the mere force of her complete availability, and could do it with a smoothness of surrender that was like an array of all the perceptions. The only thing that I might well have questioned on these occasions was the possibility on the part of a selflessness so consistently and unabatedly active of its having anything ever left *acutely* to offer; to abide so unbrokenly in such inaptness for the personal claim might have seemed to render difficult such a special show of it as any particular pointedness of hospitality would propose to represent. I dare say it was our sense of this that so often made us all, when the explicit or the categoric, the impulse of acclamation, flowered out in her, find our happiest play of filial humour in just embracing her for the sound of it; than which I can imagine no more expressive tribute to our constant depths of indebtedness. She lived in ourselves so exclusively, with such a want of use for anything in her consciousness that was not about us and for us, that I think we almost contested her being separate enough to be proud of us—it was too like our being proud of ourselves. We were delightedly derisive with her even about pride in our father—it was the most domestic of our pastimes; for what really could exceed the tenderness of our fastening on her that she *was* he, *was* each of us, was our pride and our humility, our possibility of *any* relation, and the very canvas itself on which we were floridly embroidered? How can I better express what she seemed to do for her second son in especial than by saying that even with her deepest delicacy of attention present I could still feel, while my father read, why it was that I most of all seemed to wish we might have been either much less religious or much more so? Was not the reason at bottom that I so suffered, I might almost have put it, under the impression of his style, which affected me as somehow too philosophic for life, and at the same time too living, as I made out, for thought?—since I must weirdly have opined that by so much as you were individual, which meant personal, which meant monotonous, which meant limitedly allusive and verbally repetitive, by so much you were not literary or, so to speak, *largely* figurative. My father had terms, evidently strong, but in which I presumed to feel, with a shade of irritation, a certain narrowness of exclusion as to images otherwise—and oh, since it was a question of the pen, so multitudinously!—entertainable. Variety, variety—*that* sweet ideal, *that* straight contradiction of any dialectic, hummed for me all the while as a direct, if perverse and most unedified, effect of the parental concentration, with some of its consequent, though heedless, dissociations. I heard it, felt it, saw it, both shamefully enjoyed and shamefully denied it as form, though as form only; and I owed thus supremely to my mother that I could, in whatever obscure levity, muddle out some sense of my own preoccupation under the singular softness of the connection that she kept for me, by the outward graces, with that other and truly much intenser which I was so little framed to share.

If meanwhile my father's tone, so far as that went, was to remain the same, save for a natural growth of assurance, and thereby of amplitude, all his life, I find it already, and his very voice as we were to know them, in a letter to R. W. Emerson of 1842, without more specific date, after the loose fashion of those days, but from 2 Washington Place, New York, the second house in the row between the University building and Broadway, as he was next to note to his correspondent in expressing the hope of a visit from him. (It was the house in which, the following year, his second son was born.)

I came home to-night from my lecture a little disposed to think, from the smart reduction of my audience, that I had about as well not have prepared my course, especially as I get no tidings of having interested one of the sort (the religious) for whom they are wholly designed. When I next see you I want a half-hour's support from you under this discouragement, and the purpose of this letter is to secure it. When I am *with* you I get no help from you—of the sort you can give me, I feel sure; though you must know what I want before I listen to you next. Usually the temper you show, of perfect repose and candour, free from all sickening partisanship and full of magnanimous tenderness for every creature, makes me forget my wants in your lavish plenty. But I know you have the same as I have, deep down in your breast, and it is by these I would fain know you. I am led, quite without any conscious wilfulness either, to seek the *laws* of these appearances that swim round us in God's great museum, to get hold of some central facts which may make all other facts properly circumferential and orderly; and you continually dishearten me by your apparent indifference to such law and such facts, by the dishonour you seem to cast on our intelligence as if it were what stands in our way. Now my conviction is that my intelligence is the necessary digestive apparatus for my life; that there is nihil in vita—worth anything, that is—quod non prius in intellectu. Now is it not so in truth with you? Can you not report your life to me by some intellectual symbol which my intellect appreciates? Do you not know your activity? But fudge—I cannot say what I want to say, what aches to say itself in me, and so I'll hold up till I see you, and try once more to get some better furtherance by my own effort. Here I am these thirty-one years in life, ignorant in all outward science, but having patient habits of meditation which never know disgust or weariness, and feeling a force of impulsive love toward all humanity which will not let me rest wholly mute, a force which grows against all resistance that I can muster against it. What shall I do? Shall I get me a little nook in the country and communicate with my *living* kind—not my talking kind—by life only; a word perhaps of *that* communication, a fit word once a year? Or shall I follow some commoner method—learn science and bring myself first into man's respect, that I may thus the better speak to him? I confess this last theory seems rank with earthliness—to belong to days forever past.

His appeal to Emerson at this hour was, as he elsewhere then puts it, to the "invisible" man in the matter, who affected him as somewhere behind the more or less immediately visible, the beautifully but mystifyingly audible, the Emerson of honeyed lectures and addresses, suggestive and inspiring as that one might be, and who might, as we say to-day, have something, something more at least, for him. "I will tell him that I do not value his substantive discoveries, whatever they may be, perhaps half so largely as he values them, but that I chiefly cherish that erect attitude of mind in him which in God's universe undauntedly seeks the worthiest tidings of God, and calmly defies every mumbling phantom which would challenge its freedom. Should his zeal for realities and contempt of vulgar shows abide the ordeal I have thus contrived for them I shall gladly await his visit to me. So much at least is what I have been saying to myself. Now that I have told it to you also you have become a sort of confidant between me and myself, and so bound to promote harmony there." The correspondence expands, however, beyond my space for reporting of it; I but pick out a few passages.

I am cheered by the coming of Carlyle's new book, which Greeley announces, and shall hasten off for it as soon as I have leisure.[7] The title is provokingly enigmatical, but thought enough there will be in it no doubt, whatever the name; thought heaped up to topheaviness and inevitable lopsidedness, but more interesting to me than comes from any other quarter of Europe—interesting for the man's sake whom it shows. According to my notion he is the very best interpreter of a spiritual philosophy that could be devised for *this age*, the age of transition and conflict; and what renders him so is his natural birth-and-education-place. Just to think of a Scotchman with a heart widened to German spiritualities! To have overcome his educational bigotries far enough to listen to the new ideas, this by itself was wonderful; and then to give all his native shrewdness and humour to the service of making them *tell* to the minds of his people—what more fortunate thing for the time

111

could there be? You don't look upon Calvinism as a fact at all; wherein you are to my mind philosophically infirm—impaired in your universality. I can see in Carlyle the advantage his familiarity with it gives him over you with a general audience. What is highest in him is built upon that lowest. At least so I read; I believe Jonathan Edwards redivivus in true blue would, after an honest study of the philosophy that has grown up since his day, make the best possible reconciler and critic of this philosophy—far better than Schelling redivivus.

In the autumn of 1843 the "nook in the country" above alluded to had become a question renounced, so far at least as the American country was concerned, and never again afterwards flushed into life. "I think it probable I shall winter in some mild English climate, Devonshire perhaps, and go on with my studies as at home. I shall miss the stimulus of your candid and generous society, and I confess we don't like the aspect of the journey; but one's destiny puts on many garments as it goes shaping itself in secret—so let us not cling to any particular fashion." Very marked, and above all very characteristic of my father, in this interesting relation, which I may but so imperfectly illustrate, his constant appeal to his so inspired, yet so uninflamed, so irreducible and, as it were, inapplicable, friend for intellectual and, as he would have said, spiritual help of the immediate and adjustable, the more concretely vital, kind, the kind translatable into terms of the real, the particular human terms of action and passion. "Oh you man without a *handle*! Shall one never be able to help himself out of you, according to his needs, and be dependent only upon your fitful tippings-up?"—a remarkably felicitous expression, as it strikes me, of that difficulty often felt by the passionately-living of the earlier time, as they may be called, to draw down their noble philosopher's great overhanging heaven of universal and ethereal answers to the plane of their comparatively terrestrial and personal questions; the note of the answers and their great anticipatory spirit being somehow that they seemed to anticipate everything but the unaccommodating individual case. My father, on his side, bristled with "handles"—there could scarce be a better general account of him—and tipped himself up for you almost before you could take hold of one; of which truth, for that matter, this same letter happens to give, even if just trivially, the hint. "Can I do anything for you in the way of taking parcels, no matter how large or expensive?—or for any of your friends? If you see Margaret Fuller ask her to give me some service to render her abroad, the dear noble woman: it seems a real hardship to be leaving the country now that I have just come to talk with her." Emerson, I should add, did offer personally so solid a handle that my father appears to have taken from him two introductions to be made use of in London, one to Carlyle and the other to John Sterling, the result of which shortly afterwards was as vivid and as deeply appropriated an impression of each eminent character as it was probably to be given either of them ever to have made. The impression of Carlyle was recorded but long subsequently, I note, and is included in William's gathering-in of our father's Literary Remains (1885); and of the acquaintance with Sterling no reflection remains but a passage in a letter, under date of Ventnor and of the winter of 1843, from the latter to his biographer to be; Carlyle having already mentioned in the Life that "Two American gentlemen, acquaintances also of mine, had been recommended to him, by Emerson most likely"; and that "one morning Sterling appeared here with a strenuous proposal that we should come to Knightsbridge and dine with him and them.... And accordingly we went," it goes on. "I remember it as one of the saddest dinners; though Sterling talked copiously, and our friends, Theodore Parker one of them, were pleasant and distinguished men." My father, with Theodore Parker his friend and the date fitting, would quite seem to have been one of the pair were it not that "our conversation was waste and logical, I forget quite on what, not joyful and harmoniously effusive." It is *that* that doesn't fit with any real participation of his—nothing could well do less so; unless the occasion had but too closely conformed to the biographer's darkly and richly prophetic view of it as tragic and ominous, "sad as if one had been dining in a ruin, in the crypt of a mausoleum"—all this "painfully apparent through the bright mask (Sterling) had bound himself to wear." The end of his life was then, to Carlyle's view, in sight; but his own note, in the Isle of Wight, on "Mr. James, your New-England friend," was genial enough—"I saw him several times and liked him. They went on the 24th of last month back to London—or so purposed," he adds, "because there is no pavement here for him to walk on. I want to know where he is, and thought I should be able to learn from you. I gave him a note for Mill, who may perhaps have seen him."

My main interest in which is, I confess, for the far-off germ of the odd legend, destined much to grow later on, that—already the nucleus of a household—we were New England products; which I think my parents could then have even so much as seemed only to eyes naturally unaware of our American "sectional" differences. My father, when considerably past his thirtieth year, if I am not mistaken, had travelled "East," within our borders, but once in his life—on the occasion of his spending two or three months in Boston as a very young man; there connecting itself with this for me a reminiscence so bedimmed at once and so suggestive as now almost to torment me. It must have been in '67 or '68 that, giving him my arm, of a slippery Boston day, up or down one of the steep streets that used to mount, from behind, and as slightly sullen with the effort, to Beacon Hill, and between which my now relaxed memory rather fails to discriminate, I was arrested by his pointing out to me opposite us a house in which he had for a while had rooms, long before and quite in his early time. I but recall that we were more or less skirting the base of an ancient town-reservoir, the seat of the water-supply as then constituted, a monument rugged and dark, massively granitic, perched all perversely, as it seemed to look, on the precipitous slope, and which—at least as I see it through the years—struck quite handsomely the Babylonian note. I at any rate mix up with this frowning object—it had somehow a sinister presence and suggestion—my companion's mention there in front of it that he had anciently taken refuge under its shadow from certain effects of a misunderstanding, if indeed not of a sharp rupture, for the time, with a highly generous but also on occasion strongly protesting parent at Albany, a parent displeased with some course he had taken or had declined to take (there was a tradition among us that he had been for a period quite definitely "wild"), and relief from further discussion with whom he had sought, and had more or less found, on that spot. It was an age in which a flight from Albany to Boston—there being then no Boston and Albany Railroad—counted as a far flight; though it wasn't to occur to me either then or afterwards that the ground of this manœuvre had been any plotted wildness in the Puritan air. What was clear at the moment, and what he remarked upon, was that the street-scene about us showed for all the lapse of time no scrap of change, and I remember well for myself how my first impression of Boston gave it to me under certain aspects as more expressive than I had supposed an American city could be of a seated and rooted social order, an order not complex but sensibly fixed—gathered in or folded back to intensity upon itself; and this, again and again, when the compass of the posture, its narrow field, might almost have made the fold excruciating. It had given however no sign of excruciation—that itself had been part of the Puritan stoicism; which perhaps was exactly why the local look, recognised to the point I speak of by the visitor, was so contained and yet comparatively so full: full, very nearly, I originally fancied, after the appraisable fashion of some composed town-face in one of Balzac's *villes de province*. All of which, I grant, is much to say for the occasion of that dropped confidence, on the sloshy hillside, to which I allude—and part of the action of which was that it had never been dropped before; this circumstance somehow a peculiar source of interest, an interest I the more regret to have lost my grasp of as it must have been sharp, or in other words founded, to account for the long reverberation here noted. I had still—as I was indeed to keep having through life—the good fortune that elements of interest easily sprang, to my incurable sense, from any ghost of a drama at all *presented*; though I of course can't in the least pretend to generalise on what may or may not have constituted living presentation. This felicity occurred, I make out, quite incalculably, just as it could or would; the effect depended on some particular touch of the spring, which was set in motion the instant the touch happened to be right. My father's was always right, to my receptive mind; as receptive, that is, of any scrap of enacted story or evoked picture as it was closed to the dry or the abstract proposition; so that I blush the deeper at not being able, in honour of his reference, to make the latter more vividly flower—I still so feel that I quite thrilled with it and with the standing background at the moment lighted by it. There were things in it, and other persons, old actualities, old meanings and furnishings of the other old Boston, as I by that time couldn't but appraise it; and the really archaic, the overhung and sombre and secret-keeping street, "socially" disconnected, socially mysterious—as I like at any rate to remember it—was there to testify (testify to the ancient time of tension, expansion, sore meditation or whatever) by its positively conscious gloom.

The moral of this, I fear, amounts to little more than that, putting aside the substance of his anecdote, my father had not set foot in New England till toward his thirty-fifth year, and my mother was not to do so till later still; circumstances not in the least preventing the birth of what I have called the falsifying legend. The allusion to the walking at Ventnor touches his inability to deal with rural roads and paths, then rougher things than now; by reason of an accident received in early youth and which had so lamed him for life that he could circulate to any convenience but on even surfaces and was indeed mainly reduced to driving—it had made him for all his earlier time an excellent whip. His constitution had been happily of the strongest, but as I look back I see his grave disability, which it took a strong constitution to carry, mainly in the light of a consistency of patience that we were never to have heard broken. The two acceptances melt together for me—that of the limits of his material action, his doing and enjoying, set so narrowly, and that of his scant allowance of "public recognition," or of the support and encouragement that spring, and spring so naturally and rightly, when the relation of effect to cause is close and straight, from any at all attested and glad understanding of a formula, as we say nowadays a message, richly and sincerely urged. Too many such reflections, however, beset me here by the way. My letters jump meanwhile to the summer of 1849, when I find in another of them, addressed to Emerson, a passage as characteristic as possible of one of the writer's liveliest and, as I confess it was ever to seem to me, most genially perverse idiosyncrasies, his distinctly low opinion of "mere" literary men. This note his letters in general again and again strike—not a little to the diversion of those who were to have observed and remembered his constant charmed subjection, in the matter of practice, to the masters, even quite the lighter, in the depreciated group. His sensibility to their spell was in fact so marked that it became from an early time a household game with us to detect him in evasive tears over their pages, when these were either real or romantic enough, and to publish without mercy that he had so been caught. There was a period in particular during which this pastime enjoyed, indeed quite revelled in, the form of our dragging to the light, with every circumstance of derision, the fact of his clandestine and deeply moved perusal of G. P. R. James, our nominal congener, at that time ceasing to be prescribed. It was his plea, in the "'fifties," that this romancer had been his idol in the 'forties and the 'thirties, and that under renewed, even if but experimental, surrender the associations of youth flocked back to life—so that *we*, profane about the unduly displaced master, were deplorably the poorer. He loved the novel in fine, he followed its constant course in the Revue with a beautiful inconsequence, and the more it was literature loved it the better, which was just how he loved, as well, criticism and journalism; the particular instance, with him, once he was in relation with it, quite sufficiently taking care of the invidiously-viewed type—as this was indeed viewed but a *priori* and at its most general—and making him ever so cheerfully forget to be consistent. Work was verily cut out for the particular instance, as against the type, in an air and at a time favouring so, again and again, and up and down the "literary world," a dire mediocrity. It was the distillers of *that* thinness, the "mere" ones, that must have been present to him when he wrote to Emerson in 1849: "There is nothing I dread so much as literary men, especially *our* literary men; catch them out of the range of mere personal gossip about authors and books and ask them for honest sympathy in your sentiment, or for an honest repugnancy of it, and you will find the company of stage-drivers sweeter and more comforting to your soul. In truth the questions which are beginning to fill the best books, and will fill the best for a long time to come, are not related to what we have called literature, and are as well judged—I think better— by those whom books have at all events not belittled. When a man *lives*, that is lives enough, he can scarcely write. He cannot read, I apprehend, at all. All his writing will be algebraicised, put into the form of sonnets and proverbs, and the community will feel itself insulted to be offered a big bunch of pages, as though it were stupid and wanted tedious drilling like a child." When I begin to quote my father, however, I hang over him perhaps even too historically; for his expression leads me on and on so by its force and felicity that I scarce know where to stop. "The fact is that I am afraid I am in a very bad way, for I cannot heartily engage in any topic in which I shall appear to advantage"—the question having been, *de part et d'autre*, of possible courses of lectures for which the appetite of New York and Boston already announced itself as of the largest. And it still more beguiles me that "my wife and I are obliged—so numerous has waxed our family—to enlarge our house in town and get a country house for the summer." Here came in that earnest dream of the solutional "Europe" with which I have elsewhere noted that my very youngest sensibility was fed. "These things look expensive and temporary to us, besides being an additional care; and so, considering with much pity our four stout boys, who have no play-room within doors and import shocking bad manners from the street, we gravely ponder whether it wouldn't be better to go abroad for a few years with them, allowing them to absorb French and German and get such a sensuous education as they can't get here."

In 1850, however, we had still not departed for Europe—as we were not to do for several years yet; one advantage of which was that my father remained for the time in intercourse by letter with his English friend Dr. J. J. Garth Wilkinson, first known during my parents' considerable stay in London of several years before, 1843-44; and whose admirable style of expression, in its way as personal and as vivid as Henry James's own, with an added and doubtless more perceptibly full-blooded massiveness, is so attested by his earlier writings,[8] to say nothing of the rich collection of his letters (1845-55) lately before me—notably by The Human Body and its Connection with Man, dedicated in 1851 to my father—that I wonder at the absence of such a master, in more than one happy specimen, from the common educational exhibitions of English prose. Dr. Wilkinson was a friend of Emerson's as well, which leads the latter's New York correspondent to cite to him in February 1850 a highly characteristic passage from one of the London communications.

Carlyle came up here (presumably to Hampstead) on Monday to see Neuberg, and spoke much of you with very kind recollections. He remembered your metaphysics also and asked with terrible solicitude whether they yet persevered. I couldn't absolutely say that they did not, though I did my best to stammer out something about the great social movement. He was suffering dreadfully from *malaise* and indigestion and gave with his usual force his usual putrid theory of the universe. All great men were most miserable; the day on which any man could say he was not miserable, that day he was a scoundrel; God was a Divine Sorrow; to no moment could he, Carlyle, ever say Linger, but only Goodbye and never let me see your face again. And all this interpolated with convulsive laughter, showing that joy would come into him were it even by the path of hysteria and disease. To me he is an unprofitable man, and though he gave me the most kind invitation I have too much respect for my stomach to go much into his company. Where hope is feeble genius and the human voice are on the way to die. By the next boat I will endeavour to send you over my thoughts on his recent pamphlet, the first of a series of Latter-Day-Tracts. He is very rapidly falling out with all his present admirers, for which I like them all the better; and indeed is driving fast toward social views—only his is to be a compulsory, not an attractive, socialism.

After quoting which my father comments: "Never was anything more false than this worship of sorrow by Carlyle; he has picked it up out of past history and spouts it for mere display, as a virtuoso delights in the style of his grandfather. It is the merest babble in him, as everyone who has ever talked an hour with him will acquit him of the least grain of humility. A man who has once uttered a cry of despair should ever after clothe himself in sackcloth and ashes."

The writer was to have meanwhile, before our migration of 1855, a considerable lecturing activity. A confused, yet perfectly recoverable recollection, on my own part, of these years, connects itself with our knowledge that our father engaged in that practice and that he went forth for the purpose, with my mother always in earnest and confident even though slightly fluttered attendance, at about the hour of our upward procession to bed; which fact lent to the proceeding—that is to *his*—a strange air of unnatural riot, quite as of torch-lighted and wind-blown dissipation. We went to plays and to ballets, and they had comparatively speaking no mystery; but at no lecture had we ever been present, and these put on for my fancy at least a richer light and shade, very much as if we ourselves had been on the performing side of the curtain, or the wonder of admiring (in our mother's person) and of being admired (in our father's) had been rolled for us into a single glory. This glory moreover was not menaced, but only made more of a thrill by the prime admirer's anxiety, always displayed at the last, as to whether they were not starting without the feature of features, the *corpus delicti* or manuscript itself; which it was legendary with us that the admired had been known to drive back for in an abashed flurry at the moment we

119

were launched in dreams of him as in full, though mysterious, operation. I can see him now, from the parlour window, at the door of the carriage and under the gusty street-lamp, produce it from a coat-tail pocket and shake it, for her ideal comfort, in the face of his companion. The following, to Emerson, I surmise, is of some early date in the autumn of '52.

I give three lectures in Boston at the Masonic Temple; the first and second on Nov. 5th and 8th respectively. I should be greatly appalled in some respects, but still charmed, to have you for an auditor, seeing thus a hundred empty seats obliterated; but, I beg of you, don't let any engagement suffer by such kindness to me. Looking over the lectures again they horrify me with their loud-mouthed imbecility!—but I hope they may fall upon less hardened ears in some cases. I am sure that the thought which is in them, or rather seems to me to struggle to be in them, is worthy of all men's rapturous homage, and I will trust that a glimpse of it may somehow befall my patient auditory. The fact is that a vital truth can never be transferred from one mind to another, because life alone appreciates it. The most one can do for another is to plant some rude formula of such truths in his memory, leaving his own spiritual chemistry to set free the germ whenever the demands of his life exact it. The reason why the gods seem so powerless to the sensuous understanding, and suffer themselves to be so long defamed by our crazy theologies, is that they are life, and can consequently be revealed only to life. But life is simply the passage of idea into action; and our crazy theologies forbid ideas to come into action any further than our existing institutions warrant. Hence man leads a mere limping life, and the poor gods who are dependent upon his manliness for their true revelation and for their real knowledge, are doomed to remain forever unknown, and even denied by such solemn pedants as Mr. Atkinson and Miss Martineau. However, I shall try to convert *myself* at least into an army of Goths and Huns, to overcome and destroy our existing sanctities, that the supernal splendours may at length become credible and even visible. Good-bye till we meet in Boston, and cultivate your goodnature according to my extensive needs.

I bridge the interval before our migration of 1855 exactly for the sake of certain further passages addressed to the same correspondent, from London, in the following year. The letter is a long one and highly significant of the writer's familiar frankness, but I must keep down my examples—the first of which glances at his general sense of the men he mainly met.

They are all of them depressed or embittered by the public embarrassments that beset them; deflected, distorted, somehow despoiled of their rich individual manliness by the necessity of providing for these imbecile old inheritances of church and state. Carlyle is the same old sausage, fizzing and sputtering in his own grease, only infinitely *more* unreconciled to the blest Providence which guides human affairs. He names God frequently and alludes to the highest things as if they were realities, but all only as for a picturesque effect, so completely does he seem to regard them as habitually circumvented and set at naught by the politicians. I took our friend M. to see him, and he came away greatly distressed and désillusionné, Carlyle having taken the utmost pains to deny and descry and deride the idea of his having done the least good to anybody, and to profess indeed the utmost contempt for everybody who thought he had, and poor M. being intent on giving him a plenary assurance of this fact in his own case.... Arthur Helps seems an amiable kindly little man with friendly offers, but I told him I had no intention to bore him, and would at most apply to him when I might want a good hatter or bootmaker. He fancied a little—at least I thought this was the case—that I was going to make a book, and might be indiscreet enough to put him in!.... —— disappoints me, he is so eaten up with the "spirits" and all that. His imagination is so vast as to dwarf all the higher faculties, and his sympathy as narrow as Dr. Cheever's or Brownson's. No reasonable man, it is true, likes the clergy or the philosophers, but ——'s dislike of them seems as envenomed as that between rival tradesmen or rival beauties. One can't endure the nonsense they talk, to be sure, but when one considers the dear human meaning and effort struggling at the bottom of it all one can feel still less any personal separation from the men themselves. ——'s sarcasm is of the fiercest, and on the whole he is only now at last sowing his intellectual wild oats—he will grow more genial in good time. This is it: I think he is but now finding his youth! That which we on our side of the water find so early and exhaust so prodigally he has found thus much later—I mean an emancipation from the shackles of custom; and the kicking up of his heels

121

consequently is proportionate to his greater maturity of muscle. Mrs. ——
is a dear little goose of a thing, who fancies the divine providence in closer
league with herself than with others, giving her intimations of events about
to happen and endowing her with peculiar perspicacity in the intuition of
remedies for disease; and ——, the great brawny fellow, sits by and says never
a word in abatement of this enormous domestic inflation, though the visitor
feels himself crowded by it into the most inconsiderable of corners. A sweet,
loving, innocent woman like Mrs. —— oughtn't to grow egotistical in the
company of a truly wise man, and this accordingly is another quarrel I have
with ——. In short I am getting to the time of life when one values one's
friends for what they are more than for what they do. I am just as much
impressed as ever by his enormous power, but the goodness out of which it
is born and the wisdom by which it is nurtured and bred are things I don't
so much see.

The correspondence grew more interspaced, and with the year 1861 and
the following, when we were at home again, became a matter of the occasional
note. I have before me a series of beautiful examples of Emerson's share in
it—during the earlier time copious enough; but these belong essentially to
another case. I am all but limited, for any further show of the interesting
relation than I have already given, to reproducing a few lines from Emerson's
Diary, passages unpublished at the moment I write, and the first of them of
April 1850. "I have made no note of these long weary absences at New York
and Philadelphia. I am a bad traveller, and the hotels are mortifications to all
sense of well-being in me. The people who fill them oppress me with their
excessive virility, and would soon become intolerable if it were not for a few
friends who, like women, tempered the acrid mass. Henry James was true
comfort—wise, gentle, polished, with heroic manners and a serenity like the
sun." The hotels of those days may well have been an ordeal—distinct to me
still, from no few childish glimpses of their bareness of ease and rudeness
of *acceuil*; yet that our justly fastidious friend was not wholly left to their
mercy seems signified by my not less vivid remembrance of his staying with us
on occasion in New York; some occasion, or occasions, I infer, of his coming
on to lecture there. Do I roll several occasions into one, or amplify one beyond
reason?—this last being ever, I allow, the waiting pitfall of a chronicler too

memory-ridden. I "visualise" at any rate the winter firelight of our back-parlour at dusk and the great Emerson—I knew he was great, greater than any of our friends—sitting in it between my parents, before the lamps had been lighted, as a visitor consentingly housed only could have done, and affecting me the more as an apparition sinuously and, I held, elegantly slim, benevolently aquiline, and commanding a tone alien, beautifully alien, to any we heard roundabout, that he bent this benignity upon me by an invitation to draw nearer to him, off the hearth-rug, and know myself as never yet, as I was not indeed to know myself again for years, in touch with the wonder of Boston. The wonder of Boston was above all just then and there for me in the sweetness of the voice and the finish of the speech—this latter through a sort of attenuated emphasis which at the same time made sounds more important, more interesting in themselves, than by any revelation yet vouchsafed us. Was not this my first glimmer of a sense that the human tone *could*, in that independent and original way, be interesting? and didn't it for a long time keep me going, however unwittingly, in that faith, carrying me in fact more or less on to my day of recognising that it took much more than simply not being of New York to produce the music I had listened to. The point was that, however that might be, I had had given me there in the firelight an absolutely abiding measure. If I didn't know from that hour forth quite all it was to *not* utter sounds worth mentioning, I make out that I had at least the opposite knowledge. And all by the operation of those signal moments—the truth of which I find somehow reflected in the fact of my afterwards knowing one of our household rooms for the time—it must have been our only guest-chamber—as "Mr. Emerson's room." The evening firelight played so long for me upon the door—that is to the length probably of three days, the length of a child's impression. But I must not let this carry me beyond the second note of the Diary, this time of May 1852. "'I do not wish this or that thing my fortune will procure, I wish the great fortune,' said Henry James, and said it in the noblest sense." The report has a beauty to me without my quite understanding it; the union of the two voices in it signifies quite enough. The last very relevant echo of my father's by itself, in the connection, I hasten now to find in a communication that must have been of the summer of 1869, when Dr. Wilkinson paid his only visit to America—this apparently of the briefest. The letter to Emerson from Cambridge notes that his appearance there had been delayed.

He may come to-morrow possibly: if in the morning I will telegraph you; if in the evening I shall try to keep him over Monday that you may meet him here at dinner on that day. But I fear this bothersome Sabbath and its motionless cars may play us a trick. I shall hope for a generous Monday all the same, and if that hope is baulked shall owe Sunday a black-eye—and will pay my debt on the first suitable occasion, I warrant you. What an awkward story (the letter continues) The Nation to-day tells of Charles Sumner! Charles's burly voice has always had for me a dreadfully hollow sound, as if it came from a great copper vat, and I have loved him but with fear and trembling accordingly. Is he _really_, like all American politicians, tricky, or is The Nation—so careful about facts ordinarily—only slanderous?... Carlyle nowadays is a palpable nuisance. If he holds to his present mouthing ways to the end he will find no showman là-bas to match him, for I hold Barnum a much more innocent personage. I shouldn't wonder if Barnum grew regenerate in some far off day by mere force of his democracy. But Carlyle's intellectual pride is so stupid that one can hardly imagine anything able to cope with it.

The following, in so different a key, is of some seven years earlier date—apparently '62; but I have let it stand over, for reasons, that it may figure here as the last of the communications addressed to Emerson that I shall cite. Written at an hotel, the Tremont House, in Boston, it marks his having come up from Newport for attendance at some meeting of a dining-club, highly distinguished in composition, as it still happily remains, of which he was a member—though but so occasionally present that this circumstance perhaps explains a little the even more than usual vivacity of his impression. Not indeed, I may add, that mustered reasons or apologies were ever much called for in any case of the play of that really prime note of his spontaneity.

I go to Concord in the morning, but shall have barely time to see you there, even if I do as much as that; so that I can't forbear to say to you now the word I wanted as to my impression of yesterday about Hawthorne and Ellery Channing. Hawthorne isn't to me a prepossessing figure, nor apparently at all an *enjoying* person in any way: he has all the while the look—or would have to the unknowing—of a rogue who suddenly finds himself in a company of detectives. But in spite of his rusticity I felt a sympathy for him fairly amounting to anguish, and couldn't take my eyes off him all dinner, nor my rapt attention: as that indecisive little Dr. Hedge[9] found, I am afraid, to his cost, for I hardly heard a word of what he kept on saying to me, and resented his maliciously putting his artificial person between me and the profitable object of study. (It isn't however that I now feel any ill-will to him—I could recommend anyone but myself to go and hear him preach. The thing was that Hawthorne seemed to me to possess human substance and not to have dissipated it all away like that culturally debauched ———, or even like good inoffensive comforting Longfellow.) John Forbes and you kept up the human balance at the other end of the table, but my region was a desert with H. for its only oasis. It was so pathetic to see him, contented sprawling Concord owl that he was and always has been, brought blindfold into that brilliant daylight and expected to wink and be lively, like some dapper Tommy Titmouse. I felt him bury his eyes in his plate and eat with such voracity that no one should dare to speak to him. My heart broke for him as his attenuated left-hand neighbour kept putting forth *his* long antennae to stroke his face and try whether his eyes were open. It was heavenly to see him persist in ignoring the spectral smiles—in eating his dinner and doing nothing but that, and then go home to his Concord den to fall upon his knees and ask his heavenly Father why it was that an owl couldn't remain an owl and not be forced into the diversions of a canary. I have no doubt that all the tenderest angels saw to his case that night and poured oil into his wounds more soothing than gentlemen ever know. W. Ellery Channing too seemed so human and good—sweet as summer and fragrant as pinewoods. He is more sophisticated than Hawthorne of course, but still he was kin; and I felt the world richer by two *men*, who had not yet lost themselves in mere members of society. This is what I suspect—that we are fast getting so fearful one to another, we "members of society" that we shall ere long begin to kill one another in self-defence and give place in that way at last to a more veracious state of things. The old world is breaking up on all hands: the glimpse of the everlasting granite I caught in H. and W. E. shows me that there is stock enough left

125

for fifty better. Let the old impostors go, bag and baggage, for a very real and substantial one is aching to come in, in which the churl shall not be exalted to a place of dignity, in which innocence shall never be tarnished nor trafficked in, in which every man's freedom shall be respected down to its feeblest filament as the radiant altar of God. To the angels, says Swedenborg, death means resurrection to life; by that necessary rule of inversion which keeps them separate from us and us from them, and so prevents our being mutual nuisances. Let us then accept political and all other distraction that chooses to come; because what is disorder and wrath and contention on the surface is sure to be the greatest peace at the centre, working its way thus to a surface that shall never be disorderly.

But it is in the postscript that the mixture and the transition strike me as most inevitable.

Weren't you shocked at ——'s engagement? To think of that prim old snuffers imposing himself on that pure young flame! What a world, what a world! But once we get rid of Slavery the new heavens and new earth will swim into reality.

No better example could there be, I think, of my father's remarkable and constant belief, proof against all confusion, in the imminence of a transformation-scene in human affairs—"spiritually" speaking of course always—which was to be enacted somehow without gross or vulgar visibility, or at least violence, as I have said, but was none the less straining to the front, and all by reason of the world's being, deep within and at heart, as he conceived, so achingly anxious for it. He had the happiness—though not so untroubled, all the while, doubtless, as some of his declarations would appear to represent—of being able to see his own period and environment as the field of the sensible change, and thereby as a great historic hour; that is, I at once subjoin, I more or less *suppose* he had. His measure of the imminent and immediate, of the socially and historically visible and sensible was not a thing easy to answer for, and when treated to any one of the loud vaticinations or particular revolutionary messages and promises our age was to have so much abounded in, all his sense of proportion and of the whole, of the real and the ridiculous, asserted itself with the last emphasis. In that

126

mixture in him of faith and humour, criticism and conviction, that mark of a love of his kind which fed on discriminations and was never so moved to a certain extravagance as by an exhibited, above all by a cultivated or in the least sententious vagueness in respect to these, dwelt largely the original charm, the peculiarly social and living challenge (in that it was so straight and bright a reflection of life) of his talk and temper. Almost all of my father shines for me at any rate in the above passages, and in another that follows, with their so easy glide from discrimination, as I have called it, that is from analytic play, in the outward sphere, to serenity of synthesis and confidence and high joy in the inward. It was as if he might have liked so to see his fellow-humans, fellow-diners, fellow-celebrities or whatever, in that acuity of individual salience, in order to proceed thence to some enormous final doubt or dry renouncement—instead of concluding, on the contrary, and on the same free and familiar note, to the eminently "worth while" character of life, or its susceptibility to vast and happy conversions. With which too, more than I can say, have I the sense here of his so finely contentious or genially perverse impulse to carry his wares of observation to the market in which they would on the whole bring least rather than most—where his offering them at all would produce rather a flurry (there might have been markets in which it had been known to produce almost a scandal), and where he would in fact give them away for nothing if thereby he might show that such produce grew. Never was there more of a case of the direct friendliness to startling growths—if so they might be held—of the very soil that lies under our windows. I don't think he liked to scandalise—certainly he didn't in the least for scandal's sake; but nothing inspired him more to the act and the pleasure of appreciation for appropriation, as it might be termed, than the deprecating attitude of others on such ground—that degree of shyness of appropriation on their part which practically left appreciation vague. It was true that the appreciation for a human use, as it might be called—that is for the high optimistic transition—could here carry the writer far.

VII

I find markedly relevant at this point a letter from Newport in the autumn of '61 to another correspondent, one of a series several other examples of which no less successfully appeal to me, even though it involve my going back a little to place three or four of these latter, written at Geneva in 1860. Mrs. William Tappan, primarily Caroline Sturgis of Boston, was for long years and to the end of her life our very great friend and one of my father's most constant and most considered interlocutors, both on the ground of his gravity and on that of his pleasantry. She had spent in Europe with her husband and her two small daughters very much the same years, from early in the summer of '55 till late in the autumn of '60, that we had been spending; and like ourselves, though with less continuity for the time, she had come to live at Newport, where, with no shadow of contention, but with an admirable intelligence, of the incurably ironic or mocking order, she was such a light, free, somewhat intellectually perverse but socially impulsive presence (always for instance insatiably hospitable) as our mustered circle could ill have spared. If play of mind, which she carried to any point of quietly-smiling audacity that might be, had not already become a noted, in fact I think the very most noted, value among us, it would have seated itself there in her person with a nervous animation, a refinement of what might have been called soundable sincerity, that left mere plump assurance in such directions far in the lurch. And she was interesting, she became fairly historic, with the drawing-out of the years, as almost the only survivor of that young band of the ardent and uplifted who had rallied in the other time to the "transcendental" standard, the movement for organised candour of conversation on almost all conceivable or inconceivable things which appeared, with whatever looseness, to find its prime inspirer in Emerson and become more familiarly, if a shade less authentically, vocal in Margaret Fuller. Hungry, ever so cheerfully and confidently hungry, had been much of the New England, and peculiarly the Boston, of those days; but with no such outreaching of the well-scoured empty platter, it probably would have struck one, as by the occasional and quite individual agitation of it from some ruefully-observed doorstep of the best society. It was from such a doorstep that Caroline Sturgis had originally taken her restless flight, just as it was on such another that, after a course of infinite freedom of inquiry and irony, she in the later time, with a fortune inherited, an hospitality extended and a genial gravity of expression confirmed, alighted again, to the no small re-enrichment of a company of friends who had had meanwhile scarce any such intellectual adventures as she was to retain, in a delicate and casual irreverence, the just slightly sharp fragrance or fine asperity of, but who might cultivate with complacency and in support of the general claim to comprehensive culture and awareness unafraid the legend of her vicarious exposure.

Mr. Frank Sanborn's school, which I have already mentioned and to which the following alludes, was during the years immediately preceding the War, as during those of the War itself, the last word of what was then accounted the undauntedly modern, flourishing as it did under the patronage of the most "advanced" thought. The "coeducational" idea had up to that time, if I mistake not, taken on no such confident and consistent, certainly no such graceful or plausible form; small boys and big boys, boys from near and boys from far, consorted there and cohabited, so far as community of board and lodging and of study and sport went, with little girls and great girls, mainly under the earnest tutoring and elder-sistering of young women accomplished as scholarly accomplishment in such cases was then understood, but with Mr. Sanborn himself of course predominantly active and instructional, and above all with the further felicity of the participation of the generous Emerson family by sympathy and interest and the protective spread of the rich mantle of their presence. The case had been from the first a frank and high-toned experiment, a step down from the tonic air, as was so considerably felt, of radical conviction to the firm ground of radical application, that is of happy demonstration—an admittedly new and trustful thing, but all the brighter and wiser, all the more nobly and beautifully workable for that. With but the scantest direct observation of the attempted demonstration—demonstration, that is, of the excellent fruit such a grafting might produce—I yet imagine the enacted and considerably prolonged scene (it lasted a whole decade) to have heaped perfectly full the measure of what it proposed. The interesting, the curious, the characteristic thing was just, however, I seem to make out—I seemed to have made out even at the time—in the almost complete absence of difficulty. It might almost then be said of the affair that it hadn't been difficult enough for interest even should one insist on treating it as sufficiently complicated or composed for picture. The great War was to leave so many things changed, the country over, so many elements added, to say nothing of others subtracted, in the American consciousness at large, that even though the coeducational idea, taking to itself strength, has during these later years pushed its conquests to the very verge of demonstration of its inevitable limits, my memory speaks to me of the Concord school rather as of a supreme artless word on the part of the old social order than as a charged intimation or announcement on the part of the new. The later arrangements, more or less in its likeness and when on a considerable scale, have appeared, to attentive observation, I think, mere endlessly multiplied notes of the range of high spirits in the light heart of communities more aware on the whole of the size and number of their opportunity, of the boundless spaces, the possible undertakings, the uncritical minds and the absent standards about them, than of matters to be closely and preparedly reckoned with. They have been, comparatively speaking, experiments in the void—the great void that may spread so smilingly between wide natural borders before complications have begun to grow. The name of the complication before the fact is very apt to be the discovery—which latter term was so promptly to figure for the faith that living and working more intimately together than had up to then been conceived possible would infinitely improve both the condition and the performance of the brother and sister sexes. It takes long in new communities for discoveries to become complications—though complications become discoveries doubtless often in advance of this; the large vague area, with its vast marginal ease, over which confidence could run riot and new kinds of human relation, elatedly proposed, flourish in the sun, was to shift to different ground the question the Concord school had played with, during its term of life, on its smaller stage, under the great New England elms and maples and in the preoccupied New England air.

The preoccupation had been in a large measure, it is true, exactly with such possibilities, such bright fresh answers to old stale riddles, as Mr.

Sanborn and his friends clubbed together to supply; but I can only, for my argument, recover the sense of my single visit to the scene, which must have been in the winter of '62-'63, I think, and which put before me, as I seem now to make out, some suggested fit of perversity—not desperate, quite harmless rather, and almost frivolously futile, on the part of a particular little world that had been thrown back upon itself for very boredom and, after a spell of much admired talking and other beating of the air, wanted for a change to "do" something. The question it "played" with I just advisedly said—for what could my impression have been, personally if indirectly gathered, and with my admirably communicative younger brother to testify, but that if as a school, in strict parlance, the thing was scarce more than naught, as a prolonged pastime it was scarce less than charming and quite filled up in that direction its ample and original measure? I have to reckon, I here allow, with the trick of what I used irrepressibly to read into things in front of which I found myself, for gaping purposes, planted by some unquestioned outer force: it seemed so prescribed to me, so imposed on me, to read more, as through some ever-felt claim for roundness of aspect and intensity of effect in presented matters, whatever they might be, than the conscience of the particular affair itself was perhaps developed enough to ask of it. The experience of many of the Concord pupils during the freshness of the experiment must have represented for them a free and yet ever so conveniently conditioned taste of the idyllic—such possibilities of perfect good comradeship between unsuspected and unalarmed youths and maidens (on a comprehensive ground that really exposed the business to a light and put it to a test) as they were never again to see so favoured in every way by circumstance and, one may quite emphatically say, by atmosphere. It is the atmosphere that comes back to me as most of all the making of the story, even when inhaled but by an occasional whiff and from afar—the manner of my own inhaling. In that air of charmed and cultivated good faith nothing for which the beautiful might be so presumingly claimed—if only claimed with a sufficiently brave clean emphasis—wouldn't have *worked*, which was the great thing; every one must have felt that what was aspired to did work, and as I catch the many-voiced report of it again (many-voiced but pretty well suffused with one clear tone, this of inflections irreproducible now) I seem to

131

listen in convinced admiration, though not by any means in stirred envy, to the cheerful clatter of its working. My failure of envy has, however, no mite of historic importance, proving as it does nothing at all but that if we had, in the family sense, so distinctly turned our back on Europe, the distinctness was at no point so marked as in our facing so straight to such a picture, by which I mean to such an exhibition, as my father's letter throws off. Without knowledge of the letter at the time I yet measured the situation much as he did and enjoyed it as he did, because it would have been stupid not to; but from that to any wishful vision of being in it or of it would have been a long jump, of which I was unabashedly incapable. To have broken so personally, so all but catastrophically, with Europe as we had done affected me as the jump sufficient; we had landed somewhere in quite another world or at least on the sharp edge of one; and in the single particular sense could I, as time then went on, feel myself at all moved, with the helpless, the baffled visionary way of it, to push further in. What straight solicitation *that* phase of the American scene could exert—more coercive to the imagination than any we were ever again, as Americans, to know—I shall presently try to explain; but this was an intensely different matter.

I buried two of my children yesterday—at Concord, Mass., and feel so heartbroken this morning that I shall need to adopt two more instantly to supply their place; and lo and behold you and William present yourselves, or if you decline the honour Ellen and Baby. Mary and I trotted forth last Wednesday, bearing Wilky and Bob in our arms to surrender them to the famous Mr. Sanborn. The yellowest sunshine and an atmosphere of balm were all over the goodly land, while the maple, the oak and the dogwood showered such splendours upon the eye as made the Champs Elysées and the Bois appear parvenus and comical. Mrs. Clark is a graceless enough woman outwardly, but so tenderly feathered inwardly, so unaffectedly kind and motherly toward the urchins under her roof, that one was glad to leave them in that provident nest. She has three or four other school-boarders, one of them a daughter of John Brown—tall, erect, long-haired and freckled, as John Brown's daughter has a right to be. I kissed her (inwardly) between the eyes, and inwardly heard the martyred Johannes chuckle over the fat inheritance of love and tenderness he had after all bequeathed to his children in all good men's minds. An arch little Miss Plumley also lives there, with eyes full of laughter and a mouth like a bed of lilies bordered with roses. How it is going to be possible for my two boys to pursue their studies in the midst of that bewilderment I don't clearly see. I am only sure of one thing, which is that if I had had such educational advantages as that in my youth I should probably have been now far more nearly ripe for this world's business. We asked to see Miss Waterman, one of the teachers quartered in the house, in order to say to her how much we should thank her if she would occasionally put out any too lively spark she might see fall on the expectant tinder of my poor boys' bosoms; but Miss W. herself proved of so siliceous a quality on inspection—with round tender eyes, young, fair and womanly—that I saw in her only new danger and no promise of safety. My present conviction is that a general conflagration is inevitable, ending in the total combustion of all that I hold dear on that spot. Yet I can't but felicitate our native land that such magnificent experiments in education go on among us.

Then we drove to Emerson's and waded up to our knees through a harvest of apples and pears, which, tired of their mere outward or carnal growth, had descended to the loving bosom of the lawn, there or elsewhere to grow inwardly meet for their heavenly rest in the veins of Ellen the saintly and others; until at last we found the cordial Pan himself in the midst of his household, breezy with hospitality and blowing exhilarating trumpets of welcome. Age has just the least in the world dimmed the lustre we once knew, but an unmistakable breath of the morning still encircles him, and the odour of primaeval woods. Pitchpine is not more pagan than he continues to be, and acorns as little confess the gardener's skill. Still I insist that he is a voluntary Pan, that it is a condition of mere wilfulness and insurrection on his part, contingent upon a mercilessly sound digestion and an uncommon imaginative influx, and I have no doubt that even he, as the years ripen, will at last admit Nature to be tributary and not supreme. However this be, we consumed juicy pears to the diligent music of Pan's pipe, while Ellen and Edith softly gathered themselves upon two low stools in the chimney-corner, saying never a word nor looking a look, but apparently hemming their handkerchiefs; and good Mrs. Stearns, who sat by the window and seemed to be the village dressmaker, ever and anon glanced at us over her spectacles as if to say that never before has she seen this wondrous Pan so glistening with dewdrops. Then and upon the waves of that friendly music we were duly wafted to our educational Zion and carefully made over our good and promising and affectionate boys to the school-master's keeping. Out into the field beside his house Sanborn incontinently took us to show how his girls and boys perform together their worship of Hygeia. It was a glimpse into that new world wherein dwelleth righteousness and which is full surely fast coming upon our children and our children's children; and I could hardly keep myself, as I saw my children's eyes drink in the mingled work and play of the inspiring scene, from shouting out a joyful Nunc Dimittis. The short of the story is that we left them and rode home robbed of our plumage, feeling sore and ugly and only hoping that they wouldn't die, any of these cold winter days, before the parental breast could get there to warm them back to life or cheer them on to a better.

Mrs. William Hunt has just come in to tell the good news of your near advent and that she has found the exact house for you; instigated to that activity by one of your angels, of the Hooper band, with whom she has been in correspondence. I don't thank angel Hooper for putting angel Hunt upon that errand, since I should like to have had the merit of it myself. I suspect the rent is what it ought to be: if it's not I will lay by something every week for you toward it, and have no doubt we shall stagger through the cold weather.

I gather from the above the very flower of my father's irrepressible utterance of his constitutional optimism, that optimism fed so little by any sense of things as they were or are, but rich in its vision of the facility with which they might become almost at any moment or from one day to the other totally and splendidly different. A less vague or vain idealist couldn't, I think, have been encountered; it was given him to catch in the fact at almost any turn right or left some flagrant assurance or promise of the state of man transfigured. The Concord school could be to him for the hour—there were hours and hours!—such a promise; could even figure in that light, to his amplifying sympathy, in a degree disproportionate to its genial, but after all limited, after all not so intensely "inflated," as he would have said, sense of itself. In which light it is that I recognise, and even to elation, how little, practically, of the idea of the Revolution in the vulgar or violent sense was involved in his seeing so many things, in the whole social order about him, and in the interest of their being more or less immediately altered, as lamentably, and yet at the same time and under such a coloured light, as amusingly and illustratively, wrong—wrong, that is, with a blundering helpless human salience that kept criticism humorous, kept it, so to speak, sociable and almost "sympathetic" even when readiest. The case was really of his rather feeling so vast a rightness close at hand or lurking immediately behind actual arrangements that a single turn of the inward wheel, one real response to pressure of the spiritual spring, would bridge the chasms, straighten the distortions, rectify the relations and, in a word, redeem and vivify the whole mass—after a far sounder, yet, one seemed to see, also far subtler, fashion than any that our spasmodic annals had yet shown us. It was of course the old story that we had only to *be* with more intelligence and faith—an immense deal more, certainly—in order to work off, in the happiest manner, the many-sided ugliness of life; which was a process that might go on, blessedly, in the quietest of all quiet ways. *That* wouldn't be blood and fire and tears, or would be none of these things stupidly precipitated; it would simply have taken place by *enjoyed* communication and contact, enjoyed concussion or convulsion even—since pangs and agitations, the very agitations of perception itself, are of the highest privilege of the soul and there is always, thank goodness, a saving sharpness of play or complexity of consequence in the intelligence completely alive. The meaning of which remarks for myself, I must be content to add, is that the optimists of the world, the constructive idealists, as one has mainly known them, have too often struck one as overlooking more of the aspects of the real than they recognise; whereas our indefeasible impression, William's and mine, of our parent was that he by his very constitution and intimate heritage recognised many more of those than he overlooked. What was the finest part of our intercourse with him—that is the most nutritive—but a positive record of that? Such a matter as that the factitious had absolutely no hold on him was the truest thing about him, and it was all the while present to us, I think, as backing up his moral authority and play of vision that never, for instance, had there been a more numerous and candid exhibition of all the human susceptibilities than in the nest of his original nurture. I have spoken of the fashion in which I still see him, after the years, attentively bent over those much re-written "papers," that we had, even at our stupidest, this warrant for going in vague admiration of that they caught the eye, even the most filially detached, with a final face of wrought clarity, and thereby of beauty, that there *could* be no thinking unimportant—and see him also fall back from the patient posture, again and again, in long fits of remoter consideration, wondering, pondering sessions into which I think I was more often than not moved to read, for the fine interest and colour of it, some story of acute inward difficulty amounting for the time to discouragement. If one wanted drama *there* was drama, and of the most concrete and most immediately offered to one's view and one's suspense; to the point verily, as might often occur, of making one go roundabout it on troubled tiptoe even as one would have held one's breath at the play.

These opposed glimpses, I say, hang before me as I look back, but really fuse together in the vivid picture of the fond scribe separated but by a pane of glass—his particular preference was always directly to face the window—from the general human condition he was so devoutly concerned with. He *saw* it, through the near glass, saw it in such detail and with a feeling for it that broke down nowhere—that was the great thing; which truth it confirmed that his very fallings back and long waits and stays and almost stricken musings witnessed exactly to his intensity, the intensity that would "come out," after all, and make his passionate philosophy and the fullest array of the appearances that couldn't be blinked fit together and harmonise. Detached as I could during all those years perhaps queerly enough believe myself, it would still have done my young mind the very greatest violence to have to suppose that any plane of conclusion for him, however rich and harmonious he might tend to make conclusion, could be in the nature of a fool's paradise. Small vague outsider as I was, I couldn't have borne *that* possibility; and I see, as I return to the case, how little I really could ever have feared it. This would have amounted to fearing it on account of his geniality—a shocking supposition; as if his geniality had been thin and *bête*, patched up and poor, and not by the straightest connections, nominal and other, of the very stuff of his genius. No, I feel myself complacently look back to *my* never having, even at my small poorest, been so *bête*, either, as to conceive he might be "wrong," wrong as a thinker-out, in his own way, of the great mysteries, because of the interest and amusement and vividness his attesting spirit could fling over the immediate ground. What he saw *there* at least could be so enlightening, so evocatory, could fall in so—which was to the most inspiring effect within the range of perception of a scant son who was doubtless, as to the essential, already more than anything else a novelist *en herbe*. If it didn't sound in a manner patronising I should say that I saw that my father saw; and that I couldn't but have given my own case away by not believing, however obscurely, in the virtue of his consequent and ultimate synthesis. Of course I never dreamed of any such name for it—I only thought of it as something very great and fine founded on those forces in him that came home to us and that touched us all the while. As these were extraordinary forces of sympathy and generosity, and that yet knew how to be such without falsifying any minutest measure, the structure raised upon them might well, it would seem, and even to the uppermost sublime reaches, be as valid as it was beautiful. If he so endeared himself wasn't it, one asked as time went on, through his never having sentimentalised or merely meditated away, so to call it, the least embarrassment of the actual about him, and having with a passion peculiarly his own kept together his stream of thought, however transcendent and the stream of life, however humanised? There was a kind of experiential authority in his basis, as he felt his basis—there being no human predicament he couldn't by a sympathy more *like* direct experience than any I have known enter into; and this authority, which concluded so to a widening and brightening of the philosophic—for him the spiritual—sky, made his character, as intercourse disclosed it, in a high degree fascinating. These things, I think, however, are so happily illustrated in his letters that they look out from almost any continuous passage in such a series for instance as those addressed in the earlier time to Mrs. Tappan. His *tone*, that is, always so effectually looks out, and the living parts of him so singularly hung together, that one may fairly say his philosophy *was* his tone. To cite a few passages here is at the same time to go back to a previous year or two—which my examples, I hold, make worth while. He had been on a visit to Paris toward the winter's end of '60, and had returned to Geneva, whence he writes early in April.

So sleepy have I been ever since my return from Paris that I am utterly unfit to write letters. I was thoroughly poisoned by tobacco in those horrid railway carriages, and this with want of sleep knocked me down. I am only half awake still, and will not engage consequently in any of those profound inquiries which your remembrance always suggests.

I am very sorry for you that you live in an excommunicated country, or next door to it; and I don't wonder at your wanting to get away. But it is provoking to think that but for your other plan Switzerland might possess you all for the summer. It is doubtless in part this disappointment that will unsettle us in our present moorings and take us probably soon to Germany. What after that I have no idea, and am always so little wilful about our movements that I am ready the young ones should settle them. So we may be in Europe a good while yet, always providing that war keep smooth his wrinkled front and allow us quiet newspapers. They must fight in Italy for some time to come, but between England and France is the main point. If *they* can hold aloof from tearing each other we shall manage; otherwise we go home at once, to escape the universal spatter that must then ensue.

What is the meaning of all these wars and rumours of wars? No respectable person ever seems to occupy himself with the question, but I can't help feeling it more interesting than anything in Homer or Plato or the gallery of the Vatican. I long daily with unappeasable longing for a righteous life, such a life as I am sure is implied in every human possibility, and myriads are bearing me company. What does this show but that the issue is near out of all our existing chaos? All our evil is fossil and comes from the mere persistence of diseased institutions in pretending to rule us when we ought to be left free to be living spirits of God. There is no *fresh* evil in the world. No one now steals or commits murder or any other offence with the least relish for it, but only to revenge his poor starved opportunities. The superiority of America in respect to freedom of thought over Europe comes from this fact that she has so nearly achieved her deliverance from such tyrannies. All she now needs to make her right is simply an intelligent recognition of her spiritual whereabouts. If she had this she would put her hand to the work splendidly. You and I when we get home will try to quicken her intelligence in that respect, will do at any rate *our* best to put away this pestilent munching of the tree of knowledge of good and evil, and persuade to the belief of man's unmixed innocence.

138

Which, it will easily be seen, was optimism with a vengeance, and marked especially in the immediacy, the state of being at hand for him, of a social redemption. What made this the more signal was its being so unattended with visions the least Apocalyptic or convulsional; the better order slipping in amid the worse, and superseding it, so insidiously, so quietly and, by a fair measure, so easily. It was a faith and an accompanying philosophy that couldn't be said not to be together simplifying; and yet nothing was more unmistakable when we saw them at close range, I repeat, than that they weren't unnourished, weren't what he himself would, as I hear him, have called the "flatulent" fruit of sentimentality.

His correspondent had in a high degree, by her vivacity of expression, the art of challenging his—as is markedly apparent from a letter the date of which fails beyond its being of the same stay at Geneva and of the winter's end.

If I had really imagined that I had bored you and your husband so very little while I was in Paris in December I should long since have repeated the experiment; the more surely that I want so much to see again my darling nieces and delight myself in the abundance of their large-eyed belief.... Our Alice is still under discipline—preparing to fulfil some high destiny or other in the future by reducing decimal fractions to their lowest possible rate of subsistence, where they often grow so attenuated under her rapid little fingers that my poor old eyes can no longer see them at all. I shall go before long to England, and then perhaps—! But I shan't promise anything on *her* behalf.

You ask me "why I do not brandish my tomahawk and, like Walt Whitman, raise my barbaric yawp over the roofs of all the houses." It is because I am not yet a "cosmos" as that gentleman avowedly is, but only a very dim nebula, doing its modest best, no doubt, to solidify into cosmical dimensions, but still requiring an "awful sight" of time and pains and patience on the part of its friends. You evidently fancy that cosmoses are born to all the faculty they shall ever have, like ducks: no such thing. There is no respectable cosmos but what is born to such a vapoury and even gaseous inheritance as requires long centuries of conflict on its part to overcome the same and become pronounced or educated in its proper mineral, vegatable or animal

139

order. Ducks are born perfect; that is to say they utter the same unmodified unimproved quack on their dying pillow that they uttered on their natal day; whereas cosmoses are destined to a life of such surprising change that you may say their career is an incessant disavowal of their birth, or that their highest maturation consists in their utter renunciation of their natural father and mother. You transcendentalists make the fatal mistake of denying education, of sundering present from past and future from present. These things are indissolubly one, the present deriving its consciousness only from the past, and the future drawing all its distinctive wisdom from our present experience. The law is the same with the individual as it is with the race: none of us can dodge the necessity of regeneration, of disavowing our natural ancestry in order to come forth in our own divinely-given proportions. The secret of this necessity ought to reconcile us to it, however onerous the obligation it imposes; for that secret is nothing more nor less than this, that we cosmoses have a plenary divine origin and are bound eventually to see that divinity reproduced in our most familiar and trivial experience, even down to the length of our shoe-ties. If the Deity were an immense Duck capable only of emitting an eternal quack we of course should all have been born webfooted, each as infallible in his way as the Pope, nor ever have been at the expense and bother of swimming-schools. But He is a perfect man, incapable of the slightest quackery, capable only of every honest and modest and helpful purpose, and these are perfections to which manifestly no one is born, but only *re*-born. We come to such states not by learning, only by *unlearning*. No natural edification issues in spiritual architecture of this splendour, but only a natural demolition or undoing. I dimly recognise this great truth, and hence hold more to a present imbecility than to a too eager efficiency. I feel myself more fit to be knocked about for some time yet and vastated of my natural vigour than to commence cosmos and raise the barbaric yawp. Time enough for that when I am fairly finished. Say what we will, you and I are all the while at school just now. The genial pedagogue may give you so little of the ferule as to leave you to doubt whether you really are there; but this only proves what a wonderful pedagogue it is, and how capable of adapting himself to everyone.

His friend in Paris found herself at that time, like many other persons, much interested in the exercise of automatic writing, of which we have since so abundantly heard and as to which she had communicated some striking observations.

...Your letter is full of details that interest but don't fascinate. I haven't a doubt of a single experience you allege, and do not agree with your friend Count S. (your writing of this name is obscure) that the world of spirits is not an element in your writing. I am persuaded now for a long time of the truth of these phenomena and feel no inclination to dispute or disparage them; but at the same time I feel to such a degree my own remoteness from them that I am sure I could never get any personal contact with them. The state of mind exposing one to influences of this nature, and which makes them beneficial to it, is a sceptical state; and this I have never known for a moment. Spiritual existence has always been more real to me (I was going to say) than natural; and when accordingly I am asked to believe in the spiritual world because my senses are getting to reveal it I feel as if the ground of my conviction were going to be weakened rather than strengthened. Of course I should have very little respect for spiritual things which didn't ultimately report themselves to sense, which didn't indeed subside into things of sense as logically as a house into its foundations. But what I deny is that spiritual existence can be directly known on earth—known otherwise than by correspondence or inversely. The letter of every revelation must be directly hostile to its spirit, and only inversely accordant, because the very pretension of revelation is that it's a descent, an absolute coming down, of truth, a humiliation of it from its own elevated and habitual plane to a lower one.

Admit therefore that the facts of "spiritualism" are all true; admit that persons really deceased have been communicating with you about the state of Europe, the approaching crisis and the persons known to us whom you name; in that case I should insist that, to possess the slightest spiritual interest, their revelation should be re-translated into the spiritual tongue by correspondences; because as to any spirit knowing or caring to know those persons, or being bothered about any crisis of ours, that is to me simply incredible. Such matters have in each case doubtless some spiritual or substantial counterpart answering in every particular to its superficial features; and Wilkinson and Emerson, for instance, with the others, are of

141

course shadows of some greater or less spiritual quantities. But I'll be hanged if there's the slightest *sensible* accord between the substance and the semblance on either hand. Your spirits, no doubt, give you the very communications you report to me; only Wilkinson spiritually interpreted and Emerson spiritually interpreted mean things so very different from our two friends of those denominations that if our spiritual eye were for a moment open to discern the difference I think it highly probable—I'm sure it is infinitely possible—we should renounce their acquaintance.

But I have harped on this string long enough; let me change the tune. Your spirits tell you to repose in what they are doing for you and, with a pathos to which I am not insensible, say "Rest now, poor child; your struggles have been great; clasp peace to your bosom at last." And as a general thing our ears are saluted by assurances that these communications are all urged by philanthropy and that everyone so addressing us wants in some way to help and elevate us. But just this is to my mind the unpleasant side of the business. I have been so long accustomed to see the most arrant deviltry transact itself in the name of benevolence that the moment I hear a profession of good-will from almost any quarter I instinctively look about for a constable or place my hand within reach of the bell-rope. My ideal of human intercourse would be a state of things in which no man will ever stand in need of any other man's help, but will derive all his satisfaction from the great social tides which own no individual names. I am sure no man can be put in a position of dependence upon another without that other's very soon becoming—if he accepts the duties of the relation—utterly degraded out of his just human proportions. No man can play the Deity to his fellow man with impunity—I mean spiritual impunity of course. For see: if I am at all satisfied with that relation, if it contents me to be in a position of generosity toward others, I must be remarkably indifferent at bottom to the gross social inequality which permits that position, and instead of resenting the enforced humiliation of my fellow man to myself, in the interests of humanity, I acquiesce in it for the sake of the profit it yields to my own self-complacency. I do hope the reign of benevolence is over; until that event occurs I am sure the reign of God will be impossible. But I have a shocking bad cold that racks my head to bursting almost; I can't think to any purpose. Let me hear soon from you that I have not been misunderstood. I wouldn't for the world seem wilfully to depreciate what you set a high value on. No, I really can't help my judgments. And I always soften them to within an inch of their life as it is.

The following, no longer from the Hotel de l'Ecu, but from 5 Quai du Mont Blanc, would indicate that his "Dear Queen Caroline," as he addresses her, was at no loss to defend her own view of the matters in discussion between them: in which warm light indeed it is that I was myself in the after years ever most amusedly to see her.

Don't scold a fellow so! Exert your royal gifts in exalting only the lowly and humbling only the proud. Precisely what I like, to get extricated from metaphysics, is encouragement from a few persons like yourself, such encouragement as would lie in your intelligent apprehension and acknowledgment of the great *result* of metaphysics, which is a godly and spotless life on earth. If I could find anyone apt to that doctrine I should not work so hard metaphysically to convince the world of its truth. And as for being a metaphysical Jack Horner, the thing is contradictory, as no metaphysician whose studies are sincere ever felt tempted to self-complacency or disposed to reckon himself a good boy. Such exaltations are not for him, but only for the artists and poets, who dazzle the eyes of mankind and *don't* recoil from the darkness they themselves produce—as Dryden says, or Collins.

Mrs. Tappan, spending the month of June in London, continued to impute for the time, I infer (I seem to remember a later complete detachment), a livelier importance to the supernatural authors of her "writing" than her correspondent was disposed to admit; but almost anything was a quickener of the correspondent's own rich, that is always so animated, earnestness. He had to feel an interlocutor's general sympathy, or recognise a moral relation, even if a disturbed one, for the deep tide of his conviction to rise outwardly higher; but when that happened the tide overflowed indeed.

MY DEAR CAROLINA—Neither North nor South, but an eminently free State, with no exulting shout of master and no groan of captive to be heard in all its borders, but only the cheerful hum

143

of happy husband and children—how do you find London? Here in Geneva we are so saturate with sunshine that we would fain dive to the depths of the lake to learn coolness of the little fishes. Still, we don't envy your two weeks of unbroken rain in dear dismal London. What a preparation for doing justice to Lenox! You see I know—through Mary Tweedy, who has a hearty appreciation of her London privileges. How are A. D. and all the rest of them? *Familiar* spirits, are they not, on a short acquaintance?— and how pleasant an aspect it gives to the middle kingdom to think you shall be sure to find there such lovers and friends! Only let us keep them at a proper distance. It doesn't do for us ever to accept another only at that other's own estimate of himself. If we do we may as well plunge into Tartarus at once. No human being can afford to commit his happiness to another's keeping, or, what is the same thing, forego his own individuality with all that it imports. The first requisite of our true relationship to each other (spiritually speaking) is that we be wholly independent of each other: then we may give ourselves away as much as we please, we shall do neither them nor ourselves any harm. But until that blessed day comes, by the advance of a scientific society among men, we shall be utterly unworthy to love each other or be loved in return. We shall do nothing but prey upon each other and turn each other's life to perfect weariness.

The more of it then just now the better! The more we bite and devour each other, the more horribly the newspapers abound in all the evidences of our disgusting disorganisation, the disorganisation of the old world, the readier will our dull ears be to listen to the tidings of the new world which is aching to appear, the world wherein dwelleth righteousness. Don't abuse the newspapers therefore publicly, but tell everybody of the use they are destined to promote, and set others upon the look-out. A. D. is a very good woman, I haven't a doubt, but will fast grow a better one if she would let herself alone, and me also, and all other mere persons, while she diligently inquires about the Lord; that is about that

lustrous universal life which God's providence is now forcing
upon men's attention and which will obliterate for ever all this
exaggeration of our personalities. It is very well for lovers to abase
themselves in this way to each other; because love is a *passion* of one's
nature—that is to say the lover is not self-possessed, but is lifted
for a passing moment to the level of the Lord's life in the race, and
so attuned to higher issues ever after in his own proper sphere. But
these experiences are purely disciplinary and not final. All passion is
a mere inducement to action, and when at last activity really dawns
in us we drop this faculty of hallucination that we have been under
about persons and see and adore the abounding divinity which is
in all persons alike. Who will then ever be caught in that foolish
snare again? I did nothing but tumble into it from my boyhood up
to my marriage; since which great disillusioning—yes!—I feel that
the only lovable person is one who will never permit himself to be
loved. But I have written on without any intention and have now
no time to say what alone I intended, how charming and kind and
long to be remembered you were all those Paris days. Give my love
to honest William and tell my small nieces that I pine to pluck
again the polished cherries of their cheeks. My wife admires and
loves you.

From which I jump considerably forward, for its (privately) historic
value, to a communication from Newport of the middle of August '63. My
father's two younger sons had, one the previous and one at the beginning of
the current, year obtained commissions in the Volunteer Army; as a sequel to
which my next younger brother, as Adjutant of the Fifty-fourth Massachusetts,
Colonel Robert Shaw's regiment, the first body of coloured soldiers raised in
the North, had received two grave wounds in that unsuccessful attack on
Fort Wagner from which the gallant young leader of the movement was not
to return.

Wilky had a bad day yesterday and kept me busy or I shouldn't have
delayed answering your inquiries till to-day. He is very severely wounded

both in the ankle and in the side—where he doesn't heal so fast as the doctor wishes in consequence of the shell having made a pouch which collects matter and retards nature. They cut it open yesterday, and to-day he is better, or will be. The wound in the ankle was made by a cannister ball an inch and a half in diameter, which lodged eight days in the foot and was finally dislodged by cutting down through (the foot) and taking it out at the sole. He is excessively weak, unable to do anything but lie passive, even to turn himself on his pillow. He will probably have a slow and tedious recovery—the doctors say of a year at least; but he knows nothing of this himself and speaks, so far as he does talk, but of going back in the Fall. If you write please say nothing of this; he is so distressed at the thought of a long sickness. He is vastly attached to the negro-soldier cause; believes (I think) that the world has existed for it; and is sure that enormous results to civilisation are coming out of it. We heard from Bob this morning at Morris Island; with his regiment, building earthworks and mounting guns. Hot, he says, but breezy; also that the shells make for them every few minutes—while he and his men betake themselves to the trenches and holes in the earth "like so many land-crabs in distress." He writes in the highest spirits. Cabot Russell, Wilky's dearest friend, is, we fear, a prisoner and wounded. We hear nothing decisive, but the indications point that way. Poor Wilky cries aloud for his friends gone and missing, and I could hardly have supposed he might be educated so suddenly up to serious manhood altogether as he appears to have been. I hear from Frank Shaw this morning, and they are all well—and admirable.

This goes beyond the moment I had lately, and doubtless too lingeringly, reached, as I say; just as I shall here find convenience in borrowing a few passages from my small handful of letters of the time to follow—to the extent of its not following by a very long stretch. Such a course keeps these fragments of record together, as scattering them would perhaps conduce to some leakage in their characteristic tone, for which I desire all the fulness it can keep. Impossible moreover not in some degree to yield on the spot to *any* brush of the huge procession of those particular months and years, even though I shall presently take occasion to speak as I may of my own so inevitably contracted consciousness of what the brush, with its tremendous possibilities of violence, could consist of in the given case. I had, under stress, to content myself with knowing it in a more indirect and muffled fashion than might easily have been—even should one speak of it but as a matter of mere vision of the eyes or quickened wonder of the mind or heaviness of the heart, as a matter in fine of the closer and more inquiring, to say nothing of the more agitated, approach. All of which, none the less, was not to prevent the whole quite indescribably intensified time—intensified through all lapses of occasion and frustrations of contact—from remaining with me as a more constituted and sustained act of living, in proportion to my powers and opportunities, than any other homogeneous stretch of experience that my memory now recovers. The case had to be in a peculiar degree, alas, that of living inwardly—like so many of my other cases; in a peculiar degree compared, that is, to the immense and prolonged outwardness, outwardness naturally at the very highest pitch, that was the general sign of the situation. To which I may add that my "alas" just uttered is in the key altogether of my then current consciousness, and not in the least in that of my present appreciation of the same—so that I leave it, even while I thus put my mark against it, as I should restore tenderly to the shelf any odd rococo object that might have slipped from a reliquary. My appreciation of what I presume at the risk of any apparent fatuity to call my "relation to" the War is at present a thing exquisite to me, a thing of the last refinement of romance, whereas it had to be at the time a sore and troubled, a mixed and oppressive thing—though I promptly see, on reflection, how it must frequently have flushed with emotions, with small scraps of direct perception even, with particular sharpnesses in the generalised pang of participation, that were all but touched in themselves as with the full experience. Clear as some object presented in high relief against the evening sky of the west, at all events, is the presence for me beside the stretcher on which my young brother was to lie for so many days before he could be moved, and on which he had lain during his boat-journey from the South to New York and thence again to Newport, of lost Cabot Russell's stricken father, who, failing, up and down the searched field, in respect of his own irrecoverable boy—then dying, or dead, as afterwards appeared, well within the enemy's works—had with an admirable charity brought Wilky back to a waiting home instead, and merged the parental ache in the next nearest devotion he could find. Vivid to me still is one's almost ashamed sense of this at the hurried disordered time, and of how it was impossible not to impute to his grave steady gentleness and judgment a full awareness of the difference it would have made for him, all the same, to be doing such things with a still more intimate pity. Unobliterated for me, in spite of vaguenesses, this quasi-twilight vision of the good bereft man, bereft, if I rightly recall, of his only son, as he sat erect and dry-eyed at the guarded feast of our relief; and so much doubtless partly because of the image that hovers to me across the years of Cabot Russell himself, my brother's so close comrade—dark-eyed, youthfully brown, heartily bright, actively handsome, and with the arrested expression, the indefinable shining stigma, worn, to the regard that travels back to them, by those of the young figures of the fallen that memory and fancy, wanting, never ceasing to want, to "do" something for them, set as upright and clear-faced as may be, each in his sacred niche. They have each to such a degree, so ranged, the strange property or privilege—one scarce knows what to call it—of exquisitely, for all our time, facing us out, quite blandly ignoring us, looking through us or straight over us at something they partake of together but that we mayn't pretend to know. We walk thus, I think, rather ruefully before them—those of us at least who didn't at the time share more happily their risk. William, during those first critical days, while the stretcher itself, set down with its load just within the entrance to our house, mightn't be moved further, preserved our poor lacerated brother's aspect in a drawing of great and tender truth which I permit myself to reproduce. It tells for me the double story—I mean both of Wilky's then condition and of the draughtsman's admirable hand.

But I find waiting my father's last letter of the small group to Mrs. Tappan. We were by that time, the autumn of 1865, settled in Boston for a couple of years.

MY DEAR CARRY—Are you a carry*atid* that you consider yourself bound to uphold that Lenox edifice through the cold winter as well as the hot summer? Why don't you come to town? I can't *write* what I want to say. My brain is tired, and I gladly forego all writing that costs thought or attention. But I have no day forgotten your question, and am eager always to make a conquest of you; you are so full both of the upper and the nether might as always greatly to excite my interest and make me feel how little is accomplished while you are left not so. I make no prayer to you; I would have no assistance from your own vows; or the pleasure of my intercourse with you would be slain. I would rather outrage than conciliate your sympathies, that I might have all the joy of winning you over at last. Hate me on my ideal side, the side that menaces you, as much as you please meanwhile, but keep a warm corner in your regard for me personally, as I always do for you, until we meet again. It's a delight to know a person of your sense and depth; even the *gaudia certaminis* are more cheering with you than ordinary agreements with other people.

On which note I may leave the exchange in question, feeling how equal an honour it does to the parties.

VIII

I judge best to place together here several passages from my father's letters belonging to this general period, even though they again carry me to points beyond my story proper. It is not for the story's sake that I am moved to gather them, but for their happy illustration, once more, of something quite else, the human beauty of the writer's spirit and the fine breadth of his expression. This latter virtue is most striking, doubtless, when he addresses his women correspondents, of whom there were many, yet it so pervades for instance various notes, longer and shorter, to Mrs. James T. Fields, wife of the eminent Boston publisher and editor, much commended to us as founder and, for a time, chief conductor of the Atlantic Monthly, our most adopted and enjoyed native *recueil* of that series of years. The Atlantic seemed somehow, while the good season lasted, to live with us, whereas our relation to the two or three other like organs, homegrown or foreign, of which there could be any question, and most of all, naturally, to the great French Revue, was that we lived with *them*. The light of literature, as we then invoked or at any rate received it, seemed to beat into the delightful Fields salon from a nearer heaven than upon any other scene, and played there over a museum of relics and treasures and apparitions (these last whether reflected and by that time legendary, or directly protrusive and presented, wearers of the bay) with an intensity, I feel again as I look back, every resting ray of which was a challenge to dreaming ambition. I am bound to note, none the less, oddly enough, that my father's communications with the charming mistress of the scene are more often than not a bright profession of sad reasons for inability to mingle in it. He mingled with reluctance in scenes designed and preappointed, and was, I think, mostly content to feel almost anything near at hand become a scene for him from the moment he had happened to cast into the arena (which he preferred without flags or festoons) the golden apple of the unexpected—in humorous talk, that is, in reaction without preparation, in sincerity which was itself sociability. It was not nevertheless that he didn't now and then "accept"—with attenuations.

Henry James

...If therefore you will let Alice and me come to you on Wednesday evening I shall still rejoice in the benignant fate that befalls my house—even though my wife, indisposed, "feels reluctantly constrained to count herself out of the sphere of your hospitality;" and I will bind myself moreover by solemn vows not to perplex the happy atmosphere which almost reigns in yours by risking a syllable of the incongruous polemic your husband wots of. I will listen devotedly to you and him all the evening if thereby I may early go home repaired in my own esteem, and not dilapidated, as has been hitherto too often the case.

He could resist persuasion even in the insidious form of an expressed desire that he should read something, "something he was writing," to a chosen company.

Your charming note is irresistible at first sight, and I had almost uttered a profligate Yes!—that is a promise irrespective of a power to perform; when my good angel arrested me by the stern inquiry: What have you got to give them? And I could only say in reply to this intermeddling but blest spirit: Nothing, my dear friend, absolutely nothing! Whereupon the veracious one said again: Sit you down immediately therefore and, confessing your literary indigence to this lovely lady, pray her to postpone the fulfilment of her desire to some future flood-tide in the little stream of your inspiration, when you will be ready to serve her.

The following refers to the question of his attending with my mother at some session of a Social Club, at which a prepared performance of some sort was always offered, but of which they had lately found it convenient to cease to be members.

I snatch the pen from my wife's hand to enjoy, myself, the satisfaction of saying to you how good and kind and charming you always are, and how we never grow tired of recounting the fact among ourselves here, and yet how we still shall be unable to accept your hospitality. Why? Simply because we have a due sense of what becomes us after our late secession, and would not willingly be seen at two successive meetings, lest the carnal observer should argue that we had left the Club by the front door of obligation only to be readmitted at the back door of indulgence: I put it as Fields would phrase it. To speak of him always reminds me of various things, so richly endowed is the creature in all good gifts; but the dominant consideration evoked in my mind by his name is just his beautiful home and that atmosphere of faultless womanly worth and dignity which fills it with light and warmth, and makes it a blessing to one's heart whenever one enters its precincts. Please felicitate the wretch for me—!

However earnest these deprecations he could embroider them with a rare grace.

My wife—who has just received your kind note in rapid route for the Dedham Profane Asylum, or something of that sort— begs leave to say, through me as a willing and sensitive medium, that you are one of those *arva beata*, renowned in poetry, which, visit them never so often, one is always glad to *re*visit, which are attractive in all seasons by their own absolute light and without any Emersonian pansies and buttercups to make them so. This enthusiastic Dedhamite says further in effect that while she is duly grateful for your courteous offer of a seat upon your sofa to hear the conquered sage, she yet prefers the material banquet you summon us to in your dining-room, since there we should be out of the mist and able to discern between nature and cookery, between what eats and what is eaten, at all events, and feel a thankful mind that we were in solid comfortable Charles Street, instead of in the vague and wide weltering galaxy, and should be sure to deem A. and J. (*I* am sure of A., and I think my wife feels equally sure of J.), finer fireflies than ever sparkled in the old empyrean. But alas who shall control his destiny? Not my wife, whom multitudinous cares enthrall; nor yet myself, whom a couple of months' enforced idleness now constrains to a preternatural activity, lest the world fail of salvation. Please accept then our united apologies and regrets....

P.S. Who contrived the comical title for E.'s lectures?—"Philosophy of the People!" May it not have been a joke of J. T. F.'s? It would be no less absurd for Emerson himself to think of philosophising than for the rose to think of botanising. He is the divinely pompous rose of the philosophic garden, gorgeous with colour and fragrance; so what a sad look-out for tulip and violet and lily, and the humbler grasses, if the rose should turn out philosophic gardener as well.

There connects itself with a passage in another letter to the same correspondent a memory of my own that I have always superlatively cherished and that remains in consequence vivid enough for some light reflection here. But I first give the passage, which is of date of November '67. "What a charming impression of Dickens the other night at the Nortons' dinner! How innocent and honest and sweet he is maugre his fame! Fields was merely superb on the occasion, but Dickens was saintly." As a young person of twenty-four I took part, restrictedly yet exaltedly, in that occasion—and an immense privilege I held it to slip in at all—from after dinner on; at which stage of the evening I presented myself, in the company of my excellent friend Arthur Sedgwick, brother to our hostess and who still lives to testify, for the honour of introduction to the tremendous guest. How tremendously it had been laid upon young persons of our generation to feel Dickens, down to the soles of our shoes, no more modern instance that I might try to muster would give, I think, the least measure of; I can imagine no actual young person of my then age, and however like myself, so ineffably agitated, so mystically moved, in the presence of any exhibited idol of the mind who should be in that character at all conceivably "like" the author of Pickwick and of Copperfield. There has been since his extinction no corresponding case—as to the relation between benefactor and beneficiary, or debtor and creditor; no other debt in our time has been piled so high, for those carrying it, as the long, the purely "Victorian" pressure of that obligation. It was the pressure, the feeling, that made it—as it made the feeling, and no operation of feeling on any such ground has within my observation so much as attempted to emulate it. So that on the evening I speak of at Shady Hill it was as a slim and shaken vessel of the feeling that one stood there—of the feeling in the first place diffused, public and universal, and in the second place all unfathomably, undemonstrably, unassistedly and, as it were, unrewardedly, proper to one's self as an already groping and fumbling, already dreaming and yearning dabbler in the mystery, the creative, that of comedy, tragedy, evocation, representation, erect and concrete before us there as in a sublimity of mastership. I saw the master—nothing could be more evident—in the light of an intense emotion, and I trembled, I remember, in every limb, while at the same time, by a blest fortune, emotion produced no luminous blur, but left him shining indeed, only shining with august particulars. It was to be remarked that those of his dress, which managed to be splendid even while remaining the general spare uniform of the diner-out, had the effect of higher refinements, of accents stronger and better placed, than we had ever in such a connection seen so much as hinted. But the offered inscrutable mask was the great thing, the extremely handsome face, the face of symmetry yet of formidable character, as I at once recognised, and which met my dumb homage with a straight inscrutability, a merciless *military* eye, I might have pronounced it, an automatic hardness, in fine, which at once indicated to me, and in the most interesting way in the world, a kind of economy of apprehension. Wonderful was it thus to see, and thrilling inwardly to note, that since the question was of personal values so great no faintest fraction of the whole could succeed in *not* counting for interest. The confrontation was but of a moment; our introduction, my companion's and mine, once effected, by an arrest in a doorway, nothing followed, as it were, or happened (what *might* have happened it remained in fact impossible to conceive); but intense though the positive perception there was an immensity more left to understand—for the long aftersense, I mean; and one, or the chief, of these later things was that if our hero neither shook hands nor spoke, only meeting us by the barest act, so to say, of the trained eye, the penetration of which, to my sense, revealed again a world, there was a grim beauty, to one's subsequently panting imagination, in that very truth of his then so knowing himself (committed to his monstrous "readings" and with the force required for them ominously ebbing) on the outer edge of his once magnificent margin. So at any rate I was to like for long to consider of it; I was to like to let the essential radiance which had nevertheless reached me measure itself by this accompaniment of the pitying vision. He couldn't loosely spend for grace what he had to keep for life—which was the awful nightly, or all but nightly, exhibition: such the economy, as I have called it, in which I was afterwards to feel sure he had been locked up—in spite of the appearance, in the passage from my father's letter, of the opened gates of the hour or two before. These were but a reason the more, really, for the so exquisitely complicated image which was to remain with me to this day and which couldn't on any other terms have made itself nearly so important. For that was the whole sense of the matter. It hadn't been in the least important that we should have shaken hands or exchanged platitudes—it had only been supremely so that one should have had the essence of the hour, the knowledge enriched by proof that whatever the multifold or absolute reason, no accession to sensibility from any other at all "similar" source could have compared, for penetration, to the intimacy of this particular and prodigious glimpse. It was as if I had carried off my strange treasure just exactly from under the merciless military eye—placed there on guard of the secret. All of which I recount for illustration of the force of action, unless I call it passion, that may reside in a single pulse of time.

I allow myself not to hang back in gathering several passages from another series for fear of their crossing in a manner the line of privacy and giving a distinctness to old intimate things. The distinctness is in the first place all to the honour of the persons and the interests thus glimmering through; and I hold, in the second, that the light touch under which they revive positively adds, by the magic of memory, a composite fineness. The only thing is that to speak of my father's correspondent here is to be more or less involved at once in the vision of her frame and situation, and that to get at all into relation with "the Nortons," as they were known to us at that period, to say nothing of all the years to follow, is to find on my hands a much heavier weight of reference than my scale at this point can carry. The relation had ripened for us with the settlement of my parents at Cambridge in the autumn of '66, and might I attempt even a sketch of the happy fashion in which the University circle consciously accepted, for its better satisfaction, or in other words just from a sense of what was, within its range, in the highest degree interesting, the social predominance of Shady Hill and the master there, and the ladies of the master's family, I should find myself rich in material. That institution and its administrators, however, became at once, under whatever recall of them, a picture of great inclusions and implications; so true is it of any community, and so true above all of one of the American communities best to be studied fifty years ago in their homogeneous form and native essence and identity, that a strong character reinforced by a great culture, a culture great in the given conditions, obeys an inevitable law in simply standing out. Charles Eliot Norton stood out, in the air of the place and time—which for that matter, I think, changed much as he changed, and couldn't change much beyond his own range of experiment—with a greater salience, granting his background, I should say, than I have ever known a human figure stand out with from any: an effect involved of course in the nature of the background as well as in that of the figure. He profited at any rate, to a degree that was a lesson in all the civilities, by the fact that he represented an ampler and easier, above all a more curious, play of the civil relation than was to be detected anywhere about, and a play by which that relation had the charming art of becoming extraordinarily multifold and various without appearing to lose the note of rarity. It is not of course through any exhibition of mere multiplicity that the instinct for relations becomes a great example and bears its best fruit; the weight of the example and the nature of the benefit depending so much as they do on the achieved and preserved terms of intercourse. Here it was that the curiosity, as I have called it, of Shady Hill was justified—so did its action prove largely humanising. This was all the witchcraft it had used—that of manners understood with all the extensions at once and all the particularisations to which it is the privilege of the highest conception of manners to lend itself. What it all came back to, naturally, was the fact that, on so happy a ground, the application of such an ideal and such a genius *could* find agents expressive and proportionate, and the least that could be said of the ladies of the house was that they had in perfection the imagination of their opportunity. History still at comparatively close range lays to its lips, I admit, a warning finger—yet how can I help looking it bravely in the face as I name in common courtesy Jane Norton? She distilled civility and sympathy and charm, she exhaled humanity and invitation to friendship, which latter she went through the world leaving at mortal doors as in effect the revelation of a new amenity altogether—something to wait, most other matters being meanwhile suspended, for her to come back on a turn of the genial tide and take up again, according to the stirred desire, with each beneficiary. All this to the extent, moreover, I confess, that it takes the whole of one's measure of her rendered service and her admirable life, cut so much too short—it takes the full list of her fond acclaimers, the shyest with the clearest, those who most waited or most followed, not to think almost more of the way her blest influence went to waste as by its mere uneconomised and selfless spread than of what would have been called (what was by the simply-seeing freely enough called) her achieved success. It was given her at once to shine for the simply-seeing and to abide forever with the subtly; which latter, so far as they survive, are left again to recognise how there plays inveterately within the beautiful, if it but go far enough, the fine strain of the tragic. The household at Shady Hill was leaving that residence early in the summer of '68 for a long stay in Europe, and the following is of that moment.

When I heard the other day that you had been at our house to say farewell I was glad and also sorry, glad because I couldn't say before all the world so easily what I wanted to say to you in parting, and sorry because I longed for another sight of your beautiful countenance. And then I consoled myself with thinking that I should write you the next morning and be able to do my feelings better justice. But when the morning came I saw how you would, with all your wealth of friends, scarcely value a puny chirrup from one of my like, and by no means probably expect it, and so I desisted. And now comes your heavenly letter this moment to renew my happiness in showing me once more your undimmed friendly face. How delightful that face has ever been to me since first I beheld it; how your frank and gracious and healing manners have shed on my soul a celestial dew whenever I have encountered you: I despair to tell you in fitting words. You are the largest and more generous nature I know, and one that remains always, at the same time, so womanly; and while you leave behind you such a memory you needn't fear that our affectionate wishes will ever fail you for a moment. I for my part shall rest in my affection for you till we meet where to love is to live.

Shady Hill was meanwhile occupied by other friends, out of the group of which, especially as reflected in another of my father's letters to Miss Norton, there rise for me beckoning ghosts; against whose deep appeal to me to let them lead me on I have absolutely to steel myself—so far, for the interest of it, I feel that they might take me.

We dined the other night at Shady Hill, where the Gurneys were charming and the company excellent; but there was a perpetual suggestion of the Elysian Fields about the banquet to me, and we seemed met together to celebrate a memory rather than applaud a hope. Godkin and his wife were there, and they heartily lent themselves to discourse of you all. Ever and anon his friendship gave itself such an emphatic *jerk* to your address that you might have heard it on your window-panes if you had not been asleep. As for her— what a great clot she is of womanly health, beauty and benignity! That is a most unwonted word to use in such a connection, but it came of itself, and I won't refuse it, as it means to express a wealth that seems chaotic—seems so because apparently not enough exercised or put to specific use. The Ashburners and Sedgwicks continue your tradition and even ornament or variegate it with their own original force. I go there of a Sunday afternoon, whenever possible, to read anew the gospel of their beautiful life and manners and bring away a text for the good of my own household. No one disputes the authenticity of that gospel, and I have no difficulty in spreading its knowledge.

On which follows, as if inevitably, the tragic note re-echoed; news having come from Dresden, in March '72, of the death of Mrs. Charles Norton, still young, delightful, inestimable.

What a blow we have all had in the deeper blow that has prostrated you! I despair to tell you how keen and how real a grief is felt here by all who have heard the desolating news. With my own family the brooding presence of the calamity is almost as obvious as it is in the Kirkland Street home, and I have to make a perpetual effort to reason it down. Reflectively, I confess, I am somewhat surprised that I could have been so *much* surprised by an event of this order. I know very well that death is the secret of life spiritually, and that this outward image of death which has just obtruded itself upon our gaze is *only* an image—is wholly unreal from a spiritual point of view. I know in short that your lovely sister lives at present more livingly than she has ever lived before. And yet my life is so low, habitually, that when I am called upon to put my knowledge into practice I am as superstitious as anybody else and grovel instead of soaring. Keep me in your own sweet and fragrant memory, for nowhere else could I feel myself more embalmed to my own self-respect. Indeed if anything could relieve a personal sorrow to me it would be the sense that it was shared by a being so infinitely tender and true as yourself.

Of the mass of letters by the same hand that I further turn over too many are of a domestic strain inconsistent with other application; but a page here and there emerges clear, with elements of interest and notes of the characteristic that rather invite than deprecate an emphasis. From these I briefly glean, not minding that later dates are involved—no particular hour at that time being far out of touch with any other, and the value of everything gaining here, as I feel, by my keeping my examples together. The following, addressed to me in England early in '69, beautifully illustrates, to my sense, our father's close participation in any once quite positive case that either one or the other of his still somewhat undetermined, but none the less interesting sons—interesting to themselves, to each other and to *him*—might appear for the time to insist on constituting. William had in '68 been appointed to an instructorship in Psychology at Harvard.

He gets on greatly with his teaching; his students—fifty-seven of them— are elated with their luck in having him, and I feel sure he will have next year a still larger number attracted by his fame. He came in the other afternoon while I was sitting alone, and, after walking the floor in an animated way for a moment, broke out: "Bless my soul, what a difference between me as I am now and as I was last spring at this time! Then so hypochondriachal"—he used that word, though perhaps less in substance than form—"and now with my mind so cleared up and restored to sanity. It's the difference between death and life." He had a great effusion. I was afraid of interfering with it, or possibly checking it, but I ventured to ask what especially in his opinion had produced the change. He said several things: the reading of Renouvier (particularly his vindication of the freedom of the will) and of Wordsworth, whom he has been feeding on now for a good while; but more than anything else his having given up the notion that all mental disorder requires to have a physical basis. This had become perfectly untrue to him. He saw that the mind does act irrespectively of material coercion, and could be dealt with

159

therefore at first hand, and this was health to his bones. It was a splendid declaration, and though I had known from unerring signs of the *fact* of the change I never had been more delighted than by hearing of it so unreservedly from his own lips. He has been shaking off his respect for men of mere science as such, and is even more universal and impartial in his mental judgments than I have known him before.

Nothing in such a report could affect me more, at a distance, as indeed nothing shines for me more sacredly now, than the writer's perfect perception of what it would richly say to me, even if a little to my comparative confusion and bewilderment; engaged as I must rightly have appeared in working out, not to say in tentatively playing with, much thinner things. I like to remember, as I do, ineffaceably, that my attention attached itself, intensely and on the spot, to the very picture, with whatever else, conveyed, which for that matter hangs before me still: the vision of my brother, agitated by the growth of his genius, moving in his burst of confidence, his bright earnestness, about the room I knew, which must have been our admirable parent's study—with that admirable parent himself almost holding his breath for the charm and the accepted peace of it, after earlier discussions and reserves; to say nothing too, if charm was in question, of the fact of rarity and beauty I must have felt, or in any case at present feel, in the resource for such an intellectually living and fermenting son of such a spiritually perceiving and responding sire. What was the whole passage but a vision of the fine private luxury of each?—with the fine private luxury of my own almost blurred image of it superadded. Of that same spring of '69 is another page addressed to myself in Europe. My memory must at the very time have connected itself with what had remained to me of our common or certainly of my own inveterate, childish appeal to him, in early New York days, for repetition, in the winter afternoon firelight, of his most personal, most remembering and picture-recovering "story"; that of a visit paid by him about in his nineteenth year, as I make it out, to his Irish relatives, his father's nephews, nieces and cousins, with a younger brother or two perhaps, as I set the scene forth—which it conduced to our liveliest interest to see "Billy Taylor," the negro servant accompanying him from Albany, altogether rule from the point of view of effect. The dignity of this apparition indeed, I must parenthesise, would have yielded in general to the source of a glamour still more marked—the very air in which the young emissary would have moved as the son of his father and the representative of an American connection prodigious surely in its power to dazzle. William James of Albany was at that time approaching the term of his remarkably fruitful career, and as I see the fruits of it stated on the morrow of his death—in the New York Evening Post of December 20th 1832, for instance, I find myself envying the friendly youth who could bring his modest Irish kin such a fairytale from over the sea. I attach as I hang upon the passage a melancholy gaze to the cloud of images of what might have been for us all that it distractingly throws off. Our grandfather's energy, exercised in Albany from the great year 1789, appears promptly to have begun with his arrival there. "Everywhere we see his footsteps, turn where we may, and these are the results of his informing mind and his vast wealth. His plans of improvement embraced the entire city, and there is scarcely a street or a square which does not exhibit some mark of his hand or some proof of his opulence. With the exception of Mr. Astor," this delightful report goes on to declare, "no other business man has acquired so great a fortune in this State. To his enormous estate of three millions of dollars there are nine surviving heirs. His enterprises have for the last ten years furnished constant employment for hundreds of our mechanics and labourers." The enterprises appear, alas, to have definitely ceased, or to have fallen into less able hands, with his death—and to the mass of property so handsomely computed the heirs were, more exactly, not nine but a good dozen. Which fact, however, reduces but by a little the rich ambiguity of the question that was to flit before my father's children, as they grew up, with an air of impenetrability that I remember no attempt on his own part to mitigate. I doubt, for that matter, whether he could in the least have appeased our all but haunting wonder as to what had become even in the hands of twelve heirs, he himself naturally being one, of the admirable three millions. The various happy and rapid courses of most of the participants accounted for much, but did they account for the full beautiful value, and would even the furthest stretch of the charming legend of his own early taste for the amusements of the town really tell us what had been the disposition, by such a measure, of *his* share? Our dear parent, we were later quite to feel, could have told us very little, in all probability, under whatever pressure, what had become of anything. There had been, by our inference, a general history—not on the whole exhilarating, and pressure for information could never, I think, have been applied; wherefore the question arrests me only through the brightly associated presumption that the Irish visit was made, to its extreme enlivening, in the character of a gilded youth, a youth gilded an inch thick and shining to effulgence on the scene not otherwise brilliant. Which image appeals to my filial fidelity—even though I hasten not to sacrifice the circle evoked, that for which I a trifle unassuredly figure a small town in county Cavan as forming an horizon, and which consisted, we used to delight to hear with every contributive circumstance, of the local lawyer, the doctor and the (let us hope—for we *did* hope) principal "merchant," whose conjoined hospitality appeared, as it was again agreeable to know, to have more than graced the occasion: the main definite pictorial touches that have lingered with me being that all the doors always stood open, with the vistas mostly raking the provision of whiskey on every table, and that these opportunities were much less tempting (to our narrator) than that of the quest of gooseberries in the garden with a certain beautiful Barbara, otherwise anonymous, who was not of the kin but on a visit from a distance at one of the genial houses. We liked to hear about Barbara, liked the sound of her still richer rarer surname; which in spite of the fine Irish harmony it even then struck me as making I have frivolously forgotten. She had been matchlessly fair and she ate gooseberries with a charm that was in itself of the nature of a brogue—so that, as I say, we couldn't have too much of her; yet even her measure dwindled, for our appetite, beside the almost epic shape of black Billy Taylor carrying off at every juncture alike the laurel and the bay. He singularly appealed, it was clear, to the Irish imagination, performing in a manner never to disappoint it; his young master—in those days, even in the North, young mastership hadn't too long since lapsed to have lost every grace of its tradition—had been all cordially acclaimed, but not least, it appeared, because so histrionically attended: he had been the ringmaster, as it were, of the American circus, the small circus of two, but the other had been the inimitable clown. My point is that we repaired retrospectively to the circus as insatiably as our Irish cousins had of old attended it in person—even for the interest of which fact, however, my father's words have led me too far. What here follows, I must nevertheless add, would carry me on again, for development of reference, should I weakly allow it. The allusion to my brother Wilky's vividly independent verbal collocations and commentative flights re-echoes afresh, for instance, as one of the fond by-words that spoke most of our whole humorous harmony. Just so might the glance at the next visitor prompt a further raising of the curtain, save that this is a portrait to which, for lack of acquaintance with the original, I have nothing to contribute—beyond repeating again that it was ever the sign of my father's portraits to supply almost more than anything else material for a vision of himself.

Your enjoyment of England reminds me of my feelings on my first visit there forty years ago nearly, when I landed in Devonshire in the month of May or June and was so intoxicated with the roads and lanes and hedges and fields and cottages and castles and inns that I thought I should fairly expire with delight. You can't expatiate too much for our entertainment on your impressions, though you make us want consumedly to go over and follow in your footsteps. Wilky has been at home now for 2 or 3 days and is very philosophic and enthusiastic over your letters. I hoped to remember some of his turns of speech for you, but one chases another out of my memory and it is now all a blank. I will consult Alice's livelier one before I close.

My friend —— is a tropical phenomenon, a favourite of nature whatever his fellow man may say of him. His face and person are handsome rather than otherwise, and it's obvious that he is a very unsoiled and pure piece of humanity in all *personal* regards. And with such a gift of oratory— such a boundless wealth of diction set off by copious and not ungraceful gesticulation! Here is where he belongs to the tropics, where nature claims him for her own and flings him like a cascade in the face of conventional good-breeding. I can't begin to describe him, he is what I have never before met. I see that he can't help turning out excessively tiresome, but he is not at all vulgar. He has a genius for elocution, that is all; but a real genius and no mistake. In comparison with Mr. F. L. or Mr. Longfellow or the restrained Boston style of address generally, he is what the sunflower is to the snowdrop; but on the whole, if I could kick his shins whenever I should like to and so reduce him to silence, I prefer him to the others.

What mainly commends to me certain other passages of other dates (these still reaching on a little) is doubtless the fact that I myself show in them as the object of attention and even in a manner as a claimant for esthetic aid. This latter active sympathy overflows in a letter of the spring of '70, which would be open to more elucidation than I have, alas, space for. Let the sentence with which it begins merely remind me that Forrest, the American actor, of high renown in his time, and of several of whose appearances toward the close of his career I keep a memory uneffaced—the impression as of a deep-toned thunderous organ, a prodigious instrument pounded by a rank barbarian—had been literally, from what we gathered, an early comrade of our parent: literally, I say, because the association could seem to me, at my hours of ease, so bravely incongruous. By my hours of ease I mean those doubtless too devoted to that habit of wanton dispersed embroidery for which any scrap of the human canvas would serve. From one particular peg, I at the same time allow, the strongest sense of the incongruity depended—my remembrance, long entertained, of my father's relating how, on an occasion, which must have been betimes in the morning, of his calling on the great tragedian, a man of enormous build and strength, the latter, fresh and dripping from the bath, had entered the room absolutely upside down, or by the rare gymnastic feat of throwing his heels into the air and walking, as with strides, on his hands; an extraordinary performance if kept up for more than a second or two, and the result at any rate of mere exuberance of muscle and pride and robustious joie de vivre. It had affected me, the picture, as one of those notes of high colour that the experience of a young Albany viveur, the like of which I felt I was never to come in for, alone could strike off; but what was of the finer profit in it was less the direct illustration of the mighty mountebank than of its being delightful on the part of a domestic character we so respected to have had, with everything else a Bohemian past too—since I couldn't have borne at such moments to hear it argued as not Bohemian. What did his having dropped in after such a fashion and at a late breakfast-hour on the glory of the footlights and the idol of the town, what did it fall in with but the kind of thing one had caught glimpses and echoes of from the diaries and memoirs, so far as these had been subject to the passing peep, of the giftedly idle and the fashionably great, the Byrons, the Bulwers, the Pelhams, the Coningsbys, or even, for a nearer vividness perhaps, the N. P. Willises?—of all of whom it was somehow more characteristic than anything else, to the imagination, that they always began their day in some such fashion. Even if I cite this as a fair example of one's instinct for making much of a little—once this little, a chance handful of sand, could show the twinkle of the objective, or even the reflective, grain of gold—I still claim value for that instanced felicity, as I felt it, of being able to yearn, thanks to whatever chance support, over Bohemia, and yet to have proof in the paternal presence close at hand of how well even the real frequentation of it, when achieved in romantic youth, might enable a person at last to turn out. The lesson may now indeed seem to have been one of those that rather more strictly adorn a tale than point a moral; but with me, at that period, I think, the moral ever came first and the tale more brilliantly followed. As for the recital, in such detail, of the theme of a possible literary effort which the rest of my letter represents, how could I feel this, when it had reached me, as anything but a sign of the admirable anxiety with which thought could be taken, even though "amateurishly," in my professional interest?—since professional I by that time appeared able to pass for being. And how above all can it not serve as an exhibition again of the manner in which all my benevolent backer's inveterate original *malaise* in face of betrayed symptoms of the impulse to "narrow down" on the part of his young found its solution always, or its almost droll simplification, as soon as the case might reach for him a *personal* enough, or "social" enough, as he would have said, relation to its fruits? Then the malaise might promptly be felt as changed, by a wave of that wand, to the extremity of active and expatiative confidence.

Horatio Alger is writing a Life of Edwin Forrest, and I am afraid will give him a Bowery appreciation. He reports his hero as a very "fine" talker— in which light I myself don't so much recall him, though he had a native breadth—as when telling Alger for example of old Gilbert Stuart's having when in a state of dilapidation asked him to let him paint his portrait. "I consented," said Forrest, "and went to his studio. He was an old white lion, so blind that he had to ask me the colour of my eyes and my hair; but he threw his brush at the canvas, and every stroke was life." Alger talks freely about his own late insanity—which he in fact appears to enjoy as a subject of conversation and in which I believe he has somewhat interested William, who has talked with him a good deal of his experience at the Somerville Asylum. Charles Grinnell—though not à propos of the crazy—has become a great reader and apparently a considerable understander of my productions; Alger aforesaid aussi. Everyone hopes that J. G. hasn't caught a Rosamund Vincy in Miss M. I don't know whether this hope means affection to J. or disaffection to the young lady.

I have written to Gail Hamilton to send me your story; but she does it not as yet. I will renew my invitation to her in a day or two if necessary. I went to see Osgood lately about his publishing a selection from your tales. He repeated what he had told you—that he would give you 15 per cent and do all the advertising, etc., you paying for the plates; or he would pay everything and give you 10 per cent on every copy sold after the first thousand. I shall be glad (in case you would like to publish, and I think it time for you to do so) to meet the expense of your stereotyping, and if you will pick out what you would like to be included we shall set to work at once and have the book ready by next autumn. I have meanwhile the materials of a story for you which I was telling William of the other day as a regular Tourgéneff subject, and he urged me to send it off to you at once—he was so struck with it.

Matthew Henry W. was a very cultivated and accomplished young man in Albany at the time I was growing up. He belonged to a highly respectable family of booksellers and publishers and was himself bred to the law; but had such a love of literature, and more especially of the natural sciences, that he never devoted himself strictly to his profession. He was the intimate friend of my dear old tutor, Joseph Henry of the Smithsonian, and of other distinguished men of science; he corresponded with foreign scientific bodies, and his contributions to science generally were of so original a cast as to suggest great hopes of his future eminence. He was a thorough gentleman, of perfect address and perfect courage—utterly unegotistic, and one's wonder was how he had ever grown up in Albany or resigned himself to living there. One day he invested his money, of which he had a certain quantity, in a scheme much favoured by the president of the bank in which he deposited, and this adventure proved a fortune. There lived near us as well a family of the name of K——, your cousin Mary Minturn Post's stepmother being of its members; and this family reckoned upon a great social sensation in bringing out their youngest daughter, Lydia Sibyl, who had never been seen by mortal eye outside her own immediate circle, save that of a physician who reported that she was fabulously beautiful. She *was* the most beautiful girl I think I ever saw, at a little distance. Well, she made her sensation and brought Matthew Henry promptly to her feet. Her family wanted wealth above all things for her; but here was wealth and something more, very much more, and they smiled upon his suit. Everything went merrily for a while—M. H. was deeply intoxicated with his prize. Never was man so enamoured, and never was beauty better fitted to receive adoration. She was of an exquisite Grecian outline as to face, with a countenance like the tender dawn and form and manners ravishingly graceful. But W. was not content with his adventure— he embarked again and lost almost all he owned. The girl's father—or her mother rather, being the ruler of the family and as hard as the nether world at heart—gave the cue to her daughter and my friend was dismissed. He couldn't believe his senses, he raved and cursed his fate, but it was inexorable. What was to be done? With a bitterness of heart inconceivable he plucked his revenge by marrying at once a stout and blooming jade who was to Lydia Sibyl as a peony to a violet, absolutely nothing but flesh and blood. Her he bore upon his arm at fashionable hours through the streets; her he took to church, preserving his admirable ease and courtesy to everyone, as if absolutely nothing had occurred; and her he pretended to take to his bosom in private, with what a shudder one can imagine. Everybody stood aghast. He went daily about his affairs, as serene and unconscious apparently as the moon in the heavens. Soon his poverty showed itself in certain economies of his attire, which had always been most recherché. Soon again he broke his leg and went about on crutches, but neither poverty nor accident had the least power to ruffle his air of equanimity. He was always superior to his circumstances, met you exactly as he had always done, impressed you always as the best-bred man you knew, and left you wondering what a heart and what a brain lay behind such a fortune. One morning we all read in the newspaper at breakfast that Mr. M. H. W. had appealed the day before to the protection of the police against his wife, who had taken to beating him and whom as a woman he couldn't deal with by striking back; and the police responded properly to his appeal. He went about his affairs as usual that day and every day, never saying a word to any one of his trouble nor even indirectly asking sympathy, but making you feel that here if anywhere was a rare kind of manhood, a self-respect so eminent as to look down with scorn on the refuges open to ordinary human weakness. This lasted five or six years. He never drank or took to other vices, and lived a life of such decorum, so far as his own action was concerned, a life of such interest and science and literature, as to be the most delightful and unconscious of companions even when his coat was at the last shabbiness and you didn't dare to look at him for fear of betraying your own vulgar misintelligence. Finally Lydia Sibyl died smitten with smallpox and all her beauty gone to hideousness. He lingered awhile, his charming manners undismayed still, his eye as undaunted as at the beginning, and then he suddenly died. I never knew his equal for a manly force competent to itself in every emergency and seeking none of the ordinary subterfuges that men so often seek to hide their imbecility. I think it a good basis....

Returning from Europe in June '70, after a stay there of some fifteen months, I had crossed the sea eastward again two years later, with my sister and our admirable aunt as companions—leaving them, I may mention, to return home at the end of six months while I betook myself to Italy, where I chiefly remained till the autumn of '74. The following expresses our father's liberality of recognition and constant tenderness of tone in a manner that no comment need emphasise, but at one or two of his references I allow myself to glance. I happen to remember perfectly for instance the appearance of the novel of Madame Sand's that he so invidiously alludes to in one of the first numbers of the cherished Revue that reached us after the siege of Paris had been raised— such a pathetically scant starved pale number, I quite recall, as expressed the share even of the proud periodical in the late general and so tragic dearth; with which it comes back to me that I had myself a bit critically mused on the characteristic queerness, the oddity of the light thrown on the stricken French consciousness by the prompt sprouting of *such* a flower of the native imagination in the chill air of discipline accepted and after the administration to that consciousness of a supposedly clarifying dose. But I hadn't gone the length of my father, who must have taken up the tale in its republished form, a so slim salmon-coloured volume this time: oh the repeated arrival, during those years, of the salmon-coloured volumes in their habit as they lived, a habit reserved, to my extreme appreciation, for this particular series, and that, enclosing the extraordinarily fresh fruit of their author's benign maturity, left Tamaris and Valvèdre and Mademoiselle La Quintinie in no degree ever "discounted" for us as devotees of the Revue, I make out, by their being but renewals of acquaintance. The sense of the salmon-coloured distinctive of Madame Sand was even to come back to me long years after on my hearing Edmond de Goncourt speak reminiscentially and, I permit myself to note, not at all reverently, of the *robe de satin fleur-de-pêcher* that the illustrious and infatuated lady, whose more peculiar or native tint, as Blanche Amory used to say, didn't contribute to a harmony, *s'était fait faire* in order to fix as much as possible the attention of Gustave Flaubert at the Dîner Magny; of Gustave Flaubert, who, according to this most invidious of reporters, disembroiled from each other with too scant ease his tangle of possibly incurred ridicule from the declared sentiment of so old a woman, even in a peach-blossom dress, and the glory reflected on him by his admirer's immense distinction. Which vision of a complicated past, recovered even as I write—and of a past indeed contemporary with the early complacencies I attribute to ourselves—doesn't at all blur its also coming back to me that I was to have found my parent "hard on" poor Francia in spite of my own comparative reserves; these being questions and shades that I rejoice to think of our having had so discussionally, and well at home for the most part, the social education of. I see that general period as quite flushed and toned by the salmon-coloured covers; so that a kind of domestic loyalty would ever operate, as we must have all felt, to make us take the thick with the thin and not *y regarder* for a Francia the more or the less. When I say all indeed I doubtless have in mind especially my parents and myself, with my sister and our admirable aunt (in her times of presence) thrown in—to the extent of our subjection to the charm of such matters in particular as La Famille de Germandre, La Ville Noire, Nanon and L'Homme de Neige, round which last above all we sat ranged in united ecstasy; so that I was to wonder through the after years, and I think perhaps to this day, how it could come that a case of the "story" strain at its finest and purest, a gush of imaginative force so free and yet so artfully directed, shouldn't have somehow "stood out" more in literary history. Perhaps indeed L'Homme de Neige does essentially stand out in the unwritten parts of that record—which are content to be mere tacit tender tradition; for all the world as if, since there are more or less dreadful perpetuated books, by the hundred, dreadful from whatever baseness or whatever scantness, that for shame, as it were, we never mention, so one may figure others as closeted in dimness (than which there is nothing safer) by the very scruple of respect at its richest. I hover for instance about the closet of L'Homme de Neige, I stand outside a moment as if listening for a breath from within; but I don't open the door, you see—which must mean, in all probability, that I wouldn't for the world inconsiderately finger again one of the three volumes; *that* meaning, in its turn, doubtless, that I have heard the breath I had listened for and that it can only have been what my argument wants, the breath of life unquenched. Isn't it relevant to this that when she was not reading Trollope our dear mother was reading "over" La Famille de Germandre, which, with several of its companions of the same bland period, confirmed her in the sense that there was no one like their author for a "love-story"?—a conviction, however, that when made articulate exposed her to the imputation of a larger tolerance than she doubtless intended to project; till the matter was cleared up by our generally embracing her for so sweetly not knowing about Valentine and Jacques and suchlike, and having only begun at La Mare au Diable and even thereafter been occasionally obliged to skip.

So far do I let myself go while, to recur to my letter, Chauncey Wright sits for me in his customary corner of the deep library sofa and his strange conflictingly conscious light blue eyes, appealing across the years from under the splendid arch of his fair head, one of the handsomest for representation of amplitude of thought that it was possible to see, seems to say to me with a softness more aimed at the heart than any alarm or any challenge: "But what then are you going to do for me?" I find myself simply ache, I fear, as almost the only answer to this—beyond his figuring for me as the most wasted and doomed, the biggest at once and the gentlest, of the great intending and unproducing (in anything like the just degree) bachelors of philosophy, bachelors of attitude and of life. And as he so sits, loved and befriended and welcomed, valued and invoked and vainly guarded and infinitely pitied, till the end couldn't but come, he renews that appeal to the old kindness left over, as I may say, and which must be more or less known to all of us, for the good society that was helplessly to miss a right chronicler, and the names of which, so full at the time of their fine sense, were yet to be writ in water. Chauncey Wright, of the great imperfectly-attested mind; Jane Norton, of the train, so markedly, of the distinguished, the sacrificial, devoted; exquisite Mrs. Gurney, of the infallible taste, the beautiful hands and the tragic fate; Gurney himself, for so long Dean of the Faculty at Harvard and trusted judge of all judgments (this latter pair the subject of my father's glance at the tenantship of Shady Hill in the Nortons' absence:) they would delightfully adorn a page and appease a piety that is still athirst if I hadn't to let them pass. Harshly condemned to let them pass, and looking wistfully after them as they go, how can I yet not have inconsequently asked them to turn a moment more before disappearing?

My heart turns to you this morning, so radiant in the paternal panoply you wear toward Alice and your aunt, and I would give a great deal to see you. The enclosed scrap of a letter from William is sent to show you how vastly improved are his eyes, especially when you shall have learned that he has written us within the last four or five days twenty pages of like density to these. He would fain persuade us to go to Mount Desert; perhaps later we may go to Quebec, but we are so comfortable together reading Trollope and talking philosophy that we cheerfully drop the future from our regard. Mamma is free and active and bracing. She is a domestic nor'wester, carrying balm and bloom into every nook and corner of her empire.... She hangs over The Eustace Diamonds while I try vainly to read George Sand's Francia. I have come across nothing of that lady's that reflects a baser light on her personal history. What must a woman have been through to want to grovel at this time of day in such uncleanness? Don't buy it—I wish I hadn't! The new North American is out, with a not too interesting article of Chauncey Wright's on Mivart, a scandalous (in point of taste) essay of Mr. Stirling on Buckle, full of Scotch conceit, insolence and "wut;" a very very laboured article by James Lowell on Dante, in which he determines to exhaust all knowledge; and these are all I have read. Mr. Stirling of course makes Buckle ridiculous, but he stamps himself a shabby creature.

I find the following, addressed to his daughter in August '72, so beautifully characteristic of our parents' always explicit admonition to us, in our dependent years, against too abject an impulse to be frugal in their interests, that I may fairly let it stand as a monument to this particular aspect of their affection.

Your and H.'s last letters bring tears of joy to our eyes. It's a delight above all delights to feel one's children turn out all that the heart covets in children. Your conviction is not up to the truth. Our "tender thoughts" of you are so constant that I have hardly been able to settle to anything since you have been gone. I can do little else than recount to myself "the tender mercies of the Lord" to me and my household. Still I am not wholly useless; I try to write every day, and though I haven't my daughter at hand to look after my style and occasionally after my ideas, I manage to do a little. Your conscientious economy is excessively touching, but it's a little overstrained. You needn't be afraid of putting us to any embarrassment so long as your expenses don't exceed their present rate; and you can buy all you want in Paris without stretching your tether a particle. This is Mamma's message as well as mine. Charles Atkinson wishes me to say that Monte Genneroso above Lugano Lake—the P.O. Mendrisio—offers a wondrous climate; and Mamma thinks—so fearful is she that you will descend into Italy before the warm weather is over and so compromise your strength—that you had either better go there awhile first or else be ready to retreat on it in case you find the summer heat in Venice impossible.

Nor does this scrap from a letter to myself at the same season breathe a spirit less liberal—so far as the sympathy with whatever might pass for my fondest preoccupations was concerned. These were now quite frankly recognised as the arduous attempt to learn somehow or other to write.

I send you The Nation, though there seems nothing in it of your own, and I think I never fail to recognise you. A notice of Gustave Droz's Babolain (by T. S. P., I suppose) there is; which book I read the other day. This fumbling in the cadaver of the old world, however, only disgusts me when so unrelieved as in this case by any contrast or any souffle of inspiration such as you get in Tourguéneff. It's curious to observe how uncertain the author's step is in this story—how he seems always on the look-out for some chance to break away. But it has mastered him, he can't lay the ghost he has conjured.

To which I should limit myself for the commemoration of that group of years by the gentle aid of the always vivid excerpt, were it not that I have before me a considerable cluster of letters addressed by the writer of the foregoing to Mr. J. Eliot Cabot, most accomplished of Bostonians, most "cultivated" even among the cultivated, as we used to say, and of a philosophic acuteness to which my father highly testified, with which indeed he earnestly contended. The correspondence in question covered, during the years I include, philosophic ground and none other; but though no further exhibition of it than this reference may convey is to my purpose I lay it under contribution to the extent of a passage or two just for the pleasure of inviting recognition, as I invite it wherever we meet an instance, of the fashion after which the intensely animated soul can scarce fail of a harmony and a consistency of expression that are nothing less than interesting, that in fact become at once beautiful, in themselves. By which remark I nevertheless do not mean to limit the significance of the writer's side of his long argument with Mr. Eliot Cabot, into which I may not pretend to enter, nor the part that in any such case a rare gift for style must inveterately play.

I grant then that I am often tempted to conceive, as I read your letters, that we differ only in your terms being more abstract, mine more concrete; and yet I really don't think this difference is exhaustive. If I thought Philosophy capable ever of being reduced to logical compass or realising itself as science, I should give in at once. But this is just what I cannot think. Philosophy is the doctrine exclusively of the infinite in the finite, and deals with the latter therefore only as a mask, only as *harbouring* the former. But if you formulate it scientifically your terms are necessarily all finite, as furnished by experience, and the infinite is excluded or at most creeps in as the indefinite—Hegel's *becoming* for example. Thus Hegel's dialectic modulates only in the sphere of his distance. His *being* is universal existence, and, as universals have only a logical truth, being in se is equivalent to Nothing. But Nothing hasn't even a logical basis. Lithe as human thought is it can't compass the conception. It is a mere brutum fulmen devised to disguise the absence of thought or its inanition; and Hegel, if he had been wise, would have said no-thought instead of no-thing. For no-thing doesn't express the complete absence of existence. Existence is of two sorts, real and personal, sensible and conscious, quantitative and qualitative. The most you are entitled to say therefore when existence disappears in quantitative, real or sensible, form is that it has been taken up into purely qualitative, personal or conscious form; no-thing being the logical equivalent of all-person. Thus I, who in Hegel's formula presumably extract existence from being, survive the operation as person, and though I am most clearly no-thing I am yet not *being*. Indeed I am not even existence any longer, since by knocking thing out of being I have forfeited my own reality, and consent henceforth to be pure personality, *i.e.* phenomenality. And personal or phenomenal existence is constituted by referring itself to a foreign source, or, what is the same thing, confessing itself created: so that the fundamental word of Philosophy, by Hegel's own formula, is creation; which, however, as I understand him, he denies in any objective sense of the word. This then is what I complain of in him—with deference of course to your better knowledge, which, however, you do not urge as yet in what seems to me a silencing way—that he makes existence *essential* to being, so that take existence away and being becomes nothing. It would not be a whit less preposterous in me to say that thought is essential to thing, subject to object, marble to statue, canvas to picture, woman to wife, mother to child. It is literally putting the cart before the horse and converting Philosophy to a practical quagmire. Being implies existence of course just as picture implies canvas, or as personality implies reality, or as chick implies egg; but it implies it only to a lower intelligence than itself, an unspiritual intelligence to wit, which has no direct or inward intuition of being, and requires to be agitated to discerning it. When I recognise the spiritual life of Art I never think of marble or canvas as entering even conditionally into its manifestations.

But I hold my case for a rare command of manner thus proved, and need go no further; the more that I have dropped too many of those threads of my rather niggled tapestry that belong but to the experience of my own weaving hand and the interplay of which represents thereby a certain gained authority. I disentangle these again, if the term be not portentous, though reflecting too, and again with complacency, that though I thus prize them as involved most in my own consciousness, this is just because of their attachment somewhere else to other matters and other lives.

IX

I went up from Newport to Cambridge early in the autumn of '62, and on one of the oddest errands, I think, that, given the several circumstances, I could possibly have undertaken. I was nineteen years old, and it had seemed to me for some time past that some such step as my entering for instance the Harvard Law School more or less urgently concerned what I could but try to help myself out by still putting forward as my indispensable education—I am not sure indeed that the claim didn't explicitly figure, or at least successfully dangle, as that of my possibly graceful mere "culture." I had somehow—by which I mean for reasons quite sufficient—to fall back on the merciful "mere" for any statement of my pretensions even to myself: so little they seemed to fit into any scheme of the conventional maximum as compared with those I saw so variously and strongly asserted about me, especially since the outbreak of the War. I am not sure whether I yet made bold to say it, but I should surely be good for nothing, all my days, if not for projecting into the concrete, by hook or by crook—that is my imagination shamelessly aiding—some show of (again) mere life. This impression was not in the least the flag I publicly brandished; in fact I must have come as near as possible to brandishing none whatever, a sound instinct always hinting to me, I gather, that the tune for such a performance was much more after than before—before the perfect place had been found for the real planting of the standard and the giving of its folds to the air. No such happy spot had been marked, decidedly, at that period, to my inquiring eye; in consequence of which the emblazoned morsel (hoisted sooner or later by all of us, I think, somehow and somewhere), might have passed for the hour as a light extravagant bandanna rolled into the tight ball that fits it for hiding in the pocket. There it considerably stayed, so far as I was concerned; and all the more easily as I can but have felt how little any particular thing I might meanwhile "do" would matter—save for some specious appearance in it. This last, I recognise, had for me a virtue—principally that of somehow gaining time; though I hasten to add that my approach to the Law School can scarcely, as a means to this end, in the air of it that comes back to me, have been in the least deceptive. By which I mean that my appearance of intentions, qualifications, possibilities, or whatever else, in the connection, hadn't surely so much as the grace of the specious. I spoke above of the assumed "indispensability" of some show of my being further subject to the "education" theory, but this was for the moment only under failure to ask to whom, or for what, such a tribute *was* indispensable. The interest to myself would seem to have been, as I recover the sense of the time, that of all the impossibilities of action my proceeding to Cambridge on the very vaguest grounds that probably ever determined a residence there might pass for the least flagrant; as I breathe over again at any rate the comparative confidence in which I so moved I feel it as a confidence in the positive saving virtue of vagueness. Could I but work that force as an ideal I felt it must see me through, for the beauty of it in that form was that it should absolutely superabound. I wouldn't have allowed, either, that it was vaguer to do nothing; for in the first place just staying at home when everyone was on the move couldn't in any degree show the right mark: to be properly and perfectly vague one had to be vague *about* something; mere inaction quite lacked the note—it was nothing but definite and dull. I thought of the Law School experiment, I remember, in all sorts of conceivable connections, but in the connection of dulness surely never for an hour. I thought of it under the head of "life"—by which term at the same time, I blush to confess, I didn't in the least mean free evening access to Boston in a jangling horse-car, with whatever extension this might give to the joy of the liberated senses. I simply meant—well, what was monstrously to happen; which I shall be better inspired here to deal with as a demonstration made in its course than as a premonition relatively crude and at the time still to be verified. Marked in the whole matter, however these things might be, was that irony of fate under the ugly grin of which I found my father reply in the most offhand and liberal manner to my remark that the step in question—my joining, in a sense, my brother at Cambridge—wouldn't be wholly impracticable. It might have been, from his large assent to it, a masterstroke of high policy. A certain inconsequence in this left me wondering why then if the matter was now so natural it hadn't been to his mind a year before equally simple that I should go to college, and to *that* College, after a more showy, even though I see it would have been at the same time a less presumptuous, fashion. To have deprecated the "college course" with such emphasis only so soon afterwards to forswear all emphasis and practically smile, in mild oblivion, on *any* Harvard connection I might find it in me to take up, was to bring it home, I well recall, that the case might originally have been much better managed.

All of which would seem to kick up more dust than need quite have hung about so simple a matter as my setting forth to the Cambridge scene with no design that I could honourably exhibit. A superficial account of the matter would have been that my father had a year or two earlier appeared to think so ill of it as to reduce me, given the "delicacy," the inward, not then the outward, which I have glanced at, to mild renunciation—mild I say because I remember in fact, rather to my mystification now, no great pang of disappointment, no soreness of submission. I didn't want anything so much as I wanted a certain good (or wanted thus supremely *to* want it, if I may say so), with which a conventional going to college wouldn't have so tremendously much to do as for the giving it up to break my heart—or an unconventional not-going so tremendously much either. What I "wanted to want" to be was, all intimately, just *literary*; a decent respect for the standard hadn't yet made my approach so straight that there weren't still difficulties that might seem to meet it, questions it would have to depend on. Passing the Harvard portal positively failed in fact to strike me as the shorter cut to literature; the sounds that rose from the scene as I caught them appeared on the contrary the most detached from any such interest that had ever reached my ear. Merely to open the door of the big square closet, the ample American closet, to the like of which Europe had never treated us, on the shelves and round the walls of which the pink Revues sat with the air, row upon row, of a choir of breathing angels, was to take up that particular, that sacred, connection in a way that put the coarser process to shame. The drop of the Harvard question had of a truth really meant, as I recover it, a renewed consecration of the rites of that chapel where the taper always twinkled—which circumstance I mention as not only qualifying my sense of loss, but as symbolising, after a queer fashion, the independence, blest vision (to the extent, that is, of its being a closer compact with the life of the imagination), that I should thus both luckily come in for and designingly cultivate: cultivate in other words under the rich cover of obscurity. I have already noted how the independence was, ever so few months later, by so quaint a turn, another mere shake of the tree, to drop into my lap in the form of a great golden apple—a value not a simple windfall only through the fact that my father's hand had after all just lightly loosened it. This accession pointed the moral that there was no difficulty about anything, no intrinsic difficulty; so that, to re-emphasise the sweet bewilderment, I was to "go" where I liked in the Harvard direction and do what I liked in the Harvard relation. Such was the situation as offered me; though as I had to take it and use it I found in it no little difference. Two things and more had come up—the biggest of which, and very wondrous as bearing on any circumstance of mine, as having a grain of weight to spare for it, was the breaking out of the War. The other, the infinitely small affair in comparison, was a passage of personal history the most entirely personal, but between which, as a private catastrophe or difficulty, bristling with embarrassments, and the great public convulsion that announced itself in bigger terms each day, I felt from the very first an association of the closest, yet withal, I fear, almost of the least clearly expressible. Scarce at all to be stated, to begin with, the queer fusion or confusion established in my consciousness during the soft spring of '61 by the firing on Fort Sumter, Mr. Lincoln's instant first call for volunteers and a physical mishap, already referred to as having overtaken me at the same dark hour, and the effects of which were to draw themselves out incalculably and intolerably. Beyond all present notation the interlaced, undivided way in which what had happened to me, by a turn of fortune's hand, in twenty odious minutes, kept company of the most unnatural—I can call it nothing less—with my view of what was happening, with the question of what might still happen, to everyone about me, to the country at large: it so made of these marked disparities a single vast visitation. One had the sense, I mean, of a huge comprehensive ache, and there were hours at which one could scarce have told whether it came most from one's own poor organism, still so young and so meant for better things, but which had suffered particular wrong, or from the enclosing social body, a body rent with a thousand wounds and that thus treated one to the honour of a sort of tragic fellowship. The twenty minutes had sufficed, at all events, to establish a relation—a relation to everything occurring round me not only for the next four years but for long afterward—that was at once extraordinarily intimate and quite awkwardly irrelevant. I must have felt in some befooled way in presence of a crisis—the smoke of Charleston Bay still so acrid in the air—at which the likely young should be up and doing or, as familiarly put, lend a hand much wanted; the willing youths, all round, were mostly starting to their feet, and to have trumped up a lameness at such a juncture could be made to pass in no light for graceful. Jammed into the acute angle between two high fences, where the rhythmic play of my arms, in tune with that of several other pairs, but at a dire disadvantage of position, induced a rural, a rusty, a quasi-extemporised old engine to work and a saving stream to flow, I had done myself, in face of a shabby conflagration, a horrid even if an obscure hurt; and what was interesting from the first was my not doubting in the least its duration—though what seemed equally clear was that I needn't as a matter of course adopt and appropriate it, so to speak, or place it for increase of interest on exhibition. The interest of it, I very presently knew, would certainly be of the greatest, would even in conditions kept as simple as I might make them become little less than absorbing. The shortest account of what was to follow for a long time after is therefore to plead that the interest never did fail. It was naturally what is called a painful one, but it consistently declined, as an influence at play, to drop for a single instant. Circumstances, by a wonderful chance, overwhelmingly favoured it—as an interest, an inexhaustible, I mean; since I also felt in the whole enveloping tonic atmosphere a force promoting its growth. Interest, the interest of life and of death, of our national existence, of the fate of those, the vastly numerous, whom it closely concerned, the interest of the extending War, in fine, the hurrying troops, the transfigured scene, formed a cover for every sort of intensity, made tension itself in fact contagious—so that almost any tension would do, would serve for one's share.

I have here, I allow, not a little to foreshorten—have to skip sundry particulars, certain of the steps by which I came to think of my relation to my injury as a *modus vivendi* workable for the time. These steps had after the first flush of reaction inevitably *had* to be communications of my state, recognitions and admissions; which had the effect, I hasten to add, of producing sympathies, supports and reassurances. I gladly took these things, I perfectly remember, at that value; distinct to me as it still is nevertheless that the indulgence they conveyed lost part of its balm by involving a degree of publication. Direfully distinct have remained to me the conditions of a pilgrimage to Boston made that summer under my father's care for consultation of a great surgeon, the head of his profession there; whose opinion and advice—the more that he was a guaranteed friend of my father's—had seemed the best light to invoke on the less and less bearable affliction with which I had been for three or four months seeking to strike some sort of bargain: mainly, up to that time, under protection of a theory of temporary supine "rest" against which everything inward and outward tended equally to conspire. Agitated scraps of rest, snatched, to my consciousness, by the liveliest violence, were to show for futile almost to the degree in which the effort of our interview with the high expert was afterwards so to show; the truth being that this interview settled my sad business, settled it just in that saddest sense, for ever so long to come. This was so much the case that, as the mere scene of our main appeal, the house from which we had after its making dejectedly emerged put forth to me as I passed it in many a subsequent season an ironic smug symbolism of its action on my fate. That action had come from the complete failure of our approached oracle either to warn, to comfort or to command—to do anything but make quite unassistingly light of the bewilderment exposed to him. In default of other attention or suggestion he might by a mere warning as to gravities only too possible, and already well advanced, have made such a difference; but I have little forgotten how I felt myself, the warning absent, treated but to a comparative pooh-pooh—an impression I long looked back to as a sharp parting of the ways, with an adoption of the wrong one distinctly determined. It was not simply small comfort, it was only a mystification the more, that the inconvenience of my state had to reckon with the strange fact of there being nothing to speak of the matter with me. The graceful course, on the whole ground again (and where moreover was delicacy, the proposed, the intended, without grace?) was to behave accordingly, in good set terms, as if the assurance were true; since the time left no margin at all for one's gainsaying with the right confidence so high an authority. There were a hundred ways to behave—in the general sense so freely suggested, I mean; and I think of the second half of that summer of '62 as my attempt at selection of the best. The best still remained, under closer comparisons,

181

very much what it had at first seemed, and there was in fact this charm in it that to prepare for an ordeal essentially intellectual, as I surmised, might justly involve, in the public eye, a season of some retirement. The beauty was—I can fairly see it now, through the haze of time, even as beauty!—that studious retirement and preparatory hours did after all supply the supine attitude, did invest the ruefulness, did deck out the cynicism of lying down book in hand with a certain fine plausibility. This was at least a negative of combat, an organised, not a loose and empty one, something definitely and firmly parallel to action in the tented field; and I well recall, for that matter, how, when early in the autumn I had in fact become the queerest of forensic recruits, the bristling horde of my Law School comrades fairly produced the illusion of a mustered army. The Cambridge campus was tented field enough for a conscript starting so compromised; and I can scarce say moreover how easily it let me down that when it came to the point one had still fine fierce young men, in great numbers, for company, there being at the worst so many such who hadn't flown to arms. I was to find my fancy of the merely relative right in any way to figure, or even on such terms just to exist, I was to find it in due course quite drop from me as the Cambridge year played itself out, leaving me all aware that, full though the air might be of stiffer realities, one had yet a rare handful of one's own to face and deal with.

At Cambridge of course, when I got there, I was further to find my brother on the scene and already at a stage of possession of its contents that I was resigned in advance never to reach; so thoroughly I seemed to feel a sort of quickening savoury meal in any cold scrap of his own experience that he might pass on to my palate. This figure has definite truth, that is, but for association at the board literally yielding us nourishment—the happiest as to social composition and freedom of supply of all the *tables d'hôte* of those days, a veritable haunt of conversation ruled by that gently fatuous Miss Upham something of whose angular grace and antique attitude has lived again for us in William's letters. I place him, if not at the moment of my to that extent joining him then at least from a short time afterwards, in quarters that he occupied for the next two or three years—quiet cloistered rooms, as they almost appeared to me, in the comparatively sequestered Divinity Hall of that still virtually rustic age; which, though mainly affected to the use of post-graduates and others, of a Unitarian colour, enrolled under Harvard's theological Faculty, offered chance accommodation, much appreciated for a certain supposedly separate charm, not to say a finer dignity, by the more maturely studious in other branches as well. The superstition or aftertaste of Europe had then neither left me nor hinted that it ever might; yet I recall as a distinct source of interest, to be desperately dealt with, and dealt with somehow to my inward advantage, the special force of the circumstance that I was now for the first time in presence of matters normally, entirely, consistently American, and that more particularly I found myself sniff up straight from the sources, such as they unmistakably were, the sense of that New England which had been to me till then but a name. This from the first instant was what I most took in, and quite apart from the question of what one was going to make of it, of whether one was going, in the simple formula, to like it, and of what would come, could the impression so triumph, of such monstrous assimilations. Clear to me in the light thus kindled that my American consciousness had hitherto been after all and at the best singularly starved, and that Newport for instance, during the couple of years, had fed it but with sips of an adulterated strain. Newport, with its opera-glass turned for ever across the sea—for Newport, or at least *our* Newport, even during the War, lived mainly, and quite visibly, by the opera-glass—was comparatively, and in its degree incurably, cosmopolite; and though on our first alighting there I had more or less successfully, as I fancied, invited the local historic sense to vibrate, it was at present left me to feel myself a poor uninitiated creature. However, an initiation, at least by the intelligence, into some given thing—almost anything really given would do—was essentially what I was, as we nowadays say, after; the fault with my previous data in the American kind had been that they weren't sufficiently given; so that here would be Boston and Cambridge giving as with absolute authority. The War had by itself of course, on the ground I speak of, communicated something of the quality, or rather of the quantity, otherwise deficient; only this was for my case, of which alone I speak, an apprehension without a language or a channel—a revelation as sublime as one would like to feel it, but spreading abroad as a whole and not, alas, by any practice of mine, reducible to parts. What I promptly made out at Cambridge was that "America" would be given, as I have called it, to a tune altogether fresh, so that to hear this tune wholly played out might well become on the spot an inspiring privilege. If I indeed, I should add, said to myself "wholly," this was of course not a little straining a point; since, putting my initiation, my grasp of the exhibition, at its conceivable liveliest, far more of the supposed total was I inevitably to miss than to gather to my use. But I might gather what I could, and therein was exactly the adventure. To rinse my mouth of the European aftertaste *in order* to do justice to whatever of the native bitter-sweet might offer itself in congruous vessels—such a brave dash for discovery, and such only, would give a sense to my posture. With which it was unmistakable that I shouldn't in the least have painfully to strive; of such a force of impact was each impression clearly capable that I had much rather to steady myself, at any moment, where I stood, and quite to a sense of the luxury of the occasion, than to cultivate inquiry at the aggressive pitch. There was no need for curiosity—it was met by every object, I seemed to see, so much more than half way; unless indeed I put it better by saying that as *all* my vision partook of that principle the impulse and the object perpetually melted together. It wasn't for instance by the faintest process of inquiry that the *maison* Upham, where I three times daily sat at meat, had scarce to wait an hour to become as vivid a translation into American terms of Balzac's Maison Vauquer, in Le Père Goriot, as I could have desired to deal with.

It would have been at once uplifting to see in the American terms a vast improvement on the prime version, had I not been here a bit baffled by the sense that the correspondence was not quite, after all, of like with like, and that the main scene of Balzac's action was confessedly and curiously sordid and even sinister, whereas its equivalent under the Harvard elms would rank decidedly as what we had *de mieux*, or in other words of most refined, in the "boarding" line, to show. I must have been further conscious that what we had de mieux in the social line appeared quite liable, on occasion, to board wherever it might—the situation in Balzac's world being on this head as different as possible. No one not deeply distressed or dismally involved or all but fatally compromised could have taken the chances of such an establishment at all; so that any comparison to our own particular advantage had to be, on reflection, nipped in the bud. There was a generic sameness, none the less, I might still reason; enough of that at least to show the two pictures as each in its way interesting—which was all that was required. The Maison Vauquer, its musty air thick with heavier social elements, might have been more so, for the Harvard elms overhung no strange Vautrin, no old Goriot, no young Rastignac; yet the interest of the Kirkland Street company couldn't, so to speak, help itself either, any more than I could help taking advantage of it. In one respect certainly, in the matter of talk as talk, we shone incomparably brighter; and if it took what we had de mieux to make our so regular resort a scene essentially of conversation, the point was none the less that our materials were there. I found the effect of this, very easily, as American as I liked—liked, that is, to think of it and to make all I might of it for being; about which in truth all difficulty vanished from the moment the local colour of the War broke in. So of course this element did at that season come back to us through every outward opening, and mean enough by contrast had been the questions amid which the Vauquer boarders grubbed. Anything even indirectly touched by our public story, stretching now into volume after volume of the very biggest print, took on that reflected light of dignity, of importance, or of mere gross salience, which passion charged with criticism, and criticism charged with the thousand menaced affections and connections, the whole of the reaction—charged in short with immediate intimate life—have a power, in such conditions, to fling as from a waving torch. The torch flared sufficiently about Miss Upham's board—save that she herself, ancient spinster, pushed it in dismay from her top of the table, blew upon it with vain scared sighs, and would have nothing to do with a matter so disturbing to the right temperature of her *plats*. We others passed it from hand to hand, so that it couldn't go quite out—since I must in fairness add that the element of the casual and the more *generally* ironic, the play of the studious or the irrepressibly social intelligence at large, couldn't fail to insist pretty constantly on its rights. There were quarters as well, I should note, in which the sense of local colour proceeding at all straight from the source I have named—reflected, that is, from camp and field—could but very soon run short; sharply enough do I recall for instance the felt, even if all so privately felt, limits of *my* poor stream of contributive remark (despite my habit, so fondly practised in the connection, of expatiating *in petto*). My poor stream would have trickled, truly, had it been able to trickle at all, from the most effective of my few occasions of "realising," up to that time, as to field and camp; literally as to camp in fact, since the occasion had consisted of a visit paid, or a pilgrimage, rather, ever so piously, so tenderly made, one August afternoon of the summer just ended, to a vast gathering of invalid and convalescent troops, under canvas and in roughly improvised shanties, at some point of the Rhode Island shore that figures to my memory, though with a certain vagueness, as Portsmouth Grove. (American local names lend themselves strangely little to retention, I find, if one has happened to deal for long years with almost any group of European designations—these latter springing, as it has almost always come to seem, straight from the soil where natural causes were anciently to root them, each with its rare identity. The bite into interest of the borrowed, the imposed, the "faked" label, growing but as by a dab of glue on an article of trade, is inevitably much less sharp.) Vagueness at best attends, however, the queer experience I glance at; what lives of it, in the ineffaceable way, being again, by my incurable perversity, my ambiguous economy, much less a matter of the "facts of the case," as they should, even though so dead and buried now, revive to help me through an anecdote, than the prodigiously subjective side of the experience, thanks to which it still presumes to flush with the grand air of an adventure. If I had not already so often brazened out my confession of the far from "showy" in the terms on which impressions could become indelibly momentous to me I might blush indeed for the thin tatter dragged in thus as an affair of record. It consisted at the time simply of an emotion—though the emotion, I should add, appeared to consist of everything in the whole world that my consciousness could hold. By *that* intensity did it hang as bravely as possible together, and by the title so made good has it handed itself endlessly down.

Owing to which it is that I don't at all know what troops were in question, a "mere" couple of Rhode Island regiments (nothing in those days could be too big to escape the application of the "mere,") or a congeries of the temporarily incapacitated, the more or less broken, picked from the veterans—so far as there already were such—of the East at large and directed upon the Grove as upon a place of stowage and sanitation. Discriminations of the prosaic order had little to do with my first and all but sole vision of the

American soldier in his multitude, and above all—for that was markedly the colour of the whole thing—in his depression, his wasted melancholy almost; an effect that somehow corresponds for memory, I bethink myself, with the tender elegiac tone in which Walt Whitman was later on so admirably to commemorate him. The restrictions I confess to are abject, but both my sense and my aftersense of the exhibition I here allude to had, thanks to my situation, to do all the work they could in the way of representation to me of what was most publicly, most heroically, most wastefully, tragically, terribly going on. It had so to serve for my particular nearest approach to a "contact" with the active drama—I mean of course the collectively and scenically active, since the brush of interest against the soldier single and salient was an affair of every day—that were it not for just one other strange spasm of awareness, scarce relaxed to this hour, I should have been left all but pitifully void of any scrap of a substitute for the concrete experience. The long hot July 1st of '63, on which the huge battle of Gettysburg had begun, could really be—or rather couldn't possibly not be—a scrap of concrete experience for any group of united persons, New York cousins and all, who, in a Newport garden, restlessly strolling, sitting, neither daring quite to move nor quite to rest, quite to go in nor quite to stay out, actually *listened* together, in their almost ignobly safe stillness, as to the boom of far-away guns. This *was*, as it were, the War—the War palpably in Pennsylvania; not less than my hour of a felt rage of repining at my doomed absence from the sight of that march of the 54th Massachusetts out of Boston, "Bob" Shaw at its head and our exalted Wilky among its officers, of which a great sculptor was, on the spot of their vividest passing, to set the image aloft forever. Poor other visitations, comparatively, had had to suffice for me; I could take in fact for amusing, most of all (since that, thank goodness, was high gaiety), a couple of impressions of the brief preliminary camp life at Readville during which we admired the charming composition of the 44th of the same State, under Colonel Frank Lee, and which fairly made romantic for me Wilky's quick spring out of mere juvenility and into such brightly-bristling ranks. He had begun by volunteering in a company that gave him half the ingenuous youth of the circle within our social ken for brothers-in-arms, and it was to that pair of Readville afternoons I must have owed my all so emphasised vision of handsome young Cabot

187

Russell, who, again to be his closest brother-in-arms in the 54th, irrecoverably lost himself, as we have seen, at Fort Wagner. A dry desert, one must suppose, the life in which, for memory and appreciation made one, certain single hours or compressed groups of hours have found their reason for standing out through everything, for insistently living on, in the cabinet of intimate reference, the museum, as it were, of the soul's curiosities—where doubtless at the same time an exhibition of them to mere other eyes or ears or questioning logical minds may effect itself in no plain terms. We recognise such occasions more and more as we go on, and are surely, as a general thing, glad when, for the interest of memory—which it's such a business to *keep* interesting—they constitute something of a cluster. In my queer cluster, at any rate, that flower of the connection which answers to the name of Portsmouth Grove still overtops other members of its class, so that to finger it again for a moment is to make it perceptibly exhale its very principle of life. This was, for me, at the time, neither more nor less than that the American soldier in his multitude was the most attaching and affecting and withal the most amusing figure of romance conceivable; the great sense of my vision being thus that, as the afternoon light of the place and time lingered upon him, both to the seeming enhancement of his quality and of its own, romance of a more confused kind than I shall now attempt words for attended his every movement. It was the charmingest, touchingest, dreadfullest thing in the world that my impression of him should have to be somehow of his abandonment to a rueful humour, to a stoic reserve which could yet melt, a relation with him once established, into a rich communicative confidence; and, in particular, all over the place, of his own scanted and more or less baffled, though constantly and, as I couldn't not have it, pathetically, "knowing" devices.

The great point remained for me at all events that I could afterwards appear to myself to have done nothing but establish with him a relation, that I established it, to my imagination, in several cases—and all in the three or four hours—even to the pitch of the last tenderness of friendship. I recover that, strolling about with honest and so superior fellow-citizens, or sitting with them by the improvised couches of their languid rest, I drew from each his troubled tale, listened to his plaint on his special hard case—taking form, this, in what seemed to me the very poetry of the esoteric vernacular—and sealed the beautiful tie, the responsive sympathy, by an earnest offer, in no instance waved away, of such pecuniary solace as I might at brief notice draw on my poor pocket for. Yet again, as I indulge this memory, do I feel that I might if pushed a little rejoice in having to such an extent coincided with, not to say perhaps positively anticipated, dear old Walt—even if I hadn't come armed like him with oranges and peppermints. I ministered much more summarily, though possibly in proportion to the time and thanks to my better luck more pecuniarily; but I like to treat myself to making out that I can scarce have brought to the occasion (in proportion to the time again and to other elements of the case) less of the consecrating sentiment than he. I like further to put it in a light that, ever so curiously, if the good Walt was most inwardly stirred to his later commemorative accents by his participating in the common Americanism of his hospital friends, the familiar note and shared sound of which formed its ground of appeal, I found myself victim to a like moving force through quite another logic. It was literally, I fear, because our common Americanism carried with it, to my imagination, such a disclosed freshness and strangeness, working, as I might say, over such gulfs of dissociation, that I reached across to *their*, these hospital friends', side of the matter, even at the risk of an imperilled consistency. It had for me, the state in question, colour and form, accent and quality, with scarce less "authority" than if instead of the rough tracks or worn paths of my casual labyrinth I had trod the glazed halls of some school of natural history. What holds me now indeed is that such an institution might have exemplified then almost nothing but the aspects strictly native to our social and seasonal air; so simply and easily conceivable to the kindly mind were at that time these reciprocities, so great the freedom and pleasure of them compared with the restrictions imposed on directness of sympathy by the awful admixtures of to-day, those which offer to the would-be participant among us, on returns from sojourns wherever homogeneity and its entailed fraternity, its easy contacts, still may be seen to work, the strange shock of such amenities declined on any terms. Really not possible then, I think, the perception now accompanying, on American ground, this shock—the recognition, by any sensibility at all reflective, of the point where our national theory of absorption, assimilation and conversion appallingly breaks down; appallingly, that is, for those to

189

whom the *consecrated* association, of the sort still at play where community has not been blighted, strongly speaks. Which remarks may reinforce the note of my unconsciousness of any difficulty for knowing in the old, the comparatively brothering, conditions what an American at least *was*. Absurd thus, no doubt, that the scant experience over which I perversely linger insists on figuring to me as quite a revel of the right confidence.

The revel, though I didn't for the moment yet know it, was to be renewed for me at Cambridge with less of a romantic intensity perhaps, but more usefully, so to put it, and more informingly; surrounded as I presently found myself at the Law School with young types, or rather with young members of a single type, not one of whom but would have enriched my imagined hall of congruous specimens. *That*, with the many months of it, was to be the real disclosure, the larger revelation; that was to be the fresh picture for a young person reaching the age of twenty in wellnigh grotesque unawareness of the properties of the atmosphere in which he but wanted to claim that he had been nourished. Of what I mean by this I shall in a moment have more to say—after pointing a trifle more, for our patience, the sense of my dilatation upon Portsmouth Grove. Perfectly distinct has remained the sail back to Newport by that evening's steamboat; the mere memory of which indeed—and I recall that I felt it inordinately long—must have been for me, just above, the spring of the whole reference. The sail was long, measured by my acute consciousness of paying physically for my excursion—which hadn't answered the least little bit for my impaired state. This last disobliging fact became one, at the same time, with an intensity, indeed a strange rapture, of reflection, which I may not in the least pretend to offer as a clear or coherent or logical thing, and of which I can only say, leaving myself there through the summer twilight, in too scant rest on a deck stool and against the bulwark, that it somehow crowned my little adventure of sympathy and wonder with a shining round of resignation—a realisation, as we nowadays put it, that, measuring wounds against wounds, or the compromised, the particular taxed condition, at the least, against all the rest of the debt then so generally and enormously due, one was no less exaltedly than wastefully engaged in the common fact of endurance. There are memories in truth too fine or too peculiar for notation, too intensely individual and supersubtle—call them what one will; yet which one may thus no more give up confusedly than one may insist on them vainly. Their kind is nothing ever to a present purpose unless they are in a manner statable, but is at the same time ruefully aware of threatened ridicule if they are overstated. Not that I in the least mind such a menace, however, in just adding that, soothed as I have called the admirable ache of my afternoon with that inward interpretation of it, I felt the latter—or rather doubtless simply the entire affair—absolutely overarched by the majestic manner in which the distress of our return drew out into the lucid charm of the night. To which I must further add that the hour seemed, by some wondrous secret, to know itself marked and charged and unforgettable—hinting so in its very own terms of cool beauty at something portentous in it, an exquisite claim then and there for lasting value and high authority.

X

All of which foregoing makes, I grant, a long parenthesis in my recovery of the more immediate Cambridge impressions. I have left them awaiting me, yet I am happy to say not sensibly the worse for it, in their cluster roundabout Miss Upham and her board of beneficiary images; which latter start up afresh and with the softest submission to any convenient neglect—that ineffably touching and confessed dependence of such apparitions on one's "pleasure," save the mark! for the flicker of restorative light. The image most vividly restored is doubtless that of Professor F. J. Child, head of the "English Department" at Harvard and master of that great modern science of folk-lore to his accomplishment in which his vast and slowly-published collection of the Ballad literature of our language is a recognised monument; delightful man, rounded character, passionate patriot, admirable talker, above all thorough humanist and humorist. He was the genial autocrat of that breakfast-table not only, but of our symposia otherwise timed, and as he comes back to me with the fresh and quite circular countenance of the time before the personal cares and complications of life had gravely thickened for him, his aspect *all* finely circular, with its close rings of the fairest hair, its golden rims of the largest glasses, its finished rotundity of figure and attitude, I see that *there* was the American spirit—since I was "after" it—of a quality deeply inbred, beautifully adjusted to all extensions of knowledge and taste and, as seemed to me, quite sublimely quickened by everything that was at the time so tremendously in question. That vision of him was never afterwards to yield to other lights—though these, even had occasion for them been more frequent with me, couldn't much have interfered with it; so that what I still most retain of him is the very flush and mobility, the living expansion and contraction, the bright comedy and almost lunar eclipse, of his cherubic face according as things appeared to be going for the country. I was always just across from him, as my brother, beside whom I took my place, had been, and I remember well how vivid a clock-face it became to me; I found still, as in my younger time, matter enough everywhere for gaping, but greatest of all, I think, while that tense season lasted, was my wonder for the signs and portents, the quips and cranks, the wreathèd smiles, or otherwise the candid obscurations, of our prime talker's presented visage. I set, as it were, the small tick of my own poor watch by it—which private register would thump or intermit in agreement with these indications. I recover it that, thanks to the perpetual play of his sympathy and irony, confidence and scorn, as well as to that of my own less certainly directed sensibility, he struck me on the bad days, which were then so many, as fairly august, cherubism and all, for sincerity of association with every light and shade, every ebb and flow, of our Cause. Where he most shone out, indeed, so that depression then wasn't a gloom in him but a darting flame, was in the icy air of the attitude of the nations to us, that of the couple, the most potent, across the sea, with which we were especially concerned and which, as during the whole earlier half of the War and still longer it more and more defined itself, drew from him at once all the drolleries and all the asperities of his sarcasm. Nothing more particularly touched me in him, I make out—for it lingers in a light of its own—than the fashion after which he struck me as a fond grave guardian, not so much of the memory and the ashes yet awhile, as of the promise, in all its flower, of the sacrificial young men whom the University connection had passed through his hands and whom he looked out for with a tenderness of interest, a nursing pride, that was as contagious as I could possibly have wished it. I didn't myself know the young men, save three or four, and could only, at our distance, hold my tongue and do them homage; never afterwards (as I even then foreknew would be the case) missing, when I could help it, or failing to pick up, a single brush, a scattered leaf, of their growing or their riper legend. Certain of them whom I had neither seen nor, as they fell in battle, was destined ever to see, have lived for me since just as communicated images, figures created by his tone about them—which, I admit, mightn't or needn't have mattered to me for all the years, yet which couldn't help so doing from the moment the right touch had handed them over to my restless claim.

It was not meanwhile for want of other figures that these were gathered in, for I have again to grant that in those days figures became such for me on easy terms, and that in particular William had only to let the light of *his* attention, his interest, his curiosity, his aversion even (could he indeed

have passingly lived in the helplessness of mere aversion) visibly rest on them
for me entirely to feel that they must count for as much as might be—so far
at least as my perception was concerned, contact being truly another affair.
That was the truth at that season, if it wasn't always to remain the truth; I felt
his interpretations, his personal allowances, so largely and inveterately liberal,
always impose themselves: it was not till ever so much later, and then only little
by little, that I came to accept the strange circumstance of my not invariably
"liking," in homely parlance, his people, and his not invariably liking mine.
The process represented by that word was for each of us, I think, a process
so involved with other operations of the spirit, so beautifully complicated
and deformed by them, that our results in this sort doubtless eventually
lost themselves in the labyrinth of our reasons; which latter, eventually—
the labyrinth, I mean—could be a frequent and not other than animated
meeting-place in spite of the play of divergence. The true case, I all the while
plentifully felt, and still more feel now, was that *I* diverged and my brother
almost never; in the sense, that is, that no man can well have cared less for the
question, or made less of the consciousness, of dislike—have valued less their
developments and comforts. Even the opposite of that complacency scarce
seemed a recognised, or at least in any degree a cultivated, state with him;
his passion, and that a passion of the intelligence, was justice unafraid—and
this, as it were, almost unformulatedly, altogether unpedantically: it simply
made him utterly not "mind" numberless things that with most people serve
as dim lights, warnings or attractions, in the grope of appreciation or the
adventure of instinct. His luminous indifference kept his course thus, as I was
later to recognise, extraordinarily straight—to the increase, as I have noted,
of my own poor sense of weakly straggling, unaccompanied as this at the
same time was by the least envy of such a deficiency in what is roughly called
prejudice, and what I, to save my face, in my ups and downs of sociability or
curiosity, could perhaps have found no better term for than the play of taste
as taste. Wonderful, and to me in the last resort admirable, was William's fine
heritage and awareness of that principle without its yet affecting him on the
human, the more largely social, just the conversable and workable ground—
in presence of some other principle that might do so, whether this validly or
but speciously interfered. The triumph over *dis*taste, in one's relations, one's

exposures, one's judgments, *that* I could understand as high virtue, strained heroism, the ideal groaningly applied; but what left me always impressed, to put it mildly, was the fact that in my brother's case the incorruptibility of his candour would have had to be explained to him, and with scant presumption too of his taking it in or having patience while one spoke. Such an enterprise, I was well aware, would at any rate have left *me* a sorry enough figure afterwards. What one would have had to be, what one could in the least decently be, *except* candid without alternative—this, with other like matters, I should have had to be prepared to set forth; and, more and more addressed as I eventually found myself to a cultivation of the absolute in taste as taste, to repeat my expression, I was far from the wish to contend for it as against any appearance whatever of a better way. Such was part of the experience, or call it even the discipline, of association with a genius so marked for the process known as giving the benefit of the doubt—and giving it (for that was the irritating charm), not in smug charity or for a pointed moral, but through the very nature of a mind incapable of the shut door in any direction and of a habit of hospitality so free that it might again and again have been observed, in contact and intercourse, to supply weaker and less graced vessels with the very means of bringing in response, often absolutely in retort. This last of course was not so much the benefit of the doubt as the displayed unconsciousness of any doubt, a perpetual aid rendered the doubtful, especially when incarnate in persons, to be more right or more true, more clever or more charming or whatever, than mere grudging love of "form," standing by, could at all see it entitled to become. Anything like William's unawareness of exertion after having helped the lame dog of converse over stile after stile I have in no other case met. Together with which, however, I may not forbear to add, the very occasional and comparatively small flare in him of some blest perversity of prejudice that one might enjoy on one's own side the vulgar luxury of naming as such was a thing which, conformably to that elation, one reached out for as one might for the white glint of the rare edelweiss on some high Alpine ledge.

If these remarks illustrate in their number the inevitable bent of the remark to multiply within me as an effect of fraternal evocation I thereby but stick the more to my subject, or in other words to the much-peopled scene, as I found it; which I should scarce have found without him. Peopled as it was with *his* people, which they at first struck me as markedly being, it led me then to take the company, apart from F. J. Child, for whatever he all vividly and possessively pronounced it; I having for a long time but the scantest company of my own, even at the Law School, where my fellow-disciples could bear the name for me only as a troop of actors might have done on that further side of footlights to which I never went round. This last at least with few exceptions, while there were none to the exquisite rule, as I positively to-day feel it, of my apprehension of William's cluster as a concern of his—interesting exactly because of that reference. Any concern of his was thus a thing already charged with life, *his* life over and above its own, if it happened by grace to have any comparable; which, as I pick out the elements again from the savoury Upham shades, could indeed be claimed for several of these. I pick out the ardent and delicate and firm John May, son, as he comes back to me, of a distinguished Abolitionist of New York State—rare bird; and seen by that fact in a sort of glamour of picturesque justification, an air deriving colour from the pre-established gallantry, yet the quiet and gentlemanly triumph, of his attitude. So at least do I read back into blurred visions the richest meanings they could have. I pick out for a not less baffled tribute a particular friend of my brother's and a comrade of May's, whom I identify on the superficial side but by his name of Salter and the fact of his studentship in theology; which pursuit, it comes over me as I write, he must have shared, of homely, almost of sickly, New England type as he was, with May of the fine features, the handsome smile, by my resolute recollection, the developed moustache and short dark pointed beard, the property of vaguely recalling in fine some old portrait supposedly Spanish (supposedly, and perhaps to a fantastic tune, by *me*—for I dare say it was by no one else). Salter had no such references—it even appalled me to have a bit intelligently to imagine to what origins starved of amenity or colour his aspect and air, the slope of his shoulders, the mode of growth of his hair, the relation of his clothes to his person and the relation of his person to the inevitable needs of intercourse, might refer him; but there played about him a bright force in the highest and extraordinarily quick flares of which one felt nothing, while the exhibition lasted, but his intellectual elegance. He had the distinction of wit—so rare, we ever feel it to be, when we see it beautifully act; and I remember well how, as that was indeed for me almost the whole of intellectual elegance, I fell back on the idea that such an odd assortment of marks in him was at least picturesque, or much in the Maison Vauquer line: pinched as I must have been by the question of whether a person of that type and cut had the "right" to be witty. On what else but the power the right rested I couldn't doubtless have said; I but recall my sense that wit was somehow the finest of all social matters and that it seemed impossible to be less connected with such than this product of New England at its sparest and dryest; which fact was a sort of bad mark for the higher civilisation. I was prepared to recognise that you might be witty and ugly, ugly with the highest finish of ugliness—hadn't the celebrated Voltaire been one of the scrappiest of men as well as of the most immortally quoted?—but it cost a wrench to have to take it that you could shine to admiration out of such a platitude of the mere "plain." It was William in especial who guaranteed to me Salter's superior gift, of which in the free commerce of Divinity Hall he had frequent illustration—so that what I really most apprehended, I think, was the circumstance of *his* apprehending: this too with a much finer intellectual need and competence than mine, after all, and in the course of debates and discussions, ardent young symposia of the spirit, which struck me as falling in with all I had ever curiously conceived of those hours that foster the generous youth of minds preappointed to greatness. *There* was the note of the effective quaint on which I could put my finger: catch a poor student only dreary enough and then light in him the flame of irony at its intensest, the range of question and the command of figure at their bravest, and one might, with one's appetite for character, feed on the bold antithesis. I had only to like for my brother, and verily almost with pride, his assured experience of any queer concretion—his experience of abstractions I was to rise to much more feebly and belatedly, scarce more indeed ever than most imperfectly—to find the very scene of action, or at least of passion, enjoyed by these my elders and betters, enriched and toned and consecrated after the fashion of places referred to in literature and legend.

I thus live back of a sudden—for I insist on just yielding to it—into the odd hours when the poor little old Divinity Hall of the overgrown present faced me as through the haze of all the past Indian summers it had opened its brooding study-windows to; when the "avenue" of approach to it from the outer world was a thing of dignity, a positive vista in a composition; when the Norton woods, near by, massed themselves in scarlet and orange, and when to penetrate and mount a stair and knock at a door and, enjoying response, then sink into a window-bench and inhale at once the vague golden November and the thick suggestion of the room where nascent "thought" had again and again piped or wailed, was to taste as I had never done before the poetry of the prime initiation and of associated growth. With cards of such pale pasteboard could the trick, to my vision, play itself—by which I mean that I admire under this memory the constant "dodges" of an imagination reduced to such straits for picking up a living. It was as if one's sense of "Europe," sufficiently sure of itself to risk the strategic retreat, had backed away on tiptoe just to see how the sense of what was there facing one would manage without it—manage for luxury, that is, with the mere indispensable doubtless otherwise provided for. That the sense in question did manage beautifully, when at last so hard pressed, and that the plasticity and variety of my vision draw from me now this murmur of elation, are truths constituting together for me the perhaps even overloaded moral of my tale. With which I scarce need note that so elastic a fancy, so perverse a little passion for finding good in everything—good for what I thought of as history, which was the consideration of life, while the given thing, whatever it was, had only to be before me—was inevitably to work a storage of other material for memory close-packed enough to make such disengagement as I thus attempt at the end of time almost an act of violence. I couldn't do without the *scene*, as I have elsewhere had occasion to hint, whether actually or but possibly peopled (the people always calling for the background and the background insisting on the people); and thanks to this harmless extravagance, or thanks in other words to the visionary liberties I constantly took (so that the plate of sense was at the time I speak of more overscored and figured for me than sense was in the least practically required to have it), my path is even now beset to inconvenience with the personal image unextinct. It presents itself, I feel, beyond reason, and yet if I turn from it the ease is less, and I am divided when I further press the spring between compunction at not pausing before some shade that seems individually and even hopefully to wait, and the fear of its feeling after all scanted of service should I name it only to leave it. I name for instance, just to hover a little, silent Vanderpool, the mutest presence at the Upham board, and quite with no sense of the invidious in so doing. He was save for myself, by my remembrance, the only member of the Law School there present; I see him moreover altogether remarkably, just incorruptibly and exquisitely dumb, though with a "gentlemanly" presence, a quasi-conservative New Jersey finish (so delicate those dim discriminations!) that would have seemed naturally to go with a certain forensic assurance. He looked so as if he came from "good people"—which was no very common appearance on the Harvard scene of those days, as indeed it is to a positive degree no so very common appearance on any scene at any time: it was a note of aspect which one in any case found one's self, to whatever vague tune, apt quite to treasure or save up. So it was impossible not to recognise in our soundless *commensal* the very finest flower of shyness, the very richest shade of the deprecating blush, that one had perhaps ever encountered; one ended in fact by fairly hanging on the question of whether the perfection of his modesty—for it was all a true welter of modesty, not a grain of it anything stiffer—would beautifully hold out or would give way to comparatively brute pressure from some point of our circle. I longed to bet on him, to see him through without a lapse; and this in fact was so thoroughly reserved to me that my eventual relief and homage doubtless account for the blest roundness of my impression. He had so much "for" him, was tall and fine, equipped and appointed, born, quite to an effect of ultimately basking, in the light of the Law, acquainted, one couldn't fail of seeing, with a tradition of manners, not to mention that of the forensic as aforesaid, and not to name either the use of "means," equally imputable: how rare accordingly would be the *quality*, letting even the quantity alone, of his inhibitions, and how interesting in the event the fact that he was absolutely never to have deviated! He disappeared without having spoken, and yet why should I now be noting it if he hadn't nevertheless admirably expressed himself? What this consisted of was that there was scarce anything he wouldn't have done for us had it been possible, and I think, in view of the distinctness with which he still faces me, the tenderness with which he inspires my muse and the assurance with which I have "gone into" him, that I can never in all my life since have seen so precious a message delivered under such difficulties. Admirable, ineffaceable, because so essentially all *decipherable*, Vanderpool!

199

It wasn't either that John Bancroft tossed the ball of talk—which but for the presence of the supremely retentive agent just commemorated would have appeared on occasion to remain in his keeping by a preference, on its own part, not to be outwitted; this more or less at all times too, but especially during the first weeks of his dawning on us straight out of Germany and France, flushed with the alarm, as one might have read it, of having to justify rare opportunities and account for the time he had inordinately, obscurely, or at least not a little mysteriously, spent—the implication of every inch of him being that he had spent it seriously. Odd enough it certainly was that we should have been appointed to unveil, so far as we might, a *pair* of such marked monuments to modesty, marble statues, as they might have been, on either side of the portal of talk; what I at any rate preserve of my immediate vision of Bancroft—whose very promptest identity indeed had been his sonship to the eminent historian of our country and earlier and later diplomatist—was an opposition, trying to me rather than engaging as its like had been in the composition of Vanderpool, between what we somehow wanted from him (or what I at least did) and what we too scantly gathered. This excellent friend, as he was later on to become, with his handsome high head, large colourable brow and eyes widely divided—brave contribution ever to a fine countenance—sat there in a sort of glory of experience which, had he been capable of anything so akin to a demonstration, he would have appeared all unsociably to repudiate. It was bruited of him that, like John La Farge, whose friend he was admiringly to become—for he too had a Newport connection—he "painted," that is persisted (which was the wondrous thing!) in painting; and that this practice had grown upon him in France, where, *en province*, his brother had entirely taken root and where the whole art-life, as well as the rural life, of the country had been opened to him; besides its a little later coming to light that he had romantically practised at Dusseldorf, where too he had personally known and tremendously liked George du Maurier, whose first so distinguished appearances as an illustrator had already engaged our fondest attention—were they most dawningly in the early Cornhill, or in Punch, or in Once a Week? They glimmer upon me, darkly and richly, as from the pages of the last named. Not to be rendered, I may again parenthesise, our little thrilled awareness, William's and mine, though mine indeed but panting after his, of such peeping phenomena of the European day as the outbreak of a "new man" upon our yearning view of the field of letters and of the arts. I am moved to wonder at how we came by it, shifting all for ourselves, and with the parental *flair*, so far as the sensibility of home was concerned, turned but to directions of its own and much less restless on the whole than ours. More touching to me now than I can say, at all events, this recapture of the hour at which Du Maurier, consecrated to much later, to then still far-off intimate affection, became the new man so significantly as to make a great importance of John Bancroft's news of him, which already bore, among many marvels, upon the supreme wonder of his working, as he was all his life bravely to work, under impaired and gravely menaced eyesight. When I speak, as just above, of what, through so many veils, "came to light," I should further add, I use a figure representing a considerable lapse of time and shading off, for full evocation, into more associations than I can here make place for. Nothing in this connection came *soon* to light at least but that endless amazement might lie in the strange facts of difference between our companion and his distinguished sire—the latter so supremely, so quaintly yet so brilliantly, social a figure, I apprehended, when gaped at, a still more angular, but more polished and pacific Don Quixote, on the sleekest of Rosinantes, with white-tipped chin protrusive, with high sharp elbows raised and long straight legs beautifully pointed, all after the gallantest fashion, against the clear sunset sky of old Newport cavalcades. Mr. Bancroft the elder, the "great," was a comfort, that is a fine high identity, a cluster of strong accents, the sort of thing one's vision followed, in the light of history, if not of mere misguided fancy, for illustration of conceived type—type, say in this case, of superior person of the ancient and the more or less alien public order, the world of affairs transacted at courts and *chancelleries*, in which renown, one had gathered from the perusal of memoirs, allowed for much development of detail and much incision of outline, when not even directly resting on them. As it had been a positive bliss to me that words and names might prove in extremity sources of support, so it comes back to me that I had drawn mystic strength from just obscurely sighing "Metternich!" or "Talleyrand!" as Mr. Bancroft bounced by me— so far as a pair of widely-opened compasses might bounce—in the August gloaming. The value of which, for reflection, moreover, was not in the least in

201

its being that if his son remained so long pleadingly inscrutable any derived Metternich suggestion had contributed to keep him so—for quite *there* was the curiosity of the case, that among the imputations John appeared most to repudiate was that of having at any moment breathed the air either of records or of protocols. If he persisted in painting for years after his return to America without, as the legend grew, the smallest disclosure of his work or confession of his progress to human eye or ear, he drew the rigour of this course wholly from his singleness of nature, in the aftertime to be so much approved to us. However, I pause before the aftertime, into the lap of which more than one sort of stored soundness and sweetness was to fall from him drop by drop.

I scarce know whether my impulse to lead forth these most shrinking of my apparitions be more perverse or more natural—mainly feeling, I confess, however it appear, that the rest of my impression of the animated Cambridge scene, so far as I could take it in, was anything but a vision of unasserted forces. It was only I, as now appears to me, who, ready as yet to assert nothing, hung back, and for reasons even more appreciable to me to-day than then; wondering, almost regretting as I do, that I didn't with a still sharper promptness throw up the sponge for stoppage of the absurd little boxing-match within me between the ostensible and the real—this I mean because I might afterwards thereby have winced a couple of times the less in haunting remembrance of exhibited inaptitude. My condition of having nothing to exhibit was blessedly one that there was nobody to quarrel with—and I couldn't have sufficiently let it alone. I didn't in truth, under a misleading light, reconsider it much; yet I have kept to this hour a black little memory of my having attempted to argue one afternoon, by way of exercise and under what seemed to me a perfect glare of publicity, the fierce light of a "moot-court," some case proposed to me by a fellow-student—who can only have been one of the most benign of men unless he was darkly the designingest, and to whom I was at any rate to owe it that I figured my shame for years much in the image of my having stood forth before an audience with a fiddle and bow and trusted myself to rub them together desperately enough (after the fashion of Rousseau in a passage of the Confessions,) to make some appearance of music. My music, I recall, before the look on the faces around me, quavered away into mere collapse and cessation, a void now engulfing memory itself, so that I liken it all to a merciful fall of the curtain on some actor stricken and stammering. The sense of the brief glare, as I have called the luckless exposure, revives even on this hither side of the wide gulf of time; but I must have outlived every witness—I was so obviously there the very youngest of all aspirants—and, in truth, save for one or two minor and merely comparative miscarriages of the sacrificial act before my false gods, my connection with the temple was to remain as consistently superficial as could be possible to a relation still restlessly perceptive through all its profaneness. Perceiving, even with its accompaniments of noting, wondering, fantasticating, kicked up no glare, but went on much rather under richest shades or in many-coloured lights—a *tone* of opportunity that I look back on as somehow at once deliciously soothing to myself and favourable to the clearness of each item of the picture even as the cool grey sky of a landscape is equalising. That was of course especially when I had let everything slide—everything but the mere act of rather difficultly living (by reason of my scant physical ease,) and fallen back again on the hard sofa of certain ancient rooms in the Winthrop Square, contracted nook, of a local order now quite abolished, and held to my nose for long and sustaining sniffs the scented flower of independence. I took my independence for romantic, or at least for a happy form of yawning vessel into which romance, even should it perforce consist but of mere loose observational play, might drop in the shape of ripe fruit from a shaken tree. Winthrop Square, as I had occasion to note a couple of years since, is a forgotten name, and the disappearance of my lodging spares me doubtless a reminder, possibly ironic, of the debility of those few constructional and pictorial elements that, mustering a wondrous good-will, I had invited myself to rejoice in as "colonial." The house was indeed very old, as antiquity in Cambridge went, with everything in it slanting and gaping and creaking, but with humble antique "points" and a dignity in its decay; above all with the deep recess or alcove, a sweet "irregularity" (so could irregularities of architectural conception then and there count,) thrust forth from its sitting-room toward what I supposed to be the Brighton hills and forming, by the aid of a large window and that commanding view, not to mention the grace of an ancient expansive bureau or secretary-desk (this such a piece, I now venture to figure, as would to-day be pounced on at any cunning dealer's,) a veritable bower toward which even so shy a dreamer as I still then had to take myself for might perhaps hope to woo the muse. The muse was of course the muse of prose fiction—never for the briefest hour in my case the presumable, not to say the presuming, the much-taking-for-granted muse of rhyme, with whom I had never had, even in thought, the faintest flirtation; and she did, in the event, I note, yield to the seduction of so appointed a nook—as to which romantic passage, however, I may not here anticipate. I but lose myself in the recovered sense of what it richly "meant" to me just to *have* a place where I could so handsomely receive her, where I could remark with complacency that the distant horizon, an horizon long since rudely obliterated, was not, after all, too humble to be blue, purple, tawny, changeable in short, everything an horizon should be, and that over the intervening marshes of the Charles (if I don't go astray in so much geography) there was all the fine complicated cloud-scenery I could wish—so extravagantly did I then conceive more or less associational cloud-scenery, after the fashion, I mean, of that feature of remembered English and Boulognese water-colours, to promote the atmosphere of literary composition as the act had begun to glimmer for me.

Everything, however, meant, as I say, more quite other things than I can pretend now to treat of. The mere fact of a sudden rupture, as by the happiest thought, with the "form" of bringing home from the Law-library sheepskin volumes that might give my table, if not, for sufficiency of emphasis, my afflicted self, a temporary countenance, heaped up the measure of my general intention—from the moment I embraced instead of it the practice of resorting to Gore Hall exclusively for my reading-matter; a practice in the light of which my general intention took on the air of absolutely basking. To get somehow, and in spite of everything, in spite especially of being so much disabled, at life, *that* was my brooding purpose, straight out of which the College library, with its sparse bristle of aspiring granite, stood open to far more enchanted distances than any represented by the leathery walls, with never a breach amid their labelled and numbered blocks, that I might pretend to beat against in the other quarter. Yet, happily enough, on this basis of general rather than of special culture, I still loosely rejoiced in being where I was, and by way of proof that it was all right the swim into my ken of Sainte-Beuve, for whose presence on my table, in still other literary company,

Gore Hall aiding, I succeeded in not at all blushing, became in the highest degree congruous with regular attendance at lectures. The forenoon lectures at Dane Hall I never in all my time missed, that I can recollect, and I look back on it now as quite prodigious that I should have been so systematically faithful to them without my understanding the first word of what they were about. They contrived—or at least my attendance at them did, inimitably—to be "life;" and as my wondering dips into the vast deep well of the French critic to whom all my roused response went out brought up that mystery to me in cupfuls of extraordinary savour, where was the incongruity of the two rites? That the Causeries du Lundi, wholly fresh then to my grateful lips, should so have overflowed for me was certainly no marvel—that prime acquaintance absolutely *having*, by my measure, to form a really sacred date in the development of any historic or aesthetic consciousness worth mentioning; but that I could be to the very end more or less thrilled by simply sitting, all stupid and sentient, in the thick company of my merely nominal associates and under the strange ministrations of Dr. Theophilus Parsons, "Governor" Washburn and Professor Joel Parker, would have appeared to defy explanation only for those by whom the phenomena of certain kinds of living and working sensibility are unsuspected. For myself at any rate there was no anomaly—the anomaly would have been much rather in any prompter consciousness of a sated perception; I knew why I liked to "go," I knew even why I could unabashedly keep going in face of the fact that if I had learned my reason I had learned, and was still to learn, absolutely nothing else; and that sufficiently supported me through a stretch of bodily overstrain that I only afterwards allowed myself dejectedly to measure. The mere sitting at attention for two or three hours—such attention as I achieved—was paid for by sorry pain; yet it was but later on that I wondered how I could have found what I "got" an equivalent for the condition produced. The condition was one of many, and the others for the most part declared themselves with much of an equal, though a different, sharpness. It was acute, that is, that one was so incommoded, but it had broken upon me with force from the first of my taking my seat—which had the advantage, I acknowledge, of the rim of the circle, symbolising thereby all the detachment I had been foredoomed to—that the whole scene was going to be, and again and again, as "American," and above all as suffused with New England colour, however one might finally estimate that, as I could possibly have wished. Such was the effect of one's offering such a plate for impressions to play on at their will; as well as of one's so failing to ask in advance what they would matter, so taking for granted that they would all matter somehow. It would matter somehow for instance that just a queer dusky half smothered light, as from windows placed too low, or too many interposing heads, should hang upon our old auditorium—long since voided of its then use and, with all its accessory chambers, seated elsewhere afresh and in much greater state; which glimpse of a scheme of values might well have given the measure of the sort of profit I was, or rather wasn't, to derive. It doubtless quite ought to have confounded me that I had come up to *faire mon droit* by appreciations predominantly of the local chiaroscuro and other like quantities; but I remember no alarm—I only remember with what complacency my range of perception on those general lines was able to spread.

It mattered, by the same law, no end that Dr. Theophilus Parsons, whose rich, if slightly quavering, old accents were the first to fall upon my ear from the chair of instruction beneath a huge hot portrait of Daniel Webster should at once approve himself a vivid and curiously-composed person, an *illustrative* figure, as who should say—exactly with all the marks one might have wished him, marks of a social order, a general air, a whole history of things, or in other words of people; since there was nothing one mightn't, by my sentiment, do with such a subject from the moment it gave out character. Character thus was all over the place, as it could scarce fail to be when the general subject, the one gone in for, had become identical with the persons of all its votaries. Such was the interest of the source of edification just named, not one ray of whose merely professed value so much as entered my mind. Governor Washburn was of a different, but of a no less complete consistency— queer, ingenuous, more candidly confiding, especially as to his own pleasant fallibility, than I had ever before known a chaired dispenser of knowledge, and all after a fashion that endeared him to his young hearers, whose resounding relish of the frequent tangle of his apologetic returns upon himself, quite, almost always, to inextricability, was really affectionate in its freedom. I could understand and admire that—it seemed to have for me legendary precedents;

whereas of the third of our instructors I mainly recall that he represented dryness and hardness, prose unrelieved, at their deadliest—partly perhaps because he was most master of his subject. He was none the less placeable for these things withal, and what mainly comes back to me of him is the full sufficiency with which he made me ask myself how I *could* for a moment have seen myself really browse in any field where the marks of the shepherd were such an oblong dome of a bare cranium, such a fringe of dropping little ringlets toward its base, and a mouth so meanly retentive, so ignorant of style, as I made out, above a chin so indifferent to the duty, or at least to the opportunity, of chins. If I had put it to myself that there was no excuse for the presence of a young person so affected by the idea of how people looked on a scene where the issue was altogether what they usefully taught, as well as intelligently learned and wanted to learn, I feel I should, after my first flush of confusion, have replied assuredly enough that just the beauty of the former of these questions was in its being of equal application everywhere; which was far from the case with the latter. The question of how people looked, and of how their look counted for a thousand relations, had risen before me too early and kept me company too long for me not to have made a fight over it, from the very shame of appearing at all likely to give it up, had some fleeting delusion led me to cast a slur upon it. It would do, I was already sure, half the work of carrying me through life, and where was better proof of all it would have to give than just in the fact of what it was then and there doing? It worked for appreciation—not one of the uses of which as an act of intelligence had, all round, finer connections; and on the day, in short, when one should cease to live in large measure by one's eyes (with the imagination of course all the while waiting on this) one would have taken the longest step towards not living at all. My companions—however scantly indeed they were to become such—were subject to my so practising in a degree which represented well-nigh the whole of my relation with them, small reciprocity for them as there may have been in it; since vision, and nothing but vision, was from beginning to end the fruit of my situation among them. There was not one of them as to whom it didn't matter that he "looked," by my fancy of him, thus or so; the key to this disposition of the accents being for me to such an extent that, as I have said, I was with all intensity taking in New England

and that I knew no better *immediate* way than to take it in by my senses. What that name really comprehended had been a mystery, daily growing less, to which everything that fell upon those senses referred itself, making the innumerable appearances hang together ever so densely. Theophilus Parsons, with his tone, his unction, his homage still to some ancient superstition, some standard of manners, reached back as to a state of provincialism rounded and compact, quite self-supporting, which gave it serenity and quality, something comparatively rich and urban; the good ex-Governor, on the other hand, of whom I think with singular tenderness, opened through every note of aspect and expression straight into those depths of rusticity which more and more unmistakably underlay the social order at large and out of which one felt it to have emerged in any degree but at scattered points. Where it did emerge, I seemed to see, it held itself as high as possible, conscious, panting a little, elate with the fact of having cleared its skirts, saved its life, consolidated its Boston, yet as with wastes unredeemed, roundabout it, propping up and pushing in—all so insistently that the light in which one for the most part considered the scene was strongly coloured by their action. This was one's clue to the labyrinth, if labyrinth it was to be called—a generalisation into which everything fitted, first to surprise and then indubitably to relief, from the moment one had begun to make it. Under its law the Puritan capital, however visibly disposed to spread and take on new disguises, affected me as a rural centre even to a point at which I had never known anything as rural; there being involved with this too much further food for curiosity and wonder. Boston was in a manner of its own stoutly and vividly urban, not only a town, but a town of history—so that how did it manage to be such different things at the same time? That was doubtless its secret—more and more interesting to study in proportion as, on closer acquaintance, yet an acquaintance before which the sense of one's preferred view from outside never gave way, one felt the equilibrium attained as on the whole an odd fusion and intermixture, of the chemical sort as it were, and not a matter of elements or aspects sharply alternating. There was in the exhibition at its best distinctly a savour—an excellent thing for a community to have, and part of the savour was, as who should say, the breath of the fields and woods and waters, though at their domesticated and familiarised stage, or the echo of a tone which had somehow become that of the most educated of our societies without ceasing to be that of the village.

Of so much from the first I felt sure, and this all the more that by my recollection of New York, even indeed by my recollection of Albany, we had been aware in those places of no such strain. New York at least had been whatever disagreeable, not to say whatever agreeable, other thing one might have declared it—it might even have been vulgar, though that cheap substitute for an account of anything didn't, I think, in the connection, then exist for me; but the last reference to its nature likely to crop up in its social soil was beyond question the flower of the homely. New England had, by one's impression, cropped up there, but had done so just *as* New England, New England unabsorbed and unreconciled; which was exactly a note in the striated, the piebald or, more gracefully, cosmopolite local character. I am not sure that the comparatively—I say comparatively—market-town suggestion of the city by the Charles came out for me as a positive richness, but it did essentially contribute to what had become so highly desirable, the reinforcement of my vision of American life by the idea of variety. I apparently required of anything I should take to my heart that it should be, approached at different angles, "like" as many other things as possible—in accordance with which it made for a various "America" that Boston should seem really strong, really in not having, for better or worse, the same irrepressible likenesses as New York. I invoked, I called down the revelation of, new likenesses by the simple act of threading the Boston streets, whether by garish day (the afterglow of the great snowfalls of winter was to turn in particular to a blinding glare, an unequalled hardness of light,) or under that mantle of night which draped as with the garb of adventure our long-drawn townward little rumbles in the interest of the theatre or of Parker's—oh the sordid, yet never in the least deterrent conditions of transit in that age of the unabbreviated, the dividing desert and the primitive horse-car! (The desert is indeed, despite other local developments and the general theory of the rate at which civilisation spreads and ugliness wanes, still very much what it was in the last mid-century, but the act of passage through it has been made to some extent easier.) Parker's played in the intercourse of Cambridge with Boston a part of a preponderance that I look back upon, I confess, as the very condition of the purest felicity we knew—I knew at any rate myself none, whether of a finer or a grosser strain, that competed with this precious relation. Competition has thickened since and proportions have altered—to no small darkening of the air, but the time was surely happier; a single such *point de repère* not only sufficed but richly heaped up the measure. Parker's, on the whole side of the joy of life, *was* Boston—speaking as under the thrill of early occasions recaptured; Boston could be therefore, in the acutest connections, those of young comradeship and young esthetic experience, heaven save the mark, fondly prepared or properly crowned, but the enjoyed and shared repast, literally the American feast, as I then appraised such values; a basis of native abundance on which everything else rested. The theatre, resorted to whenever possible, rested indeed doubtless most, though with its heaviest weight thrown perhaps at a somewhat later time; the theatre my uncanny appetite for which strikes me as almost abnormal in the light of what I braved to reach it from the studious suburb, or more particularly braved to return from it. I touch alas no spring that doesn't make a hum of memories, and pick them over as I will three or four of that scenic strain linger on my sense. The extraordinary fact about these—which plays into my generalisation a little way back—was that, for all the connection of such occasions with the great interest of the theatre at large, there was scarce an impression of the stage wrung from current opportunity that didn't somehow underscore itself with the special Boston emphasis; and this in spite of the fact that plays and performers in those days were but a shade less raggedly itinerant over the land than they are now. The implication of the provincial in the theatric air, and of the rustic in the provincial, may have been a matter of the "house" itself, with its twenty kinds of redolence of barbarism—with the kind determined by the very audience perhaps indeed plainest; vivid to me at all events is it how I felt even at the time, in repairing to the Howard Atheneum to admire Miss Maggie Mitchell and Miss Kate Bateman, that one would have had only to scratch a little below the surface of the affair to come upon the but half-buried Puritan curse not so very long before devoted to such perversities. Wasn't the curse still in the air, and could anything less than a curse, weighing from far back on the general conscience, have accounted for one could scarce say what want of self-respect in the total exhibition?—for that intimation more than anything else perhaps of the underhand snicker with which one sat so oddly associated. By the blest law of youth and fancy withal one did admire the actress— the young need to admire as flatly as one could broke through all crowding apprehensions. I like to put it down that nothing in the world qualified my wonder at the rendering by the first of the performers I have named of the figure of "Fanchon the Cricket" in a piece so entitled, an artless translation from a German original, if I rightly remember, which original had been an arrangement for the stage of La Petite Fadette, George Sand's charming rustic idyll. I like to put it down that Miss Maggie Mitchell's having for years, as I gathered, twanged that one string and none other; every night of her theatric life, over the huge country, before she was revealed to us—just as Mr. Joe Jefferson, with no word of audible reprehension ever once addressed to him, was to have twanged his—did nothing to bedim the brightness of our vision or the apparent freshness of her art, and that above all it seemed a privilege critically to disengage the delicacy of this art and the rare effect of the natural in it from the baseness in which it was framed: so golden a glimmer is shed, as one looks back, from any shaky little torch lighted, by whatever fond stretch, at the high esthetic flame. Upon these faint sparks in the night of time would I gently breathe, just to see them again distinguishably glow, rather than leave their momentary function uncommemorated. Strange doubtless were some of the things that represented these momentary functions—strange I mean in proportion to the fires they lighted. The small bower of the muse in Winthrop Square was first to know the fluttered descent of the goddess to my appeal for her aid in the composition of a letter from which the admired Miss Maggie should gather the full force of my impression. Particularly do I incline even now to mention that she testified to her having gratefully gathered it by the despatch to me in return of a little printed copy of the play, a scant pamphlet of "acting edition" humility, addressed in a hand which assumed a romantic cast as soon as I had bethought myself of finding for it a happy precedent in that of Pendennis's Miss Fotheringay.

It had been perhaps to the person of this heroine that Pendennis especially rendered homage, while I, without illusions, or at least without confusions, was fain to discriminate in favour of the magic of method, that is of genius, itself; which exactly, more than anything else could have done (success, as I considered, crowning my demonstration,) contributed to consecrate to an exquisite use, *the* exquisite, my auspicious *réduit* aforesaid. For an esthetic vibration to whatever touch had but to be intense enough to tremble on into other reactions under other blest contacts and commotions. It was by the operation again of the impulse shaking me up to an expression of what the elder star of the Howard Atheneum had artistically "meant" to me that I first sat down beside my view of the Brighton hills to enrol myself in the bright band of the fondly hoping and fearfully doubting who count the days after the despatch of manuscripts. I formally addressed myself under the protection, not to say the inspiration, of Winthrop Square to the profession of literature, though nothing would induce me now to name the periodical on whose protracted silence I had thus begun to hang with my own treasures of reserve to match it. The bearing of which shy ecstasies—shy of exhibition then, that is, save as achievements recognised—is on their having thus begun, at any rate, to supply all the undertone one needed to whatever positive perfunctory show; the show proceeding as it could, all the while, thanks to much help from the undertone, which felt called upon at times to be copious. It is not, I allow, that memory may pretend for me to keep the two elements of the under and the over always quite distinct—it would have been a pity all round, in truth, should they have altogether escaped mixing and fraternising. The positive perfunctory show, at all events, to repeat my term, hitched itself along from point to point, and could have no lack of outside support to complain of, I reflect, from the moment I could make my own every image and incitement—those, as I have noted, of the supply breaking upon me with my first glimpse of the Cambridge scene. If I seem to make too much of these it is because I at the time made still more, more even than my pious record has presumed to set down. The air of truth doubtless hangs uneasy, as the matter stands, over so queer a case as my having, by my intimation above, found appreciability in life at the Law School even under the failure for me of everything generally drawn upon for it, whether the glee of study, the ardour of battle or the joy of associated adventure. Not to have felt earlier sated with the mere mechanic amusement or vain form of regularity at lectures would strike me to-day as a fact too "rum" for belief if certain gathered flowers by the way, flowers of perverse appreciation though they might but be, didn't give out again as I turn them over their unspeakable freshness. They were perforce gathered (what makes it still more wondrous) all too languidly; yet they massed themselves for my sense, through the lapsing months, to the final semblance of an intimate secret garden. Such was the odd, the almost overwhelming consequence—or one of these, for they are many—of an imagination to which literally everything obligingly signified. One of the actual penalties of this is that so few of such ancient importances remain definable or presentable. It may in the fulness of time simply sound *bête* that, with the crash of greater questions about one, I should have been positively occupied with such an affair as the degree and the exact shade to which the blest figures in the School array, each quite for himself, might settle and fix the weight, the interest, the function, as it were, of his Americanism. I could scarce have cleared up even for myself, I dare say, the profit, or more pertinently the charm, of that extravagance—and the fact was of course that I didn't feel it as extravagance, but quite as homely thrift, moral, social, esthetic, or indeed, as I might have been quite ready to say, practical and professional. It was practical at least in the sense that it probably more helped to pass the time than all other pursuits together. The real proof of which would be of course my being able now to string together for exhibition some of these pearls of differentiation—since it was to differentiation exactly that I was then, in my innocence, most prompted; not dreaming of the stiff law by which, on the whole American ground, division of *type*, in the light of opposition and contrast, was more and more to break down for me and fail: so that verily the recital of my mere concomitant efforts to pick it up again and piece its parts together and make them somehow show and serve would be a record of clinging courage. I may note at once, however, as a light on the anomaly, that there hung about *all* young appearances at that period something ever so finely derivative and which at this day rather defies re-expression—the common character or shared function of the precious clay so largely making up the holocausts of battle; an advantage working for them circuitously or perhaps ambiguously enough, I grant, but still placing them more or less under the play of its wing even when the arts of peace happened for the hour to engage them. They potentially, they conceivably, they indirectly paid, and nothing was for the most part more ascertainable of them individually than

213

that, with brothers or other near relatives in the ranks or in commands, they came, to their credit, of paying families. All of which again may represent the high pitch of one's associated sensibility—there having been occasions of crisis, were they worth recovering, when under its action places, persons, objects animate or not, glimmered alike but through the grand idealising, the generalising, blur. At moments of less fine a strain, it may be added, the sources of interest presented themselves in looser formation. The young appearances, as I like to continue to call them, could be pleasingly, or at least robustly homogeneous, and yet, for livelier appeal to fancy, flower here and there into special cases of elegant deviation—"sports," of exotic complexion, one enjoyed denominating these (or would have enjoyed had the happy figure then flourished) thrown off from the thick stem that was rooted under our feet. Even these rare exceptions, the few apparitions referring themselves to other producing conditions than the New England, wrought by contrast no havoc in the various quantities for which that section was responsible; it was certainly refreshing—always to the fond imagination—that there were, for a change, imprints in the stuff of youth that didn't square with the imprint, virtually *one* throughout, imposed by Springfield or Worcester, by Providence or Portland, or whatever rural wastes might lie between; yet the variations, I none the less gather as I strive to recall them, beguiled the spirit (talking always of my own) rather than coerced it, and this even though fitting into life as one had already more or less known it, fitting in, that is, with more points of contact and more reciprocation of understanding than the New England relation seemed able to produce. It could in fact fairly blind me to the implication of an inferior immediate *portée* that such and such a shape of the New York heterogeneity, however simplified by silliness, or at least by special stupidity (though who was I to note *that?*) pressed a certain spring of association, waiting as I always was for such echoes, rather than left it either just soundless or bunglingly touched.

It was for example a link with the larger life, as I am afraid I must have privately called it, that a certain young New Yorker, an outsider of still more unmistakable hue than I could suppose even myself, came and went before us with an effect of cultivated detachment that I admired at the time for its perfect consistency, and that caused him, it was positively thrilling to note, not in the least to forfeit sympathy, but to shine in the high light of public favour. The richest reflections sprang for me from this, some of them inspiring even beyond the promptly grasped truth, a comparative commonplace, that the variation or opposition sufficiently embodied, the line of divergence sharply enough drawn, always achieves some triumph by the fact of its emphasis, by its putting itself through at any cost, any cost in particular of ridicule. So much one had often observed; but what really enriched the dear induction and made our friend's instance thus remain with me was the part played by the utter blandness itself of his protest, such an exhibition of the sweet in the imperturbable. This it was that enshrined him, by my vision, in a popularity than which nothing could have seemed in advance less indicated, and that makes me wonder to-day whether he was simply the luckiest of gamblers or just a conscious and consummate artist. He reappears to me as a finished fop, finished to possibilities we hadn't then dreamt of, and as taking his stand, or rather taking all his walks, on *that*, the magician's wand of his ideally tight umbrella under his arm and the magician's familiar of his bristling toy-terrier at his heels. He became thus an apparition entrancing to the mind. His clothes were of a perfection never known nor divined in that sphere, a revelation, straight and blindingly authentic, of Savile Row in its prime; his single eyeglass alone, and his inspired, his infinite use of it as at once a defensive crystal wall and a lucid window of hospitality, one couldn't say most which, might well have foredoomed him, by all likelihood, to execration and destruction. He became none the less, as I recover him, our general pride and joy; his entrances and exits were acclaimed beyond all others, and it was his rare privilege to cause the note of derision and the note of affection to melt together, beyond separation, in vague but virtual homage to the refreshment of felt type. To see it dawn upon rude breasts (for rude, comparatively, were the breasts of the typeless, or at the best of the typed but in one character, throughout the same,) that defiant and confident difference carried far enough might avert the impulse to slay, was to muse ever so agreeably on the queer means by which great morals, picking up a life as they may, can still get themselves pointed. The "connotation" of the trivial, it was thus attaching to remark, could perfectly serve when that of the important, roughly speaking, failed for a grateful *connection*—from the moment some such was massed invitingly in view. The difficulty with the type about me was that, in its monotony, beginning and ending with itself, it *had* no connections and suggested none; whereas the grace of the salient apparition I have perhaps too earnestly presented lay in its bridging over our separation from worlds, from great far-off reservoirs, of a different mixture altogether, another civility and complexity. Young as I was, I myself clearly recognised that ground of reference, saw it even to some extent in the light of experience—so could I stretch any scrap of contact; kept hold of it by fifty clues, recalls and reminders that dangled for me mainly out of books and magazines and heard talk, things of picture and story, things of prose and verse and anecdotal vividness in fine, and, as I have elsewhere allowed, for the most part hoardedly English and French. Our "character man" of the priceless monocle and the trotting terrier was "like" some type in a collection of types—that was the word for it; and, there being no collection, nor the ghost of one, roundabout us, was a lone courageous creature in the desert of our bald reiterations. The charm of which conclusion was exactly, as I have said, that the common voice did, by every show, bless him for rendered service, his dropped hint of an ideal containing the germ of other ideals—and confessed by that fact to more appetites and inward yearnings than it the least bit consciously counted up.

Not quite the same service was rendered by G. A. J., who had no ridicule to brave, and I can speak with confidence but of the connections, rather confused if they were, opened up to me by his splendid aspect and which had absolutely nothing in common with the others that hung near. It was brilliant to a degree that none other had by so much as a single shade the secret of, and it carried the mooning fancy to a further reach even, on the whole, than the figure of surprise I have just commemorated; this last comparatively scant in itself and rich only by what it made us read into it, and G. A. J. on the other hand intrinsically and actively ample and making us read wonders, as it were, into whatever it might be that was, as we used to say, "back of" him. He had such a flush of life and presence as to make that reference mysteriously and inscrutably loom—and the fascinating thing about this, as we again would have said, was that it could strike me as so beguilingly American. That too was part of the glamour, that its being so could kick up a mystery which one might have pushed on to explore, whereas our New York friend only kicked up a certainty (for those properly prepared) and left not exploration, but mere assured satisfaction, the mark of the case. G. A. J. reached westward, westward even of New York, and southward at least as far as Virginia; teeming facts that I discovered, so to speak, by my own unaided intelligence—so little were they responsibly communicated. Little was communicated that I recover—it would have had to drop from too great a personal height; so that the fun, as I may call it, was the greater for my opening all by myself to perceptions. I was getting furiously American, in the big sense I invoked, through this felt growth of an ability to reach out westward, southward, anywhere, everywhere, on that apprehension of finding myself but patriotically charmed. Thus there dawned upon me the grand possibility that, charm for charm, the American, the assumed, the postulated, would, in the particular case of its really acting, count double; whereas the European paid for being less precarious by being also less miraculous. It counted single, as one might say, and only made up for that by counting almost always. It mightn't be anything like almost always, even at the best, no doubt, that an American-grown value of aspect would so entirely emerge as G. A. J.'s seemed to do; but what did this exactly point to unless that the rarity so implied would be in the nature of the splendid? That at least was the way the cultivation of patriotism as a resource was the cultivation of workable aids to the same, however ingenious these. (Just to glow belligerently with one's country was no resource, but a primitive instinct breaking through; and besides this resources were cooling, not heating.) It might have seemed that I might after all perfectly dispense with friends when simple acquaintances, and rather feared ones at that, though feared but for excess of lustre, could kindle in the mind such bonfires of thought, feeding the flame with gestures and sounds and light accidents of passage so beyond their own supposing. In spite of all which, however, G. A. J. was marked for a friend and taken for a kinsman from the day when his blaze of colour should have sufficiently cleared itself up for me to distinguish the component shades.

XI

I am fully aware while I go, I should mention, of all that flows from the principle governing, by my measure, these recoveries and reflections—even to the effect, hoped for at least, of stringing their apparently dispersed and disordered parts upon a fine silver thread; none other than the principle of response to a long-sought occasion, now gratefully recognised, for making trial of the recording and figuring act on behalf of some case of the imaginative faculty under cultivation. The personal history, as it were, of an imagination, a lively one of course, in a given and favourable case, had always struck me as a task that a teller of tales might rejoice in, his advance through it conceivably causing at every step some rich precipitation—unless it be rather that the play of strong imaginative passion, passion strong enough to *be*, for its subject or victim, the very interest of life, constitutes in itself an endless crisis. Fed by every contact and every apprehension, and feeding in turn every motion and every act, wouldn't the light in which it might so cause the whole scene of life to unroll inevitably become as fine a thing as possible to represent? The idea of some pretext for such an attempt had again and again, naturally, haunted me; the man of imagination, and of an "awfully good" one, showed, as the creature of that force or the sport of that fate or the wielder of that arm, for the hero of a hundred possible fields—if one could but first "catch" him, after the fashion of the hare in the famous receipt. Who and what might he prove, when caught, in respect to *other* signs and conditions? He might take, it would seem, some finding and launching, let alone much handling—which itself, however, would be exactly part of the pleasure. Meanwhile, it no less appeared, there were other subjects to go on with, and even if one had to wait for him he would still perhaps come. It happened for me that he *was* belatedly to come, but that he was to turn up then in a shape almost too familiar at first for recognition, the shape of one of those residual substitutes that engage doubting eyes the day after the fair. He had been with me all the while, and only too obscurely and intimately—I had not found him in the market as an exhibited or *offered* value. I had in a word to draw him forth from within rather than meet him in the world before me, the more convenient sphere of the objective, and to make him objective, in short, had to turn nothing less than myself inside out. What was *I* thus, within and essentially, what had I ever been and could I ever be but a man of imagination at the active pitch?—so that if it was a question of treating *some* happy case, any that would give me what, artistically speaking, I wanted, here on the very spot was one at hand in default of a better. It wasn't what I should have preferred, yet it was after all the example I knew best and should feel most at home with—granting always that objectivity, the prize to be won, shouldn't just be frightened away by the odd terms of the affair. It is of course for my reader to say whether or no what I have done *has* meant defeat; yet even if this should be his judgment I fall back on the interest, at the worst, of certain sorts of failure. I shall have brought up from the deep many things probably not to have been arrived at for the benefit of these pages without my particular attempt. Sundry of such I seem still to recognise, and not least just now those involved in that visionary "assistance" at the drama of the War, from however far off, which had become a habit for us without ceasing to be a strain. I am sure I thought more things under that head, with the fine visionary ache, than I thought in all other connections together; for the simple reason that one had to *ask* leave—of one's own spirit—for these last intermissions, whereas one but took it, with both hands free, for one's sense of the bigger cause. There was not in that the least complication of consciousness. I have sufficiently noted how my apprehension of the bigger cause was at the same time, and this all through, at once quickened and kept low; to the point that positively my whole acquaintance of the personal sort even with such a matter as my brother Wilky's enrolment in the 44th Massachusetts was to reduce itself to but a single visit to him in camp.

I recall an afternoon at Readville, near Boston, and the fashion in which his state of juniority gave way, for me, on the spot, to immensities of superior difference, immensities that were at the same time intensities, varieties, supremacies, of the enviable in the all-difficult and the delightful in the impossible: such a fairy-tale seemed it, and withal such a flat revolution, that this soft companion of my childhood should have such romantic chances and should have mastered, by the mere aid of his native gaiety and sociability, such mysteries, such engines, such arts. To become first a happy soldier and then an easy officer was in particular for G. W. J. an exercise of sociability—and that above all was my extract of the Readville scene, which most came home to me as a picture, an interplay of bright breezy air and high shanty-covered levels with blue horizons, and laughing, welcoming, sunburnt young men, who seemed mainly to bristle, through their welcome, with Boston genealogies, and who had all alike turned handsome, only less handsome than their tawny-bearded Colonel, under I couldn't have said what common grace of clear blue toggery imperfectly and hitchingly donned in the midst of the camp labours that I gaped at (by the blessing of heaven I could in default of other adventures still gape) as at shining revels. I couldn't "do things," I couldn't indefinitely hang about, though on occasion I did so, as it comes back to me, verily to desperation; which had to be my dim explanation—dim as to my ever insisting on it—of so rare a snatch at opportunity for gapings the liveliest, or in better terms admirations the crudest, that I could have presumed to encumber the scene with. Scarce credible to me now, even under recall of my frustrations, that I was able in all this stretch of time to respond but to a single other summons to admire at any cost, which I think must have come again from Readville, and the occasion of which, that of my brother's assumed adjutancy of the so dramatically, so much more radically recruited 54th involved a view superficially less harmonious. The whole situation was more wound up and girded then, the formation of negro regiments affected us as a tremendous War measure, and I have glanced in another place at the consequence of it that was at the end of a few months most pointedly to touch ourselves. That second aspect of the weeks of preparation before the departure of the regiment can not at all have suggested a frolic, though at the time I don't remember it as grim, and can only gather that, as the other impression had been of something quite luminous and beautiful, so this was vaguely sinister and sad—perhaps simply through the fact that, though our sympathies, our own as a family's, were, in the current phrase, all enlisted on behalf of the race that had sat in bondage, it was impossible for the mustered presence of more specimens of it, and of stranger, than I had ever seen together, not to make the young men who were about to lead them appear sacrificed to the general tragic need in a degree beyond that of their more orthodox appearances. The air of sacrifice was, however, so to brighten as to confound itself with that of splendid privilege on the day (May 28th, '63) of the march of the 54th out of Boston, its fairest of young commanders at its head, to great reverberations of music, of fluttering banners, launched benedictions and every public sound; only from that scene, when it took place, I had to be helplessly absent—just as I see myself in a like dismal manner deprived of any nearness of view of my still younger brother's military metamorphosis and contemporary initiation. I vainly question memory for some such picture of *him*, at this stage of his adventure, as would have been certain to hang itself, for reasons of wonder and envy again, in my innermost cabinet. Our differently compacted and more variously endowed Bob, who had strained much at every tether, was so eager and ardent that it made for him a positive authority; but what most recurs to me of his start in the 45th, or of my baffled vision of it, is the marvel of our not having all just wept, more than anything else, either for his being so absurdly young or his being so absurdly strenuous—we might have had our choice of pretexts and protests. It seemed so short a time since he had been l'ingénieux petit Robertson of the domestic schoolroom, pairing with our small sister as I paired with Wilky. We didn't in the least weep, however— we smiled as over the interest of childhood at its highest bloom, and that my parents, with their consistent tenderness, should have found their surrender of their latest born so workable is doubtless a proof that we were all lifted together as on a wave that might bear us where it would. Our ingenious Robertson was but seventeen years old, but I suspect his ingenuity of having, in so good a cause, anticipated his next birthday by a few months. The 45th was a nine-months regiment, but he got himself passed out of it, in advance of its discharge, to a lieutenancy in the 55th U.S.C.T., Colonel A. P. Hallowell (transferred from lieutenant-colonelcy of the 54th) commanding; though not before he had been involved in the siege of Charleston, whence the visionary, the quite Edgar Poeish look, for my entertainment, of the camp-covered "Folly Island" of his letters. While his regiment was engaged in Seymour's raid on Florida he suffered a serious sunstroke, with such consequences that he was recommended for discharge; of which he declined to avail himself, obtaining instead a position on General Ames's staff and enjoying thus for six months the relief of being mounted. But he returned to his regiment in front

221

of Charleston (after service with the Tenth Army Corps, part of the Army of the James, before Petersburg and Richmond); and though I have too scant an echo of his letters from that scene one of the passages that I do recover is of the happiest. "It was when the line wavered and I saw Gen'l Hartwell's horse on my right rear up with a shell exploding under him that I rammed my spurs into my own beast, who, maddened with pain, carried me on through the line, throwing men down, and over the Rebel works some distance ahead of our troops." For this action he was breveted captain; and the 55th, later on, was the first body of troops to enter Charleston and march through its streets—which term of his experience, as it unfolded, presents him to my memory as again on staff duty; with Brigadier-Generals Potter, Rufus Hatch and his old superior and, at my present writing, gallant and vivid survivor, Alfred Hartwell, who had been his captain and his lieut.-colonel in the 45th and the 55th respectively.[10]

I can at all events speak perfectly of my own sense of the uplifting wave just alluded to during the couple of years that the "boys'" letters from the field came in to us—with the one abatement of glamour for them the fact that so much of their substance was in the whole air of life and their young reports of sharp experience but a minor pipe in the huge mixed concert always in our ears. Faded and touching pages, these letters are in some abundance before me now, breathing confidence and extraordinary cheer—though surviving principally but in Wilky's admirable hand, of all those I knew at that time the most humiliating to a feebler yet elder fist; and with their liveliest present action to recompose for me not by any means so much the scenes and circumstances, the passages of history concerned, as to make me know again and reinhabit the places, the hours, the stilled or stirred conditions through which I took them in. These conditions seem indeed mostly to have settled for me into the single sense of what I missed, compared to what the authors of our bulletins gained, in wondrous opportunity of vision, that is *appreciation of the thing seen*—there being clearly such a lot of this, and all of it, by my conviction, portentous and prodigious. The key to which assurance was that I longed to live by my eyes, in the midst of such far-spreading chances, in greater measure than I then had help to, and that the measure in which *they* had it gloriously overflowed. This capacity in them to deal with such an affluence of life stood out from every line, and images sprung up about them at every turn of the story. The story, the general one, of the great surge of action on which they were so early carried, was to take still other turns during the years I now speak of, some of these not of the happiest; but with the same relation to it on my own part too depressingly prolonged— that of seeing, sharing, envying, applauding, pitying, all from too far-off, and with the queer sense that, whether or no they would prove to have had the time of their lives, it seemed that the only time I should have had would stand or fall by theirs. This was to be yet more deplorably the case later on—I like to give a twitch to the curtain of a future reduced to the humility of a past: when, the War being over and we confronted with all the personal questions it had showily muffled up only to make them step forth with their sharper angles well upon us, our father, easily beguiled, acquired by purchase and for the benefit of his younger sons divers cottonlands in Florida; which scene of blighted hopes it perhaps was that cast upon me, at its defiant distance, the most provoking spell. There was provocation, at those subsequent seasons, in the very place-name of Serenola, beautiful to ear and eye; unforgettable were to remain the times, while the vain experiment dragged on for our anxiety and curiosity, and finally to our great discomfiture, when my still ingenuous young brothers, occupied in raising and selling crops that refused alike, it seemed, to come and to go, wafted northward their fluctuating faith, their constant hospitality and above all, for one of the number at home, their large unconscious evocations. The mere borrowed, and so brokenly borrowed, impression of southern fields basking in a light we didn't know, of scented sub-tropic nights, of a situation suffused with economic and social drama of the strangest and sharpest, worked in me, I dare say most deceptively, as a sign of material wasted, my material not being in the least the crops unproduced or unsold, but the precious store of images ungathered. However, the vicarious sensation had, as I say, been intense enough, from point to point, before that; a series of Wilky's letters of the autumn of '62 and the following winter during operations in North Carolina intended apparently to clear an approach to Charleston overflow with the vivacity of his interest in whatever befell, and still more in whatever promised, and reflect, in this freshness of young assurances and young delusions, the general public fatuity. The thread of interest for me here would certainly be much more in an exhibition of some such artless notes of the period, with their faded marks upon them, than in that of the spirit of my own poor perusal of them—were it not that those things shrink after years to the common measure when not testifying to some rarity of experience and expression. All experience in the field struck me indeed as then rare, and I wondered at both my brothers' military mastery of statement, through which played, on the part of the elder, a whimsicality of "turn," an oddity of verbal collocation, that we had ever cherished, in the family circle, as the sign of his address. "The next fight we have, I expect," he writes from Newberne, N. C., on New Year's Day '63, "will be a pretty big one, but I am confident that under Foster and our gunboats we will rid the State of these miserable wretches whom the Divine Providence has created in its wisdom to make men wish——! Send on then, open yourselves a recruiting establishment if necessary—all we want is numbers! *They* are the greatest help to the individual soldier on the battle-field. If he feels he has 30,000 men behind him pushing on steadily to back him he is in much more fighting trim than when away in the rear with 10,000 ahead of him fighting like madmen. It seems that Halleck told Foster when F. was in Washington that he scarcely slept for a week after learning that we were near Goldsboro', having heard previously that a reinforcement of 40,000 Rebels were coming down there to whip us. Long live Foster!"

"It was so cold this morning," he writes at another and earlier date, "that Divine service was held in our barracks instead of out-of-doors, as it generally is, and it was the most impressive that I have ever heard. The sermon was on profanity, and the chaplain, after making all the observations and doing by mouth and action as much as he could to rid the regiment of the curse, sat down, credulous being, thinking he had settled the question for ever. Colonel Lee then rose and said that the chaplain the other day accused him—most properly—of profanity and of its setting a very bad example to the regiment; also that when he took the command he had felt how very bad the thing would be in its influence on all around him. He felt that it would be the great conflict of his life. At this point his head drooped and he lifted his handkerchief to his face; but he went on in conclusion: 'Now boys, let us try one and all to vindicate the sublime principles our chaplain has just so eloquently expressed, and I will do *my* best. I hope to God I have wounded no man's feelings by an oath; if I have I humbly beg his pardon.' Here he finished." How this passage impressed me at the time signifies little; but I find myself now feel in its illustration of what could then happen among soldiers of the old Puritan Commonwealth a rich recall of some story from Cromwellian ranks. Striking the continuity, and not unworthy of it my brother's further comment. "I leave you to imagine which of these appeals did most good, the conventional address of the pastor or the honest manly heart-touching acknowledgment of our Colonel. That is the man through and through, and I heard myself say afterwards: 'Let him swear to all eternity if he *is* that sort of man, and if profanity makes such, for goodness' sake let us all swear.' This may be a bad doctrine, but is one that might after all undergo discussion." From which letter I cull further: "I really begin to think you've been hard in your judgments of McClellan. You don't know what an enemy we have to conquer. Every secesh I've seen, and all the rebel prisoners here, talk of the War with such callous earnestness." A letter from Newberne of December 2nd contains a "pathetic" record of momentary faith, the sort so abundant at the time in what was not at all to be able to happen. Moreover a name rings out of it which it is a kind of privilege to give again to the air—when one can do so with some approach to an association signified; so much did Charles Lowell's virtue and value and death represent at the season soon to come for those who stood within sight of them, and with such still unextinct emotion may the few of these who now survive turn to his admirably inspired kinsman's Harvard Commemoration Ode and find it infinitely and tenderly suffused with pride. Two gallantest nephews, particularly radiant to memory, had James Russell Lowell to commemorate.

I sweep for them a pæan, but they wane

Again and yet again

Into a dirge and die away in pain.

In these brave ranks I only see the gaps,

Thinking of dear ones whom the dumb turf wraps,

Dark to the triumph which they died to gain.

Cabot has had news that Mr. Amos Lawrence of Boston is getting up a cavalry regiment (Wilky writes), and he has sent home to try for a commission as 2nd lieutenant. Now if we could only *both* get such a commission in that regiment you can judge yourself how desirable it would be. Perkins will probably have one in the Massachusetts 2nd and our orderly stands a pretty good chance of one in the 44th. This cavalry colonelcy will probably be for Cabot's cousin, Charles Lowell.

There is a report that we start this week for Kinston, and if so we shall doubtless have a good little fight. We have just received 2 new Mass. Regiments, the 8th and the 51st. We have absolutely no time to ourselves; and what time we do have we want much more to give to lying down than to anything else. But try your best for me now, and I promise you to do *my* best wherever I am.

A homelier truth is in a few lines three weeks later.

The men as a general thing think war a mean piece of business as it's carried on in this State; we march 20 or 30 miles and find the enemy entrenched in rifle-pits or hidden away in some out-of-the-way place; we send our artillery forward, and after a brisk skirmish ahead the foe is driven back into the woods, and we march on for 20 miles more to find the same luck. We were all on the last march praying for a fight, so that we might halt and throw off our knapsacks. I don't pretend I am eager to make friends with bullets, but at Whitehall, after marching some 20 miles, I was on this account really glad when I heard cannonading ahead and the column was halted and the fight began.

The details of this engagement are missing from the letter, but we found matter of interest in two or three other passages—one in particular recording a December day's march with 15,000 men, "not including artillerymen," 70 pieces of artillery and 1100 cavalry; which, "on account of obstructions on the roads," had achieved by night but seventeen miles and resulted in a bivouac "in 3 immense cotton-fields, one about as large as Easton's Pond at Newport."

We began to see the camp fires of the advance brigade about 4 miles ahead of us, and I assure you those miles were soon got over. I think Willy's artistic eye would have enjoyed the sight—it seemed so as if the world were on fire. When we arrived on the field the stacks were made, the ranks broken and the men sent after rail fences, which fortunately abound in this region and are the only comfort we have at night. A long fire is made, the length of the stacks, and one rank is placed on one side of it and the other opposite. I try to make a picture you see, but scratch it out in despair. The fires made, we sit down and make our coffee in our tin dippers, and often is one of these pushed over by some careless wretch who hasn't noticed it on the coals or has been too tired to look. The coffee and the hard tack consumed we spread our rubber blankets and sleep as sound as any house in Christendom. At about 5 the fearful réveillé calls us to our feet, we make more coffee, drink it in a hurry, sling our knapsacks and spank down the road in one of Foster's regular old quicksteps.

Thrilling at our fireside of course were the particulars of the Kinston engagement, and still more, doubtless, the happy freshness of the writer.

At 8 A.M. we were on the road, and had hardly marched 3 miles when we knew by sounds ahead that the ball had opened. We were ordered up and deployed in an open field on the right of the road, where we remained some half an hour. Then we were moved some hundred yards further, but resumed our former position in another field. Here Foster came up to the Major, who was directly in the rear of our company and told him to advance our left wing to support Morrison's battery, which was about half a mile ahead. He also said he was pressing the Rebs hard and that they were retiring at every shell from our side. On we went, the left flank company taking the lead, and many a bullet and shell whizzed over our heads in that longest half-mile of my life. We

227

seemed to be nearing the fun, for wounded men were being carried to the rear and dead ones lay on each side of us in the woods. We were taken into another field on the left of the road, and before us were deployed the 23rd Mass., who were firing in great style. First we were ordered to lie down, and then in 5 or 10 minutes ordered up again, when we charged down that field in a manner creditable to any Waterloo legion. I felt as if this moment was the greatest of my life and as if all the devils of the Inferno were my benighted system. We halted after having charged some 60 yards, when what should we see on our left, just out of the woods and stuck up on a rail, but a flag of truce, placing under its protecting wing some 50 or 60 poor cowering wretches who, in their zeal for recognition, not only pulled out all their pocket handkerchiefs, but in the case of one man spread out his white shirt-flaps and offered them pacifically to the winds. The most demonic shouts and yells were raised by the 23rd ahead of us at this sight, in which the 44th joined; while the regiments on our right, and that of the road, greeted in the same frightful manner 200 prisoners they had cut off from retreat by the bridge. So far I was alive and the thing had lasted perhaps 3 hours; all the enemy but the 200 just named had got away over the bridge to Kinston and our cavalry were in hot pursuit. I don't think Sergeant G. W. has ever known greater glee in all his born days. At about 3 P.M. we crossed the bridge and got into the town. All along the road from bridge to town Rebel equipments, guns and cartridge-boxes lay thick, and within the place dead men and horses thickened too. We were taken ahead through the town to support the New York 3rd Artillery beyond, where it was shelling the woods around and ridding the place for the night of any troublesome wanderers. The Union pickets posted out ahead that night said the shrieks of women and children further on in the wood could be heard perfectly all night long, these unfortunates having taken refuge there from the threatened town. That night we lived like fighting-cocks—molasses, pork, butter, cheese and all sorts of different delicacies being foraged for and houses entered regardless of the commonest dues of life, and others set on fire to show Kinston was our own. She belonged to our army, and almost every man claimed a house. If I had only had your orders beforehand for trophies I could have satisfied you with anything named, from a gold watch to an old brickbat. This is the ugly part of war. A too victorious army soon goes down; but we luckily didn't have time for big demoralisation, as the next day in the afternoon we found ourselves some 17 miles away and bivouacking in a single prodigious cornfield.

To which I don't resist subjoining another characteristic passage from the same general scene as a wind-up to that small chapter of history.

The report has gained ground to-day that we leave to-morrow, and if so I suppose the next three months will be important ones in the history of the War. Four ironclads and a great many gunboats are in Beaufort Harbour; we have at present a force of 50,000 infantry, an immense artillery and upwards of 800 cavalry. Transports innumerable are filling up every spare inch of our harbour, and every man's pity and charity are exercised upon Charleston, Mobile or Wilmington. We are the only nine-months regiment going, a fact which to the sensitive is highly gratifying, showing Foster's evident high opinion of us. The expedition, I imagine, will be pretty interesting, for we shall have excitement enough without the fearful marches. To-day is Sunday, and I've been reading Hugo's account of Waterloo in Les Misérables and preparing my mind for something of the same sort at Wilmington. God grant the battle may do as much harm to the Rebels as Waterloo did to the French. If it does the fight will be worth the dreadful carnage it may involve, and the experience for the survivors an immense treasure. Men will fight forever if they are well treated. Give them little marching and keep the wounded away from them, and they'll do anything. I am very well and in capital spirits, though now and then rather blue about home. But only 5 months more and then heaven! General Foster has just issued an order permitting us to inscribe Goldsboro, Kinston and Whitehall on our banner.

On the discharge of the 44th after the term of nine months for which it had engaged and my brother's return home, he at once sought service again in the Massachusetts 54th, his connection with which I have already recorded, as well as his injuries in the assault on Fort Wagner fruitlessly made by that regiment in the summer of '63. He recovered with difficulty, but at last sufficiently, from his wounds (with one effect of which he had for the rest of his short life grievously to reckon), and made haste to rejoin his regiment in the field—to the promotion of my gathering a few more notes. From "off Graham's point, Tillapenny River, Headquarters 2nd Brigade," he writes in December '64.

We started last night from the riflepits in the front of Deveaux Neck to cross the Tillapenny and make a reconnaissance on this side and try and get round the enemy's works. It is now half-past 10 A.M., and I have been trying to wash some of my mud off. We are all a sorry crowd of beggars—I don't look as I did the night we left home. I am much of the time mud from head to foot, and my spirit is getting muddled also. But I am in excellent condition as regards my wounds and astonish myself by my powers. I rode some 26 miles yesterday and walked some 3 in thick mud, but don't feel a bit the worse for it. We're only waiting here an hour or two to get a relief of horses, when we shall start again. We shan't have a fight of any kind to-day, but to-morrow expect to give them a little trouble at Pocotaligo. Colonel Hallowell commands this reconnaissance. We have only 4 regiments and a section of artillery from the 2nd Brigade with us. We heard some fine music from the Rebel lines yesterday. They have got a stunning band over there. Prisoners tell us it's a militia band from Georgia. Most all the troops in our front are militia composed of old men and boys, the flower of the chivalry being just now engaged with Sherman at Savannah. We hear very heavy firing in that direction this morning, and I guess the chivalry is getting the worst of it. The taking of Fort McAllister the other day was a splendid thing—we got 280 prisoners and made them go out and pick up the torpedoes round the fort. Sherman was up at Oguchee and Ossahaw yesterday on another consultation with Foster. We had called our whole army out the night before in front of our works to give him three cheers. This had a marvellous effect upon the Rebs. About 20 men came in the night into our lines, thinking we had got reinforcements and were going to advance. Later. A scout has just come in and tells us the enemy are intrenched about 4 miles off, so that we *shall* have to-day a shindy of some kind. Our headquarters are now in a large house once owned by Judge Graham. The coloured troops are in high spirits and have done splendidly this campaign.

The high spirits of the coloured troops appear naturally to have been shared by their officers—"in the field, Tillapenny River," late at night on December 23rd, '64.

We have just received such bully news to comfort us that I can't help rising from my slumbers to drop you a line. A despatch just received tells us that Sherman has captured 150 guns, 250,000 dols. worth of cotton at Savannah, that Forrest is killed and routed by Rousseau, and that Thomas has walked into Hood and given him the worst kind of fits. I imagine the poor Rebel outposts in our front feel pretty blue to-night, for what with that and the thermometer at about zero I guess the night won't pass without robbing their army of some of its best and bravest. We suffer a good deal from the cold, but are now sitting round our camp fire in as good spirits as men could possibly be. A despatch received early this evening tells us to look out sharp for Hardee, but this latest news knocks that to a cocked hat, and we are only just remembering that that gentleman is round. My foot is bully.

As regards that impaired member, on which he was ever afterwards considerably to limp, he opines three days later, on Christmas evening, that "even in the palmy days of old it never *felt* better than now." And he goes on:

Though Savannah is taken I fear we shan't get much credit for having helped to take it. Yet night and day we have been at it hammer and tongs, and as we are away from the main army and somewhat isolated and cut off our work has been pretty hard. We have had only 1,200 effective men in our brigade, and out of that number have had regularly 400 on picket night and day, and the fatigue and extra guard duty have nearly used them up. Twice we have been attacked and both times held our own. Twice we attacked and once have been driven. The only prisoners we have captured on the whole expedition have been taken by this part of the column, and on the whole though we didn't march into Savannah I know you will give us a little credit for having hastened its downfall. Three prisoners that we took the other night slept at our Hdqrs, and we had a good long talk with them. We could get out of them nothing at all that helps from a military point of view, but their stories about the Confederacy were most hopeless. They were 3 officers and gentlemen of a crack S.C. cavalry company which has been used during the War simply to guard this coast, and their language and state of mind were those of the true Southern chevalier. They confessed to a great scare on finding themselves hemmed in by coloured troops, and all agree that the

niggers are the worst enemies they have had to face. On Thursday we turned
them over to the Provost-Marshal at Deveaux Neck, who took them to Gen'l
Hatch. The General had got our despatch announcing we could get nothing
at all out of them, and he came down on them most ruthlessly and told them
to draw lots, as one would have to swing before night. He told them he had
got the affidavit of an escaped Union prisoner, a man captured at Honey Hill
and who had come into our lines the day previous, to the effect that he had
witnessed the hanging of a negro soldier belonging to the 26th U.S.C.T., and
that he had determined one of them should answer for it. Two seemed very
much moved, but the third, Lee by name (cousin of Gen'l Stephen Lee of the
cavalry), said he knew nothing about it, but if it was so, so it might be. The
other two were taken from each other and Gen'l Hatch managed to draw a
good deal of information from them about our position, that is the force and
nature of the enemy and works in our front. Lee refused to the last to answer
any question whatever, and they all 3 now await at Hilton Head the issue of
the law. The hanging of the negro seems a perfectly ascertained fact—he was
hung by the 48th Georgia Infty, and the story has naturally much stirred up
our coloured troops. If Hardee should decide to come down on us I believe
he would get the worst of it, and only hope now that our men won't take
a prisoner alive. They certainly make a great mistake at Washington in not
attending to these little matters, and I am sure the moral effect of an order
from the President announcing that such things have happened, and that the
coloured troops have taken them thoroughly to heart, would be greater on
the Rebels than any physical blow we can deal them.

When I read again, "in the field before Pocotaligo," toward the middle
of January '65, that "Sherman leaves to-night from Beaufort with Logan's
Corps to cross Beaufort Ferry and come up on our right flank and push on
to Pocotaligo bridge," the stir as from great things rises again for me, wraps
about Sherman's name as with the huge hum that then surrounded it, and
in short makes me give the passage such honour as I may. "We are waiting
anxiously for the sound of his musketry announcing him." I was never in my
life to wait for any such sound, but how at that juncture I hung about with
privileged Wilky! "We all propose at Hdqrs to take our stores out and ride up
to the bank of the river and watch the fight on the other side. We are praying

to be relieved here—our men are dying for want of clothing; and when we see Morris Island again we shall utterly rejoice." He writes three days later from headquarters established in a plantation the name of which, as well as that of the stream, of whatever magnitude, that they had crossed to reach it, happens to be marked by an illegibility quite unprecedented in his splendid script—to the effect of a still intenser evocation (as was then to be felt at any rate) of all the bignesses involved. "Sherman's whole army is in our front, and they expect to move on Charleston at any moment." Sherman's whole army!—it affected me from afar off as a vast epic vision. The old vibration lives again, but with it also that of the smaller and nearer, the more intimate notes—such for instance as: "I shall go up to the 20th Corps to-morrow and try for a sight of Billy Perkins and Sam Storrow in the 2nd Mass." Into which I somehow read, under the touch of a ghostly hand no more "weirdly" laid than *that*, more volumes than I can the least account for or than I have doubtless any business to.

My visionary yearning must however, I think, have drawn most to feed on from the first of a series of missives dated from Headquarters, Department of the South, Hilton Head S.C., this particular one of the middle of February. "I write in a great hurry to tell you I have been placed on General Gillmore's staff as A.D.C. It is just the very thing for my foot under present circumstances, and I consider myself most fortunate. I greatly like the General, who is most kind and genial and very considerate. My duties will be principally the carrying of orders to Savannah, Morris Island, Fortress Monroe, Combalee(?) Florida, and the General's correspondence. Charleston is ours," he goes on two days later: "it surrendered to a negro regiment yesterday at 9 A.M. We have just come up from Sumter, where we have hoisted the American flag. We were lying off Bull's Bay yesterday noon waiting for this when the General saw through his glass the stars and stripes suddenly flown from the town hall. We immediately steamed up to Sumter and ran up the colours there. Old Gillmore was in fine feather and I am in consummate joy." The joy nevertheless, I may add, doesn't prevent the remark after a couple of days more that "Charleston isn't on the whole such a very great material victory; in fact the capture of the place is of value only in that its moral effect tends to strengthen the Union cause." After which he proceeds:

233

Governor Aiken of S.C. came up to Hdqrs to-day to call on the Gen'l, and they had a long talk. He is a "gradual Emancipationist" and says the worst of the President's acts was his sweeping Proclamation. Before that every one in this State was ready to come back on the gradual system, and would have done so if Lincoln's act hadn't driven them to madness. This is all fine talk, but there is nothing in it. They had at least 5 months' warning and could have in that time perfectly returned within the fold; in fact the strong Abolitionists of the North were afraid the President had made the thing but too easy for them and that they would get ahead of us and themselves emancipate. This poor gentleman is simple crazy and weakminded. Between Davis and us he *is* puzzled beyond measure, and doesn't know what line to take. One thing though troubled him most, namely the ingratitude of the negro. He can't conceive how the creatures he has treated with such extraordinary kindness and taken such care of should all be willing to leave him. He says he was the first man in the South to introduce religion among the blacks and that his plantation of 600 of them was a model of civilisation and peace. Just think of this immense slaveholder telling me as I drove him home that the coat he had on had been turned three times and his pantaloons the only ones he possessed. He stated this so simply and touchingly that I couldn't help offering him a pair of mine—which he refused, however. There are some 10,000 people in the town, mostly women and negroes, and it's tremendously ravaged by our shell, about which they have naturally lied from beginning to end.

"Bob has just come down from Charleston," he writes in March—"he has been commissioned captain in the 103rd U.S.C.T. I am sorry he has left his regiment, still he seemed bent on doing so and offers all kinds of reasons for it. He may judge rightly, but I fear he's hasty;" and indeed this might appear from a glimpse of our younger brother at his ease given by him in a letter of some days before, written at two o'clock in the morning and recording a day spent in a somewhat arduously performed visit to Charleston. "I drove out to the entrenchments to-day to see B., and found him with Hartwell (R. J.'s colonel) smoking their long pipes on the verandah of a neat country cottage with a beautiful garden in front of them and the birds chirping and rambling around. Bob looks remarkably well and seemed very nice indeed. He speaks very highly of Hartwell, and the latter the same of him. They seemed settled in remarkable comfort at Charleston and to be taking life easy after their 180 miles march through South Carolina." He mentions further that his visit to the captured city, begun the previous day, had been made in interesting conditions; there is in fact matter for quotation throughout the letter, the last of the small group from which I shall borrow. He had, with his general, accompanied a "large Senatorial delegation from Washington and shown them round the place." He records the delegation's "delight" in what they saw; how "a large crowd of young ladies" were of the party, so that the Senatorial presences were "somewhat relieved and lightened to the members of the staff;" and also that they all went over to Forts Sumter and Moultrie and the adjacent works. The pleasure of the whole company in the scene of desolation thus presented is one of those ingenuous historic strokes that the time-spirit, after a sufficient interval, permits itself to smile at—and is not the only such, it may be noted, in the sincere young statement.

To-morrow they go to Savannah, returning here in the evening, when there is to be a grand reception for them at Hdqrs. We expect Gen'l Robert Anderson (the loyalist commandant at Sumter when originally fired upon) by the next steamer, with Gideon Welles (secretary of the Navy) and a number of other notables from Washington. Anderson is going to raise the old flag on Sumter, and of course there will be a great shindy here—I only wish you were with us to join in it. I never go to Sumter without the deepest exhilaration—so many scenes come to my mind. It's the centre of the nest, and for one to *be* there is to feel that the whole game is up. These people have always insisted that there the last gun should be fired. But the suffering and desolation of this land is the worst feature of the whole thing. If you could see what they are reduced to you couldn't help being touched. The best people are in utter penury; they look like the poorest of the poor and they talk like them also. They are deeply demoralised, in fact degraded. Charleston is more forsaken and stricken than I can describe; it reminds me when I go through the streets of some old doomed city on which the wrath of God has rested from far back, and if it ever revives will do so simply through the infinite mercy and charity of the North. But for this generation at least the inhabitants are done for. Can't H. come down and pay us a visit of 2 or 3 weeks? I can get him a War Dept. pass approved by General Gillmore.

H. knew and well remembers the pang of his inability to accept this invitation, to the value of which for emphasis of tragic life on the scene of the great drama the next passage adds a touch. Mrs. William Young, the lady alluded to, was a friend we had known almost only on the European stage and amid the bright associations of Paris in particular. Whom did we suppose he had met on the arrival of a steamer from the North but this more or less distracted acquaintance of other days?—who had come down "to try and get her stepmother into our lines and take her home. She is accompanied by a friend from New York, and expects to succeed in her undertaking. I hardly think she will, however, as her mother is 90 miles out of our lines and a very old woman. We have sent a negro out to give her Mrs. Young's news, but how can this poor old thing travel such a distance on foot and sleep in the swamp besides? It's an absurd idea, but I shall do everything in my power to facilitate it." Of what further befell I gather no account; but I remember how a later time was to cause me to remark on the manner in which even dire tragedy may lapse, in the individual life, and leave no trace on the ground it has ravaged—none at least apparent unless pushingly searched for. The last thing to infer from appearances, on much subsequent renewal of contact with Mrs. Young in Paris again, was that this tension of a reach forth across great war-wasted and swamp-smothered spaces for recovery of an aged and half-starved pedestrian female relative counted for her as a chapter of experience: the experience of Paris dressmakers and other like matters had so revived and supervened. But let me add that I speak here of mere appearances, and have ever inclined to the more ironic and more complicating vision of them. It would doubtless have been too simple for wonder that our elegant friend should have lived, as it were, under the cloud of reminiscence—and wonder had always somewhere to come in.

XII

It had been, however, neither at Newport nor at Cambridge—the Cambridge at least of that single year—that the plot began most to thicken for me: I figure it as a sudden stride into conditions of a sort to minister and inspire much more, all round, that we early in 1864 migrated, as a family, to Boston, and that I now seem to see the scene of our existence there for a couple of years packed with drama of a finer consistency than any I had yet tasted. We settled for the interesting time in Ashburton Place—the "sympathetic" old house we occupied, one of a pair of tallish brick fronts based, as to its ground floor, upon the dignity of time-darkened granite, was lately swept away in the interest of I know not what grander cause; and when I wish to think of such intercourse as I have enjoyed with the good city at its closest and, as who should say its kindest, though this comes doubtless but to saying at its freshest, I live over again the story of that sojourn, a period bristling, while I recover my sense of it, with an unprecedented number of simultaneous particulars. To stick, as I can only do, to the point from which my own young outlook worked, the things going on for me so tremendously all at once were in the first place the last impressions of the War, a whole social relation to it crowding upon us there as for many reasons, all of the best, it couldn't have done elsewhere; and then, more personally speaking, the prodigious little assurance I found myself gathering as from one day to another that fortune had in store some response to my deeply reserved but quite unabashed design of becoming as "literary" as might be. It was as if, our whole new medium of existence aiding, I had begun to see much further into the question of how that end was gained. The vision, quickened by a wealth, a great mixture, of new appearances, became such a throbbing affair that my memory of the time from the spring of '64 to the autumn of '66 moves as through an apartment hung with garlands and lights—where I have but to breathe for an instant on the flowers again to see them flush with colour, and but tenderly to snuff the candles to see them twinkle afresh. Things happened, and happened repeatedly, the mere brush or side-wind of which was the stir of life; and the fact that I see, when I consider, how it was mostly the mere side-wind I got, doesn't draw from the picture a shade of its virtue. I literally, and under whatever felt restriction of my power to knock about, formed independent relations—several; and two or three of them, as I then thought, of the very most momentous. I may not attempt just here to go far into these, save for the exception of the easiest to treat, which I also, by good fortune, win back as by no means the least absorbing—the beautiful, the entrancing presumption that I should have but to write with sufficient difficulty and sufficient felicity to get once for all (that was the point) into the incredibility of print. I see before me, in the rich, the many-hued light of my room that overhung dear Ashburton Place from our third floor, the very greenbacks, to the total value of twelve dollars, into which I had changed the cheque representing my first earned wage. I had earned it, I couldn't but feel, with fabulous felicity: a circumstance so strangely mixed with the fact that literary composition of a high order had, at that very table where the greenbacks were spread out, quite viciously declined, and with the air of its being also once for all, to "come" on any save its own essential terms, which it seemed to distinguish in the most invidious manner conceivable from mine. It was to insist through all my course on this distinction, and sordid gain thereby never again to seem so easy as in that prime handling of my fee. Other guerdons, of the same queer, the same often rather greasy, complexion followed; for what had I done, to the accompaniment of a thrill the most ineffable, an agitation that, as I recapture it, affects me as never exceeded in all my life for fineness, but go one beautiful morning out to Shady Hill at Cambridge and there drink to the lees the offered cup of editorial sweetness?—none ever again to be more delicately mixed. I had addressed in trembling hope my first fond attempt at literary criticism to Charles Eliot Norton, who had lately, and with the highest, brightest competence, come to the rescue of the North American Review, submerged in a stale tradition and gasping for life, and he had not only published it in his very next number—the interval for me of breathless brevity—but had expressed the liveliest further hospitality, the gage of which was thus at once his welcome to me at home. I was to grow fond of regarding as a positive consecration to letters that half-hour in the long library at Shady Hill, where the winter sunshine touched serene book-shelves and arrayed pictures, the whole embrowned composition of objects in my view, with I knew not what golden light of promise, what assurance of things to come: there was to be nothing exactly like it later on—the conditions of perfect rightness for a certain fresh felicity, certain decisive pressures of the spring, *can* occur, it would seem, but once. This was on the other hand the beginning of so many intentions that it mattered little if the particular occasion was not repeated; for what did I do again and again, through all the years, but handle in plenty what I might have called the small change of it?

I despair, however, as I look back, of rendering the *fusions* in that much-mixed little time, every feature of which had something of the quality and interest of every other, and the more salient, the more "epoch-making"—I apply with complacency the portentous term—to drape themselves romantically in the purple folds of the whole. I think it must have been the sense of the various climaxes, the enjoyed, because so long postponed, revenges of the War, that lifted the moment in the largest embrace: the general consciousness was of such big things at last in sight, the huge national emergence, the widening assurance, however overdarkened, it is true, by the vast black cost of what General Grant (no light-handed artist he!) was doing for us. He was at all events working to an end, and something strange and immense, even like the light of a new day rising above a definite rim, shot its rays through the chinks of the immediate, the high-piled screen of sacrifice behind which he wrought. I fail to seize again, to my wonder, the particular scene of our acclamation of Lee's surrender, but I feel in the air the exhalation of our relief, which mingled, near and far, with the breath of the springtime itself and positively seemed to become over the land, over the world at large in fact, an element of reviving Nature. Sensible again are certain other sharpest vibrations then communicated from the public consciousness: Ashburton Place resounds for me with a wild cry, rocks as from a convulsed breast, on that early morning of our news of Lincoln's death by murder; and, in a different order, but also darkening the early day, there associates itself with my cherished chamber of application the fact that of a sudden, and while we were always and as much as ever awaiting him, Hawthorne was dead. What I have called the fusion strikes me as indeed beyond any rendering when I think of the peculiar assault on my private consciousness of *that* news: I sit once more, half-dressed, late of a summer morning and in a bedimmed light which is somehow at once that of dear old green American shutters drawn to against openest windows and that of a moral shadow projected as with violence—I sit on my belated bed, I say, and yield to the pang that made me positively and loyally cry. I didn't rise early in those days of scant ease—I now even ask myself how sometimes I rose at all; which ungrudged license withal, I thus make out, was not less blessedly effective in the harmony I glance at than several showier facts. To tell at all adequately why the pang was fine would nevertheless too closely involve my going back, as we have learned to say, on the whole rich interpenetration. I fondly felt it in those days invaluable that I had during certain last and otherwise rather blank months at Newport taken in for the first time and at one straight draught the full sweet sense of our one fine romancer's work—for sweet it then above all seemed to me; and I remember well how, while the process day after day drew itself admirably out, I found the actual exquisite taste of it, the strain of the revelation, justify up to the notch whatever had been weak in my delay. This prolonged hanging off from true knowledge had been the more odd, so that I couldn't have explained it, I felt, through the fact that The Wonder-Book and Twice-Told Tales had helped to enchant our childhood; the consequence at any rate seemed happy, since without it, very measurably, the sudden sense of recognition would have been less uplifting a wave. The joy of the recognition was to know at the time no lapse—was in fact through the years never to know one, and this by some rare action of a principle or a sentiment, I scarce know whether to call it a clinging consistency or a singular silliness, that placed the Seven Gables, the Blithedale Romance and the story of Donatello and Miriam (the accepted title of which I dislike to use, not the "marble" but very particularly the human Faun being throughout in question) somewhere on a shelf unvisited by harsh inquiry. The feeling had perhaps at the time been marked by presumption, by a touch of the fatuity of patronage; yet wasn't well-nigh the best charm of a relation with the works just named in the impulse, known from the first, somehow to stand in *between* them and harsh inquiry? If I had asked myself what I meant by that term, at which freedom of appreciation, in fact of intelligence, might have looked askance, I hope I should have found a sufficient answer in the mere plea of a sort of *bêtise* of tenderness. I recall how once, in the air of Rome at a time ever so long subsequent, a friend and countryman now no more, who had spent most of his life in Italy and who remains for me, with his accomplishment, his distinction, his extraordinary play of mind and his too early and too tragic death, the clearest case of "cosmopolitan culture" I was to have known, exclaimed with surprise on my happening to speak as from an ancient fondness for Hawthorne's treatment of the Roman scene: "Why, can you read *that* thing, and *here*?—to me it means nothing at all!" I remember well that under the breath of this disallowance of any possibility of association, and quite most of such a one as I had from far back positively cultivated, the gentle perforated book tumbled before me from its shelf very much as old Polonius, at the thrust of Hamlet's sword, must have collapsed behind the pictured arras. Of course I might have picked it up and brushed it off, but I seem to feel again that I didn't so much as want to, lost as I could only have been in the sense that the note of harsh inquiry, or in other words of the very stroke I had anciently wished to avert, *there* fell straight upon my ear. It represented everything I had so early known we must have none of; though there was interest galore at the same time (as there almost always is in lively oppositions of sensibility, with the sharpness of each, its special exclusions, well exhibited), in an "American" measure that could so reject our beautiful genius and in a Roman, as it were, that could so little see he had done anything for Rome. H. B. Brewster in truth, literary master of three tongues at least, was scarce American at all; homely superstitions had no hold on him; he was French, Italian, above all perhaps German; and there would have been small use, even had there been any importance, in my trying to tell him for instance why it had particularly been, in the gentle time, that I had settled once for all to take our author's case as simply exquisite and not budge from that taking. Which indeed scarce bears telling now, with matters of relative (if *but* of relative!) urgence on hand—consisting as it mainly did in the fact that his work was all charged with a *tone*, a full and rare tone of prose, and that this made for it an extraordinary value in an air in which absolutely nobody's else was or has shown since any aptitude for being. And the tone had been, in its beauty— for me at least—ever so appreciably American; which proved to what a use American matter could be put by an American hand: a consummation involving, it appeared, the happiest moral. For the moral was that an American could be an artist, one of the finest, without "going outside" about it, as I liked to say; quite in fact as if Hawthorne had become one just by being American *enough*, by the felicity of how the artist in him missed nothing, suspected nothing, that the ambient air didn't affect him as containing. Thus he was at once so clear and so entire—clear without thinness, for he might have seemed underfed, it was his danger; and entire without heterogeneity, which might, with less luck and to the discredit of our sufficing manners, have had to be his help. These remarks, as I say, were those I couldn't, or at any rate didn't, make to my Roman critic; if only because I was so held by the other case he offered me—that of a culture for which, in the dense medium around us, Miriam and Donatello and their friends hadn't the virtue that shines or pushes through. I tried to feel that this *constatation* left me musing— and perhaps in truth it did; though doubtless if my attachment to the arranger of those images had involved, to repeat, my not budging, my meditation, whatever it was, respected that condition.

It has renewed itself, however, but too much on this spot, and the scene viewed from Ashburton Place claims at the best more filling in than I can give it. Any illustration of anything worth illustrating has beauty, to my vision, largely by its developments; and developments, alas, are the whole flowering of the plant, while what really meets such attention as one may hope to beguile is at the best but a plucked and tossed sprig or two. That my elder brother was during these months away with Professor Agassiz, a member of the party recruited by that great naturalist for a prolonged exploration of Brazil, is one of the few blooms, I see, that I must content myself with detaching—the main sense of it being for myself, no doubt, that his absence (and he had never been at anything like such a distance from us,) left me the more exposed, and thereby the more responsive, to contact with impressions that had to learn to suffice for me in their uncorrected, when not still more in their inspiringly emphasised, state. The main sense for William himself is recorded in a series of letters from him addressed to us at home and for which, against my hope, these pages succeed in affording no space—they are to have ampler presentation; but the arrival of which at irregular intervals for the greater part of a year comes back to me as perhaps a fuller enrichment of my consciousness than it owed for the time to any other single source. We all still hung so together that this replete organ could yet go on helping itself, with whatever awkwardness, from the conception or projection of others of a like *general* strain, such as those of one's brothers might appear; thanks to which constant hum of borrowed experience, in addition to the quicker play of whatever could pass as more honestly earned, my stage of life knew no drop of the curtain. I literally came and went, I had never practised such coming and going; I went in particular, during summer weeks, and even if carrying my general difficulty with me, to the White Mountains of New Hampshire, with some repetition, and again and again back to Newport, on visits to John La Farge and to the Edmund Tweedys (*their* house almost a second summer home to us;) to say nothing of winter attempts, a little weak, but still more or less achieved, upon New York—which city was rapidly taking on the capital quality, the large worldly sense that dear old London and dear old Paris, with other matters in hand for them as time went on, the time they were "biding" for me, indulgently didn't grudge it. The matters they had in hand wandered indeed as stray vague airs across to us—this I think I have noted; but Boston itself could easily rule, in default even of New York, when to "go," in particular, was an act of such easy virtue. To go from Ashburton Place was to go verily round the corner not less than further afield; to go to the Athenæum, to the Museum, to a certain door of importances, in fact of immensities, defiant of vulgar notation, in Charles Street, at the opposite end from Beacon. The fruit of these mixed proceedings I found abundant at the time, and I think quite inveterately sweet, but to gather it in again now—by which I mean set it forth as a banquet for imaginations already provided—would be to presume too far; not least indeed even on my own cultivated art of exhibition. The fruit of golden youth is all and always golden—it touches to gold what it gathers; this was so the essence of the case that in the first place everything was in some degree an adventure, and in the second any differences of degree guiding my selection would be imperceptible at this end of time to the cold eye of criticism. Not least moreover in the third place the very terms would fail, under whatever ingenuity, for my really justifying so bland an account of the period at large. Do I speak of it as a thumping sum but to show it in the small change, the handful of separate copper and silver coin, the scattered occasions reduced to their individual cash value, that, spread upon the table as a treasure of reminiscence, might only excite derision? *Why* was "staying at Newport" so absurdly, insistently romantic, romantic out of all proportion, as we say—why unless I can truly tell in proportion to what it became so? It consisted often in my "sitting" to John La Farge, within his own precincts and in the open air of attenuated summer days, and lounging thereby just passive to the surge of culture that broke upon me in waves the most desultory and disjointed, it was true, but to an absolute effect of unceasingly scented spray. Particular hours and old (that is young!) ineffable reactions come back to me; it's like putting one's ear, doctor-fashion, to the breast of time—or say as the subtle savage puts his to the ground—and catching at its start some vibratory hum that has been going on more or less for the fifty years since. Newport, the barren isle of our return from Europe, had thus become—and at no such great expense if the shock of public affairs, everywhere making interests start to their feet, be counted out of the process—a source of fifty suggestions to me; which it would have been much less, however, I hasten to add, if the call of La Farge hadn't worked in with our other most standing attraction, and this in turn hadn't practically been part of the positive affluence of certain elements of spectacle. Why again I should have been able to see the pictorial so freely suggested, that pictorial which was ever for me the dramatic, the social, the effectively human aspect, would be doubtless a baffling inquiry in presence of the queer and dear old phenomena themselves; those that, taken together, may be described at the best, I suppose, rather as a much-mixed grope or halting struggle, call it even a competitive scramble, toward the larger, the ideal elegance, the traditional forms of good society in possession, than as a presentation of great noble assurances.

Spectacle in any case broke out, spectacle accumulated, by our then measure, many thicknesses deep, flushing in the sovereign light, as one felt it, of the waning Rhode Island afternoons of August and September with the most "evolved" material civilisation our American world could then show; the vividest note of this in those years, unconscious, even to an artless innocence, of the wider wings still to spread, being the long daily *corso* or processional drive (with cavaliers and amazons not otherwise than conveniently intermixed,) which, with a different direction for different days, offered doubtless as good an example of that gregarious exercise at any cost distinguishing "fashionable life" as was anywhere on the globe to be observed. The price paid for the sticking together was what emphasised, I mean, the wondrous resolve to stick, however scant and narrow and unadjusted for processional effect the various fields of evolution. The variety moreover was short, just as the incongruities of composition in the yearning array were marked; but the tender grace of old sunset hours, the happier breadth of old shining sands under favour of friendly tides, the glitter *quand même* of "caparisoned" animals, appointed vehicles and approved charioteers, to say nothing of the other and more freely exchanged and interrelated brightnesses then at play (in the softer ease of women, the more moustachio'd swagger of men, the braver bonhomie of the social aspect at large), melted together for fond fancy into a tone, a rhythm, a representational virtue charged, as to the amenities, with authority. The amenities thus sought their occasion to multiply even to the sound of far cannonades, and I well remember at once reflecting, in such maturity as I could muster, that the luckier half of a nation able to carry a huge war-burden without sacrifice of amusement might well overcome the fraction that had to feed but on shrinkage and privation; at the same time that the so sad and handsome face of the most frequent of our hostesses, Mary Temple the elder as she had been, now the apt image of a stern priestess of the public altar, was to leave with me for the years to come the grand expression and tragic irony of its revulsion from those who, offering us some high entertainment during days of particular tension, could fiddle, as she scathingly said, while Rome was burning. Blest again the state of youth which could appreciate that admirable look and preserve it for illustration of one of the forms of ancient piety lost to us, and yet at the same time stow away as part of the poetry of the general drama just the luxury and pride, overhanging summer seas and projecting into summer nights great shafts of light and sound, that prompted the noble scorn. The "round of pleasure" all this with a grand good conscience of course—for it always in the like case has that, had it at least when arranging performances, dramatic and musical, at ever so much a ticket, under the advantage of rare amateur talent, in aid of the great Sanitary Commission that walked in the footsteps and renewed in various forms the example of Florence Nightingale; these exhibitions taking place indeed more particularly in the tributary cities, New York, Philadelphia, Boston (we were then shut up to those,) but with the shining stars marked for triumphant appearance announced in advance on the Newport scene and glittering there as beauties, as élégantes, as vocalists, as heroines of European legend. Hadn't there broken upon us, under public stress, a refluent wave from Paris, the mid-Empire Paris of the highest pitch, which was to raise our social water-mark to a point unprecedented and there strikingly leave it? We were learning new lessons in every branch—that was the sense of the so immensely quickened general pace; and though my examples may seem rather spectral I like to believe this bigger breathing of the freshness of the future to have been what the collective rumble and shimmer of the whole business most meant. It exhaled an artless confidence which yet momently increased; it had no great sense of a direction, but gratefully took any of which the least hint was given, gathering up by the way and after the fact whatever account of itself a vague voice might strike off. There were times when the account of itself as flooding Lawton's Valley for afternoon tea was doubtless what it would most comfortably have welcomed—Lawton's Valley, at a good drive's length from the seaward quarter, being the scene of villeggiatura of the Boston muse, as it were, and the Boston muse having in those after all battle-haunted seasons an authority and a finish of accent beyond any other Tyrtaean strain. The New York and perhaps still more the Philadelphia of the time fumbled more helplessly, even if aspiringly, with the Boston evidences in general, I think, than they were to be reduced to doing later on; and by the happy pretext, certainly, that these superior signs had then a bravery they were not perhaps on their own side indefinitely to keep up.

They rustled, with the other leafage of the umbrageous grove, in the summer airs that hung over the long tea-tables; afternoon tea was itself but a new and romantic possibility, with the lesson of it gratefully learnt at hands that dispensed, with the tea and sugar and in the charmingest voice perhaps then to be heard among us, a tone of talk that New York took for exotic and inimitable, yet all the more felt "good," much better than it might if left *all* to itself, for thus flocking in every sort of conveyance to listen to. The Valley was deep, winding and pastoral—or at least looks so now to my attached vision; the infancy of a finer self-consciousness seemed cradled there;

the inconsequent vehicles fraternised, the dim, the more dejected, with the burnished and upstanding; so that I may really perhaps take most for the note of the hour the first tremor of the sense on the part of fashion that, if it could, as it already more or less suspected, get its thinking and reading and writing, almost everything in fact but its arithmetic, a bit dingily, but just by that sign cleverly, done for it, so occasion seemed easy, after all, for a nearer view, without responsibility, of the odd performers of the service. When these last were not literally all Bostonians they were New Yorkers who might have been mistaken for such—never indeed by Bostonians themselves, but only by other New Yorkers, the rich and guileless; so the effect as of a vague tribute to culture the most authentic (if I speak not too portentously) was left over for the aftertaste of simple and subtle alike. Those were comparatively thin seasons, I recognise, in the so ample career of Mrs. Howe, mistress of the Valley and wife of the eminent, the militant Phil-Hellene, Dr. S. G. of the honoured name, who reached back to the Byronic time and had dedicated his own later to still more distinguished liberating work on behalf of deaf mutes; for if she was thus the most attuned of interlocutors, most urbane of disputants, most insidious of wits, even before her gathered fame as Julia Ward and the established fortune of her elegant Battle-Hymn, she was perhaps to have served the State scarce better through final organised activities and shining optimisms and great lucky lyric hits than by having in her vale of heterogeneous hospitality undermined the blank assurance of her thicker contingent—after all too but to an *amusing* vague unrest—and thereby scattered the first rare seed of new assimilations. I am moved to add that, by the old terminology, the Avenue might have been figured, in the connection, as descending into the glen to meet the Point—which, save for a very small number of the rarest representatives of the latter, it could meet nowhere else. The difficulty was that of an encounter of birds and fishes; the two tribes were native to elements as opposed as air and water, the Avenue essentially nothing if not exalted on wheels or otherwise expertly mounted, and the Point hopelessly pedestrian and unequipped with stables, so that the very levels at which they materially moved were but upper and lower, dreadfully lower, parallels. And indeed the way to see the Point—which, without playing on the word, naturally became our highest law—was at the Point, where it appeared to much higher advantage than in its trudge through the purple haze or golden dust of supercilious parades. Of the advantage to which it did so appear, off in its own more languorous climate and on its own ground, we fairly cultivated a conviction, rejoicing by that aid very much as in certain old French towns it was possible to distinguish invidiously the Ville from the Cité. The Point was our *cité*, the primal aboriginal Newport—which, striking us on a first acquaintance as not other than dilapidated, might well have been "restored" quite as M. Viollet-le-Duc was even then restoring Carcassonne; and this all the more because our elder Newport, the only seat of history, had a dismantled grassy fort or archaic citadel that dozed over the waterside and that might (though I do take the vision, at close quarters, for horrible) be smartly waked up. The waterside, which was that of the inner bay, the ample reach toward Providence, so much more susceptible of quality than the extravagant open sea, the "old houses," the old elms, the old Quaker faces at the small-paned old windows, the appointedness of the scene for the literary and artistic people, who, by our fond constructive theory, lodged and boarded with the Quakers, always thrifty these, for the sake of all the sweetness and quaintness, for the sake above all somehow of *our* hungry felicity of view, by which I mean mine and that of a trusty friend or two, T. S. Perry in especial— those attributes, meeting a want, as the phrase is, of the decent imagination, made us perhaps overdramatise the sphere of the clever people, but made them at least also, when they unmistakably hovered, affect us as truly the finest touches in the picture. For they were in their way ironic about the rest, and that was a tremendous lift in face of an Avenue that not only, as one could see at a glance, had no irony, but hadn't yet risen, the magazines and the Point aiding, to so much as a suspicion of the effect, familiar to later generations, with which the word can conversationally come in. Oh the old clever people, with their difference of shade from that of the clever old ones—some few of these to have been discerned, no doubt, as of Avenue position: I read back into their various presences I know not what queer little functional value the exercise and privilege of which, uncontested, uncontrasted (save with the absence of everything but stables) represents a felicity for the individual that is lost to our age. It could count as functional then, it could count as felicitous, to have been reabsorbed into Boston, or to propose to absorb even, for the first time, New York, under cover of the mantle, the old artistic draped cloak, that had almost in each case trailed round in Florence, in Rome, in Venice, in conversations with Landor, in pencilled commemoration, a little niggling possibly but withal so sincere, of the "haunts" of Dante, in a general claim of having known the Brownings (ah "the Brownings" of those days!) in a disposition to arrange readings of these and the most oddly associated other poets about the great bleak parlours of the hotels. I despair, however, of any really right register of the art with which the cité ingratiated itself with me in this character of a vivid missionary Bohemia; I met it of course more than half way, as I met everything in the faintest degree ingratiating, even suggesting to it with an art of my own that it should become so—though in this matter I rather missed, I fear, a happy conversion, as if the authenticity were there but my sort of personal dash too absent.

I appear to myself none the less to have had dash for approaches to a confidence more largely seated; since I recall how, having commenced critic under Charles Norton's weighty protection, I was to find myself, on all but the very morrow, invited to the high glory, as I felt it, of aiding to launch, though on the obscurer side of the enterprise, a weekly journal which, putting forth its first leaves in the summer of '65 and under the highest auspices, was soon to enjoy a fortune and achieve an authority and a dignity of which neither newspaper nor critical review among us had hitherto so much as hinted the possibility. The New York Nation had from the first, to the enlivening of several persons consciously and ruefully astray in our desert, made no secret of a literary leaning; and indeed its few foremost months shine most for me in the light of their bestowal of one of the longest and happiest friendships of my life, a relation with Edwin Lawrence Godkin, the Nation incarnate as he was to become, which bore fruit of affection for years after it had ceased to involve the comparatively poorer exercise. Godkin's paper, Godkin's occasional presence and interesting history and vivid ability and, above all, admirably aggressive and ironic editorial humour, of a quality and authority new in the air of a journalism that had meant for the most part the heavy hand alone, these things, with the sudden sweet discovery that I might for my own part acceptedly stammer a style, are so many shades and shifting tints in the positive historic iridescence that flings itself for my

memory, as I have noted, over the "period" of Ashburton Place. Wherever
I dip, again, I pull out a plum from under the tooth of time—this at least
so to my own rapt sense that had I more space I might pull both freely and
at a venture. The strongest savour of the feast—with the fumes of a feast it
comes back—was, I need scarce once more insist, the very taste of the War
as ending and ended; through which blessing, more and more, the quantity
of military life or at least the images of military experience seemed all about
us, quite paradoxically, to grow greater. This I take to have been a result,
first of the impending, and then of the effective, break-up of the vast veteran
Army, swamping much of the scene as with the flow of a monster tide and
bringing literally home to us, in bronzed, matured faces and even more in
bronzed, matured characters, above all in the absolutely acquired and stored
resource of overwhelming reference, reference usually of most substance the
less it was immediately explicit, the more in fact it was faded and jaded to
indifference, what was meant by having patiently served. The very smell
of having so served was somehow, at least to my super-sensitive nostril, in
the larger and cooler air, where it might have been an emanation, the most
masculine, the most communicative as to associated far-off things (according
to the nature, ever, of elements vaguely exhaled), from the operation of the
general huge gesture of relief—from worn toggery put off, from old army-
cloth and other fittings at a discount, from swordbelts and buckles, from a
myriad saturated articles now not even lying about but brushed away with an
effect upon the passing breeze and all relegated to the dim state of some mere
theoretic commemorative panoply that was never in the event to be objectively
disposed. The generalisation grew richly or, as it were, quite adorably familiar,
that life was ever so handsomely reinforced, and manners, not to say manner
at large, refreshed, and personal aspects and types accented, and categories
multiplied (no category, for the dreaming painter of things, could our scene
afford not to grab at on the chance), just by the fact of the discharge upon
society of such an amount of out-of-the-way experience, as it might roughly
be termed—such a quantity and variety of possession and assimilation of
unprecedented history. It had been unprecedented at least among ourselves,
we had had it in our own highly original conditions—or "they," to be more
exact, had had it admirably in theirs; and I think I was never to know a

case in which his having been directly touched by it, or, in a word, having consistently "soldiered," learnt all about it and exhausted it, wasn't to count all the while on behalf of the happy man for one's own individual impression or attention; call it again, as everything came back to that, one's own need to interpret. The discharge upon "society" is moreover what I especially mean; it being the sense of how society in *our* image of the word was taking it all in that I was most concerned with; plenty of other images figured of course for other entertainers of such. The world immediately roundabout us at any rate bristled with more of the young, or the younger, cases I speak of, cases of "things seen" and felt, and a delectable difference in the man thereby made imputable, than I could begin here to name even had I kept the record. I think I fairly cultivated the perceiving of it all, so that nothing of it, under some face or other, shouldn't brush my sense and add to my impression; yet my point is more particularly that the body social itself was for the time so permeated, in the light I glance at, that it became to its own consciousness more interesting. As so many existent parts of it, however unstoried yet, to their minor credit, various thrilled persons could inhale the interest to their fullest capacity and feel that they too had been pushed forward—and were even to find themselves by so much the more pushable yet.

I resort thus to the lift and the push as the most expressive figures for that immensely *remonté* state which coincided for us all with the great disconcerting irony of the hour, the unforgettable death of Lincoln. I think of the springtime of '65 as it breathed through Boston streets—my remembrance of all those days is a matter, strangely enough, of the out-of-door vision, of one's constantly dropping down from Beacon Hill, to the brave edge of which we clung, for appreciation of those premonitory gusts of April that one felt most perhaps where Park Street Church stood dominant, where the mouth of the Common itself uttered promises, more signs and portents than one could count, more prodigies than one could keep apart, and where further strange matters seemed to charge up out of the lower districts and of the "business world," generative as never before of news. The streets were restless, the meeting of the seasons couldn't but be inordinately so, and one's own poor pulses matched—at the supreme pitch of that fusion, for instance, which condensed itself to blackness roundabout the dawn of April 15th: I was fairly to go in shame of its being my birthday. These would have been the hours of the streets if none others had been—when the huge general gasp filled them like a great earth-shudder and people's eyes met people's eyes without the vulgarity of speech. Even this was, all so strangely, part of the lift and the swell, as tragedy has but to be of a pure enough strain and a high enough connection to sow with its dark hand the seed of greater life. The collective sense of what had occurred was of a sadness too noble not somehow to inspire, and it was truly in the air that, whatever we had as a nation produced or failed to produce, we could at least gather round this perfection of a classic woe. True enough, as we were to see, the immediate harvest of our loss was almost too ugly to be borne—for nothing more sharply comes back to me than the tune to which the "esthetic sense," if one glanced but from *that* high window (which was after all one of many too), recoiled in dismay from the sight of Mr. Andrew Johnson perched on the stricken scene. We had given ourselves a figure-head, and the figure-head sat there in its habit as it lived, and we were to have it in our eyes for three or four years and to ask ourselves in horror what monstrous thing we had done. I speak but of aspects, those aspects which, under a certain turn of them, may be all but everything; gathered together they become a symbol of what is behind, and it was open to us to waver at shop-windows exposing the new photograph, exposing, that is, *the* photograph, and ask ourselves what we had been guilty of as a people, when all was said, to deserve the infliction of that form. It was vain to say that we had deliberately invoked the "common" in authority and must drink the wine we had drawn. No countenance, no salience of aspect nor composed symbol, could superficially have referred itself less than Lincoln's mould-smashing mask to any mere matter-of-course type of propriety; but his admirable unrelated head had itself revealed a type—as if by the very fact that what made in it for roughness of kind looked out only less than what made in it for splendid final stamp, in other words for commanding Style. The result thus determined had been precious for representation, and above all for fine suggestional function, in a degree that left behind every medal we had ever played at striking; whereas before the image now substituted representation veiled her head in silence and the element of the suggested was exactly the direst. What, however, on the further view, was to be more refreshing than to find that there were excesses of native habit which truly we couldn't bear? so that it was for the next two or three years fairly sustaining to consider that, let the reasons publicly given for the impeachment of the official in question be any that would serve, the grand inward logic or mystic law had been that we really couldn't go on offering each other before the nations the consciousness of such a presence. That was at any rate the style of reflection to which the humiliating case reduced me; just this withal now especially working, I feel, into that image of our generally quickened activity of spirit, our having by the turn of events more ideas to apply and even to play with, that I have tried to throw off. Everything I recover, I again risk repeating, fits into the vast miscellany—the detail of which I may well seem, however, too poorly to have handled.

Let it serve then for a scrap of detail that the appearance of William's further fortune enjoyed thereabouts a grasp of my attention scarce menaced even by the call on that faculty of such appearances of my own as I had naturally in some degree also to take for graces of the banquet. I associate the sense of his being, in a great cause, far away on the billow with that clearance of the air through the tremendous draught, from sea to sea, of the Northern triumph, which seemed to make a good-natured infinitude of room for all the individual interests and personal lives that might help the pot to bubble—if the expression be not too mean for the size of our confidence; that the cause on which the Agassiz expedition to South America embarked *was* of the greatest being happily a presumption altogether within my scope. It reawoke the mild divinatory rage with which I had followed, with so little to show for it, the military fortune of my younger brothers—feeding the gentle passion indeed, it must be added, thanks to the letter-writing grace of which the case had now the benefit, with report and picture of a vividness greater than any ever to be shed from a like source upon our waiting circle. Everything of the kind, for me, was company; but I dwelt, for that matter and as I put it all together, in company so constant and so enchanting that this amounted to moving, in whatever direction, with the mass—more and more aware as I was of the "fun" (to express it grossly) of living by my imagination and thereby finding that company, in countless different forms, could only swarm about me. Seeing further into the figurable world *made* company of persons and places, objects and subjects alike: it gave them all without exception chances to be somehow or other interesting, and the imaginative ply of finding interest once taken (I think I had by that time got much beyond looking for it), the whole conspiracy of aspects danced round me in a ring. It formed, by my present vision of it, a shining escort to one's possibly often hampered or mystified, but never long stayed and absolutely never wasted, steps; it hung about, after the fashion of winter evening adumbrations just outside the reach of the lamplight, while one sat writing, reading, listening, watching—perhaps even again, incurably, but dawdling and gaping; and most of all doubtless, if it supplied with colour people and things often by themselves, I dare say, neutral enough, how it painted thick, how it fairly smothered, any surface that did it the turn of showing positive and intrinsic life! Ah the things and the people, the hours and scenes and circumstances, the *inénarrables* occasions and relations, that I might still present in its light if I would, and with the enormous advantage now (for this I should unblushingly claim), of being able to mark for present irony or pity or wonder, or just for a better intelligence, or again for the high humour or extreme strangeness of the thing, the rare indebtedness, calculated by the long run, in which it could leave particular cases! This necessity I was under that everything should be interesting—for fear of the collapse otherwise of one's sustaining intention—would have confessed doubtless to a closest connection, of all the connections, with the small inkpot in which I seemed at last definitely destined to dip to the exclusion of any stream more Pactolean: a modest manner of saying that difficulty and slowness of composition were clearly by this time not in the least appointed to blight me, however inveterate they were likely to prove; that production, such as it was, floundered on in spite of them; and that, to put it frankly, if I enjoyed as much company as I have said no small part of it was of my very own earning. The freshness of first creations—since we are exalted, in art, to these arrogant expressions—never fails, I take it, to beguile the creator, in default of any other victim, even to the last extravagance; so that what happened was that one found all the swarm of one's intentions, one's projected images, quite "good enough" to mix with the rest of one's society, setting up with it terms of interpenetration, an admirable commerce of borrowing and lending, taking and giving, not to say stealing and keeping. Did it verily *all*, this freshness of felt contact, of curiosity and wonder, come back perhaps to certain small and relatively ridiculous achievements of "production" as aforesaid?—ridiculous causes, I mean, of such prodigious effects. I am divided between the shame on the one hand of claiming for them, these concocted "short stories," that they played so great a part, and a downright admiring tenderness on the other for their holding up their stiff little heads in such a bustle of life and traffic of affairs. I of course really and truly cared for them, as we say, more than for aught else whatever—cared for them with that kind of care, infatuated though it may seem, that makes it bliss for the fond votary never to so much as speak of the loved object, makes it a refinement of piety to perform his rites under cover of a perfect freedom of mind as to everything *but* them. These secrets of the imaginative life were in fact more various than I may dream of trying to tell; they referred to actual concretions of existence as well as to the supposititious; the joy of life indeed, drawbacks and all, was just in the constant quick flit of association, to and fro, and through a hundred open doors, between the two great chambers (if it be not absurd, or even base, to separate them) of direct and indirect experience. If it is of the great comprehensive *fusion* that I speak as the richest note of all those hours, what could truly have been more in the sense of it than exactly such a perfect muddle of pleasure for instance as my having (and, as I seem to remember, at his positive invitation) addressed the most presuming as yet of my fictional bids to my distinguished friend of a virtual lifetime, as he was to become, William Dean Howells, whom I rejoice to name here and who had shortly before returned from a considerable term of exile in Venice and was in the act of taking all but complete charge of the Boston "Atlantic"? The confusion was, to be plain, of more things than can hope to go into my picture with any effect of keeping distinct there—the felt felicity, literally, in my performance, the felt ecstasy, the still greater, in my receipt of Howells's message; and then, naturally, most of all, the at once to be recorded blest violence in the break upon my consciousness of his glittering response after perusal.

There was still more in it all than that, however—which is the point of my mild demonstration; I associate the passage, to press closer, with a long summer, from May to November, spent at the then rural retreat of Swampscott, forty minutes by train northward from Boston, and that scene of fermentation, in its turn, I invest with unspeakable memories. It was the summer of '66 and of the campaign of Sadowa across the sea—we had by that time got sufficiently away from our own campaigns to take some notice of those of other combatants, on which we bestowed in fact, I think, the highest competence of attention then anywhere at play; a sympathetic sense that bore us even over to the Franco-German war four years later and helped us to know what we meant when we "felt strongly" about it. No strength of feeling indeed of which the vibration had remained to us from the other time could have been greater than our woe-stricken vision of the plight of France under the portent of Sedan; I had been back to that country and some of its neighbourhoods for some fifteen months during the previous interval, and I recover again no share in a great collective pang more vividly than our particular appalled state, that of a whole company of us, while we gaped out at the cry of reiterated bulletins from the shade of an August verandah, and then again from amid boskages of more immediate consolation, during the Saratoga and the Newport seasons of 1870. I had happened to repair to Saratoga, of all inconsequent places, on my return from the Paris and the London of the weeks immediately preceding the war, and though it was not there that the worst sound of the first crash reached us, I feel around me still all the air of our dismay—which was, in the queerest way in the world, that of something so alien mixed, to the increase of horror, with something so cherished: the great hot glare of vulgarity of the aligned hotels of the place and period drenching with its crude light the apparent collapse of everything we had supposed most massive. Which forward stretch on the part of this chronicle represents, I recognise, the practice of the discursive well-nigh overmastering its principle—or would do so, rather, weren't it that the fitful and the flickering, the extravagant advance and the corrective retreat from it, the law and the lovely art of foreshortening, have had here throughout most to serve me. It is under countenance of that law that I still grasp my capricious clue, making a jump for the moment over two or three years and brushing aside by the way quite numberless appeals, claims upon tenderness of memory not less than pleas for charm of interest, against which I must steel myself, even though I account this rank disloyalty to each. There is no quarter to which I have inclined in my brief recovery of the high tide of impression flooding the "period" of Ashburton Place that might not have drawn me on and on; so that I confess I feel myself here drag my mantle, right and left, from the clutch of suppliant hands—voluminous as it may doubtless yet appear in spite of my sense of its raggedness. Wrapped in tatters it is therefore that, with three or four of William's letters of '67 and '68 kept before me, I make my stride, not only for the sake of what I still regard as their admirable interest, but for the way they bring back again to me everything they figured at the time, every flame of faith they rekindled, every gage they held out for the future. Present for me are still others than these in particular, which I keep over for another introducing, but even the pages I here preserve overflow with connections— so many that, extravagant as it may sound, I have to make an effort to breast them. These are with a hundred matters of our then actual life—little as that virtue may perhaps show on their face; but above all just with the huge small fact that the writer was by the blest description "in Europe," and that this had verily still its way of meaning for me more than aught else beside. For what sprang in especial from his situation was the proof, with its positive air, that a like, when all was said, might become again one's own; that such luck wasn't going to be for evermore perversely out of the question with us, and that in fine I too was already in a manner transported by the intimacy with which I partook of his having been. I shouldn't have overstated it, I think, in saying that I really preferred such a form of experience (of this particular one) to the simpler—given most of our current conditions; there was somehow a greater richness, a larger accession of knowledge, vision, life, whatever one might have called it, in "having him there," as we said, and in my individually getting the good of this with the peculiar degree of ease that reinforced the general quest of a special sufficiency of that boon to which I was during those years rigidly, and yet on the whole by no means abjectly, reduced.

Our parents had in the autumn of '66 settled, virtually for the rest of their days, at Cambridge, and William had concomitantly with this, that is from soon after his return from Brazil, entered upon a season of study at the Harvard Medical School, then keeping its terms in Boston and under the wide wing of—as one supposed it, or as I at any rate did—the Massachusetts General Hospital. I have to disengage my mantle here with a force in which I invite my reader to believe—for I push through a thicket of memories in which the thousand-fingered branches arrestingly catch; otherwise I should surrender, and with a passionate sense of the logic in it, to that long and crowded Swampscott summer at which its graceless name has already failed to keep me from having glanced. The place, smothered in a dense prose of prosperity now, may have been even in those days, by any high measure, a weak enough apology for an offered breast of Nature: nevertheless it ministered to me as the only "American country" save the silky Newport fringes with which my growing imagination, not to mention my specious energy, had met at all continuous occasion to play—so that I should have but to let myself go a little, as I say, to sit up to my neck again in the warm depth of its deposit. Out of this I should lift great handfuls of variety of vision; it was to have been in its way too a season of coming and going, and with its main mark, I make out, that it somehow absurdly flowered, first and last, into some intenser example of every sort of intimation up to then vouchsafed me, whether by the inward or the outward life. I think of it thus as a big bouquet of blooms the most mixed—yet from which it is to the point just here to detach the sole reminiscence, coloured to a shade I may not reproduce, of a day's excursion to see my brother up at the Hospital. Had I not now been warned off too many of the prime images brought, for their confusion, to the final proof, I should almost risk ever so briefly "evoking" the impression this mere snatch was to leave with me, the picture as of sublime activities and prodigious possibilities, of genial communities of consideration and acquisition, all in a great bright porticoed and gardened setting, that was to hang itself in my crazy cabinet for as long as the light of the hour might allow. I put my hand on the piece still—in its now so deeply obscured corner; though the true point of my reference would seem to be in the fact that if William studied medicine long enough to qualify and to take his degree (so as to have become as roundedly "scientific" as possible) he was yet immediately afterwards, by one of those quick shifts of the scene with which we were familiar, beginning philosophic study in Germany and again writing home letters of an interest that could be but re-emphasised by our having him planted out as a reflector of impressions where impressions were both strong and as different as possible from those that more directly beat upon us. I myself could do well enough with these last, I may parenthesise, so long as none others were in question; but that complacency shrank just in proportion as we were reached by the report of difference and of the foreign note, the report particularly favourable—which was indeed what any and every report perforce appeared to me. William's, from anywhere, had ever an authority for me that attended none others; even if this be not the place for more than a word of light on the apparent disconnection of his actual course. It comes back to me that the purpose of practising medicine had at no season been flagrant in him, and he was in fact, his hospital connection once over, never to practise for a day. He was on the other hand to remain grateful for his intimate experience of the laboratory and the clinic, and I was as constantly to feel that the varieties of his application had been as little wasted for him as those of my vagueness had really been for me. His months at Dresden and his winter in Berlin were of a new variety—this last even with that tinge of the old in it which came from his sharing quarters with T. S. Perry, who, his four years at Harvard ended and his ensuing grand tour of Europe, as then comprehensively carried out, performed, was giving the Universities of Berlin and Paris a highly competent attention. To whatever else of method may have underlain the apparently lawless strain of our sequences I should add the action of a sharp lapse of health on my brother's part which the tension of a year at the dissecting table seemed to have done much to determine; as well as the fond fact that Europe was again from that crisis forth to take its place for us as a standing remedy, a regular mitigation of all suffered, or at least of all wrong, stress. Of which remarks but a couple of letters addressed to myself, I have to recognise, form here the occasion; these only, in that order, have survived the accidents of time, as I the more regret that I have in my mind's eye still much of the matter of certain others; notably of one from Paris (on his way further) recounting a pair of evenings at the theatre, first for the younger Dumas and Les Idées de Madame Aubray, with Pasca and Delaporte, this latter of an exquisite truth to him, and then for something of the Palais Royal with *four* comedians, as he emphatically noted, who were each, wonderful to say, "de la force of Warren of the Boston Museum." He spent the summer of '67 partly in Dresden and partly at Bad-Teplitz in Bohemia, where he had been recommended the waters; he was to return for these again after a few months and was also to seek treatment by hydropathy at the establishment of Divonne, in the French back-country of Lake Leman, where a drawing sent home in a letter, and which I do my best to reproduce, very comically represents him as surrounded by the listening fair. I remember supposing even his Dresden of the empty weeks to bristle with precious images and every form of local character—this a little perhaps because of his treating us first of all to a pair of whimsical crayoned views of certain animated housetops seen from his window. It is the old names in the old letters, however, that now always most rewrite themselves to my eyes in colour—shades alas that defy plain notation, and if the two with which the following begins, and especially the first of them, only asked me to tell their story I but turn my back on the whole company of which they are part.

...I got last week an excellent letter from Frank Washburn who writes in such a manly way. But the greatest delight I've had was the loan of 5 Weekly Transcripts from Dick Derby. It's strange how quickly one grows away from one's old surroundings. I never should have believed that in so few months the tone of a Boston paper would seem so outlandish to me. As it was, I was in one squeal of amusement, surprise and satisfaction until deep in the night, when I went to bed tired out with patriotism. The boisterous animal good-humour, familiarity, reckless energy and self-confidence, unprincipled optimism, esthetic saplessness and intellectual imbecility, made a mixture hard to characterise, but totally different from the tone of things here and, as the Germans would say, whose "Existenz so völlig dasteht," that there was nothing to do but to let yourself feel it. The Americans themselves here too amuse me much; they have such a hungry, restless look and seem so unhooked somehow from the general framework. The other afternoon as I was sitting on the Terrace, a gentleman and two young ladies came and sat down quite near me. I knew them for Americans at a glance, and the man interested me by his exceedingly American expression: a reddish moustache and tuft on chin, a powerful nose, a small light eye, half insolent and *all* sagacious, and a sort of rowdy air of superiority that made me proud to claim him as a brother. In a few minutes I recognised him as General M'Clellan, rather different from his photographs of the War-time, but still not to be mistaken (and I afterwards learned he is here). Whatever his faults may be that of not being "one of us" is not among them.

This next is the note of a slightly earlier impression.

The Germans are certainly a most gemüthlich people. The way all the old women told me how "freundlich" their rooms were—"so freundlich mobilirt" and so forth—melted my heart. Whenever you tell an inferior here to do anything (*e.g.* a cabman) he or she replies "Schön!" or rather "Schehn!" with an accent not quick like a Frenchman's "Bien!" but so protracted, soothing and reassuring to you that you feel as if he were adopting you into his family. You say I've said nothing of the people of this house, but there is nothing to tell about them. The Doctor is an open-hearted excellent man as ever was, and wrapped up in his children; Frau Semler is a sickly, miserly, petty-spirited nonentity. The children are quite uninteresting, though the younger, Anna or Aennchen, aged five, is very handsome and fat. The following short colloquy, which I overheard one day after breakfast a few days since, may serve you as a piece of local colour. Aennchen drops a book she is carrying across the room and exclaims "Herr Jesus!"

Mother: "Ach, das sagen *Kinder* nicht, Anna!"

Aennchen (reflectively to herself, sotto voce): "Nicht fur Kinder!" ...

What here follows from Divonne—of fourteen months later—is too full and too various to need contribution or comment.

You must have envied within the last few weeks my revisiting of the sacred scenes of our youth, the shores of Leman, the Ecu de Genève, the sloping Corraterie, etc. My only pang in it all has been caused by your absence, or rather by the fact of my presence instead of yours; for I think your abstemious and poetic soul would have got much more good of the things I've seen than my hardening and definite-growing nature. I wrote a few words about Nürnberg to Alice from Montreux. I found that about as pleasant an impression as any I have had since being abroad—and this because I didn't expect it. The Americans at Dresden had told me it was quite uninteresting. I enclose you a few stereographs I got there—I don't know why, for they are totally irrelevant to the real effect of the place. This it would take Théophile Gautier to describe, so I renounce. It was strange to find how little I remembered at Geneva—I couldn't find the way I used to take up to the

Academy, and the shops and houses of the Rue du Rhône visible from our old windows left me uncertain whether they were the same or new ones. Kohler has set up a new hotel on the Quai du Mont-Blanc—you remember he's the brother of our old Madame Buscarlet there; but I went for association's sake to the Écu. The dining-room was differently hung, and the only thing in my whole 24 hours in the place that stung me, so to speak, with memory, was that kind of chinese-patterned dessert-service we used to have. So runs the world away. I didn't try to look up Ritter, Chantre or any of ces messieurs, but started off here the next morning, where I have now been a week.

My impression on gradually coming from a German into a French atmosphere of things was rather unexpected and not in all respects happy. I have been in Germany half amused and half impatient with the slowness of proceeding and the uncouthness of taste and expression that prevail there so largely in all things, but on exchanging it for the brightness and shipshapeness of these quasi-French arrangements of life and for the tart fire-cracker-like speech of those who make them I found myself inclined to retreat again on what I had left, and had for a few days quite a homesickness for the easy, ugly, substantial German ways. The "'tarnal" smartness in which the railway refreshment counters, for example, are dressed up, the tight waists and "tasteful" white caps of the female servants, the everlasting monsieur and madame, and especially the quickness and snappishness of enunciation, suggesting such an inward impatience, quite absurdly gave on my nerves. But I am getting used to it all, and the French people who sit near me here at table and who repelled me at first by the apparently cold-blooded artificiality of their address to each other, now seem less heartless and inhuman. I am struck more than ever I was with the hopelessness of us English, and a *fortiori* the Germans, ever competing with the French in matters of form or finite taste of any sort. They are sensitive to things that simply don't exist for us. I notice it here in manners and speech: how can a people who speak with no tonic accents in their words *help* being cleaner and neater in expressing themselves? On the other hand the limitations of *reach* in the French mind strike me more and more; their delight in rallying round an official standard in all matters, in counting and dating everything from certain great names, their use and love of catchwords and current phrases, their sacrifice of independence of mind for the mere sake of meeting their hearer or reader on common ground, their metaphysical incapacity not only to deal with questions but to know what the questions are, stand out plainer and plainer the more headway I make in German. One wonders where the "Versöhnung" or conciliation of all these rival national qualities is going to take place. I imagine we English stand rather between the French and the Germans both in taste and in spiritual intuition. In Germany, while unable to avoid respecting that solidity of the national mind which causes such a mass of permanent work to be produced there annually, I couldn't help consoling myself by the thought that whatever, after all, they might *do*, the Germans were a plebeian crowd and could never *be* such gentlemen as we were. I now find myself getting over the French superiority by an exactly inverse process of thought. The Frenchman must sneer at us even more than we sneer at the Germans—and which sneer is final, his at us two, or ours at him, or the Germans' at us? It seems an insoluble question, which I fortunately haven't got to settle.

I've read several novels lately, some of the irrepressible George's: La Daniella and the Beaux Messieurs de Bois-Doré. (Was it thee, by the bye that wrotest the Nation notices on her, on W. Morris's new poem and on The Spanish Gypsy? They came to me unmarked, but the thoughts seemed such as you would entertain, and the style in some places like yours—in others not.) George Sand babbles her improvisations on so that I never begin to believe a word of what she says. I've also read The Woman in White, a couple of Balzac's, etc., and a volume of tales by Mérimée which I will send you if I can by Frank Washburn. He is a big man; but the things which have given me most pleasure have been some sketches of travel by Th. Gautier. What an absolute thing genius is! That this creature, with no more soul than a healthy poodle-dog, no philosophy, no morality, no information (for I doubt exceedingly if his knowledge of architectural terms and suchlike is accurate) should give one a finer enjoyment than his betters in all these respects by mere force of good-nature, clear eyesight and felicity of phrase! His style seems to me perfect, and I should think it would pay you to study it with love— principally in the most trivial of these collections of notes of travel. T. S. P. has a couple of them for you, and another, which I've read here and is called Caprices et Zigzags, is worth buying. It contains wonderful French (in the classic sense, I mean, with all those associations) descriptions of London. I'm not sure if you know Gautier at all save by the delicious Capitaine Fracasse. But these republished feuilletons are all of as charming a quality and I should think would last as long as the language.

There are 70 or 80 people in this etablissement, no one of whom I have as yet particularly cottoned up to. It's incredible how even so slight a barrier as the difference of language with most of them, and still more as the absence of local and personal associations, range of gibes and other common ground to stand on, counts against one's scraping acquaintance. It's disgusting and humiliating. There is a lovely maiden of *etwa* 19 sits in sight of me at the table with whom I am falling deeply in love. She has never looked at me yet, and I really believe I should be quite incapable of conversing with her even were I "introduced," from a sense of the above difficulties and because one doesn't know what subjects or allusions may be possible with a jeune fille. I suppose my life for the past year would have furnished you, as the great American nouvelliste, a good many "motives" and subjects of observation—especially so in this place. I wish I could pass them over to you—such as they are you'd profit by them more than I and gather in a great many more. I should like full well an hour's, or even longer, interview with you, and with the Parents and the Sister and the Aunt and all; just so as to start afresh on a clean basis. Give my love to Wendell Holmes. I've seen —— —— several times; but what a cold-blooded cuss he is! Write me your impression of T. S. P., who will probably reach you before this letter. If Frank Washburn ever gets home be friendly to him. He is much aged by travel and experience, and is a most charming character and generous mind.

XIII

If I add to the foregoing a few lines more from my brother's hand, these are of a day separated by long years from that time of our youth of which I have treated. Addressed after the immense interval to an admirable friend whom I shall not name here, they yet so vividly refer—and with something I can only feel as the first authority—to one of the most prized interests of our youth that, under the need of still failing to rescue so many of these values from the dark gulf, I find myself insist the more on a place here, before I close, for that presence in our early lives as to which my brother's few words say so much. To have so promptly and earnestly spoken of Mary Temple the younger in this volume is indeed I think to have offered a gage for my not simply leaving her there. The opportunity not so to leave her comes at any rate very preciously into my hands, and I can not better round off this record than by making the most of it. The letter to which William alludes is one that my reader will presently recognise. It had come back to him thus clearly at the far end of time.

I am deeply thankful to you for sending me this letter, which revives all sorts of poignant memories and makes her live again in all her lightness and freedom. Few spirits have been more free than hers. I find myself wishing so that she could know me as I am now. As for knowing her as *she* is now—??!! I find that she means as much in the way of human character for me now as she ever did, being unique and with no analogue in all my subsequent experience of people. Thank you once more for what you have done.

The testimony so acknowledged was a letter in a copious succession, the product of little more than one year, January '69 to February '70, sacredly preserved by the recipient; who was not long after the day of my brother's acknowledgment to do me the honour of communicating to me the whole series. He could have done nothing to accord more with the spirit in which I have tried to gather up something of the sense of our far-off past, his own as well as that of the rest of us; and no loose clue that I have been able to recover unaided touches into life anything like such a tract of the time-smothered consciousness. More charming and interesting things emerge for me than I can point to in their order—but they will make, I think, their own appeal. It need only further be premised that our delightful young cousin had had from some months back to begin to reckon with the progressive pulmonary weakness of which the letters tell the sad story. Also, I can scarce help saying, the whole world of the old New York, that of the earlier dancing years, shimmers out for me from the least of her allusions.

I will write you as nice a letter as I can, but would much rather have a good talk with you. As I can't have the best thing I am putting up with the second-best, contrary to my pet theory. I feel as if I were in heaven to-day— all because the day is splendid and I have been driving about all the morning in a small sleigh in the fresh air and sunshine, until I found that I had in spite of myself, for the time being, stopped asking the usual inward question of why I was born. I am not going to Canada—I know no better reason for this than because I said I *was* going. My brother-in-law makes such a clamour when I propose departure that I am easily overcome by his kindness and my own want of energy. Besides, it is great fun to live here; the weather just now is grand, and I knock about all day in a sleigh, and do nothing but enjoy it and meditate. Then we are so near town that we often go in for the day to shop and lunch with some of our numerous friends, returning with a double relish for the country. We all went in on a spree the other night and stayed at the Everett House; from which, as a starting-point we poured ourselves in strong force upon Mrs. Gracie King's ball—a very grand affair, given for a very pretty Miss King, at Delmonico's. Our raid consisted of thirteen Emmets and a moderate supply of Temples, and the ball was a great success. It was two years since I had been to one and I enjoyed it so much that I mean very soon to repeat the experiment—at the next Assembly if possible. The men in society, in New York, this winter, are principally a lot of feeble-minded boys; but I was fortunate enough to escape them, as my partner for the German was a man of thirty-five, the solitary *man*, I believe, in the room. Curiously enough, I had danced my last German, two years before, in that very place and with the same person. He is a Mr. Lee, who has spent nearly all his life abroad; two of his sisters have married German princes, and from knocking about so much he has become a thorough cosmopolite. As he is intelligent, with nothing to do but amuse himself, he is a very agreeable partner, and I mean to dance with him again as soon as possible. I don't know why I have tried your patience by writing so about a person you have never seen; unless it's to show you that I haven't irrevocably given up the world, the flesh and the devil, but am conscious of a faint charm about them still when taken in small doses. I agree with you perfectly about Uncle Henry—I should think he would be very irritating to the legal mind; he is not at all satisfactory even to mine. Have you seen much of Willy James lately? That is a rare creature, and one in whom my intellect, if you will pardon the misapplication of the word, takes more solid satisfaction than in almost anybody. I haven't read Browning's new book—I mean to wait till you are by to explain it to me— which reminds me, along with what you say about wishing for the spring, that we shall go to North Conway next summer, and that in that case you may as well make up your mind to come and see us there. I can't wait longer than that for the Browning readings. (Which would have been of The Ring and the Book.) Arthur Sedgwick has sent me Matthew Arnold's photograph, which Harry had pronounced so disappointing. I don't myself, on the whole, find it so; on the contrary, after having looked at it much, I like it—it quite harmonises with my notion of him, and I have always had an affection for him. You must tell me something that you are *sure* is true—I don't care much what it may be, I will take your word for it. Things get into a muddle with me—how can I give you "a start on the way of righteousness"? You know that way better than I do, and the only advice I can give you is not to stop saying your prayers. I hope God may bless you, and beyond those things I hardly know what is right, and therefore what to wish you. Good-bye.

"North Conway" in the foregoing has almost the force for me of a wizard's wand; the figures spring up again and move in a harmony that is not of the fierce present; the sense in particular of the August of '65 shuts me in to its blest unawarenesses not less than to all that was then exquisite in its current certainties and felicities; the fraternising, endlessly conversing group of us gather under the rustling pines—and I admire, precisely, the arrival, the bright revelation as I recover it, of the so handsome young man, marked with military distinction but already, with our light American promptitude, addressed to that high art of peace in which a greater eminence awaited him, of whom this most attaching member of the circle was to make four years later so wise and steady a confidant. Our circle I fondly call it, and doubtless then called it, because in the light of that description I could most rejoice in it, and I think of it now as having formed a little world of easy and happy interchange, of unrestricted and yet all so instinctively sane and secure association and conversation, with all its liberties and delicacies, all its mirth and its earnestness protected and directed so much more from within than from without, that I ask myself, perhaps too fatuously, whether any such right conditions for the play of young intelligence and young friendship, the reading of Matthew Arnold and Browning, the discussion of a hundred human and personal things, the sense of the splendid American summer drawn out to its last generosity, survives to this more complicated age. I doubt if there be circles to-day, and seem rather to distinguish confusedly gangs and crowds and camps, more propitious, I dare say, to material affluence and physical riot than anything we knew, but not nearly so appointed for ingenious and ingenuous talk. I think of our interplay of relation as attuned to that fruitful freedom of what we took for speculation, what we didn't recoil from as boundless curiosity—as the consideration of life, that is, the personal, the moral inquiry and adventure at large, so far as matter for them had up to then met our view—I think of this fine quality in our scene with no small confidence in its having been rare, or to be more exact perhaps, in its having been possible to the general American felicity and immunity as it couldn't otherwise or elsewhere have begun to be. Merely to say, as an assurance, that such relations shone with the light of "innocence" is of itself to breathe on them wrongly or rudely, is uncouthly to "defend" them—as if the very air that consciously conceived and produced them didn't all tenderly and amusedly take care of them. I at any rate figure again, to my customary positive piety, all the aspects now; that in especial of my young orphaned cousins as mainly composing the maiden train and seeming as if they still had but yesterday brushed the morning dew of the dear old Albany naturalness; that of the venerable, genial, erect great-aunt, their more immediately active guardian, a model of antique spinsterhood appointed to cares such as even renewals of wedlock could scarce more have multiplied for her, and thus, among her many ancient and curious national references—one was tempted to call them—most impressive by her striking resemblance to the portraits, the most benignant, of General Washington. She might have represented the mother, no less adequately than he represented the father, of their country. I can only feel, however, that what particularly drew the desired circle sharpest for me was the contribution to it that I had been able to effect by introducing the companion of my own pilgrimage, who was in turn to introduce a little later the great friend of *his* then expanding situation, restored with the close of the War to civil pursuits and already deep in them; the interesting pair possessed after this fashion of a quantity of common fine experience that glittered as so much acquired and enjoyed luxury—all of a sort that I had no acquisition whatever to match. I remember being happy in that I might repeatedly point our moral, under permission (for we were always pointing morals), with this brilliant advantage of theirs even if I might with none of my own; and I of course knew—what was half the beauty—that if we were just the most delightful loose band conceivable, and immersed in a regular revel of all the harmonies, it was largely by grace of the three quite exceptional young men who, thanks in part to the final sublime coach-drive of other days, had travelled up from Boston with their preparation to admire inevitably quickened. I was quite willing to offer myself as exceptional through being able to promote such exceptions and see them justified to waiting apprehension. There was a dangling fringe, there were graceful accessories and hovering shades, but, essentially, we of the true connection made up the drama, or in other words, for the benefit of my imagination, reduced the fond figment of the Circle to terms of daily experience. If drama we could indeed feel this as being, I hasten to add, we owed it most of all to our just having such a heroine that everything else inevitably came. Mary Temple was beautifully and indescribably *that*—in the technical or logical as distinguished from the pompous or romantic sense of the word; wholly without effort or desire on her part—for never was a girl less consciously or consentingly or vulgarly dominant—everything that took place around her took place as if primarily in relation to her and in her interest: that is in the interest of drawing her out and displaying her the more. This too without her in the least caring, as I say—in the deep, the morally nostalgic indifferences that were the most finally characteristic thing about her—whether such an effect took place or not; she liked nothing in the world so much as to see others fairly exhibited; not as they might best please her by being, but as they might most fully reveal themselves, their stuff and their truth: which was the only thing that, after any first flutter for the superficial air or grace in an acquaintance, could in the least fix her attention. She had beyond any equally young creature I have known a sense for verity of character and play of life in others, for their acting out of their force or their weakness, whatever either might be, at no matter what cost to herself; and it was this instinct that made her care so for life in general, just as it was her being thereby so engaged in that tangle that made her, as I have expressed it, ever the heroine of the scene. Life claimed her and used her and beset her—made her range in her groping, her naturally immature and unlighted way from end to end of the scale. No one felt more the charm of the actual—only the actual comprised for her kinds of reality (those to which her letters perhaps most of all testify), that she saw treated round her for the most part either as irrelevant or as unpleasant. She was absolutely afraid of nothing she might come to by living with enough sincerity and enough wonder; and I think it is because one was to see her launched on that adventure in such bedimmed, such almost tragically compromised conditions that one is caught by her title to the heroic and pathetic mark. It is always difficult for us after the fact not to see young things who were soon to be lost to us as already distinguished by their fate; this particular victim of it at all events might well have made the near witness ask within himself how her restlessness of spirit, the finest reckless impatience, was to be assuaged or "met" by the common lot. One somehow saw it nowhere about us as up to her terrible young standard of the interesting—even if to say this suggests an air of tension, a sharpness of importunity, than which nothing could have been less like her. The charming, irresistible fact was that one had never seen a creature with such lightness of forms, a lightness all her own, so inconsequently grave at the core, or an asker of endless questions with such apparent lapses of care. It is true that as an effect of the state of health which during the year '69 grew steadily worse the anxious note and serious mind sound in her less intermittently than by her former wont.

This might be headed with that line of a hymn, "Hark, from the tombs etc.!"—but perhaps it won't prove as bad as that. It looks pretty doubtful still, but I have a sort of feeling that I shall come round this one time more; by which I don't mean to brag! The "it" of which I speak is of course my old enemy hemorrhage, of which I have had within the last week seven pretty big ones and several smaller, hardly worth mentioning. I don't know what has come over me—I can't stop them; but, as I said, I mean to try and beat them yet. Of course I am in bed, where I shall be indefinitely—not allowed to speak one word, literally, even in a whisper. The reason I write this is because I don't think it will hurt me at all—if I take it easy and stop when I feel tired. It is a pleasant break in the monotony of gruel and of thinking of the grave—and then too a few words from somebody who is strong and active in the good old world (as it seems to me now) would be very refreshing. But don't tell anyone I have written, because it will be sure to reach the ears of my dear relatives and will cause them to sniff the air and flounce! You see I am a good deal of a baby—in the sense of not wanting the reproaches of my relatives on this or any other subject.... All the Emmets are so good and kind that I found, when it came to the point, that there was a good deal to make life attractive, and that if the choice were given me I would much rather stay up here on the solid earth, in the air and sunshine, with an occasional sympathetic glimpse of another person's soul, than to be put down underground and say good-bye for ever to humanity, with all its laughter and its sadness. Yet you mustn't think me now in any *special* danger of dying, or even in low spirits, for it isn't so—the doctor tells me I am *not* in danger, even if the hemorrhages should keep on. However, "you can't fool a regular boarder," as Mr. Holmes would say, and I can't see why there is any reason to think they will heal a week hence, when I shall be still weaker, if they can't heal now. Still, they *may* be going to stop—I haven't had one since yesterday at 4, and now it's 3; nearly twenty-four hours. I am of a hopeful temperament and not easily scared, which is in my favour. If this *should* prove to be the last letter you get from me, why take it for a good-bye; I'll keep on the lookout for you in the spirit world, and shall be glad to see you when you come there, provided it's a better place than this. Elly is in New York, enjoying herself immensely, and I haven't let her know how ill I have been, as there were to be several parties this last week and I was afraid it might spoil her fun. I didn't mean you to infer from my particularising Willy James's intellect that the rest of him isn't to my liking—he is one of the very few people in this world that I love. He has the largest heart as well as the largest head, and is thoroughly interesting to me. He is generous and affectionate and full of sympathy and humanity—though you mustn't tell him I say so, lest he should think I have been telling you a lie to serve my own purposes. Good-bye.

I should have little heart, I confess, for what is essentially the record of a rapid illness if it were not at the same time the image of an admirable soul. Surrounded as she was with affection she had yet greatly to help herself, and nothing is thus more penetrating than the sense, as one reads, that a method of care would have been followed for her to-day, and perhaps followed with signal success, that was not in the healing or nursing range of forty years ago.

It is a week ago to-day, I think, since I last wrote to you, and I have only had one more hemorrhage—the day after. I feel pretty sure they have stopped for the present, and I am sitting up in my room, as bright as possible. Yesterday when I walked across it I thought I should never be strong again, but now it's quite different, and so nice to be out of bed that my spirits go up absurdly. As soon as I am able I am to be taken to town for another examination, and then when I know my fate I will do the best I can. This climate is trying, to be sure, but such as it is I've got to take my chance in it, as there is no one I care enough for, or who cares enough for me, to take charge of me to Italy, or to the south anywhere. I don't believe any climate, however good, would be of the least use to me with people I don't care for. You may let your moustache grow down to your toes if you like, and I shall but smile scornfully at your futile precautions.

Of the following, in spite of its length, I can bring myself to abate nothing.

....Well, "to make a long story short," as Hannah (her old nurse) says, I caught a cold, and it went to the weak spot, and I had another slight attack of hemorrhage; but I took the necessary steps at once, stayed in bed and didn't speak for six days, and then it stopped and I felt better than I had at all since I was first taken ill. But I began to tire so of such constant confinement to my room that they promised to take me to town as soon as I was well enough, and perhaps to the Opera. This of course would have been a wild excitement for me, and I had charming little plans of music by day and by night, for a week, which I meant to spend with Mrs. Griswold. Accordingly a cavalcade set out from here on Monday, consisting of myself escorted by sisters and friends, who were to see me safely installed in my new quarters and leave me. I arrived, bundled up, at Mrs. Griswold's, and had begun to consider myself already quite emancipated from bondage—so that I was discussing with my brother-in-law the propriety of my going that evening to hear Faust, this but the beginning of a mad career on which I proposed to rush headlong—when Dr. Bassett arrived, who is the medical man that I had meant to consult during my stay *incidentally* and between the pauses in the music. The first thing he said was: "What are you doing here? Go directly back to the place you came from and don't come up again till the warm weather. As for music, you mustn't hear of it or even think of it for two months." This was pleasant, but there was nothing to be done but obey; which I did a few hours later, with my trunk still unpacked and my immediate plan of life somewhat limited.

I say my immediate plan because my permanent found itself by no means curtailed, but on the contrary expanded and varied in a manner I had not even dared to hope. This came from what Dr. B. said subsequently, when he had examined my lungs; that is to say after he had laid his head affectionately first under one of my shoulders and then the other, and there kept it solemnly for about ten minutes, in a way that was irresistibly ludicrous, especially with Kitty as spectator. His verdict was that my lungs were *sound*, that he couldn't detect the least evidence of disease, and that hemorrhage couldn't have come from the lung itself, but from their membraneous lining, and that of the throat, whatever this may be. So he gave me to understand that I have as sound a pair of lungs at present as the next person; in fact from what he said one would have thought them a pair that a prize-fighter might covet. At the same time he sent me flying back to the country, with orders not to get excited, nor to listen to music, nor to speak with anybody I care for, nor to do anything in short that the unregenerate nature longs for. This struck my untutored mind as somewhat inconsistent, and I ventured a gentle remonstrance, which however was not even listened to, and I was ignominiously thrust into a car and borne back to Pelham. The problem still bothers me: either sound lungs are a very dangerous thing to have, or there is a foul conspiracy on foot to oppress me. Still, I cling to the consoling thought of my matchless lungs, and this obliterates my present sufferings.

Harry came to see me before he sailed for Europe; I'm very glad he has gone, though I don't expect to see him again for a good many years. I don't think he will come back for a long time, and I hope it will do him good and that he will enjoy himself—which he hasn't done for several years. I haven't read all of Faust, but I think I know the scenes you call divine—at least I know some that are exquisite. But why do you speak so disparagingly of King David, whom I always had a weakness for? Think how charming and lovable a person he must have been, poet, musician and so much else combined—with however their attendant imperfections. I don't think I should have cared to be *Queen* David exactly. I am possessed with an overpowering admiration and affection for George Eliot. I don't know why this has so suddenly come over me, but everything I look at of hers nowadays makes me take a deeper interest in her. I should love to see her, and I hope Harry will; I asked him to give my love to her. But I don't remember ever to have heard *you* speak of her. Good-bye. I wish conventionality would invent some other way of ending a letter than "yours truly"; I am so tired of it, and as one says it to one's shoemaker it would be rather more complimentary to one's friends to dispense with it altogether and just sign one's name without anything, after the manner of Miss Emerson and other free Boston citizens. But I am a slave to conventionality, and after all *am* yours truly....

Singularly present has remained to "Harry," as may be imagined, the rapid visit he paid her at Pelham that February; he was spending a couple of days in New York, on a quick decision, before taking ship for England. I was then to make in Europe no such stay as she had forecast—I was away but for fifteen months; though I can well believe my appetite must have struck her as open to the boundless, and can easily be touched again by her generous thought of this as the right compensatory thing for me. That indeed is what I mainly recall of the hour I spent with her—so unforgettable none the less in its general value; our so beautifully agreeing that quite the same course would be the right thing for *her* and that it was wholly detestable I should be voyaging off without her. But the precious question and the bright aspect of her own still waiting chance made our talk for the time all gaiety; it was, strangely enough, a laughing hour altogether, coloured with the vision of the next winter in Rome, where we should romantically meet: the appearance then being of particular protective friends with Roman designs, under whose wing she might happily travel. She had at that moment been for many weeks as ill as will here have been shown; but such is the priceless good faith of youth that we perfectly kept at bay together the significance of this. I recall no mortal note—nothing but the bright extravagance of her envy; and see her again, in the old-time Pelham parlours, ever so erectly slight and so more than needfully, so transparently, fair (I fatuously took this for "becoming"), glide as swiftly, toss her head as characteristically, laugh to as free a disclosure of the handsome largeish teeth that made her mouth almost the main fact of her face, as if no corner of the veil of the future had been lifted. The house was quiet and spacious for the day, after the manner of all American houses of that age at those hours, and yet spoke of such a possible muster at need of generous, gregarious, neighbouring, sympathising Emmets; in spite of which, withal, the impression was to come back to me as of a child struggling with her ignorance in a sort of pathless desert of the genial and the casual. Three months before I returned to America the struggle had ended. I *was*, as happened, soon to see in London her admiration, and my own, the great George Eliot—a brief glimpse then, but a very impressive, and wellnigh my main satisfaction in which was that I should have my cousin to tell of it. I found the Charles Nortons settled for the time in London, with social contacts and penetrations, a give and take of hospitality, that I felt as wondrous and of some elements of which they offered me, in their great kindness, the benefit; so that I was long to value having owed them in the springtime of '69 five separate impressions of distinguished persons, then in the full flush of activity and authority, that affected my young provincialism as a positive fairytale of privilege. I had a Sunday afternoon hour with Mrs. Lewes at North Bank, no second visitor but my gentle introducer, the younger Miss Norton, sharing the revelation, which had some odd and for myself peculiarly thrilling accompaniments; and then the opportunity of dining with Mr. Ruskin at Denmark Hill, an impression of uneffaced intensity and followed by a like—and yet so unlike—evening of hospitality from William Morris in the medieval mise-en-scène of Queen Square. This had been preceded by a luncheon with Charles Darwin, beautifully benignant, sublimely simple, at Down; a memory to which I find attached our incidental wondrous walk—Mrs. Charles Norton, the too near term of her earthly span then smoothly out of sight, being my guide for the happy excursion—across a private park of great oaks, which I conceive to have been the admirable Holwood and where I knew my first sense of a matter afterwards, through fortunate years, to be more fully disclosed: the springtime in such places, the adored footpath, the first primroses, the stir and scent of renascence in the watered sunshine and under spreading boughs that were somehow before aught else the still reach of remembered lines of Tennyson, ached over in nostalgic years. The rarest hour of all perhaps, or at least the strangest, strange verily to the pitch of the sinister, was a vision, provided by the same care, of D. G. Rossetti in the vernal dusk of Queen's House Chelsea—among his pictures, amid his poetry itself, his whole haunting "esthetic," and yet above all bristling with his personality, with his perversity, with anything, as it rather awfully seemed to me, but his sympathy, though it at the same time left one oddly desirous of more of him. These impressions heaped up the measure, goodness knew, of what would serve for Minnie's curiosity—she was familiarly Minnie to us; the point remaining all along, however, that, impatient at having overmuch to wait, I rejoiced in possession of the exact vivid terms in which I should image George Eliot to her. I was much later on to renew acquaintance with that great lady, but I think I scarce exceed in saying that with my so interested cousin's death half the savour of my appreciation had lost itself. Just in those days, that month of April, the latter had made a weak ineffectual move to Philadelphia in quest of physical relief—which expressed at the same time even more one of those reachings out for appeasement of the soul which were never too publicly indulged in, but by which her power to interest the true subjects of her attraction was infinitely quickened. It represented wonderments, I might well indeed have said to myself, even beyond any inspired by the high muse of North Bank.

I suppose I ought to have something special to say after having been suddenly transplanted to a new place and among new people, yet there isn't much to tell. I came because they all thought at home that the climate might do me good; I don't feel, however, any difference in my sensations between this and New York—if I do it's in favour of New York. I wish it might turn out that an inland climate isn't after all necessary for me, as I like the other sort much better and really think I feel stronger in it too. My doctor told me that Boston would kill me in six months—though he is possibly mistaken. I am going to try it a little longer here, and then go back to Pelham, where I'm pretty sure I shall find myself better again. It may be that the mental atmosphere is more to me than any other, for I feel homesick here all the while, or at least what I call so, being away from what is most *like* home to me, and what if I were there I should call tired. The chief object I had in coming was to listen to Phillips Brooks; I have heard him several times and am not, I think, disappointed. To be sure he didn't say anything new or startling, but I certainly oughtn't to have expected that, though I believe I did have a secret hope that he was going to expound to me the old beliefs with a clearness that would convince me for ever and banish doubt. I had placed all my hopes in him as the one man I had heard of who, progressive in all other ways, had yet been able to keep his faith firm in the things that most earnest men have left far behind them. Yet in preaching to his congregation he doesn't, or didn't, touch the real difficulties at all. He was leading them forward instead of trying to make it clear to *me* that I have any good reason for my feelings. Still, it was something to feel that he has them too, and isn't afraid to trust them and live for them. I wonder what he really does believe or think about it all, and whether he knows the reaction that comes to me about Thursday, after the enthusiasm and confidence made by his eloquence and earnestness on Sunday. To-morrow will be Saturday, and I shall be glad when Sunday comes to wind me up again. I feel sadly run down to-night and as if I should like to see some honest old pagan and shake him by the hand. It will seem all right and easy again soon, I know, but is it always thus? Is there no more of that undoubting faith in the world that there used to be? But I won't talk any more about it now, or I shan't sleep; it is getting late and all themes but the least interesting must be put away.

"Quaint," as we now say, it at this end of time seems to me that Phillips Brooks, the great Episcopal light of the period, first in Philadelphia and then in Boston, and superior character, excellent, even ardent, thoughtful, genial, practical man, should have appeared to play before her a light possibly of the clear strain, the rich abundance, the straight incidence, that she so desired to think attainable. A large, in fact an enormous, softly massive and sociably active presence, of capacious attention and comforting suggestion, he was a brave worker among those who didn't too passionately press their questions and claims—half the office of such a minister being, no doubt, to abate the high pitch, and the high pitch being by the same token too much Minnie's tendency. She was left with it in the smug Philadelphia visibly on her hands; she had found there after all but a closed door, to which she was blandly directed, rather than an open, and the sigh of her falling back with her disappointment seems still to reach one's ears. She found them too much all round, the stiff blank barriers that, for whatever thumping, didn't "give;" and in fine I like not too faintly to colour this image of her as failing, in her avid young sincerity, to draw from the honest pastor of more satisfied souls any assurance that she could herself honestly apply. I confess that her particular recorded case, slender enough in its lonely unrest, suggests to me a force, or at least a play, of effective criticism more vivid to-day than either of the several rich monuments, honourably as these survive, to Phillips Brooks's positive "success." She had no occasion or no chance to find the delightful harmonising friend in him—which was part of the success for so many others. But her letter goes on after a couple of days—she had apparently not sent the previous part, and it brings her back, we can rejoicingly note, to George Eliot, whose poem, alluded to, must have been The Spanish Gipsy. This work may indeed much less have counted for her than the all-engulfing Mill on the Floss, incomparably privileged production, which shone for young persons of that contemporaneity with a nobleness that nothing under our actual star begins in like case to match. These are great recognitions, but how can I slight for them a mention that has again and again all but broken through in my pages?—that of Francis Boott and his daughter (she to become later on Mrs. Frank Duveneck and to yield to the same dismal decree of death before her time that rested on so many of the friends of our youth). When I turn in thought to the happiness that our kinswoman was still to have known in her short life, for all her disaster, Elizabeth Boott, delightful, devoted and infinitely under the charm, at once hovers for me; this all the more, I hasten to add, that we too on our side, and not least Mary Temple herself, were under the charm, and that *that* charm, if less immediately pointed, affected all our young collective sensibility as a wondrous composite thing. There was the charm for us—if I must not again speak in assurance but for myself—that "Europe," the irrepressible even as the *ewig Weibliche* of literary allusion was irrepressible, had more than anything else to do with; and then there was the other that, strange to say (strange as I, once more, found myself feeling it) owed nothing of its authority to anything so markedly out of the picture. The spell to which I in any case most piously sacrificed, most cultivated the sense of, was ever of this second cast—and for the simple reason that the other, serene in its virtue, fairly insolent in its pride, needed no rites and no care. It must be allowed that there was nothing composite in any spell proceeding, whether directly or indirectly, from the great Albany connection: this form of the agreeable, through whatever appeals, could certainly not have been more of a piece, as we say—more of a single superfused complexion, an element or principle that we could in the usual case ever so easily and pleasantly account for. The case of that one in the large number of my cousins whom we have seen to be so incomparably the most interesting was of course anything but the usual; yet the Albany origin, the woodnote wild, sounded out even amid her various voices and kept her true, in her way, to something we could only have called local, or perhaps family, type. Essentially, however, she had been a free incalculable product, a vivid exception to rules and precedents; so far as she had at all the value of the "composite" it was on her own lines altogether—the composition was of things that had lain nearest to hand. It mattered enormously for such a pair as the Bootts, intimately associated father and daughter, that what had lain nearest *their* hand, or at least that of conspiring nature and fortune in preparing them for our consumption, had been the things of old Italy, of the inconceivable Tuscany, that of the but lately expropriated Grand Dukes in particular, and that when originally alighting among us *en plein* Newport they had seemed fairly to reek with a saturation, esthetic, historic, romantic, that everything roundabout made precious. I was to apprehend in due course, and not without dismay, that what they really most reeked with was the delight of finding us ourselves exactly as we were; they fell so into the wondrous class of inverted romantics, several other odd flowers of which I was later on to have anxiously to deal with: we and our large crude scene of barbaric plenty, as it might have been called, beguiled them to appreciations such as made our tribute to themselves excite at moments their impatience and strike them as almost silly. It was *our* conditions that were picturesque, and I had to make the best of a time when they themselves appeared to consent to remain so but by the beautiful gaiety of their preference. This, I remember well, I found disconcerting, so that my main affectionate business with them became, under amusement by the way, that of keeping them true to type. What above all contributed was that they really couldn't help their case, try as they would to shake off the old infection; they were of "old world" production through steps it was too late to retrace; and they were in the practical way and in the course of the very next years to plead as guilty to this as the highest proper standard for them could have prescribed. They "went back," and again and again, with a charming, smiling, pleading inconsequence—any pretext but the real one, the fact that the prime poison was in their veins, serving them at need; so that, as the case turned, all my own earlier sense, on the spot, of Florence and Rome was to mix itself with their delightfully rueful presence there. I could then perfectly put up with that flame of passion for Boston and Newport in them which still left so perfect their adaptability to Italian installations that would have been impossible save for subtle Italian reasons.

I speak of course but of the whole original view: time brings strange revenges and contradictions, and all the later history was to be a chapter by itself and of the fullest. We had been all alike accessible in the first instance to the call of those references which played through their walk and conversation with an effect that their qualifying ironies and amusing reactions, where such memories were concerned, couldn't in the least abate; for nothing in fact lent them a happier colour than just this ability to afford so carelessly to cheapen the certain treasure of their past. They had enough of that treasure to give it perpetually away—in our subsequently to be more determined, our present, sense; in short we had the fondest use for their leavings even when they themselves hadn't. Mary Temple, with her own fine quality so far from composite, rejoiced in the perception, however unassisted by any sort of experience, of what their background had "meant"; she would have liked to be able to know just that for herself, as I have already hinted, and I actually find her image most touching perhaps by its so speaking of what she with a peculiar naturalness dreamed of and missed. Of clear old English stock on her father's side, her sense for what was English in life—so we used to simplify—was an intimate part of her, little chance as it enjoyed for happy verifications. In the Bootts, despite their still ampler and more recently attested share in that racial strain, the foreign tradition had exceedingly damped the English, which didn't however in the least prevent her being caught up by it as it had stamped itself upon the admirable, the infinitely civilised and sympathetic, the markedly *produced* Lizzie. This delightful girl, educated, cultivated, accomplished, toned above all, as from steeping in a rich old medium, to a degree of the rarest among her coevals "on our side," had the further, the supreme grace that she melted into American opportunities of friendship—and small blame to her, given such as she then met—with the glee of a sudden scarce believing discoverer. Tuscany could only swoon away under comparison of its starved sociabilities and complacent puerilities, the stress of which her previous years had so known, with the multiplied welcomes and freedoms, the exquisite and easy fellowships that glorified to her the home scene. Into not the least of these quick affinities had her prompt acquaintance with Mary Temple confidently ripened; and with no one in the aftertime, so long as that too escaped the waiting shears, was I to find it more a blest and sacred rite, guarded by no stiff approaches, to celebrate my cousin's memory. That really is my apology for this evocation— which might under straighter connections have let me in still deeper; since if I have glanced on another page of the present miscellany at the traps too often successfully set for my wandering feet my reader will doubtless here recognise a perfect illustration of our danger and will accuse me of treating an inch of canvas to an acre of embroidery. Let the poor canvas figure time and the embroidery figure consciousness—the proportion will perhaps then not strike us as so wrong. Consciousness accordingly still grips me to the point of a felt pressure of interest in such a matter as the recoverable history—history in the esthetic connection at least—of its insistent dealings with a given case. How in the course of time for instance was it not insistently to deal, for a purpose of application, with the fine prime image deposited all unwittingly by the "picturesque" (as I absolutely required to feel it) Boott situation or Boott *data*? The direct or vital value of these last, in so many ways, was experiential, a stored and assimilated thing; but the seed of suggestion proved after long years to have kept itself apart in order that it should develop under a particular breath. A not other than lonely and bereft American, addicted to the arts and endowed for them, housed to an effect of long expatriation in a massive old Florentine villa with a treasured and tended little daughter by his side, *that* was the germ which for reasons beyond my sounding the case of Frank Boott had been appointed to plant deep down in my vision of things. So lodged it waited, but the special instance, as I say, had lodged it, and it lost no vitality—on the contrary it acquired every patience—by the fact that little by little each of its connections above ground, so to speak, was successively cut. Then at last after years it raised its own head into the air and found its full use for the imagination. An Italianate bereft American with a little moulded daughter in the setting of a massive old Tuscan residence was at the end of years exactly what was required by a situation of my own—conceived in the light of the Novel; and I *had* it there, in the authenticated way, with its essential fund of truth, at once all the more because my admirable old friend had given it to me and none the less because he had no single note of character or temper, not a grain of the non-essential, in common with my Gilbert Osmond. This combination of facts has its shy interest, I think, in the general imaginative or reproductive connection—testifying as it so happens to do on that whole question of the "putting of people into books" as to which any ineptitude of judgment appears always in order. I probably shouldn't have had the Gilbert Osmonds at all without the early "form" of the Frank Bootts, but I still more certainly shouldn't have had them with the *sense* of my old inspirers. The form had to be disembarrassed of that sense and to take in a thoroughly other; thanks to which account of the matter I am left feeling that I scarce know whether most to admire, for support of one's beautiful business of the picture of life, the relation of "people" to art or the relation of art to people. Adorable each time the mystery of which of these factors, as we say, has the more prevailingly conduced to a given effect—and too much adored, at any rate, I allow, when carrying me so very far away. I retrace my steps with this next.

I have made several attempts lately to write you a letter, but I have given it up after two or three pages, because I have always been in a blue state of mind at the time, and have each time charitably decided before it was too late to spare you. But if I were to wait until things change to rose-colour I might perhaps wait till I die, or longer even, in which case your next communication from me would be a spiritual one. I am going to Newport in the early part of May to meet the Bootts—Henrietta has just come back from there delighted with her visit; why, heaven knows, I suppose, but I don't—except that she is in that blissful state of babyhood peculiar to herself where everything seems delightful.... I like George Eliot not through her poem so much, not nearly so much, as through her prose. The creature interests me personally, and I feel a desire to know something of her life; how far her lofty moral sentiments have served her practically—for instance in her dealings with Lewes. I see that she understands the character of a *generous* woman, that is of a woman who believes in generosity and who must be that or nothing, and who feels keenly, notwithstanding, how hard it is practically to follow this out, and how (looking at it from the point of view of comfort as far as this world goes) it "pays" not at all. We are having weather quite like summer and rather depressing; I don't feel very well and am always catching cold—that is I suppose I am, as I have a cough nearly all the time. As for Phillips Brooks, what you say of him is, no doubt, all true—he didn't touch the main point when I heard him, at all events, and that satisfaction you so kindly wish me is, I am afraid, not to be got from any man. The mystery of this world grows and grows, and sticks out of every apparently trivial thing, instead of lessening. I hope this feeling may not be the incipient stage of insanity. Paul told the truth when he said that now we see through a glass, *very* darkly. I hope and trust that the rest may be equally true, and that some day we shall see face to face. You say it is easy to drown thought by well-doing, and is it not also the soundest philosophy (so long of course as one doesn't humbug oneself); since by simply thinking out a religion who has ever arrived at anything that did not leave one's heart empty? Do you ever see Willy James? Good-bye.

Needless enough surely to declare that such pages were essentially not love-letters: that they could scarce have been less so seems exactly part of their noble inevitability, as well as a proof singularly interesting and charming that confident friendship may obey its force and insist on its say quite as much as the sentiment we are apt to take, as to many of its occasions, for the supremely vocal. We have so often seen this latter beat distressfully about the bush for something still deficient, something in the line of positive esteem or constructive respect, whether offered or enjoyed, that an esteem and a respect such as we here apprehend, explicit enough on either side to dispense with those superlatives in which graceless reaction has been known insidiously to lurk, peculiarly refresh and instruct us. The fine special quietude of the relation thus promoted in a general consciousness of unrest—and even if it could breed questions too, since a relation that breeds none at all is not a living one—was of the highest value to the author of my letters, who had already sufficiently "lived," in her generous way, to know well enough in how different a quarter to look for the grand inconclusive. The directness, the ease, the extent of the high consideration, the felt need of it as a support, indeed one may almost say as an inspiration, in trouble, and the free gift of it as a delightful act of intelligence and justice, render the whole exhibition, to my sense, admirable in its kind. Questions luckily *could* haunt it, as I say and as we shall presently see, but only to illustrate the more all the equilibrium preserved. I confess I can imagine no tribute to a manly nature from a feminine more final even than the confidence in "mere" consideration here embodied—the comfort of the consideration being in the fact that the character with which the feminine nature was dealing lent it, could it but come, such weight. We seem to see play through the whole appeal of the younger person to the somewhat older an invocation of the weight suspended, weight of judgment, weight of experience and authority, and which may ever so quietly drop. How kindly in another relation it had been in fact capable of dropping comes back to me in the mention of my brother Wilky, as to whom this aspect of his admiring friendship for our young relative's correspondent, the fruit of their common military service roundabout Charleston, again comprehensively testifies. That comradeship was a privilege that Wilky strongly cherished, as well as what one particularly liked to think for him of his having known—he was to have known nothing more fortunate. In no less a degree was our elder brother to come to prize *his* like share in the association—this being sufficiently indicated, for that matter, in the note I have quoted from him. That I have prized my own share in it let my use of this benefit derived strongly represent. But again for Minnie herself the sadder admonition is sharp, and I find I know not what lonely pluck in her relapses shaken off as with the jangle of silver bells, her expert little efforts to live them down, Newport and other matters aiding and the general preoccupied good will all vainly at her service. Pitiful in particular her carrying her trouble experimentally back to the Newport of the first gladness of her girlhood and of the old bright spectacle.

I know quite well I don't owe you a letter, and that the custom for maidens is to mete out strictly letter for letter; but if you don't mind it I don't, and if you *do* mind that kind of thing you had better learn not to at once—if you propose to be a friend of mine; or else have your feelings from time to time severely shocked. After which preamble I will say that there is a special reason in this case, though there might not be in another.

She mentions having seen a common friend, in great bereavement and trouble, who has charged her with a message to her correspondent "if you know of anything to comfort a person when the one they love best dies, for heaven's sake say it to her—*I* hadn't a word to say." And she goes on:

I wrote to you that I was going to Newport, and I meant to go next Tuesday, but I had another hemorrhage last night, and it is impossible to say when I shall be able to leave here. I think I was feeling ill when I last wrote to you, and ever since have been coughing and feeling wretchedly, until finally the hemorrhage has come. If that goes over well I think I shall be better. I am in bed now, on the old plan of gruel and silence, and I may get off without any worse attack this time. It is a perfect day, like summer—my windows are up and the birds sing. It seems quite out of keeping that I should be in bed. I should be all right if I could only get rid of coughing. The warm weather will set me up again. I wonder what you are doing to-day. Probably taking a solitary walk and meditating—on what? Good-bye.

But she went to Newport after a few days apparently; whence comes this.

I believe I was in bed when I last wrote to you, but that attack didn't prove nearly so bad a one as the previous; I rather bullied it, and after the fourth hemorrhage it ceased; moreover my cough is better since I came here. But I am, to tell the truth, a little homesick—and am afraid I am becoming too much of a baby. Whether it's from illness or from the natural bent I know not, but there is no comfort in life away from people who care for you—not an heroic statement, I am fully aware. I hear that Wilky is at home, and dare say he will have the kindness to run down and see me while I am here; at least I hope so. But I am not in the mood for writing to-day—I am tired and can only bore you if I kept on. It is just a year since we began to write, and aren't you by this time a little tired of it? If you are, say so like a man—don't be afraid of me. Now I am going to lie down before dressing for dinner. Good-bye.

This passage more than a month later makes me ask myself of which of the correspondents it strikes me as most characteristic. The gay clearness of the one looks out—as it always looked out on the least chance given—at the several apparent screens of the other; each of which is indeed disconnectedly, independently clear, but tells too small a part (at least for her pitch of lucidity) of what they together enclose, and what was *quand même* of so fine an implication. Delightful at the same time any page from her that is not one of the huddled milestones of her rate of decline.

How can I write to you when I have forgotten all about you?—if one *can* forget what one has never known. However, I am not quite sure whether it isn't knowing you too much rather than too little that seems to prevent. Do you comprehend the difficulty? Of course you don't, so I will explain. The trouble is, I think, that to me you have no distinct personality. I don't feel sure to whom I am writing when I say to myself that I will write to you. I see mentally three men, all answering to your name, each liable to read my letters and yet differing so much from each other that if it is proper for one of them it's quite unsuitable to the others. Do you see? If you can once settle for me the question of which gets my letters I shall know better what to say in them. Is it the man I used to see (I can't say know) at Conway, who had a beard, I think, and might have been middle-aged, and who discussed Trollope's novels with Kitty and Elly? This was doubtless one of the best of men, but he didn't *interest* me, I never felt disposed to speak to him, and used to get so sleepy in his society at about eight o'clock that I wondered how the other girls could stay awake till eleven. Is it *that* person who reads my letters? Or is it the young man I recently saw at Newport, with a priestly countenance, calm and critical, with whom I had certainly no fault to find as a chance companion for three or four days, but whom I should never have dreamt of writing to or bothering with my affairs one way or the other, happiness or no happiness, as he would doubtless at once despise me for my nonsense and wonder at me for my gravity? Does *he* get my letters?—or is it finally the being who has from time to time himself written to me, signing by the same name that the other gentlemen appropriate? If my correspondent is this last I know where I stand—and, please heaven, shall stand there some time longer. Him I won't describe, but he's the only one of the three I care anything about. My only doubt is because I always address him at Pemberton Square, and I think him the least likely of the three to go there much. But good-bye, whichever you are!

It was not at any rate to be said of her that she didn't live surrounded, even though she had to go so far afield—very far it may at moments have appeared to her—for the freedom of talk that was her greatest need of all. How happily and hilariously surrounded this next, of the end of the following August, and still more its sequel of the mid-September, abundantly bring back to me; so in the habit were the numerous Emmets, it might almost be said, of marrying the numerous young women of our own then kinship: they at all events formed mainly by themselves at that time the figures and the action of her immediate scene. The marriage of her younger sister was as yet but an engagement—to the brother-in-law of the eldest, already united to Richard Emmet and with Temple kinship, into the bargain, playing between the pairs. All of which animation of prospective and past wedding-bells, with whatever consolidation of pleasant ties, couldn't quench her ceaseless instinct for the obscurer connections of things or keep passionate reflections from awaiting her at every turn. This disposition in her, and the way in which, at the least push, the gate of thought opened for her to its widest, which was to the prospect of the soul and the question of interests on *its* part that wouldn't be ignored, by no means fails to put to me that she might well have found the mystifications of life, had she been appointed to enjoy more of them, much in excess of its contentments. It easily comes up for us over the relics of those we have seen beaten, this sense that it was not for nothing they missed the ampler experience, but in no case that I have known has it come up for me so much. In none other have I so felt the naturalness of our asking ourselves what such spirits would have done with their extension and what would have satisfied them; since dire as their defeat may have been we don't see them, in the ambiguous light of some of their possibilities, at peace with victory. This may be perhaps an illusion of our interest in them, a mere part of its ingenuity; and I allow that if our doubt is excessive it does them a great wrong—which is another way in which they were not to have been righted. We soothe a little with it at any rate our sense of the tragic.

...The irretrievableness of the step (her sister E.'s marriage) comes over my mind from time to time in such an overwhelming way that it's most depressing, and I have to be constantly on my guard not to let Temple and Elly see it, as it would naturally not please them. After all, since they are not appalled at what they've done, and are quite sure of each other, as they evidently are, why should I worry myself? I am well aware that if all other women felt the seriousness of the matter to the extent I do, hardly any would *ever* marry, and the human race would stop short. So I ought perhaps to be glad so many people can find and take that "little ease" that Clough talks about, without consciously giving up the "highest thing." And may not this majority of people be the truly wise and my own notions of the subject simply fanatical and impracticable? I clearly see in how small a minority I am, and that the other side has, with Bishop Blougram, the best of it from one point of view;

but I can't help that, can I? We must be true to *ourselves*, mustn't we? though all the rest of humanity be of a contrary opinion, or else throw discredit upon the wisdom of God, who made us as we are and not like the next person. Do you remember my old hobby of the "remote possibility of the best thing" being better than a clear certainty of the second best? Well, I believe it more than ever, every day I live. Indeed I don't believe anything else—but is not that everything? And isn't it exactly what Christianity means? Wasn't Christ the only man who ever lived and died *entirely* for his faith, without a shadow of selfishness? And isn't that reason enough why we should all turn to Him after having tried everything else and found it wanting?—turn to Him as the only pure and *unmixed* manifestation of God in humanity? And if I believe this, which I think I do, how utterly inconsistent and detestable is the life I lead, which, so far from being a loving and cheerful surrender of itself once for all to God's service, is at best but a base compromise—a few moments or acts or thoughts consciously and with difficulty divested of actual selfishness. Must this always be so? Is it owing to the indissoluble mixture of the divine and the diabolical in us all, or is it because I myself am hopelessly frivolous and trifling? Or is it finally that I really don't *believe*, that I have still a doubt in my mind whether religion *is* the one exclusive thing to live for, as Christ taught us, or whether it will prove to be only *one* of the influences, though a great one, which educate the human race and help it along in that culture which Matthew Arnold thinks the most desirable thing in the world? In fine is it the meaning and end of our lives, or only a moral principle bearing a certain part in our development——?

Since I wrote this I have been having my tea and sitting on the piazza looking at the stars and thinking it most unfaithful and disloyal of me even to speak as I did just now, admitting the possibility of that faith not being everything which yet at moments is so divinely true as to light up the whole of life suddenly and make everything clear. I know the trouble is with *me* when doubt and despondency come, but on the other hand I can't altogether believe it wrong of me to have written as I have, for then what becomes of my principle of saying what one really thinks and leaving it to God to take care of his own glory? The truth will vindicate itself in spite of my voice to the contrary. If you think I am letting myself go this way without sufficient excuse I won't do it again; but I can't help it this time, I have nobody else to speak to about serious things. If by chance I say anything or ask a question that lies at all near my heart my sisters all tell me I am "queer" and that they "wouldn't be me for anything"—which is, no doubt, sensible on their part, but which puts an end to anything but conversation of the most superficial kind on mine. You know one gets lonely after a while on such a plan of living, so in sheer desperation I break out where I perhaps more safely can.

Such is the magic of old letters on its subtlest occasions that I reconstitute in every detail, to a vivid probability—even if I may not again proportionately project the bristling image—our scene of next mention; drawing for this upon my uneffaced impression of a like one, my cousin Katharine Temple's bright nuptials, in the same general setting, very much before, and in addition seeming to see the very muse of history take a fresh scroll in order to prepare to cover it, in her very handsomest hand, well before my eyes. Covered is it now for me with that abounding and interesting life of the generations then to come at the pair of preliminary flourishes ushering in the record of which I thus feel myself still assist.

But a line to-day to tell you that Elly was safely married on Wednesday. She looked simply beautiful in her wedding garment, and behaved herself throughout with a composure that was as delightful as it was surprising. I send you a photograph of myself that I had taken a few weeks ago. It looks perhaps a trifle melancholy, but I can't help that—I did the best I could. But I won't write more—it wouldn't be enlivening. Everything looks grey and blue in the world nowadays. It will all be bright again in time, I have no doubt; there is no special reason for it; I think I am simply tired with knocking about. Yet my week in Newport might have been pleasant enough if the dentist hadn't taken that occasion to break my bones for me in a barbarous manner. You are very kind and friendly to me—you don't know how much happiness your letters give me. You will be surprised, I dare say, but I shall not, at the last day, when the accounts are all settled, to find how much this counts in your favour. Good-bye.

I find my story so attaching that I prize every step of its course, each note of which hangs together with all the others. The writer is expressed to my vision in every word, and the resulting image so worth preserving. Much of one's service to it is thus a gathering-in of the ever so faded ashes of the happiness that did come to her after all in snatches. Everything could well, on occasion, look "grey and blue," as she says; yet there were stretches, even if of the briefest, when other things still were present than the active symptoms of her state. The photograph that she speaks of above is before me as I write and blessedly helpful to memory—so that I am moved to reproduce it only till I feel again how the fondness of memory must strike the light for apprehension. The plan of the journey to California for the advantage of the climate there was, with other plans taken up and helplessly dropped, but beguiling for the day, to accompany her almost to the end.

The Temple-Emmet caravan have advanced as far as Newport and now propose to retreat again to Pelham without stopping at Boston or anywhere else. My brother-in-law has business in New York and can't be away any longer. I haven't been well of late, or I should have run up to Boston for a day or two to take a sad farewell of all I love in that city and thereabouts before I cross the Rocky Mountains. This little trip has been made out for me by my friends; I have determined to go, and shall probably start with Elly and Temple in about ten days, possibly not for a fortnight, to spend the winter in San Francisco. I can't be enthusiastic about it, but suppose I might as well take all the means I can to get better: a winter in a warm climate *may* be good for me. In short I am going, and now what I want *you* to do about it is simply to come and see us before that. Kitty is going to send you a line to add her voice—perhaps that may bring you. You may never see me again, you know, and if I were to die so far away you'd be sorry you hadn't taken leave of me, wouldn't you?

The idea of California held, and with other pleasant matters really occupied the scene; out of which moreover insist on shining to me accessory connections, or connections that then were to be: intensely distinct for example the figure of Miss Crawford, afterwards Madame von Rabe, sister of my eminent friend F. Marion of the name and, in her essence, I think, but by a few shades less entire a figure than he—which is saying much. The most endowed and accomplished of men Frank Crawford, so that I have scarcely known another who had more aboundingly lived and wrought, about whom moreover there was singularly more to be said, it struck me, than at all found voice at the time he might have been commemorated. Therefore if the young lady alluded to in my cousin's anecdote was at all of the same personal style and proportion—well, I should draw the moral if it didn't represent here too speciously the mouth of a trap, one of those I have already done penance for; the effect of my yielding to which would be a shaft sunk so straight down into matters interesting and admirable and sad and strange that, with everything that was futurity to the occasion noted in our letter and is an infinitely mixed and a heavily closed past now, I hurry on without so much as a glance.

The present plan is to send me to California in about three weeks by water, under the care of one of the Emmet boys and Temple's valet—for nurse; and by the time I get there, early in December, they will be settled in San Francisco for the winter. The idea of a twenty-one days' sea-voyage is rather appalling—what do you think of it? This day is but too heavenly here. I haven't been to church, but walking by myself, as happy as possible. When one sleeps well and the sun shines, what happiness to live! I wish you were here—wouldn't I show you Pelham at high tide, on a day that is simply intoxicating, with a fresh breeze blown through the red and yellow leaves and sunshine "on field and hill, in heart and brain," as Mr. Lowell says. I suppose you remember the pony I drove, and Punch, the little Scotch terrier that tried so to insinuate himself into your affections, on the piazza, the morning you left. The former has been "cutting up," the latter *cut* up, since then. You wouldn't believe me when I told you the pony was a highly nervous creature—but she behaved as one the other day when I took the Roman Miss Crawford, who has been staying near here, a ride. She shied at a dog that frightened her, and dragged the cart into a ditch, and tried to get over a stone wall, waggon and all. I of course had to hang on to the reins, but I suggested to Miss Crawford that she should get out, as the cart was pretty steady while the horse's forefeet were on top of the wall; which she did, into a mud-puddle, and soiled her pretty striped stockings and shoes in a horrible way. It ended by the dear little beast's consenting to get back upon all fours, but I found it very amusing and have liked her better ever since.... How does Mr. Holmes persevere about smoking? I pity him if he can't sleep, and wish *I* had a vicious habit so that I might give it up. But I must finish my tale of the quadruped Punch, who was called upon in the dead of night by five dogs of the neighbourhood and torn to pieces by them. The coachman heard him crying in the night, and in the morning we found him—that is to say we gathered him together, his dear little tail from one place and his head from another etc! So went out a very sweet little spirit—I wonder where it is now. Don't tell me he hadn't more of a soul than that Kaufmann, the fat oysterman.

I find bribes to recognition and recovery quite mercilessly multiply, and with the effort to brush past them more and more difficult; with the sense for me at any rate (whatever that may be worth for wisdom or comfort) of sitting rather queerly safe and alone, though as with a dangle of legs over the edge of a precipice, on the hither side of great gulfs of history. But these things, dated toward the end of that November, speak now in a manner for themselves.

My passage for California is taken for the 4th of December; Elly and Temple have written to me to come at once—they are settled in San Francisco for the winter. My brother-in-law here has been promised that I shall be made so comfortable I shan't want to tear myself from the ship when I arrive. The captain is a friend of Temple's, and also of my uncle Captain Temple, and both of them are going to arrange so for me that I fully expect the ship to be hung with banners and flowers when I step on board.... I enjoyed my time in Boston far more than I had expected—in fact immensely, and wouldn't have missed it for anything; I feel now as if it had *necessarily* had to happen. I don't know how I should have done the winter, and especially started off for an indefinitely long absence in the west without the impetus that it gave me in certain directions—the settling down and shaking up, the dissipating of certain impressions that I had thought fixed and the strengthening of others that I hadn't been so sure of: an epoch in short. I dare say you have had such—in which a good deal of living was done in a short time, to be turned over and made fruitful in days to come. I saw Mr. Holmes once, and was very glad of that glimpse, short as it was. I went home by way of Newport, where I stayed two days—and where I was surprised to hear of Fred Jones's engagement to Miss Rawle of Philadelphia. Do you know her? When I got to New York I went to the Hones' to ask something about Fred and his affairs and found that Miss Rawle was staying next door with Mrs. Willy Duncan; so I went in to see her on the spur of the moment, very much as I had come from the boat, not particularly presentable for a first call: however, I thought if she had a soul she wouldn't mind it—and such I found the case.... Lizzie Boott was as sweet and good to me as ever; I think she is at once the most unselfish and most unegotistical girl I know—they don't always go together.

What follows here has, in its order, I think, that it still so testifies to life—if one doesn't see in it indeed rather perhaps the instinct on the writer's part, though a scarce conscious one, to wind up the affairs of her spirit, as it were, and be able to turn over with a sigh of supreme relief for an end intimately felt as at hand. The moral fermentation breaking through the bustle of outward questions even at a time when she might have thrown herself, as one feels, on the great soft breast of equalising Nature, or taken her chance of not being too wrong, is a great stroke of truth. No one really could be less "morbid"; yet she would take no chance—it wasn't in her—of not being right with the right persons; among whom she so ranked her correspondent.

My address at San Francisco will be simply Care of C. Temple Emmet, Esq.; and I am surely off this time unless heaven interposes in a miraculous way between now and Saturday. I've no great courage about it, but after all it's much the same to me where I am; life is always full of interest and mystery and happiness to me, and as for the voyage, the idea of three weeks of comparative solitude between sea and sky isn't unattractive.... I know that by my question [as to why he had written, apparently, that she was, of her nature, "far off" from him] I am putting an end to that delightful immunity I have enjoyed so much with you from sickening introspection, analysis of myself and yourself, that exhausting and nauseating subjectivity, with which most of my other friends see fit to deluge me, thereby taking much that is refreshing out of life. Don't be afraid of "hurting my feelings" by anything you can say. Our friendship has always been to my mind a one-sided thing, and if you should tell me you find me in any way unsympathetic or unsatisfactory it won't disappoint me, and I won't even allow myself to think I'm sorry. I feel so clearly that God knows best, and that we ought neither of us surely to wish to distort his creatures from the uses he made them for, just to serve our own purposes—that is to get a little more sympathy and comfort. We must each of us, after all, live out our own lives apart from everyone else; and yet, this being once understood as a fundamental truth, there is nobody's sympathy and approval that would encourage me so much as yours. I mean that if one's heart and motives could be known by another as God knows them, without disguise or extenuation, and if it should *then* prove that on the *whole* you didn't think well of me, it would, more than anything else could, shake my confidence in my own instincts, which must after all forever be my guide. And yet, as I said before, I am quite prepared for the worst, and shall listen to it, if necessary, quite humbly. I am very much inclined to trust your opinion before my own.

An hour later. *Sold* again, by all that's wonderful—I had almost said by all that's damnable, though it isn't exactly that. My brother Dick has just walked in with a telegram from Temple: "I shall be back in December—don't send M." A tremendous revulsion of feeling and a general sigh of relief have taken place on this announcement, and it's all right, I'm sure, though when I wrote you an hour ago I thought the same of the other prospect.

One catches one's breath a little, frankly, at what was to follow the above within a few days—implying as it does that she had drawn upon herself some fairly direct statement of her correspondent's reserves of view as to her human or "intellectual" composition. To have *had* such reserves at such an hour, and to have responded to the invitation to express them—for invitation there had been—is something that our actual larger light quite helps us to flatter ourselves *we* shouldn't have been capable of. But what was of the essence between these admirable persons was exactly the tone of truth; the larger light was all to wait for, and the real bearings of the hour were as unapparent as the interlocutors themselves were at home in clearness, so far as they might bring that ideal about. And whatever turn their conversation took is to the honour always of the generous girl's passion for truth. As this long letter admirably illustrates that, I withdraw from it almost nothing. The record of the rare commerce would be incomplete without it; all the more perhaps for the wonder and pain of our seeing the noble and pathetic young creature have, of all things, in her predicament, to plead for extenuations, to excuse and justify herself.

I understood your letter perfectly well—it was better than I feared it might be, but bad enough. Better because I knew already all it told me, and had been afraid there might be some new and horrible development in store for me which I hadn't myself felt; but bad enough because I find it in itself, new or old, such a disgusting fact that I am intellectually so unsympathetic. It is a fault I feel profoundly conscious of, but one that, strange to say, I have only of late been conscious of *as* a fault. I dare say I have always known, in a general way, that I am very unobservant about things and take very little interest in subjects upon which my mind doesn't naturally dwell; but it had never occurred to me before that it is a fault that ought to be corrected. Whether because I have never been given to studying myself much, but have just let myself go the way my mind was most inclined to, more interested in the subject itself than in the fact that it interested me; or whether because one is averse to set oneself down as indolent and egotistic I don't know; at all events I have of late seen the thing in all its unattractiveness, and I wish I could get over it. Do you think that, now I am fully roused to the fact, my case is hopeless? Or that if I should try hard for the next twenty-five years I might succeed in modifying it? I am speaking now of a want of interest in *all* the rest of the world; of not having the desire to investigate subjects, naturally uninteresting to me, just because they are interesting to some other human being whom I don't particularly owe anything to except that he *is* a human being, and so his thoughts and feelings ought to be respected by me and sympathised with. Not to do this is, I know, unphilosophic and selfish, conceited and altogether inhuman. To be unselfish, to live for other people, to mould our lives as much as possible on the model of Christ's all-embracing humanity, seems most clearly to my mind the one thing worth living for; and yet it is still the hardest thing for me to do, and I think I do it less than anybody else who feels the necessity of it strongly at all.

I am glad you still go to an occasional ball—I should rather like to meet you at one myself; it's a phase of life we have seen so little of together. I have been feeling so well lately that I don't know what to make of it. I don't remember ever in my life being in such good spirits. Not that they are not in general pretty natural to me when there is the slightest excuse for them, but now everything seems bright and happy, my life so full of interest, my time so thoroughly filled and such a delicious calm to have settled down on my usually restless spirit. Such an enjoyment of the *present*, such a grateful contentment, is in each new day as I see it dawn in the east, that I can only be thankful and say to myself: "Make a note of this—you are happy; don't forget it, nor to be thankful for this beautiful gift of life." This is Sunday morning, and I wonder whether you are listening to Phillips Brooks. I understand how you feel about his preaching—that it is all feeling and no reason; I found it so myself last winter in Philadelphia: he was good for those within the pale, but not good to convince outsiders that they should come in. I am glad, however, that he preaches in this way—I think his power lies in it; for it seems to me, after all, that what comfort we get from religion, and what light we have upon it, come to us through feeling, that is through trusting our instinct as the voice of God, the Holy Ghost, though it may at the same time appear to us directly against what our intellect teaches us. I don't mean by this that we should deny the conclusions arrived at by our intellect—which on the contrary I believe we should trust and stand by to the bitter end, whenever this may be. But let us fearlessly trust our *whole* nature, showing our faith in God by being true to ourselves all through, and not dishonouring Him by ignoring what our heart says because it is not carried out by our intellect, or by wilfully blunting our intellectual perception because it happens to run against some cherished wish of our heart.

"But," you will say, "how can a man live torn to pieces this way by these contrary currents?" Well, I know it is hard to keep our faith *sure* of a standpoint where these apparent inconsistencies are all reconciled and the jangle and discord sound the sweetest harmony; but I do believe there *is* one, in God, and that we must only try to have that faith and never mind how great the inconsistency may seem, nor how perplexing the maze it leads us through. Let us never give up one element of the problem for the sake of coming to a comfortable solution of it in this world. I don't blame those eager minds that are always worrying, studying, investigating, to *find* the solution here below; it is a noble work, and let them follow it out (and without a bit of compromise) to whom God has given the work. But whether we find it or not I would have them and all of us feel that it is to *be* found, if God wills—and through no other means surely than by our being *true*. Blessed are they who have not seen and who have yet believed. But I am going out now for a walk! We have had the most delightful weather this whole week, and capital sleighing, and I have spent most of my time driving myself about with that same dear little pony. I went to town yesterday to a matinée of William Tell; it was delightful and I slept all night after it too. I am reading German a little every day, and it's beginning to go pretty well. Good-bye. Don't tire yourself out between work and dissipation.

I find myself quite sit up to her, as we have it to-day, while she sits there without inconvenience, after all that has happened, under the dead weight of William Tell; the relief of seeing her sublimely capable of which, with the reprieve from her formidable flight to the Pacific doubtless not a little contributing, helps to draw down again the vision, or more exactly the sound, of the old New York and Boston Opera as our young generation knew and artlessly admired it; admired it, by my quite broken memories of the early time, in Brignoli the sweet and vague, in Susini the deep and rich, in Miss Kellogg the native and charming, in Adelaide Phillipps the universal, to say nothing of other acclaimed warblers (they appear to me to have warbled then so much more than since) whom I am afraid of not placing in the right perspective. They warbled Faust a dozen times, it comes back to me, for once of anything else; Miss Kellogg and Brignoli heaped up the measure of that success, and I well remember the great yearning with which I heard my cousin describe her first enchanted sense of it. The next in date of the letters before me, of the last day but one of December '69, is mainly an interesting expression of the part that music plays in her mental economy—though but tentatively offered to her correspondent, who, she fears, may not be musical enough to understand her, understand how much "spiritual truth has been 'borne in' upon me by means of harmony: the relation of the part to the whole, the absolute value of the individual, the absolute necessity of uncompromising and unfaltering truth, the different ways in which we like our likes and our unlikes," things all that have been so made clearer to her. Of a singular grace in movement and attitude, a grace of free mobility and activity, as original and "unconventional" as it was carelessly natural, she never looked more possessed of her best resources than at the piano in which she delighted, at which she had ardently worked, and where, slim and straight, her shoulders and head constantly, sympathetically swaying, she discoursed with an admirable touch and a long surrender that was like a profession of the safest relation she could know. Comparatively safe though it might have been, however, in the better time, she was allowed now, I gather, but little playing, and she is deep again toward the end of January '70 in a quite other exposure, the old familiar exposure to the "demon," as she calls it, "of the Why, Whence, Whither?" Long as the letter is I feel it a case again for presentation whole; the last thoughts of her life, as they appear, breathe in it with such elevation. They seem to give us her last words and impulses, and, with what follows of the middle of February, constitute the moving climax of her rich short story.

There have been times (and they will come again no doubt) when I could write to you about ordinary things in a way at least not depressing; but for a good while now I have felt so tired out, bodily and mentally, that I couldn't conscientiously ask you to share my mood. The life I live here in the country, and so very much alone, is capable of being the happiest or the unhappiest of existences, as it all depends so on oneself and is so very little interfered with by outside influences. Perhaps I am more than usually subject to extremes of happiness and of depression, yet I suppose everyone must have moments, even in the most varied and distracting life, when the old questioning spirit, the demon of the Why, Whence, Whither? stalks in like the skeleton at the feast and takes a seat beside him. I say everyone, but I must except those rare and happy souls who really believe in Christianity, who no longer strive after even goodness as it comes from one's own effort, but take refuge in the mysterious sacrifice of Christ, his merit sufficing, and in short throw themselves in the orthodox way on the consoling truth of the Atonement—to me hitherto neither comprehensible nor desirable. These people, having completely surrendered self, having lost their lives, as it were in Christ, must truly have found them, must know the rest that comes from literally casting their care of doubt and strife and thought upon the Lord.

I say hitherto the doctrine of the vicarious suffering of Christ has been to me not only incomprehensible but also unconsoling; I didn't want it and didn't understand even intellectually the feeling of people who do. I don't mean to say that the life and death of Christ and the example they set for us have not been to me always the brightest spot in history—for they have; but they have stood rather as an example that we must try to follow, that we must by constant and ceaseless effort bring our lives nearer to—but always, to some extent at least, through ourselves, that is through ourselves with God's help, got by asking Him for it and by His giving it to us straight and with no mediation. When I have seen as time went by my own shortcomings all the more instead of the less frequent, I have thought: "Well, you don't try hard enough; you are not really in earnest in thinking that you believe in the Christian life as the only true one." The more I tried, nevertheless, the less it seemed like the model life; the best things I did continued to be the more spontaneous ones; the greatest efforts had the least success; until finally I couldn't but see that if this was Christianity it was not the "rest" that Christ had promised his disciples—it was nothing more than a pagan life with a high ideal, only an ideal so high that nothing but failure and unhappiness came from trying to follow it. And one night when I was awake through all the hours it occurred to me: What if this were the need that Christianity came to fill up in our hearts? What if, after all, that old meaningless form of words that had been sounded in my unheeding ears all my days were suddenly to become invested with spirit and truth? What if this were the good tidings that have made so many hearts secure and happy in the most trying situations? For if morality and virtue were the test of a Christian, certainly Christ would never have likened the kingdom of heaven to a little child, in whose heart is no struggle, no conscious battle between right and wrong, but only unthinking love and trust.

However it may turn out, whether it shall seem true or untrue to me finally, I am at least glad to be able to put myself intellectually into the place of the long line of Christians who have felt the need and the comfort of this belief. It throws a light upon Uncle Henry's talk, which has seemed to me hitherto neither reasonable nor consoling. When I was with him it so far disgusted me that I fear I showed him plainly that I found it not only highly unpractical, but ignoble and shirking. I knew all the while that he disliked what he called my pride and conceit, but felt all the same that his views didn't touch my case a bit, didn't give me the least comfort or practical help, and seemed to me wanting in earnestness and strength. *Now* I say to myself: What if the good gentleman had all along really got hold of the higher truth, the purer spirituality? Verily there are two sides to everything in this world, and one becomes more charitable the older one grows. However, if I write at this length it is because I am feeling to-day too seedy for anything else. I had a hemorrhage a week ago, which rather took the life out of me; but as it was the only one I feel I should by this time be coming round again—and probably might if I hadn't got into a sleepless state which completely knocks me up. The old consolatory remark, "Patience, neighbour, and shuffle the cards," ought to impart a little hope to me, I suppose; but it's a long time since I've had any trumps in my hand, and you know that with the best luck the game always tired me. Willy James sometimes tells me to behave like a man and a gentleman if I wish to outwit fate. What a *real* person he is! He is to me in nearly all respects a head and shoulders above other people. How is Wendell Holmes? Elly is having the gayest winter in Washington and wants me to go to them there, which I had meant to do before the return of my last winter's illness. But it's not for me now.

Later.—I have kept my letter a day or two, thinking I might feel in tune for writing you a better one and not sending this at all. But alas I shall have to wait some time before I am like my old self again, so I may as well let this go. You see I'm not in a condition, mentally or physically, to take bright and healthy views of life. But if you really care you may as well see this mood as another, for heaven only knows when I shall get out of it. Can you understand the utter weariness of thinking about one thing all the time, so that when you wake up in the morning consciousness comes back with a sigh of "Oh yes, here it is again; another day of doubting and worrying, hoping and fearing has begun." If I don't get any sleep at all, which is too frequently the case, the strain is a "leetle" bit too hard, and I am sometimes tempted to take a drop of "pison" to put me to sleep in earnest. That momentary vision of redemption from thinking and striving, of a happy rest this side of eternity, has vanished away again. I can't help it; peaceful, desirable as it may be, the truth is that practically I don't believe it. It was such a sudden thing, such an entire change from anything that had ever come to me before, that it seemed almost like an inspiration, and I waited, almost expecting it

301

to continue, to be permanent. But it doesn't stay, and so back swings the universe to the old place—paganism, naturalism, or whatever you call the belief whose watchword is "God and our own soul." And who shall say there is not comfort in it? One at least feels that here one breathes one's native air, welcoming back the old *human* feeling, with its beautiful pride and its striving, its despair, its mystery and its faith. Write to me and tell me whether, as one goes on, one must still be tossed about more and more by these conflicting feelings, or whether they finally settle themselves quietly one way or the other and take only their proper share at least of one's life. This day is like summer, but I should enjoy it more if last night hadn't been quite the most unpleasant I ever spent. I got so thoroughly tired about two in the morning that I made up my mind in despair to give the morphine another trial, and as one dose had no effect took two; the consequence of which is that I feel as ill to-day as one could desire. I can tell you, sir, you had better prize the gift of sleep as it deserves while you have it. If I don't never write to you no more you'll know it's because I really wish to treat you kindly. But one of these days you'll get another kind of letter, brim-full perhaps with health and happiness and thoroughly ashamed of my present self. I had a long letter yesterday from Harry James at Florence—enjoying Italy but homesick. Did you see those verses in the North American translated from the Persian? Good-bye.

The last of all is full both of realities and illusions, the latter insistently living through all the distress of the former. And I should like to say, or to believe, that they remained with her to the end, which was near.

Don't be alarmed at my pencil—I am not in bed but only bundled-up on the piazza by order of the doctor.... I started for New York feeling a good deal knocked up, but hoping to get better from the change; I was to stay there over Sunday and see Dr. Metcalfe, who has a high reputation and was a friend of my father's. I left a request at his office that he would come to me on Sunday P.M.; but in the meantime my cousin Mrs. Minturn Post, with whom I was staying, urged upon me her physician, Dr. Taylor, who came on Saturday night, just as I was going to bed, and, after sounding my lungs, told me very dreadful things about them. As his verdict was worse than Metcalfe's proved I will tell you what he said first. He began very solemnly: "My dear young lady, your right lung is diseased; all your hemorrhages have come from there. It must have been bad for at least a year before they began. You must go to Europe as soon as possible." This was not cheerful, as I had been idiot enough to believe some time ago such a different explanation. But of course I wanted to learn what he absolutely thought, and told him I wasn't a bit afraid. If there weren't tubercles was I curable and if there *were*• was I hopeless? I asked him for the very worst view he had conscientiously to take, but didn't mean definitely to ask how long I should live, and so was rather unprepared for his reply of "Two or three years." I didn't however wish to make him regret his frankness, so I said, "Well, Doctor, even if my right lung were all gone I should make a stand with my left," and then, by way of showing how valiant the stand would be, fainted away. This, I should say, was owing a good deal to my previous used-up condition from want of sleep. It made him at any rate hasten to assure me that there was every possibility of my case being not after all so bad—with which he took his departure; to my great relief as I didn't think him at all nice. His grammar was bad, and he made himself generally objectionable.

The next night dear Dr. Metcalfe came, whom I love for the gentlest and kindest soul I have ever seen. To start with he's a gentleman, as well as an excellent physician, and to end with he and my father were fond of each other at West Point, and he takes a sort of paternal interest in me. He told me that my right lung is decidedly weaker than my left, which is quite sound, and that the hemorrhage has been a good thing for it and kept it from actual disease; and also that if I can keep up my general health I may get all right again. He has known a ten times worse case get entirely well. He urged me not to go to Washington, but decidedly to go to Europe; so this last is what I am to do with my cousin Mrs. Post if I am not dead before June. In a fortnight I'm to go back to New York to be for some time under Metcalfe's care. I feel tired out and hardly able to stir, but my courage is good, and I don't propose to lose it if I can help, for I know it all depends on myself whether I get through or not. That is if I begin to be indifferent to what happens I shall go down the hill fast. I have fortunately, through my mother's father, enough Irish blood in me rather to enjoy a good fight. I feel the greatest longing for summer or spring; I should like it to be always spring for the rest of my life and to have all the people I care for always with me! But who *wouldn't* like it so? Good-bye.

To the gallantry and beauty of which there is little surely to add. But there came a moment, almost immediately after, when all illusion failed; which it is not good to think of or linger on, and yet not pitiful not to note. One may have wondered rather doubtingly—and I have expressed that—what life would have had for her and how her exquisite faculty of challenge could have "worked in" with what she was likely otherwise to have encountered or been confined to. None the less did she in fact cling to consciousness; death, at the last, was dreadful to her; she would have given anything to live—and the image of this, which was long to remain with me, appeared so of the essence of tragedy that I was in the far-off aftertime to seek to lay the ghost by wrapping it, a particular occasion aiding, in the beauty and dignity of art. The figure that was to hover as the ghost has at any rate been of an extreme pertinence, I feel, to my doubtless too loose and confused general picture, vitiated perhaps by the effort to comprehend more than it contains. Much as this cherished companion's presence among us had represented for William and myself—and it is on *his* behalf I especially speak—her death made a mark that must stand here for a too waiting conclusion. We felt it together as the end of our youth.

THE END

FOOTNOTES:

[1] *A Small Boy and Others.* New York, 1913.

[2] *A Small Boy and Others*, 1913.

[3] A Small Boy and Others, 1913.

[4] Expressive drawing alas irreproducible.

[5] A drawing of figures in evening lamplight.

[6] Literary Remains of Henry James, Boston, 1885. The portrait accompanying the volume gave us, alas, but the scantest satisfaction.

[7] *Past and Present*, 1843.

[8] "But, Sir, we have yet one more scene to visit together, connected with all we have previously witnessed: a home scene, Sir Benjamin; and we must now ascend a mountain of pity high enough to command the dewy extense of three kingdoms. From thence we have to look down from every point of our warm hearts with a sight as multifold as the cherubic eyes. We are to see with equal penetration through the diverse thickness of castles, mansions, and cottages, through London and through hamlet, at young wives and at aged mothers, little children, brothers and sisters—all groups and ties that are; and at affianced maidens, ties that were to be. There are rents and tears to-day in the general life: the bulletin of the dead has come, and the groups of sorrow are constituted. Splendid Paris bends as a Niobe or as a Rachel while the corse of her much-enduring Hero is borne to the marble Invalides; other corses go earthward with a shorter procession, helped away by the spades of ruder but more instant sculptors; the rucked sod of the Alma is their urn and monument in one; yet every warrior among them is also buried to-day with swelling greatness of obsequies, if we could see them, in the everlasting ruby vaults of some human heart. You are touched, Sir Benjamin, and are justly religious on this summit. Struck down for a moment from worldliness, we both discourse without an afterthought on the immortal

state; we hope that the brave are already welcomed in the land of peace; that our laurels they could not stop to take, and our earned promotion they seem to have missed are clad upon them now by the God of battles in front of the shining armies of the just. We hope also that if their voices could now speak to the mourners, the oil of their sure gladness would heal our faithless sorrow. It is a true strain no doubt, and yet but of momentary power." War, Cholera, and the Ministry of Health. An Appeal to Sir Benjamin Hall and the British People. London, 1854.

[9] An eminent Unitarian pastor.

[10] My youngest brother's ingenuity was to know as little rest during much of his life as his strong faculty of agitation—to the employment of which it was indeed not least remarkably applied. Many illustrations of it would be to give, had I more margin; and not one of them anything less than striking, thanks to the vivacity of his intelligence, the variety of his gifts and the native ability in which he was himself so much less interested than was the case with everyone he met, however casually, that he became, many years before his death in 1910, our one gentleman of leisure: so far as this condition might consort with the easiest aptitude for admirable talk, charged with natural life, perception, humour and colour, that I have perhaps ever known. There were times when Bob's spoken overflow struck me as the equivalent, for fine animation, of William's epistolary. The note of the ingenious in him spent itself as he went, but I find an echo of one of its many incidents in the passage of verse that I am here moved to rescue from undue obscurity. It is too "amateurish" and has too many irregular lines, but images admirably the play of spirit in him which after ranging through much misadventure could at last drop to an almost effective grasp of the happiest relation.

> Although I lie so low and still
>
> Here came I by the Master's will;
>
> He smote at last to make me free,
>
> As He was smitten on the tree

And nailèd there. He knew of old
The human heart, and mine is cold;
And I know now that all we gain
Until we come to Him is vain.
Thy hands have never wrought a deed,
Thy heart has never known a need,
That went astray in His great plan
Since far-off days when youth began.
For in that vast and perfect plan
Where time is but an empty span
Our Master waits. He knows our want,
We know not his—till pale and gaunt
With weariness of life we come
And say to Him, What shall I be?
Oh Master, smite, but make me free
Perchance in these far worlds to know
The better thing we sought to be.

And then upon thy couch lie down
And fold the hands which have not sown;
And as thou liest there alone
Perhaps some breath from seraph blown
As soft as dew upon the rose

Will fall upon thee at life's close.

So thou wilt say, At last, at last!

All pain is love when pain is past!

And to the Master once again:

Oh keep my heart too weak to pray;

I ask no longer questions vain

Of life and love, of loss and gain—

These for the living are and strong;

I go to Thee, to Thee belong.

Once was I wakened by Thy light,

But years have passed, and now the night

Takes me to Thee. I am content;

So be it in Thy perfect plan

A mansion is where I am sent

To dwell among the innocent.

About Author

Henry James OM (15 April 1843 – 28 February 1916) was an American-British author regarded as a key transitional figure between literary realism and literary modernism, and is considered by many to be among the greatest novelists in the English language. He was the son of Henry James Sr. and the brother of renowned philosopher and psychologist William James and diarist Alice James.

He is best known for a number of novels dealing with the social and marital interplay between émigré Americans, English people, and continental Europeans. Examples of such novels include The Portrait of a Lady, The Ambassadors, and The Wings of the Dove. His later works were increasingly experimental. In describing the internal states of mind and social dynamics of his characters, James often made use of a style in which ambiguous or contradictory motives and impressions were overlaid or juxtaposed in the discussion of a character's psyche. For their unique ambiguity, as well as for other aspects of their composition, his late works have been compared to impressionist painting.

His novella The Turn of the Screw has garnered a reputation as the most analysed and ambiguous ghost story in the English language and remains his most widely adapted work in other media. He also wrote a number of other highly regarded ghost stories and is considered one of the greatest masters of the field.

James published articles and books of criticism, travel, biography, autobiography, and plays. Born in the United States, James largely relocated to Europe as a young man and eventually settled in England, becoming a British subject in 1915, one year before his death. James was nominated for the Nobel Prize in Literature in 1911, 1912 and 1916.

Life

Early years, 1843–1883

James was born at 2 Washington Place in New York City on 15 April 1843. His parents were Mary Walsh and Henry James Sr. His father was intelligent and steadfastly congenial. He was a lecturer and philosopher who had inherited independent means from his father, an Albany banker and investor. Mary came from a wealthy family long settled in New York City. Her sister Katherine lived with her adult family for an extended period of time. Henry Jr. had three brothers, William, who was one year his senior, and younger brothers Wilkinson (Wilkie) and Robertson. His younger sister was Alice. Both of his parents were of Irish and Scottish descent.

The family first lived in Albany, at 70 N. Pearl St., and then moved to Fourteenth Street in New York City when James was still a young boy. His education was calculated by his father to expose him to many influences, primarily scientific and philosophical; it was described by Percy Lubbock, the editor of his selected letters, as "extraordinarily haphazard and promiscuous." James did not share the usual education in Latin and Greek classics. Between 1855 and 1860, the James' household traveled to London, Paris, Geneva, Boulogne-sur-Mer and Newport, Rhode Island, according to the father's current interests and publishing ventures, retreating to the United States when funds were low. Henry studied primarily with tutors and briefly attended schools while the family traveled in Europe. Their longest stays were in France, where Henry began to feel at home and became fluent in French. He was afflicted with a stutter, which seems to have manifested itself only when he spoke English; in French, he did not stutter.

In 1860 the family returned to Newport. There Henry became a friend of the painter John La Farge, who introduced him to French literature, and in particular, to Balzac. James later called Balzac his "greatest master," and said that he had learned more about the craft of fiction from him than from anyone else.

In the autumn of 1861 Henry received an injury, probably to his back, while fighting a fire. This injury, which resurfaced at times throughout his life, made him unfit for military service in the American Civil War.

312

In 1864 the James family moved to Boston, Massachusetts to be near William, who had enrolled first in the Lawrence Scientific School at Harvard and then in the medical school. In 1862 Henry attended Harvard Law School, but realised that he was not interested in studying law. He pursued his interest in literature and associated with authors and critics William Dean Howells and Charles Eliot Norton in Boston and Cambridge, formed lifelong friendships with Oliver Wendell Holmes Jr., the future Supreme Court Justice, and with James and Annie Fields, his first professional mentors.

His first published work was a review of a stage performance, "Miss Maggie Mitchell in Fanchon the Cricket," published in 1863. About a year later, A Tragedy of Error, his first short story, was published anonymously. James's first payment was for an appreciation of Sir Walter Scott's novels, written for the North American Review. He wrote fiction and non-fiction pieces for The Nation and Atlantic Monthly, where Fields was editor. In 1871 he published his first novel, Watch and Ward, in serial form in the Atlantic Monthly. The novel was later published in book form in 1878.

During a 14-month trip through Europe in 1869–70 he met Ruskin, Dickens, Matthew Arnold, William Morris, and George Eliot. Rome impressed him profoundly. "Here I am then in the Eternal City," he wrote to his brother William. "At last—for the first time—I live!" He attempted to support himself as a freelance writer in Rome, then secured a position as Paris correspondent for the New York Tribune, through the influence of its editor John Hay. When these efforts failed he returned to New York City. During 1874 and 1875 he published Transatlantic Sketches, A Passionate Pilgrim, and Roderick Hudson. During this early period in his career he was influenced by Nathaniel Hawthorne.

In 1869 he settled in London. There he established relationships with Macmillan and other publishers, who paid for serial installments that they would later publish in book form. The audience for these serialized novels was largely made up of middle-class women, and James struggled to fashion serious literary work within the strictures imposed by editors' and publishers' notions of what was suitable for young women to read. He lived in rented rooms but was able to join gentlemen's clubs that had libraries and where he could entertain male friends. He was introduced to English society by Henry Adams and Charles Milnes Gaskell, the latter introducing him to the Travellers' and the Reform Clubs.

In the fall of 1875 he moved to the Latin Quarter of Paris. Aside from two trips to America, he spent the next three decades—the rest of his life—in Europe. In Paris he met Zola, Alphonse Daudet, Maupassant, Turgenev, and others. He stayed in Paris only a year before moving to London.

In England he met the leading figures of politics and culture. He continued to be a prolific writer, producing The American (1877), The Europeans (1878), a revision of Watch and Ward (1878), French Poets and Novelists (1878), Hawthorne (1879), and several shorter works of fiction. In 1878 Daisy Miller established his fame on both sides of the Atlantic. It drew notice perhaps mostly because it depicted a woman whose behavior is outside the social norms of Europe. He also began his first masterpiece, The Portrait of a Lady, which would appear in 1881.

In 1877 he first visited Wenlock Abbey in Shropshire, home of his friend Charles Milnes Gaskell whom he had met through Henry Adams. He was much inspired by the darkly romantic Abbey and the surrounding countryside, which features in his essay Abbeys and Castles. In particular the gloomy monastic fishponds behind the Abbey are said to have inspired the lake in The Turn of the Screw.

While living in London, James continued to follow the careers of the "French realists", Émile Zola in particular. Their stylistic methods influenced his own work in the years to come. Hawthorne's influence on him faded during this period, replaced by George Eliot and Ivan Turgenev. 1879–1882 saw the publication of The Europeans, Washington Square, Confidence, and The Portrait of a Lady. He visited America in 1882–1883, then returned to London.

The period from 1881 to 1883 was marked by several losses. His mother died in 1881, followed by his father a few months later, and then by his brother Wilkie. Emerson, an old family friend, died in 1882. His friend Turgenev died in 1883.

314

Middle years, 1884–1897

In 1884 James made another visit to Paris. There he met again with Zola, Daudet, and Goncourt. He had been following the careers of the French "realist" or "naturalist" writers, and was increasingly influenced by them. In 1886, he published The Bostonians and The Princess Casamassima, both influenced by the French writers he'd studied assiduously. Critical reaction and sales were poor. He wrote to Howells that the books had hurt his career rather than helped because they had "reduced the desire, and demand, for my productions to zero". During this time he became friends with Robert Louis Stevenson, John Singer Sargent, Edmund Gosse, George du Maurier, Paul Bourget, and Constance Fenimore Woolson. His third novel from the 1880s was The Tragic Muse. Although he was following the precepts of Zola in his novels of the '80s, their tone and attitude are closer to the fiction of Alphonse Daudet. The lack of critical and financial success for his novels during this period led him to try writing for the theatre. (His dramatic works and his experiences with theatre are discussed below.)

In the last quarter of 1889, he started translating "for pure and copious lucre" Port Tarascon, the third volume of Alphonse Daudet adventures of Tartarin de Tarascon. Serialized in Harper's Monthly Magazine from June 1890, this translation praised as "clever" by The Spectator was published in January 1891 by Sampson Low, Marston, Searle & Rivington.

After the stage failure of Guy Domville in 1895, James was near despair and thoughts of death plagued him. The years spent on dramatic works were not entirely a loss. As he moved into the last phase of his career he found ways to adapt dramatic techniques into the novel form.

In the late 1880s and throughout the 1890s James made several trips through Europe. He spent a long stay in Italy in 1887. In that year the short novel The Aspern Papers and The Reverberator were published.

Late years, 1898–1916

In 1897–1898 he moved to Rye, Sussex, and wrote The Turn of the Screw. 1899–1900 saw the publication of The Awkward Age and The Sacred

Fount. During 1902–1904 he wrote The Ambassadors, The Wings of the Dove, and The Golden Bowl.

In 1904 he revisited America and lectured on Balzac. In 1906–1910 he published The American Scene and edited the "New York Edition", a 24-volume collection of his works. In 1910 his brother William died; Henry had just joined William from an unsuccessful search for relief in Europe on what then turned out to be his (Henry's) last visit to the United States (from summer 1910 to July 1911), and was near him, according to a letter he wrote, when he died.

In 1913 he wrote his autobiographies, A Small Boy and Others, and Notes of a Son and Brother. After the outbreak of the First World War in 1914 he did war work. In 1915 he became a British subject and was awarded the Order of Merit the following year. He died on 28 February 1916, in Chelsea, London. As he requested, his ashes were buried in Cambridge Cemetery in Massachusetts.

Biographers

James regularly rejected suggestions that he should marry, and after settling in London proclaimed himself "a bachelor". F. W. Dupee, in several volumes on the James family, originated the theory that he had been in love with his cousin Mary ("Minnie") Temple, but that a neurotic fear of sex kept him from admitting such affections: "James's invalidism ... was itself the symptom of some fear of or scruple against sexual love on his part." Dupee used an episode from James's memoir A Small Boy and Others, recounting a dream of a Napoleonic image in the Louvre, to exemplify James's romanticism about Europe, a Napoleonic fantasy into which he fled.

Dupee had not had access to the James family papers and worked principally from James's published memoir of his older brother, William, and the limited collection of letters edited by Percy Lubbock, heavily weighted toward James's last years. His account therefore moved directly from James's childhood, when he trailed after his older brother, to elderly invalidism. As more material became available to scholars, including the diaries of contemporaries and hundreds of affectionate and sometimes erotic letters written by James to younger men, the picture of neurotic celibacy gave way to a portrait of a closeted homosexual.

Between 1953 and 1972, Leon Edel authored a major five-volume biography of James, which accessed unpublished letters and documents after Edel gained the permission of James's family. Edel's portrayal of James included the suggestion he was celibate. It was a view first propounded by critic Saul Rosenzweig in 1943. In 1996 Sheldon M. Novick published Henry James: The Young Master, followed by Henry James: The Mature Master (2007). The first book "caused something of an uproar in Jamesian circles" as it challenged the previous received notion of celibacy, a once-familiar paradigm in biographies of homosexuals when direct evidence was non-existent. Novick also criticised Edel for following the discounted Freudian interpretation of homosexuality "as a kind of failure." The difference of opinion erupted in a series of exchanges between Edel and Novick which were published by the online magazine Slate, with the latter arguing that even the suggestion of celibacy went against James's own injunction "live!"—not "fantasize!"

A letter James wrote in old age to Hugh Walpole has been cited as an explicit statement of this. Walpole confessed to him of indulging in "high jinks", and James wrote a reply endorsing it: "We must know, as much as possible, in our beautiful art, yours & mine, what we are talking about — & the only way to know it is to have lived & loved & cursed & floundered & enjoyed & suffered — I don't think I regret a single 'excess' of my responsive youth".

The interpretation of James as living a less austere emotional life has been subsequently explored by other scholars. The often intense politics of Jamesian scholarship has also been the subject of studies. Author Colm Tóibín has said that Eve Kosofsky Sedgwick's Epistemology of the Closet made a landmark difference to Jamesian scholarship by arguing that he be read as a homosexual writer whose desire to keep his sexuality a secret shaped his layered style and dramatic artistry. According to Tóibín such a reading "removed James from the realm of dead white males who wrote about posh people. He became our contemporary."

James's letters to expatriate American sculptor Hendrik Christian Andersen have attracted particular attention. James met the 27-year-old Andersen in Rome in 1899, when James was 56, and wrote letters to Andersen that are intensely emotional: "I hold you, dearest boy, in my innermost love, & count on your feeling me—in every throb of your soul". In a letter of 6 May 1904, to his brother William, James referred to himself as "always your hopelessly celibate even though sexagenarian Henry". How accurate that description might have been is the subject of contention among James's biographers, but the letters to Andersen were occasionally quasi-erotic: "I put, my dear boy, my arm around you, & feel the pulsation, thereby, as it were, of our excellent future & your admirable endowment." To his homosexual friend Howard Sturgis, James could write: "I repeat, almost to indiscretion, that I could live with you. Meanwhile I can only try to live without you."

His numerous letters to the many young gay men among his close male friends are more forthcoming. In a letter to Howard Sturgis, following a long visit, James refers jocularly to their "happy little congress of two" and in letters to Hugh Walpole he pursues convoluted jokes and puns about their relationship, referring to himself as an elephant who "paws you oh so benevolently" and winds about Walpole his "well meaning old trunk". His letters to Walter Berry printed by the Black Sun Press have long been celebrated for their lightly veiled eroticism.

He corresponded in almost equally extravagant language with his many female friends, writing, for example, to fellow novelist Lucy Clifford: "Dearest Lucy! What shall I say? when I love you so very, very much, and see you nine times for once that I see Others! Therefore I think that—if you want it made clear to the meanest intelligence—I love you more than I love Others." To his New York friend Mary Cadwalader Jones: "Dearest Mary Cadwalader. I yearn over you, but I yearn in vain; & your long silence really breaks my heart, mystifies, depresses, almost alarms me, to the point even of making me wonder if poor unconscious & doting old Célimare [Jones's pet name for James] has 'done' anything, in some dark somnambulism of the spirit, which has ... given you a bad moment, or a wrong impression, or a 'colourable pretext' ... However these things may be, he loves you as tenderly as ever;

nothing, to the end of time, will ever detach him from you, & he remembers those Eleventh St. matutinal intimes hours, those telephonic matinées, as the most romantic of his life ..." His long friendship with American novelist Constance Fenimore Woolson, in whose house he lived for a number of weeks in Italy in 1887, and his shock and grief over her suicide in 1894, are discussed in detail in Edel's biography and play a central role in a study by Lyndall Gordon. (Edel conjectured that Woolson was in love with James and killed herself in part because of his coldness, but Woolson's biographers have objected to Edel's account.)

Works

Style and themes

James is one of the major figures of trans-Atlantic literature. His works frequently juxtapose characters from the Old World (Europe), embodying a feudal civilisation that is beautiful, often corrupt, and alluring, and from the New World (United States), where people are often brash, open, and assertive and embody the virtues—freedom and a more highly evolved moral character—of the new American society. James explores this clash of personalities and cultures, in stories of personal relationships in which power is exercised well or badly. His protagonists were often young American women facing oppression or abuse, and as his secretary Theodora Bosanquet remarked in her monograph Henry James at Work:

> When he walked out of the refuge of his study and into the world and looked around him, he saw a place of torment, where creatures of prey perpetually thrust their claws into the quivering flesh of doomed, defenseless children of light ... His novels are a repeated exposure of this wickedness, a reiterated and passionate plea for the fullest freedom of development, unimperiled by reckless and barbarous stupidity.

Critics have jokingly described three phases in the development of James's prose: "James I, James II, and The Old Pretender." He wrote short stories and plays. Finally, in his third and last period he returned to the long, serialised novel. Beginning in the second period, but most noticeably in the third, he increasingly abandoned direct statement in favour of frequent

319

double negatives, and complex descriptive imagery. Single paragraphs began to run for page after page, in which an initial noun would be succeeded by pronouns surrounded by clouds of adjectives and prepositional clauses, far from their original referents, and verbs would be deferred and then preceded by a series of adverbs. The overall effect could be a vivid evocation of a scene as perceived by a sensitive observer. It has been debated whether this change of style was engendered by James's shifting from writing to dictating to a typist, a change made during the composition of What Maisie Knew.

In its intense focus on the consciousness of his major characters, James's later work foreshadows extensive developments in 20th century fiction. Indeed, he might have influenced stream-of-consciousness writers such as Virginia Woolf, who not only read some of his novels but also wrote essays about them. Both contemporary and modern readers have found the late style difficult and unnecessary; his friend Edith Wharton, who admired him greatly, said that there were passages in his work that were all but incomprehensible. James was harshly portrayed by H. G. Wells as a hippopotamus laboriously attempting to pick up a pea that had got into a corner of its cage. The "late James" style was ably parodied by Max Beerbohm in "The Mote in the Middle Distance".

More important for his work overall may have been his position as an expatriate, and in other ways an outsider, living in Europe. While he came from middle-class and provincial beginnings (seen from the perspective of European polite society) he worked very hard to gain access to all levels of society, and the settings of his fiction range from working class to aristocratic, and often describe the efforts of middle-class Americans to make their way in European capitals. He confessed he got some of his best story ideas from gossip at the dinner table or at country house weekends. He worked for a living, however, and lacked the experiences of select schools, university, and army service, the common bonds of masculine society. He was furthermore a man whose tastes and interests were, according to the prevailing standards of Victorian era Anglo-American culture, rather feminine, and who was shadowed by the cloud of prejudice that then and later accompanied suspicions of his homosexuality. Edmund Wilson famously compared James's objectivity to Shakespeare's:

One would be in a position to appreciate James better if one compared him with the dramatists of the seventeenth century—Racine and Molière, whom he resembles in form as well as in point of view, and even Shakespeare, when allowances are made for the most extreme differences in subject and form. These poets are not, like Dickens and Hardy, writers of melodrama—either humorous or pessimistic, nor secretaries of society like Balzac, nor prophets like Tolstoy: they are occupied simply with the presentation of conflicts of moral character, which they do not concern themselves about softening or averting. They do not indict society for these situations: they regard them as universal and inevitable. They do not even blame God for allowing them: they accept them as the conditions of life.

It is also possible to see many of James's stories as psychological thought-experiments. In his preface to the New York edition of The American he describes the development of the story in his mind as exactly such: the "situation" of an American, "some robust but insidiously beguiled and betrayed, some cruelly wronged, compatriot..." with the focus of the story being on the response of this wronged man. The Portrait of a Lady may be an experiment to see what happens when an idealistic young woman suddenly becomes very rich. In many of his tales, characters seem to exemplify alternative futures and possibilities, as most markedly in "The Jolly Corner", in which the protagonist and a ghost-doppelganger live alternative American and European lives; and in others, like The Ambassadors, an older James seems fondly to regard his own younger self facing a crucial moment.

Major novels

The first period of James's fiction, usually considered to have culminated in The Portrait of a Lady, concentrated on the contrast between Europe and America. The style of these novels is generally straightforward and, though personally characteristic, well within the norms of 19th-century fiction. Roderick Hudson (1875) is a Künstlerroman that traces the development of the title character, an extremely talented sculptor. Although the book shows some signs of immaturity—this was James's first serious attempt at a full-length novel—it has attracted favourable comment due to the vivid realisation of the three major characters: Roderick Hudson, superbly gifted but unstable and unreliable; Rowland Mallet, Roderick's limited but much more mature friend and patron; and Christina Light, one of James's most enchanting and maddening femmes fatales. The pair of Hudson and Mallet has been seen as representing the two sides of James's own nature: the wildly imaginative artist and the brooding conscientious mentor.

In The Portrait of a Lady (1881) James concluded the first phase of his career with a novel that remains his most popular piece of long fiction. The story is of a spirited young American woman, Isabel Archer, who "affronts her destiny" and finds it overwhelming. She inherits a large amount of money and subsequently becomes the victim of Machiavellian scheming by two American expatriates. The narrative is set mainly in Europe, especially in England and Italy. Generally regarded as the masterpiece of his early phase, The Portrait of a Lady is described as a psychological novel, exploring the minds of his characters, and almost a work of social science, exploring the differences between Europeans and Americans, the old and the new worlds.

The second period of James's career, which extends from the publication of The Portrait of a Lady through the end of the nineteenth century, features less popular novels including The Princess Casamassima, published serially in The Atlantic Monthly in 1885–1886, and The Bostonians, published serially in The Century Magazine during the same period. This period also featured James's celebrated Gothic novella, The Turn of the Screw.

The third period of James's career reached its most significant achievement in three novels published just around the start of the 20th century: The Wings of the Dove (1902), The Ambassadors (1903), and The Golden Bowl (1904). Critic F. O. Matthiessen called this "trilogy" James's major phase, and these novels have certainly received intense critical study. It was the second-written of the books, The Wings of the Dove (1902) that was the first published because it attracted no serialization. This novel tells the story of Milly Theale, an American heiress stricken with a serious disease, and her impact on the people around her. Some of these people befriend Milly with honourable motives, while others are more self-interested. James stated in his autobiographical books that Milly was based on Minny Temple, his beloved cousin who died at an early age of tuberculosis. He said that he attempted in the novel to wrap her memory in the "beauty and dignity of art".

Shorter narratives

James was particularly interested in what he called the "beautiful and blest nouvelle", or the longer form of short narrative. Still, he produced a number of very short stories in which he achieved notable compression of sometimes complex subjects. The following narratives are representative of James's achievement in the shorter forms of fiction.

- "A Tragedy of Error" (1864), short story
- "The Story of a Year" (1865), short story
- A Passionate Pilgrim (1871), novella
- Madame de Mauves (1874), novella
- Daisy Miller (1878), novella
- The Aspern Papers (1888), novella
- The Lesson of the Master (1888), novella
- The Pupil (1891), short story
- "The Figure in the Carpet" (1896), short story
- The Beast in the Jungle (1903), novella
- An International Episode (1878)
- Picture and Text
- Four Meetings (1885)
- A London Life, and Other Tales (1889)
- The Spoils of Poynton (1896)

- Embarrassments (1896)

- The Two Magics: The Turn of the Screw, Covering End (1898)

- A Little Tour of France (1900)

- The Sacred Fount (1901)

- Views and Reviews (1908)

- The Wings of the Dove, Volume I (1902)

- The Wings of the Dove, Volume II (1909)

- The Finer Grain (1910)

- The Outcry (1911)

- Lady Barbarina: The Siege of London, An International Episode and Other Tales (1922)

- The Birthplace (1922)

Plays

At several points in his career James wrote plays, beginning with one-act plays written for periodicals in 1869 and 1871 and a dramatisation of his popular novella Daisy Miller in 1882. From 1890 to 1892, having received a bequest that freed him from magazine publication, he made a strenuous effort to succeed on the London stage, writing a half-dozen plays of which only one, a dramatisation of his novel The American, was produced. This play was performed for several years by a touring repertory company and had a respectable run in London, but did not earn very much money for James. His other plays written at this time were not produced.

In 1893, however, he responded to a request from actor-manager George Alexander for a serious play for the opening of his renovated St. James's Theatre, and wrote a long drama, Guy Domville, which Alexander produced. There was a noisy uproar on the opening night, 5 January 1895, with hissing from the gallery when James took his bow after the final curtain, and the author was upset. The play received moderately good reviews and had a modest run of four weeks before being taken off to make way for Oscar Wilde's The Importance of Being Earnest, which Alexander thought would have better prospects for the coming season.

After the stresses and disappointment of these efforts James insisted that he would write no more for the theatre, but within weeks had agreed to write a curtain-raiser for Ellen Terry. This became the one-act "Summersoft", which he later rewrote into a short story, "Covering End", and then expanded into a full-length play, The High Bid, which had a brief run in London in 1907, when James made another concerted effort to write for the stage. He wrote three new plays, two of which were in production when the death of Edward VII on 6 May 1910 plunged London into mourning and theatres closed. Discouraged by failing health and the stresses of theatrical work, James did not renew his efforts in the theatre, but recycled his plays as successful novels. The Outcry was a best-seller in the United States when it was published in 1911. During the years 1890–1893 when he was most engaged with the theatre, James wrote a good deal of theatrical criticism and assisted Elizabeth Robins and others in translating and producing Henrik Ibsen for the first time in London.

Leon Edel argued in his psychoanalytic biography that James was traumatised by the opening night uproar that greeted Guy Domville, and that it plunged him into a prolonged depression. The successful later novels, in Edel's view, were the result of a kind of self-analysis, expressed in fiction, which partly freed him from his fears. Other biographers and scholars have not accepted this account, however; the more common view being that of F.O. Matthiessen, who wrote: "Instead of being crushed by the collapse of his hopes [for the theatre]... he felt a resurgence of new energy."

Non-fiction

Beyond his fiction, James was one of the more important literary critics in the history of the novel. In his classic essay The Art of Fiction (1884), he argued against rigid prescriptions on the novelist's choice of subject and method of treatment. He maintained that the widest possible freedom in content and approach would help ensure narrative fiction's continued vitality.

James wrote many valuable critical articles on other novelists; typical is his book-length study of Nathaniel Hawthorne, which has been the subject of critical debate. Richard Brodhead has suggested that the study was emblematic of James's struggle with Hawthorne's influence, and constituted an effort to place the elder writer "at a disadvantage." Gordon Fraser, meanwhile, has suggested that the study was part of a more commercial effort by James to introduce himself to British readers as Hawthorne's natural successor.

When James assembled the New York Edition of his fiction in his final years, he wrote a series of prefaces that subjected his own work to searching, occasionally harsh criticism.

At 22 James wrote The Noble School of Fiction for The Nation's first issue in 1865. He would write, in all, over 200 essays and book, art, and theatre reviews for the magazine.

For most of his life James harboured ambitions for success as a playwright. He converted his novel The American into a play that enjoyed modest returns in the early 1890s. In all he wrote about a dozen plays, most of which went unproduced. His costume drama Guy Domville failed disastrously on its opening night in 1895. James then largely abandoned his efforts to conquer the stage and returned to his fiction. In his Notebooks he maintained that his theatrical experiment benefited his novels and tales by helping him dramatise his characters' thoughts and emotions. James produced a small but valuable amount of theatrical criticism, including perceptive appreciations of Henrik Ibsen.

With his wide-ranging artistic interests, James occasionally wrote on the visual arts. Perhaps his most valuable contribution was his favourable assessment of fellow expatriate John Singer Sargent, a painter whose critical status has improved markedly in recent decades. James also wrote sometimes charming, sometimes brooding articles about various places he visited and lived in. His most famous books of travel writing include Italian Hours (an example of the charming approach) and The American Scene (most definitely on the brooding side).

James was one of the great letter-writers of any era. More than ten thousand of his personal letters are extant, and over three thousand have been published in a large number of collections. A complete edition of James's letters began publication in 2006, edited by Pierre Walker and Greg Zacharias. As of 2014, eight volumes have been published, covering the period from 1855 to 1880. James's correspondents included celebrated contemporaries like Robert Louis Stevenson, Edith Wharton and Joseph Conrad, along with many others in his wide circle of friends and acquaintances. The letters range from the "mere twaddle of graciousness" to serious discussions of artistic, social and personal issues.

Very late in life James began a series of autobiographical works: A Small Boy and Others, Notes of a Son and Brother, and the unfinished The Middle Years. These books portray the development of a classic observer who was passionately interested in artistic creation but was somewhat reticent about participating fully in the life around him.

Reception

Criticism, biographies and fictional treatments

James's work has remained steadily popular with the limited audience of educated readers to whom he spoke during his lifetime, and has remained firmly in the canon, but, after his death, some American critics, such as Van Wyck Brooks, expressed hostility towards James for his long expatriation and eventual naturalisation as a British subject. Other critics such as E. M. Forster complained about what they saw as James's squeamishness in the treatment of sex and other possibly controversial material, or dismissed his late style as difficult and obscure, relying heavily on extremely long sentences and excessively latinate language. Similarly Oscar Wilde criticised him for writing "fiction as if it were a painful duty". Vernon Parrington, composing a canon of American literature, condemned James for having cut himself off from America. Jorge Luis Borges wrote about him, "Despite the scruples and delicate complexities of James, his work suffers from a major defect: the absence of life." And Virginia Woolf, writing to Lytton Strachey, asked, "Please tell me what you find in Henry James. ... we have his works here, and

I read, and I can't find anything but faintly tinged rose water, urbane and sleek, but vulgar and pale as Walter Lamb. Is there really any sense in it?" The novelist W. Somerset Maugham wrote, "He did not know the English as an Englishman instinctively knows them and so his English characters never to my mind quite ring true," and argued "The great novelists, even in seclusion, have lived life passionately. Henry James was content to observe it from a window." Maugham nevertheless wrote, "The fact remains that those last novels of his, notwithstanding their unreality, make all other novels, except the very best, unreadable." Colm Tóibín observed that James "never really wrote about the English very well. His English characters don't work for me."

Despite these criticisms, James is now valued for his psychological and moral realism, his masterful creation of character, his low-key but playful humour, and his assured command of the language. In his 1983 book, The Novels of Henry James, Edward Wagenknecht offers an assessment that echoes Theodora Bosanquet's:

> "To be completely great," Henry James wrote in an early review, "a work of art must lift up the heart," and his own novels do this to an outstanding degree ... More than sixty years after his death, the great novelist who sometimes professed to have no opinions stands foursquare in the great Christian humanistic and democratic tradition. The men and women who, at the height of World War II, raided the secondhand shops for his out-of-print books knew what they were about. For no writer ever raised a braver banner to which all who love freedom might adhere.

William Dean Howells saw James as a representative of a new realist school of literary art which broke with the English romantic tradition epitomised by the works of Charles Dickens and William Makepeace Thackeray. Howells wrote that realism found "its chief exemplar in Mr. James... A novelist he is not, after the old fashion, or after any fashion but his own." F.R. Leavis championed Henry James as a novelist of "established pre-eminence" in The Great Tradition (1948), asserting that The Portrait of a Lady and The Bostonians were "the two most brilliant novels in the language." James is now prized as a master of point of view who moved literary fiction forward by insisting in showing, not telling, his stories to the reader. (Source: Wikipedia)

NOTABLE WORKS

The Whole Family (collaborative novel with eleven other authors, 1908)

The Outcry (1911)

The Ivory Tower (unfinished, published posthumously 1917)

The Sense of the Past (unfinished, published posthumously 1917)

SHORT STORIES AND NOVELLAS

A Tragedy of Error (1864)

The Story of a Year (1865)

A Landscape Painter (1866)

A Day of Days (1866)

My Friend Bingham (1867)

Poor Richard (1867)

The Story of a Masterpiece (1868)

A Most Extraordinary Case (1868)

A Problem (1868)

De Grey: A Romance (1868)

Osborne's Revenge (1868)

The Romance of Certain Old Clothes (1868)

A Light Man (1869)

Gabrielle de Bergerac (1869)

Travelling Companions (1870)

A Passionate Pilgrim (1871)

At Isella (1871)

Master Eustace (1871)

Guest's Confession (1872)

The Madonna of the Future (1873)

The Sweetheart of M. Briseux (1873)

The Last of the Valerii (1874)

Madame de Mauves (1874)

Adina (1874)

Professor Fargo (1874)

Eugene Pickering (1874)

Benvolio (1875)

Crawford's Consistency (1876)

The Ghostly Rental (1876)

Four Meetings (1877)

Rose-Agathe (1878, as Théodolinde)

Daisy Miller (1878)

Longstaff's Marriage (1878)

An International Episode (1878)

The Pension Beaurepas (1879)

A Diary of a Man of Fifty (1879)

A Bundle of Letters (1879)

The Point of View (1882)

The Siege of London (1883)

Impressions of a Cousin (1883)

Lady Barberina (1884)

Pandora (1884)

The Author of Beltraffio (1884)

Georgina's Reasons (1884)

A New England Winter (1884)

The Path of Duty (1884)

Mrs. Temperly (1887)

Louisa Pallant (1888)

The Aspern Papers (1888)

The Liar (1888)

The Modern Warning (1888, originally published as The Two Countries)

A London Life (1888)

The Patagonia (1888)

The Lesson of the Master (1888)

The Solution (1888)

The Pupil (1891)

Brooksmith (1891)

The Marriages (1891)

The Chaperon (1891)

Sir Edmund Orme (1891)

Nona Vincent (1892)

The Real Thing (1892)

The Private Life (1892)

Lord Beaupré (1892)

The Visits (1892)

Sir Dominick Ferrand (1892)

Greville Fane (1892)

Collaboration (1892)

Owen Wingrave (1892)

The Wheel of Time (1892)

The Middle Years (1893)

The Death of the Lion (1894)

The Coxon Fund (1894)

The Next Time (1895)

Glasses (1896)

The Altar of the Dead (1895)

The Figure in the Carpet (1896)

The Way It Came (1896, also published as The Friends of the Friends)

The Turn of the Screw (1898)

Covering End (1898)

In the Cage (1898)

John Delavoy (1898)

The Given Case (1898)

Europe (1899)

The Great Condition (1899)

The Real Right Thing (1899)

Paste (1899)

The Great Good Place (1900)

Maud-Evelyn (1900)

Miss Gunton of Poughkeepsie (1900)

The Tree of Knowledge (1900)

The Abasement of the Northmores (1900)

The Third Person (1900)

The Special Type (1900)

The Tone of Time (1900)

Broken Wings (1900)

The Two Faces (1900)

Mrs. Medwin (1901)

The Beldonald Holbein (1901)

The Story in It (1902)

Flickerbridge (1902)

The Birthplace (1903)

The Beast in the Jungle (1903)

The Papers (1903)

Fordham Castle (1904)

Julia Bride (1908)

The Jolly Corner (1908)

The Velvet Glove (1909)

Mora Montravers (1909)

Crapy Cornelia (1909)

The Bench of Desolation (1909)

A Round of Visits (1910)

OTHER

Transatlantic Sketches (1875)

French Poets and Novelists (1878)

Hawthorne (1879)

Portraits of Places (1883)

A Little Tour in France (1884)

Partial Portraits (1888)

Essays in London and Elsewhere (1893)

Picture and Text (1893)

Terminations (1893)

Theatricals (1894)

Theatricals: Second Series (1895)

Guy Domville (1895)

The Soft Side (1900)

William Wetmore Story and His Friends (1903)

The Better Sort (1903)

English Hours (1905)

The Question of our Speech; The Lesson of Balzac. Two Lectures (1905)

The American Scene (1907)

Views and Reviews (1908)

Italian Hours (1909)

A Small Boy and Others (1913)

Notes on Novelists (1914)

Notes of a Son and Brother (1914)

Within the Rim (1918)

Travelling Companions (1919)

Notebooks (various, published posthumously)

The Middle Years (unfinished, published posthumously 1917)

A Most Unholy Trade (1925, published posthumously)

The Art of the Novel : Critical Prefaces (1934)

CPSIA information can be obtained
at www.ICGtesting.com
Printed in the USA
LVHW042301050920
665177LV00005B/651

9 789390 295982